Neorealism and Its Critics

THE POLITICAL ECONOMY OF INTERNATIONAL CHANGE

John Gerard Ruggie, General Editor

NEOREALISM
AND ITS CRITICS

Robert O. Keohane, *editor*

New York   COLUMBIA UNIVERSITY PRESS   1986

Library of Congress Cataloging-in-Publication Data

Neorealism and its critics.

(The Political economy of international change)
Bibliography: p.
Includes index.
Contents: Realism, neorealism, and the study of
world politics / Robert O. Keohane—Laws and
theories / Kenneth N. Waltz—Reductionist and
systemic theories / Kenneth N. Waltz—[etc.]
   1. International relations—Addresses, essays,
lectures.   2. World politics—1945–   —Addresses,
essays, lectures.   I. Keohane, Robert O. (Robert
Owen), 1941–   II. Series.
JX1391.N46   1986   327′.01   86–2247
ISBN 0–231–06348–2
ISBN 0–231–06349–0 (pbk.)

Book designed by Laiying Chong.

Columbia University Press
New York   Guildford, Surrey
Copyright © 1986 Columbia University Press

Printed in the United States of America

THE POLITICAL ECONOMY OF INTERNATIONAL CHANGE
John Gerard Ruggie, General Editor

Contents

Acknowledgments

THIS VOLUME would not have been possible without the cooperation of a large number of people and institutions. The authors are grateful to Columbia University Press for seeing the scholarly potential in a book that includes a number of previously published articles—and for encouraging us to include a substantial amount of original material as well. Kate Wittenberg has been an efficient and supportive editor. Credit is due to Howard Silverman for preparing a unified bibliography and to Nicholas Humez for the index.

We are also grateful to a number of publishers and academic journals for permission to reprint material that originally appeared elsewhere. Random House gave permission for reprinting of chapters 1, and 4–6 from *Theory of International Politics* (Reading, Massachusetts: Addison-Wesley, 1979) by Kenneth Waltz, which appear as articles 2–5 of this volume. Article 6, "Continuity and Transformation in the World Polity: Toward a Neorealist Synthesis," by John Gerard Ruggie, is reprinted with permission by Princeton University Press, publisher of *World Politics,* where it originally appeared in January 1983, volume 35(2):261–285. "Theory of World Politics: Structural Realism and Beyond," by Robert O. Keohane, which constitutes article 7, appeared first in Ada Finifter, ed., *Political Science: The State of the Discipline,* pp. 503–540 (Washington: American Political Science Association), and is reprinted with the permission of the American Political Science Association.

Robert W. Cox's "Social Forces, States and World Orders: Beyond International Relations Theory" (article 8) is reprinted with permission from *Journal of International Studies: Millennium* (Summer 1981), 10(2):126–155. An edited version of "The Poverty of Neorealism," by Richard K. Ashley, which constitutes article 9, is reprinted with permission from *International Organization* (Spring 1984) 38(2):225–261; 275–281. Robert G. Gilpin's response, "The Richness of the Tradition of Political Realism" (article 10) is reprinted from the same issue of *International Organization,* pp. 287–304, also with permission.

The other material in this volume is published here for the first time: Robert O. Keohane's introduction, "Realism, Neorealism and the Study of World Politics" (article 1); Robert W. Cox's postscript to his article (included in article 8); and Kenneth N. Waltz's concluding essay, "Reflections on *Theory of International Politics*: A Response to My Critics" (article 11).

The participants in this enterprise have sought to create a volume that is coherent in style as well as in argument. Hence we have standardized our references and created a unified bibliography. Some editing of the previously published articles has been done to eliminate confusing references to material not included here. The new contributions—the introduction by Keohane, the postscript by Cox to his earlier article, and the conclusion by Waltz—refer to the other articles by page number in this volume rather than in the original, to facilitate analysis of competing arguments by our readers.

We hope that this volume will make more people aware of the importance and liveliness of contemporary theories of international relations, and that some of our readers will respond by making contributions to the debate themselves in the future. Perhaps, eventually and indirectly, our thoughts will exert a constructive impact on practice as well.

Let me conclude with a personal note. The penultimate version of this preface was completed on the same day, September 10, 1985, on which my mother was involved in an automobile accident that caused her death at the age of 81. I wish to dedicate my contributions to this volume to her memory. Mary P. Keohane was a remarkable person— teacher, author, lover of nature, deep thinker. Her spirit lives on in those who knew her.

Robert O. Keohane
Wellesley, Massachusetts
December 1985

Neorealism and Its Critics

ONE

Realism, Neorealism and the Study of World Politics

ROBERT O. KEOHANE

WORLD POLITICS today is a matter of life and death—not just for soldiers or citizens caught in the path of war, but for the whole human race. Nuclear holocaust remains a continual threat. At a less apocalyptic level, world politics has a daily impact on the lives of people throughout the globe: political forces and decisions affect patterns of international trade, investment, and production. Whether OPEC oil will be cheap or dear; whether China will export textiles to the United States; how many Americans will work in the auto industry: all depend as much on political decisions as on patterns of comparative costs and efficiencies.

The complexities of security in a nuclear age, and of economic viability in an era of interdependence and rapid technological change, have created demands by policymakers for expertise on a myriad of international political issues. Thousands of experts, in and out of governments around the world, analyze the relative military forces of the superpowers, fluctuations in supply and demand in oil markets, or shifts in international patterns of comparative advantage. These observers interpret the significance of changes in policies of governments and nongovernmental actors such as transnational corporations and international organizations, and they seek to determine their impact—on Soviet or American security, Saudi or Mexican oil revenues, inflation in the United States, or the viability of high-tech industry in Europe.

Little of this immense application of brainpower to world affairs takes any explicit account of theories about world politics. Indeed, a naïve

Note: For comments on earlier drafts of this essay I am indebted to Nannerl O. Keohane, Andy Moravcsik, Joseph S. Nye, John Gerard Ruggie, and Howard Silverman.

observer might conclude that all of the relevant theories come from other disciplines: physics, laser engineering, petroleum geology, electronics, the economics of comparative advantage or exchange-rate determination. Foundations and governments display little interest in supporting theoretical work in international relations, compared with their zest for "policy-relevant" research or the incorporation into international relations of findings from other fields.

In view of this widespread lack of interest, the reader may well ask: "Why should I care about theoretical debates among scholars of international relations? If I want to understand world politics or make policy, shouldn't I devote my efforts directly to studying nuclear deterrence, OPEC, or the international financial system?" In other words, is the enterprise represented by this volume—abstract discussion of theoretical issues in international relations—relevant to the practical tasks of interpreting the world and seeking to change it? Does the theory of international relations have implications for practice? Should it be studied by practitioners or by those who seek to become policymakers in the future?

The contributors to this volume believe that theory does have implications for practice and that it should be studied by those who seek to influence events. In the first section of this introductory essay I present my reasons for holding such beliefs. After making my argument, I will turn to the issues raised by the tradition of political realism and its contemporary offshoot, "neorealism," and then conclude with a brief overview of the contributions that constitute this volume.

I. THEORY AND PRACTICE IN INTERNATIONAL RELATIONS

One reason for an aspiring practitioner to learn international relations theory would be to absorb valuable maxims or propositions that would prove useful in specific situations. If the conditions for applicability of these maxims are sufficiently well understood, and if the practitioner knows enough history to be able to place them in context, they can furnish useful guides to the interpretation of events. Even a limited, partial theory—with only a few propositions and a number of interpretive guides—can be useful. For instance, the realist theory of the balance of power, discussed by Waltz, could have alerted American policymakers in the 1950s (who were excessively imbued with an ideological view of world politics) to the likelihood of an eventual Sino-Soviet split. Realist maxims would have counseled the United States to be in a position to make an alliance, or at least an accommodation, when feasible, with the weaker Chinese to counterbalance the Soviet Union—as Henry Kissinger and Richard Nixon eventually did.

Theory can therefore be useful: it is often better than unconscious adherence to the prejudices of the day. Nevertheless, it is necessary for any practitioner using international relations theory to remain skeptical; indeed, the more seriously the maxims are taken, the more important is the task of critical analysis. If the maxims apply only under certain conditions, or if the theory underlying them is fundamentally erroneous in its understanding of the forces affecting cooperation and discord, peace and war, they will be dangerously misleading. For example, the popular maxim in Western foreign policy after World War II, that appeasement (making concessions to others' demands) should be avoided since it breeds aggression, is by no means universally valid. Whether making concessions to others' demands breeds aggression depends, among other things, on the nature of the demands, the capabilities of the demander, and the willingness of the responding power to use force effectively, in a sustained way, as an alternative to making concessions. A policy of appeasement, disastrous when pursued by Britain and France toward Hitler, would not necessarily have been inappropriate for those two countries in their relations with Egypt in the mid-1950s or even for the United States in its relations with North Vietnam in the 1960s.

Practitioners cannot judge the validity of theories offered to them, or the conditions under which theoretical maxims might apply, without studying theory. It may appear, however, that practitioners could avoid the pitfalls of misguided or misapplied theory simply by shunning theory altogether; and indeed, most commentators on international relations avoid explicit discussion of theories of world politics. Yet to purge oneself of all traces of theory would be impossible, since even our intuitions about world politics are deeply affected by how the subject has been thought about in the past. For over 2000 years, thinkers have sought to understand, more or less systematically, the most basic questions of world politics: the sources of discord and of war and the conditions of cooperation and of peace. As Keynes said in another context, practitioners are prisoners of "academic scribblers," whose views of reality profoundly affect the contemporary actions of practical people. The choice for practitioners is not between being influenced by theory or examining each case "on its merits": it is rather between being aware of the theoretical basis for one's interpretation and action, and being unaware of it.

Even if one could eradicate theory from one's mind, it would be self-defeating to try. No one can cope with the complexities of world politics without the aid either of a theory or of implicit assumptions and propositions that substitute, however poorly, for theory. Reality has to be ordered into categories, and relationships drawn between events. To prefer atheoretical activity over theoretically informed practice would be to seek to be guided by an unexamined jumble of prejudices, yielding conclusions that may not logically follow from the assumptions, rather than by beliefs based on systematic attempts to specify one's assumptions and to derive and test propositions.

The inescapability of theory in studying world politics suggests a second reason for exploring what are labeled here political realism and neorealism. Whatever one's conclusion about the value of contemporary neorealism for the analysis of world politics in our time, it is important to understand realism and neorealism because of their widespread acceptance in contemporary scholarship and in policy circles. Political realism is deeply embedded in Western thought. Without understanding it, we can neither understand nor criticize our own tradition of thinking about international relations. Nor could we hope to change either our thinking or our practice. All people who are interested in having a sustained professional impact on world affairs should study international relations theory at some time, if only to examine prevailing assumptions and evaluate the basic propositions that they might otherwise take for granted.

The danger that one will become the prisoner of unstated assumptions is rendered particularly acute by the value-laden nature of international relations theory. This does not mean that observers simply see what they want to see: on the contrary, virtually all serious students of world politics view it as a highly imperfect realm of action in which wrongdoing is common and unimaginable evil is threatened. Nevertheless, it is hard to doubt that scholars' values, and their own personal experiences and temperaments, affect which aspects of world politics they emphasize and how strenuously, or desperately, they search for ways to mitigate the injustice and cruelty that is so evident. For this reason, as well as those mentioned above, interpretations of world politics need to be scrutinized critically—a task for which a certain degree of sophistication about the subject is essential.

An objection could be raised to the above argument. If a theory provides sufficiently accurate guidance about cause–effect relationships, and if its propositions about these relationships remain valid over time and under different conditions, practitioners may not need to study it deeply. They can learn its major theorems without being too concerned about how they were derived, or about the range of their theoretical application. A structural engineer, engaged in building bridges, can assume the validity of Newtonian physics and can apply its propositions without being able to derive them from basic premises. It is of no concern to the engineer that this same assumption would be terribly misleading for a scientist trying to understand black holes in outer space or the behavior of quarks at the subatomic level. Similarly, if the theories of world politics on which policymakers and commentators rely provided powerful, value-free explanations of outcomes in world politics, which were sure to remain valid throughout the time-horizon of policymakers, it would be unnecessary for interpreters of contemporary world politics to concern themselves with theoretical controversies. The methodological presuppositions of international political theories would be of no more concern to practitioners than are investigations of quarks or black holes to the bridge-building engineer.

But theories of world politics are not at all like those of physics. No careful analyst believes that our theories of world politics have attained either the explanatory quality or the practical usefulness of Newton's system, much less of quantum mechanics; and there is general skepticism that they will ever approximate the rigor and accuracy even of seventeenth-century physics. Furthermore, since both world politics and our values keep changing, there is no guarantee that even a well-tested theory will remain valid in the future. Each proposition of any theory of world politics should therefore be scrutinized carefully to ascertain the range of its applicability, its robustness under different conditions, and the likelihood of its being overtaken by events.

What this suggests sounds paradoxical. The problematic character of international relations theory *increases* the importance of studying it deeply. If international relations theory were as generally valid as Newtonian physics is for ordinary events, practitioners could learn only its theorems, or maxims, without exploring carefully the question of on what assumptions, and under what conditions, they will continue to be applicable. But since it is neither so generally valid nor so unchangingly applicable, we must be on our guard. Critical reevaluation is continually important in international relations—more so than copybook learning.

Even if one accepts these arguments for studying international relations theory, it remains an open question whether political realism and neorealism constitute valuable ways to enhance our understanding of international affairs. Indeed, many of the disagreements expressed in this volume revolve around this point. It is to be anticipated that readers who are primarily interested in understanding contemporary world affairs, or in giving policy advice, will answer this question differently for themselves, reacting to this volume's debate over theories of world politics in at least three ways:

1. Some may conclude that neorealist theory provides a solid basis for understanding contemporary events, and that we are unlikely to make substantial additional theoretical progress in the near future. That is, even if the contribution of neorealist theory is relatively small compared with that of well-developed theories such as those of physics, the theory is the best we can construct, given the difficulties of the subject. Such a judgment would imply that students of world politics should learn the essentials of neorealist theory in order to avoid reliance on crude oversimplifications or caricatures; but that they should not dwell too long on theory, but go on to study specific aspects of contemporary international affairs in detail.

2. A different conclusion would be that neorealist theory has value in certain situations, but that for analyzing other situations it is of quite limited use—or even misleading—and could be improved through modification. For those who believe this, continuing to work on theory holds more promise than for those in the first camp: it is worthwhile to seek to modify and extend neorealist theory in order to increase its validity and usefulness. Practitioners who adhere to this view have two tasks: to distinguish carefully the areas where neorealist theory is applicable from those in which it is irrelevant or confusing; and to reflect periodically on new at-

tempts at international theory, asking themselves whether these could be helpful in interpreting contemporary events.

3. A third view would hold that neorealist theory is fundamentally flawed and misleading to the core—an "orrery of errors," as Richard Ashley claims. From this perspective, theoretical work that fundamentally reinterprets the nature of world politics is crucially necessary; and in the meantime, policymakers and analysts of particular issues should strive to rid themselves of the pernicious biases of neorealism. From this perspective, studying neorealism is necessary in order to "know thy enemy."

Whichever view is taken, some value will have been derived from studying realism and neorealism, even if exactly what has been gained will depend on the reader's own evaluation of the theoretical contentions put forward in this volume.

II. POLITICAL REALISM AND NEOREALISM

Even as long ago as the time of Thucydides, political realism (as described in more detail in my own essay later in this volume) contained three key assumptions: (1) states (or city-states) are the key units of action; (2) they seek power, either as an end in itself or as a means to other ends; and (3) they behave in ways that are, by and large, rational, and therefore comprehensible to outsiders in rational terms. These premises do not, by themselves, constitute the basis for a science: they do not establish propositions linking causes with effects. Yet they have furnished a usable interpretative framework for observers from Thucydides onward. Indeed, all three elements can be found in Thucydides' discussion of the causes of the Peloponnesian War in the first chapter of his book. Having described the complaints and legal violations leading up to the war, Thucydides observes that "the real cause I consider to be the one which was formally most kept out of sight. The growth of the power of Athens, and the alarm which this inspired in Lacedaemon, made war inevitable" (Thucydides, ca. 400 B.C./1951, chapter 1, paragraph 24). That is, the Lacedaemonians rationally feared that Athens would at some point direct its growing power against their interests, and decided to act while they could still exert some influence over the course of events.

One of the appeals of realist thinking is its applicability to practical problems of international relations: it provides a readily comprehensible set of steps to be followed by those seeking to understand and deal with potential threats to the security of their states. Analysts working within the realist tradition will proceed as the Lacedaemonians did. They will focus on states that could constitute effective threats, alone or in coalition with one another, given the power at their disposal. They will interpret the actions of those states not on the basis simply of their announced policies or on the assumption that they will behave morally, but rather on the premise that they are seeking rationally to increase their power. And they will devise policies that would protect their own society by amassing or maintaining sufficient power, alone or in coalitions, to maintain their essential security interests.

In view of its easy applicability to a competitive interstate system, and its prudential maxims, it is not surprising that realism was regarded as intuitively plausible by statesmen in post-medieval Western Europe. After the Peace of Westphalia in 1648, with its legitimation of the state system, political realism became the generally accepted conventional wisdom, particularly in continental Europe. Critics of power politics who offered alternative plans based on loose federations of republican governments— such as Immanuel Kant, in *Perpetual Peace* (1795)—did not exercise decisive influence on the thoughts of those in power. The response of Frederick the Great to the earlier, more utopian, plan of the Abbé de Saint Pierre was rather typical: "The thing is most practicable; for its success all that is lacking is the consent of Europe and a few similar trifles" (Hinsley 1963: 45).

In Great Britain, however—and even more in the United States— there has been a greater tendency to envisage alternatives to power politics and to question the premises of political realism (Wolfers and Martin 1956). The arbitration movement, Woodrow Wilson's speeches during World War I, and the Kellogg-Briand Pact of 1927 to "outlaw war" all exemplify this institutional and legalistic approach to international relations. Yet by the late 1930s this liberal theory was in decline: 1939 marked the publication date of E. H. Carr's classic attack on the conceptions of harmony of interest, or of morality unrelated to power in world politics. As Carr stated in the second edition (1946) of *The Twenty Years' Crisis, 1919–1939,* "in the international order, the role of power is greater and that of morality less" (p. 168).

World War II elevated this realist perspective to the new orthodoxy in Anglo-American thinking on international affairs. The struggle with Nazism cast doubt on the efficacy of international law and emphasized the role of power in world politics. This shift in perspective was particularly rapid in America, since the collapse of the European balance of power meant that the United States, no longer merely an observer of European foibles, had accepted the burdens, along with the heady privileges, of becoming a hegemonic power—one with both the willingness and the ability to make and maintain rules for world politics.

It is therefore not surprising that during and immediately after World War II the tradition of power politics was revived and reinvigorated in the United States. John Herz, George F. Kennan, Walter Lippmann, and Hans J. Morgenthau articulated what Morgenthau called "political realism," in contrast to the "utopianism," "legalism," or "idealism" that they associated with liberal writers on international affairs. These self-styled realists sought to reorient United States foreign policy so that American policymakers could cope with Soviet attempts at domination without either lapsing into passive unwillingness to use force or engaging in destructive and quixotic crusades to "make the world safe for democracy." Their ideas were greeted warmly by the policymakers, who sought, in Stanley Hoffmann's words, to "exorcise isolationism, justify a permanent and global involvement in world affairs, [and] rationalize the accumulation of power."[1]

During the postwar years, political realism swept the field in the United States. Its opponents may have been overwhelmed as much by the exigencies of the Cold War as by the rhetorical brilliance of the leading realists or the power of their arguments. Yet for the most part, discussions of foreign policy have been carried on, since 1945, in the language of political realism—that is, the language of power and interests rather than of ideals or norms. In public discourse in the United States today, foreign policy prescriptions are rarely justified directly by reference to universal moral principles or utopian aspirations. When commentators wish to justify policy prescriptions on ethical grounds, they smuggle their ethics into the ambiguous and elastic concept of "the national interest."[2]

For commentators such as Kennan and Lippmann, the triumph of realism as a way of thinking about foreign policy was sufficient. They were more interested in practice than in abstract theory. Like them,

Morgenthau wished to influence contemporary foreign policy, and much of his writing critically assessed American actions in light of his conception of the "national interest." Morgenthau did not aspire to be a value-free scientist, detached from the world of power. On the contrary, he viewed realism largely as an interpretive guide, which would help us to "look over the shoulder" of a statesman, enabling us "to read and anticipate his very thoughts" (Morgenthau 1948/1978:5; Ashley 1981).

Yet Morgenthau also sought to use Realism to create what he called a "science" of international politics. He was, after all, a scholar who sought to extend knowledge as well as to apply it. Furthermore, he was well aware that political realism was at odds with the American political tradition and would therefore come under attack; when this happened, its status as a science would make it easier to defend. Thus it is not inappropriate for us to consider Morgenthau's bold attempt to create such a science, as long as we do not commit the error of assuming that this was his only aspiration, or that he can be categorized simply as a precursor of later analysts. He was, as Stanley Hoffmann points out, the founding father, if there is one, of our discipline (Hoffmann, 1977:44). Neither Kenneth N. Waltz's *Theory of International Politics,* four chapters from which are reproduced below, nor the responses of Waltz's critics, can be fully understood without some comprehension of Morgenthau's attempt to construct a theory of international politics.

Some of Morgenthau's arguments, such as his reliance on objective national interests, have been thoroughly discussed in the literature. His failure to explore problems of misperception systematically has been noted, and appropriate modifications have been introduced into the realist canon.[3] Other conceptions of his, however, require more attention. Like all realists, Morgenthau relied heavily on the concepts of power, rationality and the balance of power; accordingly, analysis of his treatment of these concepts offers insights into the strengths and weaknesses of realist theory, and therefore into the nature of the task that Waltz set for himself.

Morgenthau characterized international politics as a struggle for power and argued that it could be understood by assuming that statesmen "think and act in terms of interest defined as power" (Morgenthau 1948/1967:5). International politics is a struggle for power not only because of the inherent logic of a competitive realm such as world politics, but also because of the "limitless character of the lust for power [which] reveals a general quality of the human mind" (Morgenthau 1946:194). As Waltz (1959:34ff.) points out, Morgenthau is not content to see power as an instrument for the attainment of other ends in a competitive world, but regards it also as an end in itself, due to the nature of human beings.

Explanations of international conflict as resulting from human nature are vulnerable to severe criticism. As Waltz (1959:39) argues, they blame a small number of behavior traits for conflict, ignoring more benign aspects of human nature that point in the opposite direction. Furthermore, such theories fail to explain variations in warfare over time and space: if human nature is constant, why shouldn't warfare be constant as well?

If Morgenthau's reasons why world politics is a struggle for power are not entirely convincing, neither is his treatment of the concept of power itself. His definition of power was murky, since he failed to distinguish between power as a resource (based on tangible as well as intangible assets) and power as the ability to influence others' behavior. If the latter definition is adopted, *any* effective action in world politics will necessarily involve power; but since this is a tautology, we will have learned nothing about the capabilities that create such influence. Is others' behavior affected more by greater numbers of tanks, superior economic productivity, or by an attractive ideology? If, on the other hand, power is defined in terms of specific resources, we avoid tautology and can begin to construct and test theory. Unfortunately, however, theories based solely on definable power capabilities have proven to be notoriously poor at accounting for political outcomes (Baldwin 1979; March 1966; Keohane 1983, reprinted below in article 7).

Morgenthau's conception of rationality is clearer than his view of power. Although he does not offer a formal definition in *Politics Among Nations,* he seems to accept the conception that is standard in neoclassical economics. To say that governments act rationally in this sense means that they have consistent, ordered preferences, and that they calculate the costs and benefits of all alternative policies in order to maximize their utility in light both of those preferences and of their perceptions of the nature of reality.[4]

Morgenthau explicitly acknowledged that the assumption of rationality was not descriptively accurate—indeed, one of his purposes was to instruct leaders in order to enable them to act more rationally—but he believed that it could be used as a baseline, which could be "tested against the actual facts," making a theory of international politics possible (Morgenthau 1948/1978:5). That is, even though such an assumption is not always descriptively correct, it serves a valuable theoretical function. With it, the analyst can infer actions from interests, and thereby construct an explanatory theory of behavior. Against the baseline provided by the theory's prediction, we can ask how "imperfections" caused by misperceptions, a lack of information, bargaining perversities, or even sheer irrationality could have made actual patterns of behavior diverge from our expectations.

Morgenthau's sophisticated use of the rationality assumption was consistent both with that of Thucydides and those of later realists and neorealists, including Waltz. Yet there are alternative approaches that do not sacrifice the possibility of systemic theory. One such research strategy would be to follow the lead of Herbert Simon, who introduced the notion of bounded rationality into the study of decisionmaking (Simon 1979, 1982). Actors subject to bounded rationality cannot maximize their utilities, since they find it difficult to use available information to calculate the costs and benefits of every alternative course of action. They therefore use shortcuts such as rules of thumb in order to "satisfice"—achieving a satisfactory level of performance rather than an optimal one. In the terms of Akerlof and Yellen (1985), they may be "near rational." That is, their deviations from rationality may not be so costly as to lead them to change their behavior.

This approach seems intuitively to describe governmental behavior better than does maximizing rationality; and it is also more plausible as a description of how business firms behave (Allison 1971; Snyder and Diesing 1977; Nelson and Winter 1982). Although Waltz is content to make theoretical assumptions about units that deviate sharply from their known patterns of behavior, this is not, *pace* Milton Friedman (1953), a universally accepted practice in the natural or social sciences (Cyert and Simon 1983:101; McKeown 1986). Indeed, the correctness of an empirically testable theoretical assumption is by no means irrelevant to the adequacy of a theory. As Cyert and Simon say about neoclassical theory, there are great difficulties in "attributing, to firms, decision processes more sophisticated than those yet invented by economists" (*ibid.*, p. 103).

This objection is reinforced by recent findings that satisficing or near rational behavior at the unit level can produce substantially different system level outcomes than those characteristic of maximizing rationality. This suggests that systemic models based on maximizing assumptions may seriously distort our understanding of what happens in world politics. Students of international politics should be wary of becoming too attached to the assumptions of neoclassical microeconomics, just when these assumptions are under attack on behavioral grounds (Kahneman and Tversky 1984) and when imaginative economists are seeking to build rigorous models based on satisficing (Nelson and Winter 1982) or on near rationality (Akerlof and Yellen 1985). Conceptions of satisficing or near rationality open up the possibility of constructing systemic theories of world politics that do not rely on the implausible unit-level assumption of perfect rationality built into classical microeconomics (Keohane 1984, chapter 7).[5]

Morgenthau's third major concept was that of the balance of power, which he referred to as a "necessary outgrowth" of power politics (Morgenthau 1948/1967:161). The balance of power is for Morgenthau a "universal concept." His desire to demonstrate the universality of the balance of power may be what led him to use the term so broadly as to lead to inconsistency, as I. L. Claude (1962:25–37) showed. Morgenthau used "the balance of power" to refer to a situation of equilibrium as well as to any situation in which power struggles take place; but since Morgenthau did not regard equilibrium as inevitable, this double usage of the phrase led him into unresolvable contradictions.

Without coherent definitions of "power" and "balance of power," Morgenthau was unable to create a consistent and convincing theory. Subsequent attempts to construct better theory were made by others, notably Morton Kaplan (1957), Stanley Hoffmann (1959, 1965), and Richard Rosecrance (1963). All three of these theorists sought to use what Waltz refers to as "systemic theory" to attempt to account for state behavior. That is, they abandoned reliance on the nature of human beings to account for discord and cooperation in world politics, but focused instead on the competitive, anarchic nature of world politics as a whole. Furthermore, unlike Morgenthau—who sought general principles—they were more interested in explaining variations: alternations of war and peace, stability and instability. They asked not so much about an alleged "essence" of international politics as why international systems changed.

In chapter 3 of *Theory of International Politics* (not reprinted in this volume) Waltz agrees with these writers that a good theory of international politics must be systemic, since how the relationships among states are organized strongly affects governments' behavior toward one another. A system, for Waltz, consists of a set of interacting units exhibiting behavioral regularities and having an identity over time. Yet Waltz is severely critical of Hoffmann, Kaplan, and Rosecrance for not having gone beyond the description of international systems to identify their *structures*, defined separately from the attributes of and relations between the units. "In order to turn a systems approach into a theory, one has to move from the usual vague identification of systemic forces and effects to their more precise specification, to say what units the system comprises, to indicate the comparative weights of systemic and subsystemic causes, and to show how forces and effects change from one system to another" (Waltz 1979:40–41). And it is crucial that the analyst "carefully keep the attributes and interactions of the system's units out of the definition of its structure," if the theory is to avoid the perils of reductionism (relying for explanation on unit-level rather than system-level attributes) or tautology.

In chapters 4–6 of *Theory of International Politics,* reprinted as articles 3–5 of this volume, Waltz presents his own systemic theory.[6] The chapter on "reductionist and systemic theories" defends the analytical priority of systemic theory and indicates how such a theory could meaningfully explain state behavior. "Political structures" argues that structure "defines the arrangement, or the ordering, of the parts of a system" (p. 73). Structures vary along three dimensions: by their ordering principles, the specification of functions of formally differentiated parts, and the relative capabilities (or power) of the units themselves. International relations is an anarchic rather than hierarchic realm, populated by units (states) performing similar functions. Thus any international systems that we analyze are "ordered" by the principle of anarchy. And in such systems, we need not be concerned with the functions performed by the units, since they are functionally alike. Thus the dimension of differentiation of units "drops out."

This characterization of the first two attributes of international systems enormously simplifies the analyst's task, since it means that structures of international systems differ only along the third dimension, that of the

distribution of power. In analyzing actual international-political structures, we therefore "abstract from every attribute of states except their
capabilities." What emerges Waltz calls "a positional picture," which
portrays the placement of the units—where they stand relative to one
another—rather than their intrinsic qualities. The key changes that we
are to look for, in international politics, are changes in the distribution
of capabilities across units.

Waltz uses his definitions of system and structure in "Anarchic orders
and balances of power" to develop a theory of the balance of power that
will not be vulnerable to the criticisms leveled against Morgenthau. For
Waltz, a good theory will not merely point to the importance of power
and the balance of power, as Morgenthau did, but will account for the
recurrent formation of balances of power in world politics, and tell us
how changing power configurations affect patterns of alignments and
conflict in world politics. From the anarchic nature of the international
system, and the assumption that states "are unitary actors who, at a
minimum, seek their own preservation and, at a maximum, drive for
universal domination," Waltz deduces that balances of power must necessarily emerge. Furthermore, as states compete with each other "they
will imitate each other and become socialized to their system" (p. 129).

In the next three chapters of *Theory* (not reprinted in this volume),
Waltz applies his structural theory to issues of economic interdependence,
military relationships, and what he calls "the management of international
affairs." He argues in chapter 7 that discussions of interdependence ex-
aggerate the extent to which great powers, including the United States,
are dependent on others. In chapter 8 he contends that military power
remains as useful as ever—even that its usefulness has increased—and
that military bipolarity is remarkably stable. Chapter 9 emphasizes the
role of great powers in maintaining order: the problem "is not to say
how to manage the world, including its great powers, but to say how
the possibility that great powers will constructively manage international
affairs varies as systems change" (Waltz 1979:210).

The significance of Waltz's theory, as elaborated in the selections
reprinted here, lies less in his initiation of a new line of theoretical
inquiry or speculation than in his attempt to systematize political realism
into a rigorous, deductive systemic theory of international politics. The
Waltzian synthesis is referred to here as neorealism, to indicate both its

intellectual affinity with the classical realism of Morgenthau and Herz and its elements of originality and distinctiveness.[7]

III. CRITICISMS AND REBUTTALS

The importance of neorealism has been widely recognized, and it has been subjected to critical scrutiny from a variety of perspectives, and with varying concentration on Waltz's work. Of the articles reprinted here, only one (that of John Gerard Ruggie) actually constitutes a review essay of *Theory of International Politics.* The others all had broader purposes; but for each author, neorealism (a term coined, so far as I know, by Robert W. Cox) constitutes a central issue for discussion, and in every case Waltz's work is recognized as a major statement of neorealist doctrine. Since these articles appeared in a wide variety of publications (three different journals and one collection of works on political science as a discipline), they have often not been considered together, as major contributions to a sustained, focused debate. Thus a major purpose of this volume is to collect the debate on neorealism within one set of covers, so that students and other observers of world politics can focus coherently on the issues that it raises.

Until publication of this volume, Waltz had not responded in print to the criticisms expressed by Ruggie, Cox, Richard K. Ashley, and myself. A second purpose of *Neorealism and Its Critics,* therefore, is to provide an appropriate forum for Waltz to do this, giving readers the opportunity to judge the validity of his theory not only in light of the critics' arguments but in view of his defense and reconsideration of his views. Waltz's response clarifies his arguments, in some cases reducing the differences between himself and his critics, in others making the nature and significance of those disagreements more readily apparent. The intellectually honest and constructive character of his response both advances the debate and illustrates how genuine scholarly discourse should be carried out.

This volume begins with the principal theoretical chapters from *Theory of International Politics,* reprinted with only minor editorial changes so that each reader will have the opportunity to judge Waltz's theory, and the various criticisms of it, for himself or herself. The first commentary consists of Ruggie's review essay; the articles by Keohane, Cox, and Ashley are presented in order of their increasing divergence from Waltz's premises. Following Ashley's essay, the volume continues with a response to Ashley's critique of neorealism by Robert G. Gilpin, and Waltz's concluding essay.[8]

John Gerard Ruggie embeds his criticisms of Waltz in a larger appreciation of his work, declaring *Theory of International Politics* to be "one of the most important contributions to the theory of international relations" since Waltz's last book on the subject, *Man, the State and War* (1959). Yet Ruggie also concludes that Waltz does not fully succeed on his own terms. By truncating his own concept of structure, Waltz has (according to Ruggie) made it impossible for his theory to account for major changes in world politics, such as that between the medieval and modern period. To show this, Ruggie focuses on the concept of sovereignty, arguing that the medieval system differed from the modern one "by the principles on the basis of which the constituent units are separated from one another" (p. 142). After correcting what he regards as Waltz's misleading definition of differentiation, Ruggie uses this concept to depict what he calls an "institutional transformation" from a medieval set of arrangements to the modern conception of sovereignty. He argues that the differentiation of units does not drop out of a structural theory of world politics, but provides a way of understanding change—from the medieval to modern system, and perhaps to a future international system.

Ruggie also criticizes Waltz for overlooking Durkheim's concept of "dynamic density"—the quantity, velocity, and diversity of transactions—as a determinant of change in world politics. Such changing patterns of interdependence could, according to Ruggie, affect world politics even without changes in the structure of the system, narrowly defined. Ultimately, for Ruggie, structural change has no source other than unit-level processes. Waltz's exclusion of such processes prevents him from developing a theory of change in the form of a "generative" model that would analyze how changes in interdependence, or "dynamic density," affect the relationship between the structure of an international system and the degree of order observed within it.

Robert O. Keohane focuses on what he calls the "research program" of Structural Realism—referred to in the rest of this volume as neorealism. Keohane accepts Waltz's emphasis on system-level theory and

his acceptance of the rationality assumption as *starting-points* for theory
in international relations. Keohane argues that systemic theory is essential
both because we have to understand the context of states' actions before
accounting for the actions themselves; and because a good structural
theory can be simpler (more parsimonious) and more readily testable
than theories that rely on variations in the internal attributes of states.

Yet Keohane is dissatisfied with Waltz's theory. He seeks to show that
Waltz's theory of the balance of power is inconsistent with his assumption
that states seek to "maximize power." He points to difficulties in relying
heavily on the ambiguous concept of power, especially when the contexts
within which power is exercised are not sufficiently specified and distinguished from one another. He claims that Waltz fails to test his theory
in accordance with the standards that he set up in chapter 1. He argues
that Waltz's theory does not explain change well and agrees with Ruggie
that more attention needs to be paid to connections between the internal
attributes of states on the one hand, and the international system on the
other.

Keohane suggests the need for a revised theory that incorporates
Waltz's notion of structure but that takes seriously, as explanatory factors,
elements of the international system not included in Waltz's limited
conception of structure. Such a theory would follow the lead of earlier
work by Keohane and Nye (1977), which emphasized the significance of
economic processes and of international political institutions. Keohane
calls for "systemic theories that retain some of the parsimony of Structural Realism, but that are able to deal better with differences between
issue-areas, with institutions, and with change" (p. 197). Foreshadowing
his later work (Keohane 1984), he also calls for more serious attention
to the ways in which international systems may facilitate or inhibit the
flow of information, thereby affecting the behavior of actors and their
ability to cooperate with one another.

Robert W. Cox also focuses on the alleged inability of neorealism to
comprehend change in world politics. In Cox's view, Morgenthau and
Waltz infelicitously transformed realism from the category of historically
based critical theory to what he calls "problem-solving theory," which
regards contemporary institutions and power relations as permanent.
Such a theory is flawed by the error of "taking a form of thought derived
from a particular phase of history (and thus from a particular structure

of social relations) and assuming it to be universally valid" (p. 214). Critical theory is needed to understand change: the analyst needs to stand outside the prevailing order and inquire into how that order came about and what forces are at work to change it. The most promising form of critical theory, for Cox, is historical materialism, which sees conflict as a possible source of structural change rather than as "a recurrent consequence of a continuing structure" (p. 215). By analyzing the interplay of ideas, material capabilities, institutions, and social forces, critical theorists can understand how world orders, such as the *Pax Americana,* came about and can therefore discern some of the possible ways in which they might change.

In a postscript written especially for this volume, Cox contrasts the research programs of positivism (with which he associates Waltz's neorealism) and of historicism, or historical materialism (with which he identifies himself). Cox argues that neorealism does not sufficiently take account of human ideas and practices, and that its search for general laws prevents it from accounting for change. The research program of historicism, by contrast, involves finding connections between people's ideas and the material world, revealing the historical structures characteristic of particular eras, and ultimately explaining transformations from one structure to another. In contrast to neorealism, which is "ideologically at the service of big-power management of the international system," Cox's nondeterministic Marxism focuses on class struggle as "the heuristic model for the understanding of structural change" (p. 248).

Like Cox, Richard K. Ashley sharply distinguishes neorealism from the classical realism of Morgenthau and Herz. Neorealism, like structuralist analysis in other fields, seeks to "transcend empiricist fixations" by comprehending deeper levels of social reality through systematic social scientific investigation; yet according to Ashley, this attempt leads to contradictions and ideological narrowness. Neorealism is statist, yet the atomistic utilitarian epistemology adopted by its proponents undermines "the ideal of the state-as-actor upon which their distinction among 'levels' and their whole theory of international politics depend" (p. 279). Furthermore, the positivist commitment to technical rationality and the dichotomy between scientific knowledge and values "ties positivism to an ideology of its own" by endorsing an unquestionable faith in scientific-technical progress (p. 282). Positivism becomes committed to what Ashley calls an "actor model" of social reality, within which science cannot question the constitution or the ends of social actors, but can only provide advice about means. In the end, therefore, "politics in neorealism becomes pure technique." Neorealism thus combines the superficiality of positivistic atomism and structuralism's inability to account for change, with an ideological aversion to critical thinking about values.

Ashley's alternative is his *dialectical competence model,* which has some obvious affinities with Cox's project for the analysis of changing social forces. Ashley's model would account for the emergence of balance of power politics and explore the conditions for its continuation or transformation. In particular, it would explore the subjective aspects of the balance of power, focusing on the manipulation of symbols and on learning. It would seek to provide an account of crisis and consider alternatives to "the modern global hegemony," in the hope of transcending its conditions of dominance. And it would reinterpret neorealism as a perverse research program contributing to "the impoverishment of political imagination and the reduction of international politics to a battleground for the self-blind strategic clash of technical reason against technical reason in the service of unquestioned ends" (Ashley, p. 297).

The criticisms of neorealism made by Ruggie, Keohane, Cox, and Ashley can be summarized with the aid of an architectural metaphor. Those who accept the foundations of neorealism, and the overall shape of the building, can still argue about the exact design. If the concept of international structure is valuable, how much should it include: what should be the boundaries between unit-level and system-level variables? To what extent should system-level analysis have priority over analysis of foreign policy, and how should the analysis of these two levels be linked? More fundamental questions about the edifice itself can be raised even by scholars who accept neorealism's utilitarian, positivistic methodology. How well-crafted are the cornerstone concepts of power, the balance of power and sovereignty? Shouldn't neorealist theory take better account of institutions and the role of information? How could neorealism be reformulated to account for transformation as well as continuity? Finally, the deeper foundations of the structure can be questioned. Neorealism, in the view of its more severe critics, ignores both history and human subjectivity. It does not investigate how the order that it analyzes came about, nor does it consider the production relations on which it depends. Philosophically, according to the critics, neorealism does not rest on the solid rock of a coherent epistemology but rather is sinking into a swamp of a state-as-actor theory contradicted by its utilitarian premises.

In the symposium that accompanied "The Poverty of Neorealism" in *International Organization,* Robert G. Gilpin replied to many of Ashley's criticisms. In his essay reprinted below, Gilpin describes realism as emphasizing that "the final arbiter of things political is power," and that "the essence of social reality is the group," represented preeminently in our own time by the state. Gilpin concentrates his critique on Ashley's distinction between classical realism and neorealism. For Gilpin, continuity in the tradition of political realism is more important than differences between contemporary neorealists and their intellectual ancestors. Gilpin contends that the greatest realist writers have always appreciated "the intimate connection between international politics and international economics" (Gilpin, p. 309). Nor do neorealists adopt determinism in contrast to the classical realists' view that statesmen can change the international environment. Finally, the neorealists, like classical realists, adhere to moral values that they seek to promote: they are not guilty of "moral neutrality." On the contrary, "moral skepticism joined to a hope that reason may one day gain greater control over passions constitutes the essence of realism and unites realists of every generation" (p. 321).

Waltz, in his concluding essay, focuses principally on three issues that have attracted the attention of his critics: (1) what he calls his "spare" definition of international-political structure, criticized especially by Ruggie; (2) his view on how theories should be tested, questioned by Keohane; and (3) his attempt to construct a problem-solving international structural theory of international politics rather than a critical theory of the state—which in his view is the focus of Cox's and Ashley's principal complaints.

In defending himself from Ruggie's charge of truncating the concept of structure and overlooking "dynamic density," Waltz argues that dynamic density reflects unit-level processes rather than system structure. In Waltz's view, elegant definitions of structure (which Ruggie regards as truncated and insufficiently rich) have the great virtues of precision and parsimony: they "enable one to fashion an explanatory system having only a few variables" (p. 330). They do not tell us everything; but they do help us understand fundamental continuities in world politics that would otherwise be obscured by inclusion of too many other factors that vary from one era to another.

In responding to Ruggie's objection, Waltz is attempting also to rebut my own claim that a good systems-level theory would take into account "the institutional context of action as well as the underlying power realities and state position upon which Realist thought concentrates" (p. 195, below). Ruggie and I both seek to make systemic theory account for more of what we see by taking into account aspects of international systems that are excluded from Waltz's spare concept of structure. Waltz regards changes in the intensity of interactions among the members of a system, or in the international institutions that connect them, as unit-level phenomena because patterns of interaction are not included as part of his definition of system structure.

Yet these patterns do not depend on differences among the internal attributes of states. On the contrary, changes both in the intensity of interactions and in international institutions can take place even when states continue to be similar in their internal attributes. These changes, furthermore, may affect actors' behavior in classic systemic ways by altering the incentives and opportunities that face them. Such processes and institutions should therefore, in my view, be considered system-level rather than unit-level changes. By contrast, a unit-level theory relies on cross-national variations to explain variations in outcomes. The international system includes systemwide processes and institutions as well as a structure in Waltz's sense: this should not be forgotten when we construct systemic theories of international politics.[9]

In contrast to the continuing debate over the boundaries of systemic and unit-level explanations, Waltz's response to my points on testing seems to suggest convergence between our views. I had interpreted Waltz, in chapter 1, as believing that social science theories could be tested rigorously, and then criticized Waltz for not following his own methodological strictures. In his response, Waltz explicitly adopts a more complex and sophisticated view of social science theory-testing, one that is close to that of Lakatos, with which I am sympathetic. By renouncing the naïve falsificationism that he had seemed to adopt in chapter 1 of *Theory*, Waltz clarifies his views and removes the apparent inconsistency in his earlier argument.

In reply to Cox, Waltz affirms that he set out to construct what Cox refers to as problem-solving theory, and to do so at the level of the international system. In Waltz's view, it is these choices to which Cox objects: Cox believes in critical theory and thinks that without a theory of domestic politics and state-society relations, a theory of international structure is of limited value. To Waltz, Ashley's objections run along similar lines. Associating himself with Gilpin's response to Ashley, Waltz goes on to deny that he assumes, ahistorically, that states will always exist as they do now. "I find it hard to believe," he says, "that anyone would think that states will remain fixed in their present condition" (p. 339). He holds, however, that in building a systems-level theory, it is theoretically useful to assume unitary, purposeful states, whose internal characteristics do not vary. "A separate theory dealing with the politics and policies of states" would be valuable; but Waltz did not set himself this task.

According to Waltz, this separation of theories of international politics and theories of the state would be problematic only if one sought to combine international and domestic politics in one theory; but Waltz doubts that this is possible.

Waltz's response to Ashley takes us back to the issue that I raised earlier in this essay when discussing Morgenthau's conception of rationality. Since Waltz accepts the separation of international and domestic political theory, he is content to follow the lead of neoclassical economists, who do the same. Waltz argues that "economists get along quite well with separate theories of markets and firms" (p. 340). But a number of economists are discontented with the disjunction between our knowledge of firms' behavior and orthodox microeconomic theory. Richard Nelson and Sydney Winter view the neoclassical assumption that "economic man is a perfect mathematician" as an "affront to reason [that] is not innocuous" (1982:66). Richard Cyert and Herbert A. Simon regard this assumption as empirically indefensible and not in accord with the canons of natural science (Cyert and Simon, 1983:101). One of the issues highlighted by the debate between Waltz and his critics is precisely how serious is the disjunction between the assumptions of our systemic theory and what we know about unit-level behavior. Some of us seek eventually to build an integrated theory of world politics, linking the domestic and international levels of analysis, rather than being content with unit-level and system-level theories that are inconsistent with one another. Insofar as this is our goal, we should hesitate before following the neoclassical economists into what may be an intellectual dead-end.[10]

CONCLUSION

The issues on which the neorealist debate explicitly focuses are familiar ones to social scientists, since they have to do with levels of analysis, the precision of concepts, and philosophical underpinnings of theory. Underneath these conundrums, however, lurk questions of purposes and values, theory and practice. The reality of domination—of certain states over others, and of elites over nonelites—continues. More novel is the shadow of atomic weapons, which hangs over all students of world politics today, giving urgency to their attempts to discover how conflict could be limited and cooperation facilitated. The widespread, if varied, sense of dissatisfaction with Waltz's version of neorealism has its roots not only in the critical, idealistic tradition of commentary on world politics, but also in the enormity of nuclear war. Although the critics reject the answers of Wilsonian liberalism, they share the traditional liberal, and Marxist, sense of unease about *Realpolitik*. They seek in some sense to move, in Ernst Haas's phrase, "beyond the nation-state" (Haas 1964)— by devising new international institutions or regimes, by thinking about changes in the principles of sovereignty on the basis of which units are currently separated from one another, or by fundamentally questioning the validity of the "state as actor" model on which neorealism relies.

Thus the critics of neorealism also challenge, more or less profoundly, the adequacy of the interstate system in the contemporary era; and this challenge raises once again the questions of theory and practice discussed in the first part of this essay. If neorealism as articulated by Waltz remains an adequate theory, efficacious action in world politics will have to take account of the limitations of anarchy to which it points. But if it is seriously incomplete, as Ruggie and I argue, more attention will need to be paid to aspects of world politics that it downgrades or ignores: economic and ecological interdependence, changes in the functional capabilities of governments, variations in the availability of information, and the role of international institutions and regimes. If it is erroneous to its positivist core, as Cox and Ashley believe, the theory will need to be restructured in conjunction with massive changes in political practice. Readers' judgments about these theoretical issues must necessarily affect how they think about foreign policy and world politics.

None of these issues can be resolved here; they can only be raised. Since this volume does not enunciate an orthodoxy, its contributors can only hope that you, the reader, learn from our disagreements:

> Like or find fault, do as your pleasures are,
> Now good or bad, 'tis but the chance of war.[11]

NOTES

1. Hoffmann (1977), pp. 47–48. See Herz (1951); Kennan (1951); Lippmann (1943); Morgenthau (1946); and Morgenthau (1948/1967).

2. On the ambiguity of the "national interest," see Arnold Wolfers, "The National Interest as an Ambiguous Symbol," in Wolfers (1962:147–165). The ideological hegemony of realism is regarded as a mixed blessing by some of its original proponents. Herz has recently emphasized that he never regarded realism and idealism as incompatible: " 'Realist liberalism' renders realism 'more humane' and idealism 'less chimerical' " (Herz 1981:203). Even Morgenthau, in *Politics Among Nations,* acknowledged that international politics operates within the framework of rules and institutions, although he stressed that it "cannot be reduced to legal rules and institutions" (Morgenthau 1946/1967:16).

3. On the concept of the national interest, see Rosenau (1968) and George (1980), chapter 13. For a classic study of misperceptions, see Jervis (1976). For an attempt to incorporate the concept of misperception into realist theory, see Kindermann (1985).

4. For an enlightening discussion of "rationale explanations" in political science, see Moon (1975), especially pp. 156–166. A pathbreaking although controversial attempt to use the assumption of maximizing rationality is Bueno de Mesquita (1981). For an incisive critique of this assumption, see McKeown (1986).

5. Readers of my article "Theory of World Politics: Structural Realism and Beyond" will recognize that I have become more skeptical of the value of assuming rationality than I was when the article was written. See below, pp. 190–197.

6. Chapter 1 of *Theory,* which indicates how Waltz views social theory and the tests he regards as appropriate for it, is also reprinted below, as article 2 of this volume.

7. Since I am critical of Waltz on a number of points, it follows that I am unwilling to classify myself as a neorealist, despite my sympathy with a number of Waltz's positions and Richard Ashley's inclusion of my name as one of the contemporary neorealists. As readers of my essay reprinted in this volume, or my subsequent book, *After Hegemony* (1984), will recognize, I admire the clarity and parsimony of

Waltz's systemic theory without subscribing to many of the inferences that he draws from it.

8. When I refer to myself in this essay with reference exclusively to my 1983 essay on theories of world politics, reprinted as article 7 below, I use the third person, but when I refer to my current views, I use the first person form.

9. The theory of regime change presented in *Power and Interdependence* (1977) by Joseph S. Nye and myself is a system-level rather than a unit-level theory by the criteria outlined in this paragraph. So is my functional theory of international regimes in chapter 6 of *After Hegemony* (1984).

10. As Timothy McKeown (1986) has emphasized, the question is how much we should rely on a theory whose premises are markedly inconsistent with what we know about how choices are actually made. Admittedly, as Waltz emphasizes, every theory employs simplifying assumptions; but if a theory neither makes accurate predictions about state behavior nor helps us understand the political processes of choice, it may be inferior to potential alternatives. Illustrating his argument, McKeown points out the difficulties encountered by several generations of structural theorists who have sought to explain states' trade policies by employing the unitary actor, utility-maximizing assumptions of microeconomics.

11. William Shakespeare, *The History of Troilus and Cressida* (1603), prologue, lines 30–31.

TWO
Laws and Theories

KENNETH N. WALTZ

I WRITE THIS BOOK with three aims in mind: first, to examine
theories of international politics and approaches to the subject matter
that make some claim to being theoretically important; second, to construct a theory of international politics that remedies the defects of
present theories; and third, to examine some applications of the theory
constructed. The required preliminary to the accomplishment of these
tasks is to say what theories are and to state the requirements for testing
them.

I

Students of international politics use the term "theory" freely, often to
cover any work that departs from mere description and seldom to refer
only to work that meets philosophy-of-science standards. The aims I
intend to pursue require that definitions of the key terms *theory* and *law*
be carefully chosen. Whereas two definitions of theory vie for acceptance,
a simple definition of law is widely accepted. Laws establish relations
between variables, variables being concepts that can take different values.
If *a*, then *b*, where *a* stands for one or more independent variables and
b stands for the dependent variable: In form, this is the statement of a
law. If the relation between *a* and *b* is invariant, the law is absolute. If
the relation is highly constant, though not invariant, the law would read
like this: If *a*, then *b* with probability *x*. A law is based not simply on a
relation that has been found, but on one that has been found repeatedly.
Repetition gives rise to the expectation that if I find *a* in the future,
then with specified probability I will also find *b*. In the natural sciences
even probabilistic laws contain a strong imputation of necessity. In the

social sciences to say that persons of specified income vote Democratic with a certain probability is to make a law-like statement. The word *like* implies a lesser sense of necessity. Still, the statement would not be at all like a law unless the relation had so often and so reliably been found in the past that the expectation of its holding in the future with comparable probability is high.[1]

By one definition, theories are collections or sets of laws pertaining to a particular behavior or phenomenon. In addition to income, for example, associations may be established between voters' education, their religion, and their parents' political commitment, on the one hand, and the way they vote, on the other hand. If the probabilistic laws thus established are taken together, higher correlations are achieved between voters' characteristics (the independent variables) and choice of party (the dependent variable). Theories are, then, more complex than laws, but only quantitatively so. Between laws and theories no difference of kind appears.

This first definition of theory supports the aspiration of those many social scientists who would "build" theory by collecting carefully verified, interconnected hypotheses. The following story suggests how most political scientists think of theory:

Homer describes the walls of Troy as being eight feet thick. If his account is true, then millennia later one should be able to find those walls by careful digging. This thought occurred to Heinrich Schliemann as a boy, and as a man he put the theory to empirical test. Karl Deutsch uses the story as an example of how new-style theories are tested (1966:168–169). A theory is born in conjecture and is viable if the conjecture is confirmed. Deutsch regards theories of the simple if–then sort as "special theories," which may "later on become embedded in a grand theory." He then gives other examples and in doing so shifts "from a yes-or-no question to a how-much question." We should try to find out how much of a contribution "different variables" make to a given result (pp. 219–21).

What is possibly useful in such a pattern of thinking, and what is not? Everyone knows that a coefficient of correlation, even a high one, does not warrant saying that a causal relation exists. Squaring the coefficient, however, technically permits us to say that we have accounted for a certain percentage of the variance. It is then easy to believe that a real

causal connection has been identified and measured, to think that the
relation between an independent and a dependent variable has been
established, and to forget that something has been said only about dots
on a piece of paper and the regression line drawn through them. Is the
correlation spurious? That suggests the right question without quite asking it. Correlations are neither spurious nor genuine; they are merely
numbers that one gets by performing simple mathematical operations. A
correlation is neither spurious nor genuine, but the relation that we infer
from it may be either. Suppose someone propounds a law, for example,
by carefully establishing the relation between the amount of push im-
parted to a cart and the amount of its movement. The relation established,
if conditions are kept constant and measurement is careful, is simply a
fact of observation, a law that remains constantly valid. The *explanation*
offered for that relation of push and movement, however, is radically
different depending on whether we consult Aristotle or Galileo or Newton. The uncritical acceptance of a number as indicating that a connection
obtains is the first danger to guard against. To do so is fairly easy. The
next problem is more important and harder to solve.

Even if we have satisfied ourselves in various ways that a correlation
points to a connection that reliably holds, we still have not accounted
for that connection in the sense of having explained it. We have accounted
for it in the way—and only in the way—that Aristotelian physics accounted for the relation between push and movement. From a practical
standpoint, knowledge of the high correlation between push and movement is very useful. That descriptive knowledge may suggest clues about
the principles of motion. It may as easily be grossly misleading, as indeed
it turned out to be. Numbers may describe what goes on in the world.
But no matter how securely we nail a description down with numbers,
we still have not explained what we have described. Statistics do not
show how anything works or fits together. Statistics are simply descriptions in numerical form. The form is economical because statistics describe a universe through manipulation of samples drawn from it.
Statistics are useful because of the variety of ingenious operations that
can be performed, some of which can be used to check on the significance of others. The result, however, remains a description of some part
of the world and not an explanation of it. Statistical operations cannot
bridge the gap that lies between description and explanation. Karl

Deutsch advises us "to formulate, or reformulate, a proposition in terms of probability and to say *how much* of the outcome could be accounted for by one element and how much of the outcome could be accounted for from the other elements or is autonomous and free" (1966:220). If we follow that advice, we will behave like Aristotelian physicists. We will treat a problem as though it were like the one of trying to say to what extent a cart's movement results from push and slope and to what extent its movement is impeded by frictions. We will continue to think in sequential and correlational terms. By doing so, results that are practically useful may be achieved, although students of international politics have disappointingly little to show for such efforts, even in practical terms. And if useful information were uncovered, the more difficult task of figuring out its theoretical meaning would remain.

The "inductivist illusion," as structural anthropologist Lévi-Strauss terms it, is the belief that truth is won and explanation achieved through the accumulation of more and more data and the examination of more and more cases. If we gather more and more data and establish more and more associations, however, we will not finally find that we know something. We will simply end up having more and more data and larger sets of correlations. Data never speak for themselves. Observation and experience never lead directly to knowledge of causes. As the American pragmatist, C. S. Peirce, once said, "direct experience is neither certain nor uncertain, because it affirms nothing—it just *is*. It involves no error, because it testifies to nothing but its own appearance. For the same reason, it affords no certainty" (quoted in Nagel 1956:150). Data, seeming facts, apparent associations—these are not certain knowledge of something. They may be puzzles that can one day be explained; they may be trivia that need not be explained at all.

If we follow the inductivist route, we can deal only with pieces of problems. The belief that the pieces can be added up, that they can be treated as independent variables whose summed effects will account for a certain portion of a dependent variable's movement, rests on nothing more than faith. We do not know what to add up, and we do not know whether addition is the appropriate operation. The number of pieces that might be taken as parts of a problem is infinite, and so is the number of ways in which the pieces may be combined. Neither observationally nor experimentally can one work with an infinity of objects and combinations. In the following example, Ross Ashby offers an apt caution. Astrophysicists seek to explain the behavior of star clusters with 20,000 members. The beginner, Ashby observes, "will say simply that he wants to know what the cluster will do, i.e., he wants the trajectories of the components. If this knowledge, however, could be given to him, it would take the form of many volumes filled with numerical tables, and he would then realise that he did not really want all that." The problem, Ashby concludes, is how to find out what we really want to know without "being overwhelmed with useless detail" (1956:113). The old motto "knowledge for the sake of knowledge" is an appealing one, perhaps because one can keep busy and at the same time avoid the difficult question of knowledge for what. Because facts do not speak for themselves, because associations never contain or conclusively suggest their own explanation, the question must be faced. The idea of "knowledge for the sake of knowledge" loses its charm, and indeed its meaning, once one realizes that the possible objects of knowledge are infinite.

Today's students of politics nevertheless display a strong commitment to induction. They examine numerous cases with the hope that connections and patterns will emerge and that those connections and patterns will represent the frequently mentioned "reality that is out there." The hope apparently rests on the conviction that knowledge begins with certainties and that induction can uncover them. But we can never say with assurance that a state of affairs inductively arrived at corresponds to something objectively real. What we think of as reality is itself an elaborate conception constructed and reconstructed through the ages. Reality emerges from our selection and organization of materials that are available in infinite quantity. How can we decide which materials to select and how to arrange them? No inductive procedure can answer the question, for the very problem is to figure out the criteria by which induction can usefully proceed.

Those who believe, oddly, that knowledge begins with certainties think of theories as edifices of truth, which they would build inductively. They define theories as hypotheses that are confirmed and connected. But empirical knowledge is always problematic. Experience often misleads us. As Heinrich Hertz put it, "that which is derived from experience can again be annulled by experience" (1894:357). Nothing is ever both empirical and absolutely true, a proposition established by Immanuel Kant and now widely accepted at least by natural scientists. And since empirical knowledge is potentially infinite in extent, without some guidance we can know neither what information to gather nor how to put it together so that it becomes comprehensible. If we could directly apprehend the world that interests us, we would have no need for theory. We cannot. One can reliably find his way among infinite materials only with the guidance of theory defined in the second sense.

Rather than being mere collections of laws, theories are statements that explain them (cf. Nagel 1961:80–81; Isaak 1969:138–139). Theories are qualitatively different from laws. Laws identify invariant or probable associations. Theories show why those associations obtain. Each descriptive term in a law is directly tied to observational or experimental tests. In addition to descriptive terms, theories contain theoretical notions. Theories cannot be constructed through induction alone, for theoretical notions can only be invented, not discovered. Aristotle dealt with real motion, that is with the ratios of effort to movement that are matters of common experience. Galileo took bold steps away from the real world in order to explain it. Aristotle believed that objects are naturally at rest and that effort is required to move them; Galileo assumed that both rest and uniform circular motion are natural and that an object remains in either of these conditions in the absence of outside forces. Newton conceived of a uniform rectilinear motion. The theory he devised to explain it introduced such theoretical notions as point-mass, instantaneous acceleration, force, and absolute space and time, none of which can be observed or experimentally determined. At each step, from Aristotle through Galileo to Newton, the theoretical concepts became bolder— that is, further removed from our sense experience.

A theoretical notion may be a concept, such as force, or an assumption, such as the assumption that mass concentrates at a point. A theoretical notion does not explain or predict anything. We know, and so did Newton, that mass does not concentrate at a point. But it was not odd of Newton to assume that it did, for assumptions are not assertions of fact. They are neither true nor false. Theoretical notions find their justification in the success of the theories that employ them. Of purported laws, we ask: "Are they true?" Of theories, we ask: "How great is their explanatory power?" Newton's theory of universal gravitation provided a unified explanation of celestial and terrestrial phenomena. Its power lay in the number of previously disparate empirical generalizations and laws that could be subsumed in one explanatory system, and in the number and range of new hypotheses generated or suggested by the theory, hypotheses that in turn led to new experimental laws.

Aristotle concluded that, within limits, "a given body can be displaced in a set time through a distance proportional to the effort available" (Toulmin 1961:49). Whether by ancient or modern mechanics, the high correlation of push and movement holds true. But how is it to be explained? Such facts have remained constant; the theories accepted as adequate for their explanation have changed radically. Laws are "facts of observation"; theories are "speculative processes introduced to explain them." Experimental results are permanent; theories, however well supported, many not last (Andrade 1957:29, 242). Laws remain, theories come and go.

Since I see no reason for wasting the word "theory" by defining it as a set of two or more laws, I adopt the second meaning of the term: Theories explain laws. This meaning does not accord with usage in much of traditional political theory, which is concerned more with philosophic interpretation than with theoretical explanation. It does correspond to the definition of the term in the natural sciences and in some of the social sciences, especially economics. The definition also satisfies the need for a term to cover the explanatory activity we persistently engage in. In order to get beyond "the facts of observation," as we wish irresistibly to do, we must grapple with the problem of explanation. The urge to explain is not born of idle curiosity alone. It is produced also by the desire to control, or at least to know if control is possible, rather than merely to predict. Prediction follows from knowledge of the regularity of associations embodied in laws. Sunrises and sunsets can be reliably predicted on the basis of empirical findings alone, without benefit of theories explaining why the phenomena occur. Prediction may certainly be useful: The forces that propel two bodies headed for a collision may be inaccessible, but if we can predict the collision, we can at least get out of the way. Still, we would often like to be able to exert some control. Because a law does not say why a particular association holds, it cannot tell us whether we can exercise control and how we might go about doing so. For the latter purposes we need a theory.

A theory, though related to the world about which explanations are wanted, always remains distinct from that world. "Reality" will be congruent neither with a theory nor with a model that may represent it. Because political scientists often think that the best model is the one that reflects reality most accurately, further discussion is needed.

Model is used in two principal ways. In one sense a model represents a theory. In another sense a model pictures reality while simplifying it, say, through omission or through reduction of scale. If such a model departs too far from reality, it becomes useless. A model airplane should look like a real airplane. Explanatory power, however, is gained by moving away from "reality," not by staying close to it. A full description would be of least explanatory power; an elegant theory, of most. The latter would be at an extreme remove from reality; think of physics. Departing from reality is not necessarily good, but unless one can do so in some clever way, one can only describe and not explain. Thus James Conant once defined science as "a dynamic undertaking directed to lowering the degree of the empiricism involved in solving problems" (1952:62). A model of a theory will be about as far removed from reality as the theory it represents. In modeling a theory, one looks for suggestive ways of depicting the theory, and not the reality it deals with. The model then presents the theory, with its theoretical notions necessarily omitted, whether through organismic, mechanical, mathematical, or other expressions.

Some political scientists write of theoretical models as though they were of the model airplane sort. For example, they first criticize the state-centric model of international politics because it has supposedly become further and further removed from reality. Then they try earnestly to make models that mirror reality ever more fully. If their efforts were to succeed, the model and the real world would become one and the same. The error made is the opposite of the one Immanuel Kant so cogently warned against, that is, of thinking that what is true in theory may not be so in practice. As Kant well understood, his warning did not imply that theory and practice are identical. Theory explains some part of reality and is therefore distinct from the reality it explains. If the distinction is preserved, it becomes obvious that induction from observables cannot in itself yield a theory that explains the observed. "A theory can be tested by experience," as Albert Einstein once said, "but there is no way from experience to the setting up of a theory" (quoted in Harris

1970:121). To claim that it is possible to arrive at a theory inductively is to claim that we can understand phenomena before the means for their explanation are contrived.

The point is not to reject induction, but to ask what induction can and cannot accomplish. Induction is used at the level of hypotheses and laws rather than at the level of theories. Laws are different from theories, and the difference is reflected in the distinction between the way in which laws may be discovered and the way in which theories have to be constructed. Hypotheses may be inferred from theories. If they are confimed quite conclusively, they are called laws. Hypotheses may also be arrived at inductively. Again, if they are confirmed quite conclusively, they are called laws. Ebb and flood tides were predicted by ancient Babylonians with an accuracy unsurpassed until the end of the nineteenth century. Highly reliable knowledge of the law-like movement of tides did not enable one to explain them. Hypotheses about the association of this with that, no matter how well confirmed, do not give birth to theories. Associations never contain or conclusively suggest their own explanation.

Though in itself induction leads to a theoretical dead end, we nevertheless need some sense of the puzzling connections of things and events before we can worry about constructing theories. At the same time we need a theory, or some theories, in order to know what kind of data and connections to look for. Knowledge, it seems, must precede theory, and yet knowledge can proceed only from theory. This looks much like the dilemma suggested by the Platonic proposition that we cannot know anything until we know everything. Take this thought literally, and one is driven to despair. Take it instead as a statement of the strategic problem of gaining knowledge, and no more is suggested than the difficulties in any field of getting onto an intellectual track that promises to lead to some progress.

If induction is not the way to get onto a useful track, what is? The leap from law to theory, from the fashioning of hypotheses to the development of explanations of them, cannot be made by taking information as evidence and seeking more of it. The leap cannot be made by continuing to ask what is associated with what, but rather by trying to answer such questions as these: Why does this occur? How does that thing work? What causes what? How does it all hang together?

If a theory is not an edifice of truth and not a reproduction of reality, then what is it? A theory is a picture, mentally formed, of a bounded realm or domain of activity. A theory is a depiction of the organization of a domain and of the connections among its parts (cf. Boltzman 1905). The infinite materials of any realm can be organized in endlessly different ways. A theory indicates that some factors are more important than others and specifies relations among them. In reality, everything is related to everything else, and one domain cannot be separated from others. Theory isolates one realm from all others in order to deal with it intellectually. To isolate a realm is a precondition to developing a theory that will explain what goes on within it. If the precondition cannot be met, and that of course is a possibility, then the construction of theory for the matters at hand is impossible. The question, as ever with theories, is not whether the isolation of a realm is realistic, but whether it is useful. And usefulness is judged by the explanatory and predictive powers of the theory that may be fashioned.

Theories, though not divorced from the world of experiment and observation, are only indirectly connected with it. Thus the statement made by many that theories can never be proved true. If "truth" is the question, then we are in the realm of law, not of theory. Thus the statement made by James B. Conant, a chemist, that "a theory is only overthrown by a better theory" (1947:48). Thus the statement made by John Rader Platt, a physicist, that "the pressure of scientific determinism becomes weak and random as we approach the great unitary syntheses. For they are not only discoveries. They are also artistic creations, shaped by the taste and style of a single hand" (1956:75). And these statements can all be read as glosses on the famous proof of the mathematician Henri Poincaré that if one mechanical explanation for a phenomenon can be given, then so can an infinity of others.[2] Theories do construct *a* reality, but no one can ever say that it is *the* reality. We are therefore faced with both an infinity of data and an infinity of possible explanations of the data. The problem is a double one. Facts do not determine theories; more than one theory may fit any set of facts. Theories do not explain facts conclusively; we can never be sure that a good theory will not be replaced by a better one.

I have said what theories are and what they are not, but I have not said how theories are made. How are they made? The best, but unhelpful, short answer is this: "creatively." The word sets the problem without saying how to solve it. How does one move between observations and experiments and theories that explain them? The longest process of painful trial and error will not lead to the construction of a theory unless at some point a brilliant intuition flashes, a creative idea emerges. One cannot say how the intuition comes and how the idea is born. One can say what they will be about. They will be about the organization of the subject matter. They will convey a sense of the unobservable relations of things. They will be about connections and causes by which sense is made of things observed. A theory is not the occurrences seen and the associations recorded, but is instead the explanation of them. The formula for the acceleration of a freely falling body does not explain how the body falls. For the explanation one looks in classical physics to the whole Newtonian system—a package of interconnected concepts, an organization of the physical world in which the pertinent happenings become natural or necessary. Once the system is understood, once its principle of organization is grasped, the phenomena are explained. All of this is well summed up in words that Werner Heisenberg attributess to Wolfgang Pauli: " 'Understanding' probably means nothing more than having whatever ideas and concepts are needed to recognize that a great many different phenomena are part of a coherent whole" (1971:33).

By a theory the significance of the observed is made manifest. A theory arranges phenomena so that they are seen as mutually dependent; it connects otherwise disparate facts; it shows how changes in some of the phenomena necessarily entail changes in others. To form a theory requires envisioning a pattern where none is visible to the naked eye. The pattern is not the sum of the substance of our daily world. Scientific facts are highly special and relatively few as compared to all of the things that could conceivably be brought within explanatory systems. A theory must then be constructed through simplifying. That is made obvious by thinking of any theory, whether Isaac Newton's or Adam Smith's, or by thinking of the alternative—to seek not explanation through simplification but accurate reproduction through exhaustive description. Simplifications lay bare the essential elements in play and indicate the necessary relations of cause and interdependency—or suggest where to look for them.

Even by those who have authored them, the emergence of theories cannot be described in other than uncertain and impressionistic ways. Elements of theories can, however, be identified. The difficulty of moving from causal speculations based on factual studies to theoretical formulations that lead one to view facts in particular ways is experienced in any field. To cope with the difficulty, simplification is required. This is achieved mainly in the following four ways: (1) by isolation, which requires viewing the actions and interactions of a small number of factors and forces as though in the meantime other things remain equal; (2) by abstraction, which requires leaving some things aside in order to concentrate on others; (3) by aggregation, which requires lumping disparate elements together according to criteria derived from a theoretical purpose; (4) by idealization, which requires proceeding as though perfection were attained or a limit reached even though neither can be. Whatever the means of simplifying may be, the aim is to try to find the central tendency among a confusion of tendencies, to single out the propelling principle even though other principles operate, to seek the essential factors where innumerable factors are present.

In addition to simplifications, or as forms of them, theories embody theoretical assumptions. Imagining that mass concentrates at a point, inventing genes, mesons, and neutrinos, positing a national interest, and defining nations as unitary and purposive actors: These are examples of common assumptions. Theories are combinations of descriptive and theoretical statements. The theoretical statements are nonfactual elements of a theory. They are not introduced freely or whimsically. They are not introduced in the ancient and medieval manner as fictions invented to save a theory. They are introduced only when they make explanation possible. The worth of a theoretical notion is judged by the usefulness of the theory of which it is a part. Theoretical notions enable us to make sense of the data; the data limit the freedom with which theoretical notions are invented. Theorists create their assumptions. Whether or not they are acceptable depends on the merit of the scientific structure of which they are a part.

Constructing theories involves more than the performance of logically permissible operations on observed data. By deduction nothing can be explained, for the results of deduction follow logically from initial premises. Deduction may give certain answers, but nothing new; what is deduced is already present either in theoretical major premises or in empirical minor premises dealing with matters previously observed. Induction may give new answers, but nothing certain; the multiplication of particular observations can never support a universal statement. Theory is fruitful because it goes beyond the necessarily barren hypothetico-deductive approach. Both induction and deduction are indispensable in the construction of theory, but using them in combination gives rise to a theory only if a creative idea emerges. The task of constructing theories becomes both more consequential and more complicated, and so does the task of verifying them. The relation between theory and observation, or between theory and fact, becomes puzzling.

As an example of this puzzling relation, consider the problem of defining the terms used in a theory. Think of the distinct meanings in different physical theories of space, energy, momentum, and time. Obviously such notions have no meaning outside of the theory in which they appear (Nagel 1961:17, 127f.). That theoretical notions are defined by the theory in which they appear is easily understood. In the field of international politics, think of the different meanings commonly attached to the words in the following list: power, force, pole, relation, actor, stability, structure, and system. The meanings of such terms vary depending on their user's approach to the subject. This is necessarily so in any field where theories are contradictory. The contradiction of theories creates differences in the meanings of terms across theories. In international politics, as in the social sciences generally, theories turn out to be weak ones. The weakness of theories creates uncertainty of meanings even within a single theory. In international politics, whether because theories are contradictory or weak, discussion and argument about many important matters—the closeness of national interdependence, the stability of particular configurations of power, the usefulness of force—are made difficult or useless because the participants are talking about different things while using the same terms for them. Movement toward a remedy is impeded by disinclination to treat the question of meaning as a problem that can be solved only through the articulation and refinement of theories. The tendency instead is to turn the problem of meaning into the technical one of making terms operational. That won't help. Any of the above terms can be made operational in most of the meanings our discourse assigns to them. "Poles" have clear empirical referents, for example, whether defined as blocs or as great powers. By either definition, "poles" can become descriptive terms in the statement of laws. The technical usability of terms is unfortunately a weak criterion.

Though it is easy to see that theoretical notions are defined by the theory in which they appear, it is easy to overlook that even descriptive terms acquire different meanings as theories change. Stephen C. Pepper refers to the "close interdependence of fact and theory" (1942:324). Thomas S. Kuhn specifies what happens precisely in terms of the change of "similarity relations" in the transition from one theory to the next. Objects of the same or of different sets in one theory may be grouped in different or in the same sets by another theory, as with the sun, the moon, Mars, and the earth before and after Copernicus. As Kuhn remarks, if two men are committed to different theories, "we cannot say with any assurance that the two men even see the same thing, [that they] possess the same data, but identify or interpret it differently" (1970:266–276). Do we only know what we see, one may wonder, or do we only see what we know? Our minds cannot record and make something of all of the many things that in some sense we see. We are therefore inclined to see what we are looking for, to find what our sense of the causes of things leads us to believe significant.

Changes of theory produce changes in the meaning of terms, both theoretical and factual ones. Theories not only define terms; they also specify the operations that can rightly be performed. In the sense used a moment ago, the operational question is a minor or merely a practical one. In another sense, the operational question is fundamentally important. Theories indicate what is connected with what and how the connection is made. They convey a sense of how things work, of how they hang together, of what the structure of a realm of inquiry may be. If the organization of a realm affects the interactions of variables within it, it makes no sense to manipulate data until the question of how variables may be connected is answered. Nevertheless, correlational labors proceed as though in the international realm variables are directly connected without structural constraints operating on them—as though the phenomena we deal with are all at one level. Coefficients of correlation are amassed without asking which theories lead one to expect *what kind* of a connection among *which* variables.

Much pointless work is done because the three questions that should be asked at the outset of an inquiry are so often ignored. They are:

• Does the object of investigation permit use of the analytic method of

classical physics—examining the attributes and interactions of two variables while others are kept constant?
- Does it permit the application of statistics in ways commonly used when
the number of variables becomes very large?
- Does the object of study permit neither approach, but instead require a
systemic one?

The answer to the last question will be "yes" if the object of study is
both complex and organized. Organized complexity, to use Warren Weaver's terms, precludes the use of traditional modes of investigation
(1947:6–7). One must choose an approach that is appropriate to the
subject matter. The rules by which one's inquiry proceeds vary from one
approach to another. "Due process of inquiry," as Martin Landau has
said, requires one to follow the logic and procedures that one's methodology prescribes (1972:219–221). Most students of international politics have not observed "due process of inquiry." Worse still, they have
not been able to figure out what the due process of their inquiries might
be. They have been much concerned with methods and little concerned
with the logic of their use. This reverses the proper priority of concern,
for once a methodology is adopted, the choice of methods becomes
merely a tactical matter. It makes no sense to start the journey that is
to bring us to an understanding of the phenomena without asking which
methodological routes might possibly lead there. Before setting out we
need to ask what different theoretical maps of the subject matter might
show. If we are not to waste time laboring without any idea of whether
the labor is mere muscular exercise, theoretical questions must be raised
at the outset of inquiry.

II

In order to test a theory, one must do the following:

1 State the theory being tested.
2 Infer hypotheses from it.
3 Subject the hypotheses to experimental or observational tests.
4 In taking steps 2 and 3, use the definitions of terms found in the theory
being tested.

5 Eliminate or control perturbing variables not included in the theory under test.

6 Devise a number of distinct and demanding tests.

7 If a test is not passed, ask whether the theory flunks completely, needs repair and restatement, or requires a narrowing of the scope of its explanatory claims.

The apparent failure of a theory may result from the improper accomplishment of one of these steps. Several of them require special emphasis. Since a hypothesis derived from a theory is being tested (there being no way to test a theory directly), a hypothesis proved wrong should lead one to reexamine the second and seventh operations. Was the hypothesis rightly inferred from the theory? How, and to what extent, does the invalidation of a properly drawn hypothesis bring the theory into question? The unfavorable results of tests should not lead to the hasty rejection of theories. Nor should favorable results lead to their easy acceptance. Even if all tests are passed, one must remember that a theory is made credible only in proportion to the variety and difficulty of the tests, and that no theory can ever be proved true.[3]

Efforts by political scientists to infer hypotheses from theories and test them have become commonplace. Much of the testing is done in basically the same way. One effort to test propositions, an effort more careful than most, can therefore serve as an illustration of how the above requirements go unobserved. Singer, Bremer, and Stuckey (1972) set out to evaluate "a number of equally plausible, but logically incompatible, theoretical formulations" about certain conditions that are said to be associated with peace and stability, or, alternatively, with war and instability. Having consolidated the "viewpoints" of the opposing "schools," they offer "predictive models" in which concentration of capability within the set of major powers, changes of that concentration, and changes of capability among the powers are the three independent variables. They then reach conclusions about whether and when the "parity-fluidity" model or the "preponderance-stability" model makes the better predictions. The questions asked are these: Will international politics be more or less peaceful and stable if power is more or less closely concentrated and if the ranking of great powers changes more or less rapidly? What can one make of the answers given? Very little. The deficiencies that account for this disappointing answer are revealed by running down our list of rules for the testing of theories.

Many testers of theories seem to believe that the major difficulties lie in the devising of tests. Instead, one must insist that the first big difficulty lies in finding or stating theories with enough precision and plausibility to make testing worthwhile. Few theories of international politics define terms and specify the connection of variables with the clarity and logic that would make testing the theories worthwhile. Before a claim can be made to have tested something, one must have something to test. In testing their models, Singer, Bremer, and Stuckey fail to examine the theories they have attempted to model. The theories the authors apparently have in mind are contradictory and confused about whether it is war and peace, or conflict and harmony, or instability and stability that are the expected alternative outcomes. One may, for example, think of a stable system as one that survives the waging of wars. Singer and his associates nevertheless finesse the question of what outcome should be expected by identifying war with instability and letting it go at that. They fail to explain how their expectations accord with expectations derived from any particular theory.

The authors claim to be systematically and quantitatively evaluating contradictory "theoretical formulations." In gathering their data they necessarily fix upon certain definitions of the variables involved. As their key independent variable they choose concentration of power or of capabilities. They mention no theory that in fact employs such a variable, and I know of none that does. The well-known theories dealing with these matters refer to numbers of great powers or to polarities. "Polarity," moreover, is variously defined in terms of countries or of blocs. "Poles" are counted sometimes according to the physical capabilities of nations or of alliances, sometimes by looking at the pattern of national interrelations, and sometimes by awarding or denying top status to those who get or fail to get their ways. Unless the confused, vague, and fluctuating definitions of variables are remedied, no tests of anything can properly be conducted. The authors have nevertheless arbitrarily introduced their new variables without even considering how they may alter one's expectation of outcomes. Though this crucial problem is not even discussed, Singer and his associates announce that correlations between power-concentration variables, on the one hand, and war, on the other hand, confirm or disconfirm the expectations of the two schools they so vaguely refer to.

Rules one, two, and four are thus blithely ignored. The theories being tested are not stated. How hypotheses may have been inferred from them is not explained. Observations are made and data are generated without any effort to define variables as they were defined in the theories presumably being dealt with. The authors may be accomplishing something, but that something cannot be the confirming or disconfirming of any school's expectations.

In the face of such failures, one finds it hard to believe that here, as so often in the correlational labors undertaken by students of international politics, no thought is given to the possible presence of perturbing variables. An exception does not prove a rule or a theory, but if something can be shown to be exceptional, it does not provide any disproof either. One would expect variation in results achieved to prompt a search for possible sources of perturbation omitted from the models. In the instance before us, the "findings" for the nineteenth century differ from those for the twentieth. The discrepancy leads the authors only to the barest speculation about what may have been omitted and to no speculation at all about what may have gone wrong in the way variables were originally defined and interconnected. Rule five is no more heeded than the preceding ones.

Rule six calls for a number of different tests and for demanding ones. One might think this instruction more than usually important since the model consists merely of three highly similar and arbitrarily chosen variables and since the results of the tests are inconclusive. The dubious quality of the results, however, does not lead the authors to devise or to suggest further tests that might challenge their models with some force.

The seventh rule calls for care in the drawing of conclusions from the negative results of tests. Do they defeat the theory, require its amendment, or call for a narrowing of explanatory claims? Singer and his associates fail to consider such questions. Instead they simply report the different correlations between power-concentration and war in the nineteenth and twentieth centuries. Their conclusions are modest enough, but then what more could they say?

A general word of caution should be added to the many words of caution just uttered. One would be scientifically most satisfied if rigorous, experimental tests could be made. If a theory is stated in general terms, however, and if it gives rise to expectations that fall within a range that is identifiable but unfortunately wide, then to draw precise inferences and to try to check them experimentally is to place more weight on the theory than it can bear. Rigorous testing of vague theory is an exercise in the use of methods rather than a useful effort to test theory. The early application of demanding tests may, moreover, cause poorly developed theories to be discarded before their potential has unfolded (cf. Rapoport, 1968).

What then can one do? Simply negotiate the seven steps set forth above in ways appropriate to the theory at hand. Ask what the theory leads one to expect rather than fixing arbitrarily on expectations that one's data and methods can cope with. Check expectations against one's (often historical) observations before trying for precise refinements and using elaborate methods. Unless a theory is shown to be logical, coherent, and plausible, it is silly to subject it to elaborate tests. It a theory is seen to be logical, coherent, and plausible, the rigor and complication of tests must be geared to the precision or to the generality of the expectations inferred from the theory.[4]

III

I have dealt so far with the meaning of theory and with theory construction and testing. Theories do not emerge from efforts to establish laws, even when those efforts succeed. The construction of theory is a primary task. One must decide which things to concentrate on in order to have a good chance of devising some explanations of the international patterns and events that interest us. To believe that we can proceed otherwise is to take the profoundly unscientific view that everything that varies is a variable. Without at least a sketchy theory, we cannot say what it is that needs to be explained, how it might be explained, and which data, how formulated, are to be accepted as evidence for or against hypotheses (cf. Scheffler 1967:64–66; Lakatos 1970:154–177). To proceed by looking for associations without at least some glimmering of a theory is like shooting a gun in the general direction of an invisible target. Not only would much ammunition be used up before hitting it, but also, if the bull's-eye were hit, no one would know it!

The trick, obviously, is to link theoretical concepts with a few variables in order to contrive explanations from which hypotheses can then be inferred and tested.

NOTES

1. One must be careful. The above statement is law-like only if it can be verified in various ways. Counterfactual conditions, for example, would have to be met in this way: Person b is in the income category of likely Republicans; if b's income were reduced to a certain level, he would probably become a Democrat. More precisely, the law-like statement establishes these expectations: If b is an R with probability x, and if a is a D with probability y, then if b becomes a, he thereby becomes a D with probability y.

2. The proof is simply presented by Nagel (1961:116n). One should add that the explanations will not be equally simple and useful.

3. For consideration of testing procedures and explanation of their importance, see Stinchcombe (1968 ch. 2).

4. See article 5, part III, for further thoughts about testing.

THREE

Reductionist and Systemic Theories

KENNETH N. WALTZ

I

IN ONE WAY or another, theories of international politics, whether reductionist or systemic, deal with events at all levels, from the subnational to the supranational. Theories are reductionist or systemic, not according to what they deal with, but according to how they arrange their materials. Reductionist theories explain international outcomes through elements and combinations of elements located at national or subnational levels. That internal forces produce external outcomes is the claim of such theories. $N \rightarrow X$ is their pattern. The international system, if conceived of at all, is taken to be merely an outcome.

A reductionist theory is a theory about the behavior of parts. Once the theory that explains the behavior of the parts is fashioned, no further effort is required. According to the theories of imperialism examined in chapter 2 [not reprinted here: ed.], for example, international outcomes are simply the sum of the results produced by the separate states, and the behavior of each of them is explained through its internal characteristics. Hobson's theory (1902), taken as a general one, is a theory about the workings of national economies. Given certain conditions, it explains why demand slackens, why production falls, and why resources are underemployed. From a knowledge of how capitalist economies work, Hobson believed he could infer the external behavior of capitalist states. He made the error of predicting outcomes from attributes. To try to do that amounts to overlooking the difference between these two statements: "He is a troublemaker." "He makes trouble." The second statement does not follow from the first one if the attributes of actors do not uniquely determine outcomes. Just as peacemakers may fail to make peace, so troublemakers may fail to make trouble. From attributes one cannot predict outcomes if outcomes depend on the situations of the actors as well as on their attributes.

Few, it seems, can consistently escape from the belief that international-political outcomes are determined, rather than merely affected, by what states are like. Hobson's error has been made by almost everyone, at least from the nineteenth century onward. In the earlier history of modern great-power politics, all of the states were monarchies, and most of them absolute ones. Was the power-political game played because of international-political imperatives or simply because authoritarian states are power-minded? If the answer to the latter part of the question were "yes," then profound national changes would transform international politics. Such changes began to take place in Europe and America most strikingly in 1789. For some, democracy became the form of the state that would make the world a peaceful one; for others, later, it was socialism that would turn the trick. Not simply war and peace, moreover, but international politics in general was to be understood through study of the states and the statesmen, the elites and the bureaucracies, the subnational and the transnational actors whose behaviors and interactions form the substance of international affairs.

Political scientists, whether traditional or modern in orientation, reify their systems by reducing them to their interacting parts. For two reasons, the lumping of historically minded traditionalists and scientifically oriented modernists together may seem odd. First, the difference in the methods they use obscures the similarity of their methodology, that is, of the logic their inquiries follow. Second, their different descriptions of the objects of their inquiries reinforce the impression that the difference of methods is a difference of methodology. Traditionalists emphasize the structural distinction between domestic and international politics, a distinction that modernists usually deny. The distinction turns on the difference between politics conducted in a condition of settled rules and politics conducted in a condition of anarchy. Raymond Aron, for example, finds the distinctive quality of international politics in "the absence of a tribunal or police force, the right to resort to force, the plurality of autonomous centers of decision, the alternation and continual interplay between peace and war" (1967:192). With this view, contrast J. David Singer's examination of the descriptive, explanatory, and predictive potentialities of two different levels of analysis: the national and the international (1961). In his examination, he fails even to mention the contextual difference between organized politics within states and formally unorganized politics among them. If the contextual difference is overlooked or denied, then the qualitative difference of internal and external politics disappears or never was. And that is indeed the conclusion that modernists reach. The difference between the global system and its subsystems is said to lie not in the anarchy of the former and the formal organization of the latter, but in there being, as Singer puts it, only one international system "on and around the planet Earth" (1969:30). If one believes that, then "the level-of-analysis problem in international relations" is solved by turning the problem into a matter of choice, a choice made according to the investigator's interest (1961:90).

Traditionalists keep harping on the anarchic character of international politics as marking the distinction between internal and external realms, and modernists do not. If we listen to what members of the two camps *say,* the gulf between them is wide. If we look at what members of both camps *do,* methods aside, the gulf narrows and almost disappears. All of them drift to the "subsystem dominant pole." Their attention focuses on the behaving units. They concentrate on finding out who is doing what to produce the outcomes. When Aron and other traditionalists insist that theorists' categories be consonant with actors' motives and perceptions, they are affirming the preeminently behavioral logic that their inquiries follow. Modernists and traditionalists are struck from the same mold. They share the belief that explanations of international-political outcomes can be drawn by examining the actions and interactions of nations and other actors.

The similarity of traditional and modern approaches to the study of international politics is easily shown. Analysts who confine their attention to interacting units, without recognizing that systemic causes are in play, compensate for the omissions by assigning such causes arbitrarily to the level of interacting units and parcelling them out among actors. The effects of relegating systemic causes to the level of interacting units are practical as well as theoretical. Domestic politics are made into matters of direct international concern. This was clearly shown in 1973 and after when détente became something of an issue in American politics. Could détente, some wondered, survive American pressure on Russian political leaders to govern a little more liberally? Hans Morgenthau, not unexpectedly, turned the argument around. American concern with Russia's internal politics, he claimed, is not "meddling in the domestic affairs of another country. Rather it reflects the recognition that a stable peace, founded upon a stable balance of power, is predicated upon a common moral framework that expresses the commitment of all the nations concerned to certain basic moral principles, of which the preservation of that balance of power is one" (1974:39). If the international-political outcomes are determined by what states are like, then we must be concerned with, and if necessary do something to change, the internal dispositions of the internationally important ones.

As a policymaker, Secretary of State Henry Kissinger rejected Morgenthau's argument. As a political scientist, however, Kissinger had earlier agreed with Morgenthau in believing that the preservation of peace and the maintenance of international stability depend on the attitudes and the internal characteristics of states. Kissinger defined an international order as "legitimate" if it is accepted by all of the major powers and as "revolutionary" if one or more of them rejects it. In contrast to a legitimate order, a revolutionary order is one in which one or more of the major states refuses to deal with other states according to the conventional rules of the game. The quality of the order depends on the dispositions of the states that constitute it. A legitimate international order tends toward stability and peace; a revolutionary international order, toward instability and war. Revolutionary states make international systems revolutionary; a revolutionary system is one that contains one or more revolutionary states (Kissinger 1957:316–20; 1964:1–6, 145–147; 1968:899). The reasoning is circular, and naturally so. Once the system is reduced to its interacting parts, the fate of the system can be determined only by the characteristics of its major units.[1]

Among political scientists, Morgenthau and Kissinger are considered to be traditionalists—scholars turned toward history and concerned more with policy than with theory and scientific methods. The practice in question, however, is common among social scientists of different orientations. Kaplan's reasoning (1957) is Morgenthau's, although Kaplan's vocabulary, borrowed from general-systems theory, has obscured this. Marion Levy, a sociologist who at times writes about international politics, provides another example. He asserts that the "problem foci" of international affairs "are those of the modernization of the relatively nonmodernized societies and of the maintenance of stability within (and consequently among) the relatively modernized societies" (1966:734).

Inside-out explanations always produce the results that these examples illustrate. Kissinger's saying that international instability and war are caused by the existence of revolutionary states amounts to saying that wars occur because some states are warlike. And yet revolutionary regimes may obey international rules—or, more simply, tend toward peaceful coexistence—because the pressures of their external situations overwhelm their internally generated aims. Revolutionary international orders are at times stable and peaceful. Conversely, legitimate international orders are at times unstable and war prone. Levy's effort to predict international outcomes from national characteristics leads to similarly unimpressive results. Saying that stable states make for a stable world amounts to no more than saying that order prevails if most states are orderly. But even if every state were stable, the world of states might not be. If each state, being stable, strove only for security and had no designs on its neighbors, all states would nevertheless remain insecure; for the means of security for one state are, in their very existence, the means by which other states are threatened. One cannot infer the condition of international politics from the internal composition of states, nor can one arrive at an understanding of international politics by summing the foreign policies and the external behaviors of states.

Differences across traditional and modern schools are wide enough to obscure their fundamental similarity. The similarity, once seen, is striking: Members of both schools reveal themselves as behavioralists under the skin. Members of both schools offer explanations in terms of behaving units while leaving aside the effect that their situations may have. Veblen (1915) and Schumpeter (1919) explain imperialism and war according to internal social development; Hobson and his vast progeny, by internal economic arrangement. Levy thinks national stability determines international stability. Kaplan declares international politics to be subsystem dominant. Aron says that what the poles of the system are like is more important than how many poles there may be. As scholar, though not as public official, Kissinger identified revolutionary states with internal instability and war. Because he agrees with Kissinger as scholar, Morgenthau advises intervention in the domestic affairs of other states in the name of international-political necessity. Rosecrance (1963) makes the international system all effect, and not at all cause, and turns his examination of international politics into a "correlating" of internal conditions and international outcomes and a tracing of sequential effects. Many modern students spend much of the time calculating Pearsonian coefficients of correlation. This often amounts to attaching numbers to the kinds of impressionistic associations between internal conditions and international outcomes that traditionalists so frequently offer. International-political studies that conform to the inside-out pattern proceed by correlational logic, whatever the methods used. Scholars who may or may not think of themselves as systems theorists, and formulations that seem to be more scientific or less so, follow the same line of reasoning. They examine international politics in terms of what states are like and how they interact, but not in terms of how they stand in relation to each other. They commit C. F. A. Pantin's "analytic fallacy" by confining their studies to factors that bear on their phenomena without considering that "higher-order configurations may have properties to be studied in their own right" (1968:175).

It is not possible to understand world politics simply by looking inside of states. If the aims, policies, and actions of states become matters of exclusive attention or even of central concern, then we are forced back to the descriptive level; and from simple descriptions no valid generalizations can logically be drawn. We can say what we see, but we cannot know what it may mean. Every time we think that we see something different or new, we will have to designate another unit-level "variable" as its cause. If the situation of actors affects their behavior and influences their interactions, then attempted explanation at the unit level will lead to the infinite proliferation of variables, because at that level no one variable, or set of variables, is sufficient to produce the observed result. So-called variables proliferate wildly when the adopted approach fails to comprehend what is causally important in the subject matter. Variables are added to account for seemingly uncaused effects. What is omitted at the systems level is recaptured—if it is recaptured at all—by attributing characteristics, motives, duties, or whatever to the separate actors. The result observed is turned into a cause, which is then assigned to the actors. There is, however, no logically sound and traceable process by which effects that derive from the system can be attributed to the units. Variables then have to be added subjectively, according to the good or bad judgment of the author. This makes for endless arguments that are doomed to being inconclusive.

In order to take Morgenthau, Kissinger, Levy, and the rest seriously, we would have to believe that no important causes intervene between the aims and actions of states and the results their actions produce. In the history of international relations, however, results achieved seldom correspond to the intentions of actors. Why are they repeatedly thwarted? The apparent answer is that causes not found in their *individual* characters and motives do operate among the actors collectively. Each state arrives at policies and decides on actions according to its own internal processes, but its decisions are shaped by the very presence of other states as well as by interactions with them. When and how internal forces find external expression, if they do, cannot be explained in terms of the interacting parties if the situation in which they act and interact constrains them from some actions, disposes them toward others, and affects the outcomes of their interactions.

If changes in international outcomes are linked directly to changes in actors, how can one account for similarities of outcome that persist or recur even as actors vary? One who believes that he can account for changes in international politics must also ask how continuities can be explained. International politics is sometimes described as the realm of accident and upheaval, of rapid and unpredictable change. Although changes abound, continuities are as impressive, or more so, a proposition that can be illustrated in a number of ways. One who reads the apocryphal book of First Maccabees with events in and after World War I in mind will gain a sense of the continuity that characterizes international politics. Whether in the second century before Christ or in the twentieth century after, Arabs and Jews fought among themselves and over the residues of northern empire, while states outside of the arena warily watched or actively intervened. To illustrate the point more generally, one may cite the famous case of Hobbes experiencing the contemporaneity of Thucydides. Less famous, but equally striking, is the realization by Louis J. Halle of the relevance of Thucydides in the era of nuclear weapons and superpowers (1955, Appendix). In the two world wars of this century, to choose a different type of illustration, the same principal countries lined up against each other, despite the domestic political upheavals that took place in the interwar period. The texture of international politics remains highly constant, patterns recur, and events repeat themselves endlessly. The relations that prevail internationally seldom shift rapidly in type or in quality. They are marked instead by dismaying persistence, a persistence that one must expect so long as none of the competing units is able to convert the anarchic international realm into a hierarchic one.

The enduring anarchic character of international politics accounts for the striking sameness in the quality of international life through the millennia, a statement that will meet with wide assent. Why then do we find such a persistent pull toward reduction? The answer is that usually reduction results not from a scholar's intent but from his errors. The study of interacting units is thought to exhaust the subject, to include all that can be included both at the level of the unit and at the level of the system. Some political scientists claim that a systems perspective draws attention to the relational aspects of international politics. But interacting states have always been the objects of study. Others say that to complete an analysis done in terms of interacting states one need only add consideration of nonstate actors. They may need to be included, but including them will leave us at the unit level or lower. Interactions occur at the level of the units, not at the level of the system. Like the outcome of states' actions, the implications of interactions cannot be known, or intelligently guessed at, without knowledge of the situation within which interactions occur. The sporadic interactions of states may, for example, be more important than the daily conduct of routine business. The fate of states whose economic and touristic relations are sparse may be closely linked. We know that this holds for the United States and the Soviet Union. We could not reach that conclusion by counting transactions and by measuring the interactions that take place. This does not mean that counting and measuring are useless activities. It does mean that conclusions about the condition of international politics cannot be directly inferred from data about the formal or informal relations of states. In fact, we more often proceed in the opposite direction. We say, for example, that the United States and the Soviet Union, or the United States, the Soviet Union, and China, interact closely because we believe that actions separately taken strongly affect the pair, or the trio, whether or not there are relations to observe and transactions to count. We save ourselves from the absurdity of saying that a low level of observed interactions between or among certain states indicates the unimportance of their relations by falling back on what we already know.

Continuities and repetitions defeat efforts to explain international politics by following the familiar inside-out formula. Think of the various causes of war discovered by students. Governmental forms, economic systems, social institutions, political ideologies: These are but a few examples of where causes have been found. And yet, though causes are specifically assigned, we know that states with every imaginable variation of economic institution, social custom, and political ideology have fought wars. More strikingly still, many different sorts of organizations fight wars, whether those organizations be tribes, petty principalities, empires, nations, or street gangs. If an indicated condition seems to have caused a given war, one must wonder what accounts for the repetition of wars even as their causes vary. Variations in the quality of the units are not linked directly to the outcomes their behaviors produce, nor are variations in patterns of interaction. Many, for example, have claimed that World War I was caused by the interaction of two opposed and closely balanced coalitions. But then many have claimed that World War II was caused by the failure of some states to right an imbalance of power by combining to counter an alliance in being.

II

Nations change in form and in purpose; technological advances are made; weaponry is radically transformed; alliances are forged and disrupted. These are changes within systems, and such changes help to explain variations in international-political outcomes. In chapter 3 [not reprinted here: ed.] we found that aspiring systems theorists think of such within-system changes as marking shifts from one system to another. Once structure is clearly defined, a task for the next chapter, changes at the level of structure can be kept separate from changes at the level of units. One may wonder, however, whether inadvertent reductions that result in calling unit-level changes structural ones can be remedied by a change of vocabulary. Unfortunately they cannot be. The problem of showing how structural causes produce their effects would be left unsolved.

Low-level explanations are repeatedly defeated, for the similarity and repetition of international outcomes persist despite wide variations in the attributes and in the interactions of the agents that supposedly cause them. How can one account for the disjunction of observed causes and effects? When seeming causes vary more than their supposed effects, we know that causes have been incorrectly or incompletely specified. The repeated failure of attempts to explain international outcomes analyti-cally—that is, through examination of interacting units—strongly signals the need for a systems approach. If the same effects follow from different causes, then constraints must be operating on the independent variables in ways that affect outcomes. One cannot incorporate the constraints by treating them as one or more of the independent variables with all of them at the same level, because the constraints may operate on all of the independent variables and because they do so in different ways as systems change. Because one cannot achieve that incorporation, reduction is not possibly adequate, and an analytic approach must give way to a systemic one. One can believe that some causes of international outcomes are located at the level of the interacting units. Since variations in pre-sumed causes do not correspond very closely to variations in observed outcomes, however, one has to believe that some causes are located at a different level as well. Causes at the level of units and of systems interact, and because they do so explanation at the level of units alone is bound to mislead. If one's approach allows for the handling of both unit-level and systems-level causes, then it can cope with both the changes and the continuities that occur in a system. It can do so, moreover, without proliferating variables and multiplying categories.

From chapter 1 we know how theories are constructed. To construct a theory we have to abstract from reality, that is, to leave aside most of what we see and experience. Students of international politics have tried to get closer to the reality of international practice and to increase the empirical content of their studies. Natural science, in contrast, has advanced over the millennia by moving away from everyday reality and by fulfilling Conant's previously mentioned aspiration to lower "the degree of the empiricism involved in solving problems." Natural scientists look for simplicities: elemental units and elegant theories about them. Students of international politics complicate their studies and claim to locate more and more variables. The subject matters of the social and natural sciences are profoundly different. The difference does not obliterate certain possibilities and necessities. No matter what the subject, we have to bound the domain of our concern, to organize it, to simplify the materials we deal with, to concentrate on central tendencies, and to single out the strongest propelling forces.

From the first part of this article, we know that the theory we want to construct has to be a systemic one. What will a systems theory of international politics look like? What scope will it have? What will it be able, and unable, to explain?

Theory explains regularities of behavior and leads one to expect that the outcomes produced by interacting units will fall within specified ranges. The behavior of states and of statesmen, however, is indeterminate. How can a theory of international politics, which has to comprehend behavior that is indeterminate, possibly be constructed? This is the great unanswered, and many say unanswerable, question of international-political studies. The question cannot be answered by those whose approach is reductionist or behavioral, as we have seen. They try to explain international politics in terms of its principal actors. The dominant behavioral approach to constructing international-political theory proceeds by fram-

ing propositions about the behavior, the strategies, and the interactions
of states. But propositions at the unit level do not account for the
phenomena observed at the systems level. Since the variety of actors and
the variations in their actions are not matched by the variety of outcomes,
we know that systemic causes are in play. Knowing that, we know further
that a systems theory is both needed and possible. To realize the possibility requires conceiving of an international system's structure and
showing how it works its effects. We have to bring off the Copernican
revolution that others have called for by showing how much of states'
actions and interactions, and how much of the outcomes their actions
and interactions produce, can be explained by forces that operate at the
level of the system, rather than at the level of the units.

What do I mean by *explain*? I mean explain in these senses: to say
why the range of expected outcomes falls within certain limits; to say
why patterns of behavior recur; to say why events repeat themselves,
including events that none or few of the actors may like. The structure
of a system acts as a constraining and disposing force, and because it
does so systems theories explain and predict continuity within a system.
A systems theory shows why changes at the unit level produce less change
of outcomes than one would expect in the absence of systemic constraints. A theory of international politics can tell us some things about
expected international-political outcomes, about the resilience systems
may show in response to the unpredictable acts of a varied set of states,
and about the expected effects of systems on states.

A theory has explanatory and predictive power. A theory also has
elegance. Elegance in social-science theories means that explanations and
predictions will be general. A theory of international politics will, for
example, explain why war recurs, and it will indicate some of the conditions that make war more or less likely; but it will not predict the
oubreak of particular wars. Within a system, a theory explains continuities. It tells one what to expect and why to expect it. Within a system,
a theory explains recurrences and repetitions, not change. At times one
is told that structural approaches have proved disappointing, that from
the study of structure not much can be learned. This is supposedly so
for two reasons. Structure is said to be largely a static concept and nearly
an empty one. Though neither point is quite right, both points are
suggestive. Structures appear to be static because they often endure for

long periods. Even when structures do not change, they are dynamic, not static, in that they alter the behavior of actors and affect the outcome of their interactions. Given a durable structure, it becomes easy to overlook structural effects because they are repeatedly the same. Thus one expects the same broad range of outcomes to result from the actions of states in an anarchic condition. What continues and repeats is surely not less important than what changes. A constancy of structure explains the recurrent patterns and features of international-political life. Is structure nevertheless an empty concept? Pretty much so, and because it is it gains in elegance and power. Structure is certainly no good on detail. Structural concepts, although they lack detailed content, help to explain some big, important, and enduring patterns.

Structures, moreover, may suddenly change. A structural change is a revolution, whether or not violently produced, and it is so because it gives rise to new expectations about the outcomes that will be produced by the acts and interactions of units whose placement in the system varies with changes in structure. Across systems, a theory explains change. A theory of international politics can succeed only if political structures are defined in ways that identify their causal effects and show how those effects vary as structures change. From anarchy one infers broad expectations about the quality of international-political life. Distinguishing between anarchic structures of different type permits somewhat narrower and more precise definitions of expected outcomes.

Consider, for example, the effects on European states of the shift from a multipolar to a bipolar system. So long as European states were the world's great powers, unity among them could only be dreamt of. Politics among the European great powers tended toward the model of a zero-sum game. Each power viewed another's loss as its own gain. Faced with the temptation to cooperate for mutual benefit, each state became wary and was inclined to draw back. When on occasion some of the great powers did move toward cooperation, they did so in order to oppose other powers more strongly. The emergence of the Russian and American superpowers created a situation that permitted wider ranging and more effective cooperation among the states of Western Europe. They became consumers of security, to use an expression common in the days of the League of Nations. For the first time in modern history, the determinants of war and peace lay outside the arena of European states, and the means of their preservation were provided by others. These new circumstances made possible the famous "upgrading of the common interest," a phrase which conveys the thought that all should work together to improve everyone's lot rather than being obsessively concerned with the precise division of benefits. Not all impediments to cooperation were removed, but one important one was—the feat that the greater advantage of one would be translated into military force to be used against the others. Living in the superpowers' shadow, Britain, France, Germany, and Italy quickly saw that war among them would be fruitless and soon began to believe it impossible. Because the security of all of them came to depend ultimately on the policies of others, rather than on their own, unity could effectively be worked for, although not easily achieved.

Once the possibility of war among states disappears, all of them can more freely run the risk of suffering a relative loss. Enterprises more beneficial to some parties than others can be engaged in, partly in the hope for the latter that other activities will reverse the balance of benefits, and partly in the belief that overall the enterprise itself is valuable. Economic gains may be granted by one state to another in exchange for expected political advantages, including the benefit of strengthening the structure of European cooperation. The removal of worries about security among the states of Western Europe does not mean the termination of conflict; it does produce a change in its content. Hard bargaining within the European Economic Community (by France over agricultural policies, for example) indicates that governments do not lose interest in who will gain more and who will gain less. Conflicts of interest remain, but not the expectation that someone will use force to resolve them. Politics among European states became different in quality after World War II because the international system changed from a multipolar to a bipolar one. The limited progress made in economic and other ways toward the unity of Western Europe cannot be understood without considering the effects that followed from the changed structure of international politics. The example helps to show what a theory of international politics can and cannot tell us. It can describe the range of likely outcomes of the actions and interactions of states within a given system and show how the range of expectations varies as systems change. It can tell us what pressures are exerted and what possibilities are posed by systems of different structure, but it cannot tell us just how, and how effectively, the units of a system will respond to those pressures and possibilities.

Structurally we can describe and understand the pressures states are subject to. We cannot predict how they will react to the pressures without knowledge of their internal dispositions. A systems theory explains changes across systems, not within them, and yet international life within a given system is by no means all repetition. Important discontinuities occur. If they occur within a system that endures, their causes are found at the unit level. Because something happens that is outside a theory's purview, a deviation from the expected occurs.

A systems theory of international politics deals with the forces that are in play at the international, and not at the national, level. This question then arises: With both systems-level and unit-level forces in play, how can one construct a theory of international politics without simultaneously constructing a theory of foreign policy? The question is exactly like asking how an economic theory of markets can be written in the absence of a theory of the firm. The answer is "very easily." Market theory is a structural theory showing how firms are pressed by market forces to do certain things in certain ways. Whether and how well they will do them varies from firm to firm, with variations depending on their different internal organization and management. An international-political theory does not imply or require a theory of foreign policy any more than a market theory implies or requires a theory of the firm. Systems theories, whether political or economic, are theories that explain how the organization of a realm acts as a constraining and disposing force on the interacting units within it. Such theories tell us about the forces the units are subject to. From them, we can infer some things about the expected behavior and fate of the units: namely, how they will have to compete with and adjust to one another if they are to survive and flourish. To the extent that dynamics of a system limit the freedom of its units, their behavior and the outcomes of their behavior become predictable. How do we expect firms to respond to differently structured markets, and states to differently structured international-political systems? These theoretical questions require us to take firms as firms, and states as states, without paying attention to differences among them. The questions are then answered by reference to the placement of the units in their system and not by reference to their internal qualities. Systems theories explain why different units behave similarly and, despite their variations, produce outcomes that fall within expected ranges. Conversely, theories at the unit level tell us why different units behave differently despite their similar placement in a system. A theory about foreign policy is a theory at the national level. It leads to expectations about the responses that dissimilar polities will make to external pressures. A theory of international politics bears on the foreign policies of nations while claiming to explain only certain aspects of them. It can tell us what international conditions national policies have to cope with. To think that a theory of international politics can in itself say how the coping is likely to be done is the opposite of the reductionist error.

The theory, like the story, of international politics is written in terms of the great powers of an era. This is the fashion among political scientists as among historians, but fashion does not reveal the reason lying behind the habit. In international politics, as in any self-help system, the units of greatest capability set the scene of action for others as well as for themselves. In systems theory, structure is a generative notion; and the structure of a system is generated by the interactions of its principal parts. Theories that apply to self-help systems are written in terms of the systems' principal parts. It would be as ridiculous to construct a theory of international politics based on Malaysia and Costa Rica as it would be to construct an economic theory of oligopolistic competition based on the minor firms in a sector of an economy. The fates of all the states and of all the firms in a system are affected much more by the acts and the interactions of the major ones than of the minor ones. At the turn of the century, one who was concerned with the prospects for international politics as a system, and for large and small nations within it, did not concentrate attention on the foreign and military policies of Switzerland, Denmark, and Norway, but rather on those of Britain and Germany, of Russia and France. To focus on great powers is not to lose sight of lesser ones. Concern with the latter's fate requires paying most attention to the former. Concern with international politics as a system requires concentration on the states that make the most difference. A general theory of international politics is necessarily based on the great powers. The theory once written also applies to lesser states that interact insofar as their interactions are insulated from the intervention of the

great powers of a system, whether by the relative indifference of the
latter or by difficulties of communication and transportation.

III

In a systems theory, some part of the explanation of behaviors and
outcomes is found in the system's structure. A political structure is akin
to a field of forces in physics: Interactions within a field have properties
different from those they would have if they occurred outside of it, and
as the field affects the objects, so the objects affect the field. How can
one give clear and useful political meaning to such a concept as structure?
How do structures work their effects? In considering structures as causes,
it is useful to draw a distinction between two definitions.

The term "structure" is now a social-science favorite. As such, its
meaning has become all inclusive. In meaning everything, it has ceased
to mean anything in particular. Its casual and vacuous uses aside, the
term has two important meanings. First, it may designate a compensating
device that works to produce a uniformity of outcomes despite the variety
of inputs. Bodily organs keep variations within tolerable ranges despite
changes of condition. One's liver, for example, keeps the blood-sugar
level within a certain range despite the variety of food and drink ingested.
Similarly, negative and progressive income taxes narrow disparities of
income despite variations in people's skill, energy, and luck. Because such
structures bring leveling processes into play, those who experience the
leveling effects need be aware neither of the structure nor of how its
effects are produced. Structures of this sort are agents or contrivances
that work within systems. They are structures of the sort that political
scientists usually have in mind. They do share one quality with structures
as I shall define them: They work to keep outcomes within narrow ranges.
They differ in being designed by nature or man to operate for particular
purposes within larger systems. When referring to such devices, I use
terms such as agent, agency, and compensating device. I use the word
"structure" only in its second sense.

In the second sense structure designates a set of constraining conditions. Such a structure acts as a selector, but it cannot be seen, examined, and observed at work as livers and income taxes can be. Freely

formed economic markets and international-political structures are se-
lectors, but they are not agents. Because structures select by rewarding
some behaviors and punishing others, outcomes cannot be inferred from
intentions and behaviors. This is simple logic that everyone will understand. What is not so simple is to say just what it is politically that
disjoins behavior and result. Structures are causes, but they are not causes
in the sense meant by saying that A causes X and B causes Y. X and Y
are different outcomes produced by different actions or agents. A and B
are stronger, faster, earlier, or weightier than X and Y. By observing the
values of variables, by calculating their covariance, and by tracing sequences, such causes are fixed.[2] Because A and B are different, they
produce different effects. In contrast, structures limit and mold agents
and agencies and point them in ways that tend toward a common quality
of outcomes even though the efforts and aims of agents and agencies
vary. Structures do not work their effects directly. Structures do not act
as agents and agencies do. How then can structural forces be understood?
How can one think of structural causes as being more than vague social
propensities or ill-defined political tendencies?

Agents and agencies act; systems as a whole do not. But the actions
of agents and agencies are affected by the system's structure. In itself a
structure does not directly lead to one outcome rather than another.
Structure affects behavior within the system, but does so indirectly. The
effects are produced in two ways: through socialization of the actors and
through competition among them. These two pervasive processes occur
in international politics as they do in societies of all sorts. Because they
are fundamental processes, I shall risk stating the obvious by explaining
each of them in elementary terms.

Consider the process of socialization in the simplest case of a pair of
persons, or for that matter of firms or of states. A influences B. B, made
different by A's influence, influences A. As Mary Parker Follett, an organization theorist, put it: "A's own activity enters into the stimulus
which is causing his activity" (1941:194). This is an example of the
familiar structural-functional logic by which consequences become causes
(cf. Stinchcombe 1968:80–101). B's attributes and actions are affected
by A, and vice versa. Each is not just influencing the other: both are
being influenced by the situation their interaction creates. Extending the
example makes the logic clearer. George and Martha, the principal char-

acters in Edward Albee's play, *Who's Afraid of Virginia Woolf?*, through their behavior and interaction create a condition that neither can control by individual acts and decisions. In a profound study of Albee's play, Paul Watzlawick and his associates show that George's and Martha's activities cannot be understood without considering the system that emerges from their interactions. They put it this way:

> That which is George or Martha, individually, does not explain what is compounded between them, nor how. To break this whole into individual personality traits . . . is essentially to separate them from each other, to deny that their behaviors have special meaning in the context of this interaction—that in fact the pattern of the interaction perpetuates these (1967:156).

The behavior of the pair cannot be apprehended by taking a unilateral view of either member. The behavior of the pair cannot, moreover, be resolved into a set of two-way relations because each element of behavior that contributes to the interaction is itself shaped by their being a pair. They have become parts of a system. To say simply that George and Martha are interacting, with the action of one eliciting a response from the other, obscures the circularity of their interactions. Each acts and reacts to the other. Stimulus and response are part of the story. But also the two of them act together in a game, which—no less because they have "devised" it—motivates and shapes their behavior. Each is playing a game, *and* they are playing the game together. They react to each other and to the tensions their interactions produce.

These are descriptions and examples of what we all know and experience. One may firmly intend to end an argument, may announce the intention, may insist on it, and yet may be carried along by the argument. One may firmly predict one's action and yet be led to act in ways that surprise onself as well as others. Years ago, Gustave Le Bon said this about the effect of the group on the individual:

> The most striking peculiarity presented by a psychological crowd is the following: Whoever be the individuals that compose it, however like or unlike be their mode of life, their occupations, their character, or their intelligence, the fact that they have been transformed into a crowd puts them in possession of a sort of collective mind which makes them feel, think, and act in a manner quite different from that in which each

individual of them would feel, think, and act were he in a state of isolation (1896:29–30).

We do not cease to be ourselves when situations strongly affect us, but we become ourselves and something else as well. We become different, but we cannot say that any agent or agency caused us to do so.

Pairs and crowds provide microcosmic and transitory examples of the socialization that takes place in organizations and in societies on larger scales and over longer periods. Nobody tells all of the teenagers in a given school or town to dress alike, but most of them do. They do so, indeed, despite the fact that many people—their parents—are ordinarily telling them not to. In spontaneous and informal ways, societies establish norms of behavior. A group's opinion controls its members. Heroes and leaders emerge and are emulated. Praise for behavior that conforms to group norms reinforces them. Socialization brings members of a group into conformity with its norms. Some members of the group will find this repressive and incline toward deviant behavior. Ridicule may bring deviants into line or cause them to leave the group. Either way the group's homogeneity is preserved. In various ways, societies establish norms and encourage conformity. Socialization reduces variety. The differences of society's members are greater than the differences in their observed behavior. The persistent characteristics of group behavior result in one part from the qualities of its members. They result in another part from the characteristics of the society their interactions produce.

The first way in which structures work their effects is through a process of socialization that limits and molds behavior. The second way is through competition. In social sectors that are loosely organized or segmented, socialization takes place within segments and competition takes place among them. Socialization encourages similarities of attributes and of behavior. So does competition. Competition generates an order, the units of which adjust their relations through their autonomous decisions and acts. Adam Smith published *The Wealth of Nations* in 1776. He did not claim to explain economic behavior and outcomes only from then onward. He did not develop a theory that applies only to the economic activities of those who read, understand, and follow his book. His economic theory applies wherever indicated conditions prevail, and it applies aside from the state of producers' and consumers' knowledge.[3]

This is so because the theory Smith fashioned deals with structural constraints. Insofar as selection rules, results can be predicted whether or not one knows the actors' intentions and whether or not they understand structural constraints. Consider an example. Suppose I plan to open a shoe store. Where should I put it? I might notice that shoe stores tend to cluster. Following common political-science reasoning, I would infer either that towns pass laws regulating the location of shoe stores or that shoe-store owners are familiar with the location theory of economists, which tells them generally how to locate their stores in order to catch the attention of the largest number of shoppers. Neither inference is justified. Following common economic reasoning, I would say that market conditions reward those who wittingly or not place their stores in the right places and punish those who do not. Behaviors are selected for their consequences. Individual entreprenuers need not know how to increase their chances of turning a profit. They can blunder along, if they wish to, and rely on the market selector to sort out the ones who happen to operate intelligently from those who do not.

Firms are assumed to be maximizing units. In practice, some of them may not even be trying to maximize anything. Others may be trying, but their ineptitude may make this hard to discern. Competitive systems are regulated, so to speak, by the "rationality" of the more successful competitors. What does rationality mean? It means only that some do better than others—whether through intelligence, skill, hard work, or dumb luck. They succeed in providing a wanted good or service more attractively and more cheaply than others do. Either their competitors emulate them or they fall by the wayside. The demand for their product shrinks, their profits fall, and ultimately they go bankrupt. To break this unwanted chain of events, they must change their ways. And thus the units that survive come to look like one another. Patterns are formed in the location of firms, in their organization, in their modes of production, in the design of their products, and in their marketing methods. The orderliness is in the outcomes and not necessarily in the inputs. Those who survive share certain characteristics. Those who go bankrupt lack them. Competition spurs the actors to accommodate their ways to the socially most acceptable and successful practices. Socialization and competition are two aspects of a process by which the variety of behaviors and of outcomes is reduced.

Where selection according to consequences rules, patterns emerge and endure without anyone arranging the parts to form patterns or striving to maintain them. The acts and the relations of parties may be regulated through the accommodations they mutually make. Order may prevail without an orderer; adjustments may be made without an adjuster; tasks may be allocated without an allocator. The mayor of New York City does not phone the truck gardeners of southern New Jersey and tell them to grow more tomatoes next year because too few were recently supplied. Supply and demand are more sensitively and reliably adjusted through the self-interested responses of numerous buyers and sellers than they are by mayors' instructions. An example of a somewhat different sort is provided by considering Montesquieu's response when presented with a scheme for an ideal society. "Who," he is said to have asked, "will empty the chamber pots?" As an equivalent question, we might ask: Who will collect the trash? The buyers of the trash-collecting service want to buy the service cheaply. The sellers want to sell their service dearly. What happens? Cities take steps to make the trash detail more attractive: cleaner and simpler through moves toward automation, and socially more acceptable through increasing the status of the job, for example, by providing classy uniforms for the workers. Insofar as trash collecting remains unattractive, society pays more in relation to the talents required than it does for other services. The real society becomes hard to distinguish from the ideal.

IV

Different structures may cause the same outcomes to occur even as units and interactions vary. Thus throughout a market the price of any good or service is uniform if many firms compete, if a few oligopolists engage in collusive pricing, or if the government controls prices. Perfect competition, complete collusion, absolute control: These different causes produce identical results. From uniformity of outcomes one cannot infer that the attributes and the interactions of the parts of a system have remained constant. Structure may determine outcomes aside from changes at the level of the units and aside from the disappearance of some of them and the emergence of others. Different "causes" may

produce the same effect; the same "causes" may have different consequences. Unless one knows how a realm is organized, one can hardly
tell the causes from the effects.

The effect of an organization may predominate over the attributes and
the interactions of the elements within it. A system that is independent
of initial conditions is said to display equifinality. If it does, "*the system
is then its own best explanation,*" and the study of its present organization
the appropriate methodology" (Watzlawick *et al.* 1967:129; cf. p. 32). If
structure influences without determining, then one must ask how and
to what extent the structure of a realm accounts for outcomes and how
and to what extent the units account for outcomes. Structure has to be
studied in its own right as do units. To claim to be following a systems
approach or to be constructing a systems theory requires one to show
how system and unit levels can be distinctly defined. Failure to mark
and preserve the distinction between structure, on the one hand, and
units and processes, on the other, makes it impossible to disentangle
causes of different sorts and to distinguish between causes and effects.
Blurring the distinction between the different levels of a system has, I
believe, been the major impediment to the development of theories about
international politics. The next chapter shows how to define political
structures in a way that makes the construction of a systems theory
possible.

NOTES

1. What Kissinger learned as a statesman is dramatically different from the
conclusions he had reached as a scholar. Statements revealing his new views abound,
but one example will suffice. When interviewed while Secretary of State by
William F. Buckley Jr., Kissinger made the following points in three successive paragraphs: "Communist societies are morally, in their internal structure, not acceptable to us. . . ." Though our and their ideologies continue to be incompatible, we
can nevertheless make practical and peace-preserving accommodations in our foreign
policy. We should, indeed, "avoid creating the illusion that progress on some foreign
policy questions . . . means that there has been a change in the domestic structure"
(September 13, 1975, p. 5).

The link between internal attributes and external results is not seen as an un-
breakable one. Internal conditions and commitments no longer determine the quality
of international life.

2. A variable, contrary to political-science usage, is not just anything that varies.

It is a concept that takes different values, a concept developed as part of a highly simplified model of some part of the world.

3. In saying that the theory applies, I leave aside the question of the theory's validity.

FOUR

Political Structures

KENNETH N. WALTZ

W E LEARNED in chapters 2, 3, and 4 [article 3 here] that international-political outcomes cannot be explained reductively. We found in chapter 3 that even avowedly systemic approaches mingle and confuse systems-level with unit-level causes. Reflecting on theories that follow the general-systems model, we concluded at once that international politics does not fit the model closely enough to make the model useful and that only through some sort of systems theory can international politics be understood. To be a success, such a theory has to show how international politics can be conceived of as a domain distinct from the economic, social, and other international domains that one may conceive of. To mark international-political systems off from other international systems, and to distinguish systems-level from unit-level forces, requires showing how political structures are generated and how they affect, and are affected by, the units of the system. How can we conceive of international politics as a distinct system? What is it that intervenes between interacting units and the results that their acts and interactions produce? To answer these questions, this chapter first examines the concept of social structure and then defines structure as a concept appropriate for national and for international politics.

I

A system is composed of a structure and of interacting units. The structure is the system-wide component that makes it possible to think of the system as a whole. The problem, unsolved by the systems theorists considered in chapter 3 [not reprinted here: ed.], is to contrive a definition of structure free of the attributes and the interactions of units.

Definitions of structure must leave aside, or abstract from, the characteristics of units, their behavior, and their interactions. Why must those obviously important matters be omitted? They must be omitted so that we can distinguish between variables at the level of the units and variables at the level of the system. The problem is to develop theoretically useful concepts to replace the vague and varying systemic notions that are customarily employed—notions such as environment, situation, context, and milieu. Structure is a useful concept if it gives clear and fixed meaning to such vague and varying terms.

We know what we have to omit from any definition of structure if the definition is to be useful theoretically. Abstracting from the attributes of units means leaving aside questions about the kinds of political leaders, social and economic institutions, and ideological commitments states may have. Abstracting from relations means leaving aside questions about the cultural, economic, political, and military interactions of states. To say what is to be left out does not indicate what is to be put in. The negative point is important nevertheless because the instruction to omit attributes is often violated and the instruction to omit interactions almost always goes unobserved. But if attributes and interactions are omitted, what is left? The question is answered by considering the double meaning of the term "relation." As S. F. Nadel points out, ordinary language obscures a distinction that is important in theory. "Relation" is used to mean both the interaction of units and the positions they occupy vis-à-vis each other (1957:8–11). To define a structure requires ignoring how units relate with one another (how they interact) and concentrating on how they stand in relation to one another (how they are arranged or positioned). Interactions, as I have insisted, take place at the level of the units. How units stand in relation to one another, the way they are arranged or positioned, is not a property of the units. The arrangement of units is a property of the system.

By leaving aside the personality of actors, their behavior, and their interactions, one arrives at a purely positional picture of society. Three propositions follow from this. First, structures may endure while personality, behavior, and interactions vary widely. Structure is sharply distinguished from actions and interactions. Second, a structural definition applies to realms of widely different substance so long as the arrangement of parts is similar (cf. Nadel:104–109). Third, because this is so, theories developed for one realm may with some modification be applicable to other realms as well.

A structure is defined by the arrangement of its parts. Only changes of arrangement are structural changes. A system is composed of a structure and of interacting parts. Both the structure and the parts are concepts, related to, but not identical with, real agents and agencies. Structure is not something we see. The anthropologist Meyer Fortes put this well. "When we describe structure," he said, "we are in the realm of grammar and syntax, not of the spoken word. We discern structure in the 'concrete reality' of social events only by virtue of having first established structure by abstraction from 'concrete reality'" (Fortes 1949:56). Since structure is an abstraction, it cannot be defined by enumerating material characteristics of the system. It must instead be defined by the arrangement of the system's parts and by the principle of that arrangement.

This is an uncommon way to think of political systems, although structural notions are familiar enough to anthropologists, to economists, and even to political scientists who deal with political systems in general but with such of their parts as political parties and bureaucracies. In defining structures, anthropologists do not ask about the habits and the values of the chiefs and the Indians; economists do not ask about the organization and the efficiency of particular firms and the exchanges among them; and political scientists do not ask about the personalities and the interests of the individuals occupying various offices. They leave aside the qualities, the motives, and the interactions of the actors, not because those matters are uninteresting or unimportant, but because they want to know how the qualities, the motives, and the interactions of tribal units are affected by tribal structure, how decisions of firms are influenced by their market, and how people's behavior is molded by the offices they hold.

II

The concept of structure is based on the fact that units differently juxtaposed and combined behave differently and in interacting produce different outcomes. I first want to show how internal political structure can be defined. In a book on international-political theory, domestic political structure has to be examined in order to draw a distinction between expectations about behavior and outcomes in the internal and external realms. Moreover, considering domestic political structure now will make the elusive international-political structure easier to catch later on.

Structure defines the arrangement, or the ordering, of the parts of a system. Structure is not a collection of political institutions but rather the arrangement of them. How is the arrangement defined? The constitution of a state describes some parts of the arrangement, but political structures as they develop are not identical with formal constitutions. In defining structures, the first question to answer is this: What is the principle by which the parts are arranged?

Domestic politics is hierarchically ordered. The units—institutions and agencies—stand vis-à-vis each other in relations of super- and subordination. The ordering principle of a system gives the first, and basic, bit of information about how the parts of a realm are related to each other. In a polity the hierarchy of offices is by no means completely articulated, nor all all ambiguities about relations of super- and subordination removed. Nevertheless, political actors are formally differentiated according to the degrees of their authority, and their distinct functions are specified. By "specified" I do not mean that the law of the land fully describes the duties that different agencies perform, but only that broad agreement prevails on the tasks that various parts of a government are to undertake and on the extent of the power they legitimately wield. Thus Congress supplies the military forces; the President commands them. Congress makes the laws; the executive branch enforces them; agencies administer laws; judges interpret them. Such specification of roles and differentiation of functions is found in any state, the more fully so as the state is more highly developed. The specification of functions of formally differentiated parts gives the second bit of structural information. This second part of the definition adds some content to the structure, but only enough to say more fully how the units stand in relation to one another. The roles and the functions of the British Prime Minister and Parliament, for example, differ from those of the American

President and Congress. When offices are juxtaposed and functions are combined in different ways, different behaviors and outcomes result, as I shall shortly show.

The placement of units in relation to one another is not fully defined by a system's ordering principle and by the formal differentiation of its parts. The standing of the units also changes with changes in their relative capabilities. In the performance of their functions, agencies may gain capabilities or lose them. The relation of Prime Minister to Parliament and of President to Congress depends on, and varies with, their relative capabilities. The third part of the definition of structure acknowledges that even while specified functions remain unchanged, units come to stand in different relation to each other through changes in relative capability.

A domestic political structure is thus defined, first, according to the principle by which it is ordered; second, by specification of the functions of formally differentiated units; and third, by the distribution of capabilities across those units. Structure is a highly abstract notion, but the definition of structure does not abstract from everything. To do so would be to leave everything aside and to include nothing at all. The three-part definition of structure includes only what is required to show how the units of the system are positioned or arranged. Everything else is omitted. Concern for tradition and culture, analysis of the character and personality of political actors, consideration of the conflictive and accommodative processes of politics, description of the making and execution of policy—all such matters are left aside. Their omission does not imply their unimportance. They are omitted because we want to figure out the expected effects of structure on process and of process on structure. That can be done only if structure and process are distinctly defined.

Political structures shape political processes, as can best be seen by comparing different governmental systems. In Britain and America legislative and executive offices are differently juxtaposed and combined. In England they are fused; in America they are separated and in many ways placed in opposition to each other. Differences in the distribution of power and authority among formal and informal agencies affect the chief executives' power and help to account for persistent differences in their performance. I have shown elsewhere how structural differences explain contrasts in the patterns of British and American political behavior. Repeating a few points in summary form will make preceding definitional statements politically concrete. I shall take just political leadership as an example and concentrate more on Britain than on America so as to be able to go into some small amount of detail (1967; I draw mainly on chapters 3 and 11).

Prime Ministers have been described, at least since the late nineteenth century, as gaining ever more power to the point where one should no longer refer to parliamentary or even to cabinet government. The Prime Minister alone now carries the day, or so one is told. One must then wonder why these increasingly strong Prime Ministers react so slowly to events, do the same ineffective things over and over again, and in general govern so weakly. The answers are not found in the different personalities of Prime Ministers, for the patterns I refer to embrace all of them and extend backward to the 1860s, that is, to the time when the discipline of parties began to emerge as a strong feature of British governance. The formal powers of Prime Ministers appear to be ample, and yet their behavior is more closely constrained than that of American Presidents. The constraints are found in the structure of British government, especially in the relation of leader to party. Two points are of major importance: the way leaders are recruited and the effect of their having to manage their parties so carefully.

In both countries, directly or indirectly, the effective choice of a chief executive lies between the leaders of two major parties. How do they become the two from whom the choice is made? An MP becomes leader of his party or Prime Minister by long service in Parliament, by proving his ability in successive steps up the ministerial ladder, and by displaying the qualities that the House of Commons deems important. The members of the two major parliamentary parties determine who will rise to the highest office. They select the person who will lead their party when it is out of power and become Prime Minister when it is triumphant. The MP who would be Prime Minister must satisfy his first constituents, the members of his party who sit in the Commons, that he would be competent and, according to the lights of the party, safe and reliable in office. They will look for someone who has shown over the years that he will displease few of his fellow MPs. Given no limits on length of service as Prime Minister, MP's will, moreover, be reluctant to support a younger person, whose successful candidacy might block the road to the highest office for decades.

Like most countries of settled political institutions, the British apprentice their rulers. The system by which Britain apprentices her rulers is more likely than America's quite different system to produce not only older chief executives but also ones who are safer and surer. Since the Second Reform Act, in 1867, Britain has had 20 Prime Ministers. Their average age in office is 62 years. Their average service in Parliament prior to becoming Prime Minister is 28 years, during which time they served their apprenticeships in various high Cabinet posts. In England the one way of attaining the highest office is to climb the ministerial ladder.[1] Since the Civil War, America has had 22 Presidents. Their average age in office is 56 years.[2] Since Congress is not a direct route to executive preferment, it is pointless to compare congressional with parliamentary service. It is, however, safe and significant to say that the Presidency draws on a wider field of experience, occasionally—as with Grant and Eisenhower—on a field not political at all.

The British mode of recruitment creates a condition that serves as a gross restraint on executive power. The Prime Minister, insofar as he has great powers, is likely to be of an age and experience, a worldly wisdom if you like, that makes his exercising them with force and vigor improbable. If it is true that England muddles through, here is part of the explanation, a bigger part than the oft-cited national character to which ideological commitment and programmatic politics are supposedly alien.

The limitations that come to bear on Prime Ministers in the very process by which they are selected are as important as they are subtle, elusive, and generally overlooked. These qualities also characterize the limitations that derive from the Prime Minister's relation to his party and to Parliament, where his strength is often thought to be greatest. The situation in the two countries can be put as follows: The President can lead but has trouble getting his party to follow; the Prime Minister has the followers but on condition that he not be too far in front of, or to the side of, his party, which makes it difficult for him to lead. The requisite art for a Prime Minister is to manage the party in ways that avoid the defiance of the many or the rebellion of the few, if those few are important, rather than to levy penalties after rebellion has occurred.

Most often the Prime Minister's worry is less that some members will defy him than that his real and effective support will dwindle in the years between general elections, as happened to Churchill and Macmillan in their last governments, and even more obviously to Eden and Heath. It is wrong to see the parliamentary party as a brake on the government only when the party is split and the Prime Minister faces an unruly faction, for a party is never monolithic. A well-managed party will appear to be almost passively obedient, but the managerial arts are difficult to master. The effective Prime Minister or party leader moves in ways that avoid dissent, if possible, by anticipating it. Concessions are made; issues are postponed and at times evaded entirely. If we think of the two parties as disciplined armies marching obediently at their leaders' commands, we not only ignore much important history but we also overlook the infinite care and calculation that goes into getting groups, be they armies, football teams, or political parties, to act in concert. The Prime Minister can ordinarily count on his party to support him, but only within limits that are set in part by the party members collectively. The Prime Minister can only ask for what his party will give. He cannot say: "The trade unions must be disciplined." He cannot say: "The relations of labor and management must be recast." He cannot say: "Industry must be ratio- nalized." He cannot make such statements, even if he believes them. He can give a bold lead only if he is sure that his party will come around without a major faction splitting off. But by the time a Prime Minister is sure of that, any lead given is no longer a bold one. One can be a bold Prime Minister only at the cost of being a bad party manager. "A Party has to be managed, and he who can manage it best, will probably be its best leader. The subordinate task of legislation and of executive government may well fall into the inferior hands of less astute practitio- ners."[3] Such were the reflections of Anthony Trollope on the career of Sir Timothy Beeswax, a party manager of near magical skills (1880, 3:169; cf. 1:216). The roles of leader of the country and manager of a party easily come into conflict. In the absence of formal checks and balances of the American sort, the party that would act can do so. Because the party in power acts on the word of its leader, the leader must be cautious about the words he chooses to utter.

The leadership problem coupled with the apprenticeship factor goes far to describe the texture of British politics. The Prime Minister must preserve the unity of his party, for it is not possible for him to perpetuate his rule by constructing a series of majorities whose composition varies from issue to issue. Prime Ministers must be, and must take pains to remain, acceptable to their parliamentary parties. By the political system within which he operates, the Prime Minister is impelled to seek the support of his entire party, at the cost of considerably reducing his freedom of action. He is constrained to crawl along cautiously, to let situations develop until the near necessity of decision blunts inclinations to quarrel about just what the decision should be. Leadership characteristics are built into the system. The typical Prime Minister is a weak national leader but an expert party manager—characteristics that he ordinarily must have in order to gain office and retain it.

In contrast, consider Presidents. Because their tenure does not depend on securing majority support in Congress, because they can be defeated on policies and still remain in office, and because obstruction is an ordinary and accepted part of the system, they are encouraged to ask for what at the moment may well not be granted. Presidents are expected to educate and inform, to explain that the legislation Congress refuses to pass is actually what the interest of the country requires; they may, indeed, ask for more than they want, hoping that the half-loaf they often get will conform roughly to their private estimate of need. The gap between promise and performance, between presidential request and congressional acquiescence is thus often illusory. Prime Ministers get all that they ask, and yet major social and economic legislation in Britain is ordinarily a long time maturing. Presidents ask for much that they do not get, and yet the pace of reform is not slower, the flexibility and response of American government are not less, than those of Great Britain.

Appearances are often deceptive. Prime Ministers are thought to be strong leaders because they are in public so ineffectively opposed. The fusion of powers, however, tempts the Prime Minister to place his concern for the unity of the party above his regard for the public interest and in rendering the party responsible in the eyes of the voter makes the government unresponsive to the needs of the nation. "A public man is responsible," as a character in one of Disraeli's novels once said, "and a responsible man is a slave" (1880:156). To be clearly responsible is to be highly visible. In America, the congressional show detracts in some measure from the attention the President receives; in Britain, the public concentrates its gaze with single-minded intensity on the Prime Minister. Fairly or not, he is praised or blamed for the good or ill health of the polity. Responsibility is concentrated rather than diffused. The leader who is responsible then has to husband his power; the onus for the risky policy that fails to come off falls entirely on him.

Americans, accustomed to rule by strong Presidents, naturally think only in terms of limits that are institutionally imposed and overlook the structural constraints on British government. Indeed in the two countries, the term "leadership" has different political meanings: in the United States, that strong men occupy the Presidency; in Britain, that the will of the Prime Minister becomes the law of the land. To say that the will of the leader becomes law should not be taken to mean that the system is one of strong leadership in the American sense; instead everything depends on the leader's identity and on the forces that shape his decisions. The British system goes far to ensure that the leader is moderate and will behave with propriety. This is not seen by simply observing political processes. One has first to relate political structure to process, to consider the ways in which political offices and institutions are juxtaposed and combined. Power is concentrated in the hands of the Prime Minister and yet with great, though informal, checks against its impetuous use: the apprentice system by which parliamentarians rise to office; the subtle restraints of party that work upon the Prime Minister; the habit, institutionally encouraged, of moving slowly with events and of postponing changes in policy until their necessity is widely accepted.

The endurance of patterns over the decades is striking. Think of the Prime Ministers Britain has known since the turn of the century. They are Balfour, Campbell-Bannerman, Asquith, Lloyd George, Bonar Law, Baldwin, MacDonald, Chamberlain, Churchill, Attlee, Eden, Macmillan, Home, Wilson, Heath, and Callaghan. Two failed to fit the pattern— Lloyd George and Winston Churchill. Both had long sat in the Commons. Both had worked their ways up the ladder. They had served their apprenticeships, but doing so had not tamed them. In normal times each of them appeared unreliable at best, and perhaps downright dangerous, to fractions of their parties large enough to deny them the highest office. Back benchers in large number thought of them as being unlikely to balance the interests and convictions of various groups within the party, to calculate nicely whose services and support merited higher or lower ministerial positions, and to show a gentlemanly respect for the opinions of others even when they were thought to be ill-founded. A few comments on Winston Churchill will show what I mean. Member of Parliament since 1900 and the holder of more ministerial posts than any politician in British history, he was richly qualified for the highest office. But he had been a maverick for most of his political life. A Conservative at the outset of his political career, he became a Liberal in 1906 and did not return to the Conservative fold until the middle 1920s. In the 1930s, he was at odds with his party on great matters of state policy, first on Indian and then on European affairs. Nothing less than a crisis big enough to turn his party liabilities into national assets could elevate him to the highest office. The events required to raise him to prime ministerial office, by virtue of their exceptional quality, cause the normal practice to stand out more clearly. Accidents do occur, but it takes great crises to produce them. To pull someone from outside the normal lines of succession is not easily done.

Political structure produces a similarity in process and performance so long as a structure endures. Similarity is not uniformity. Structure operates as a cause, but it is not the only cause in play. How can one know whether observed effects are caused by the structure of national politics rather than by a changing cast of political characters, by variations of nonpolitical circumstances, and by a host of other factors? How can one separate structural from other causes? One does it by extending the comparative method that I have just used. Look, for example, at British political behavior where structure differs. Contrast the behavior of the Labour movement with that of the Parliamentary Labour Party. In the Labour movement, where power is checked and balanced, the practice of politics, especially when the party is out of power, is strikingly similar to the political conduct that prevails in America. In the face of conflict and open dissension, the leaders of the party are stimulated actually to lead, to explore the ground and try to work out compromises, to set a line of policy, to exhort and persuade, to threaten and cajole, to inform and educate, all with the hope that the parts of the party—the National Executive Committee, the trade unions, and the constituency parties, as well as the Members of Parliament—can be brought to follow the leader.

Within a country one can identify the effects of structure by noticing *differences* of behavior in differently structured parts of the polity. From one country to another, one can identify the effects of structure by noticing *similarities* of behavior in polities of similar structure. Thus Chihiro Hosoya's description of the behavior of Prime Ministers in postwar Japan's parliamentary system exactly fits British Prime Ministers (1974:366–369). Despite cultural and other differences, similar structures produce similar effects.

III

I defined domestic political structures first by the principle according to which they are organized or ordered, second by the differentiation of units and the specification of their functions, and third by the distribution of capabilities across units. Let us see how the three terms of the definition apply to international politics.

1. Ordering Principles

Structural questions are questions about the arrangement of the parts of a system. The parts of domestic political systems stand in relations of super- and subordination. Some are entitled to command; others are required to obey. Domestic systems are centralized and hierarchic. The parts of international-political systems stand in relations of coordination. Formally, each is the equal of all the others. None is entitled to command; none is required to obey. International systems are decentralized and anarchic. The ordering principles of the two structures are distinctly different, indeed, contrary to each other. Domestic political structures have governmental institutions and offices as their concrete counterparts. International politics, in contrast, has been called "politics in the absence of government" (Fox 1959:35). International organizations do exist, and in evergrowing numbers. Supranational agents able to act effectively, however, either themselves acquire some of the attributes and capabilities of states, as did the medieval papacy in the era of Innocent III, or they soon reveal their inability to act in important ways except with the support, or at least the acquiescence, of the principal states concerned with the matters at hand. Whatever elements of authority emerge internationally are barely once removed from the capability that provides the foundation for the appearance of those elements. Authority quickly reduces to a particular expression of capability. In the absence of agents with system-wide authority, formal relations of super- and subordination fail to develop.

The first term of a structural definition states the principle by which the system is ordered. Structure is an organizational concept. The prominent characteristic of international politics, however, seems to be the lack of order and of organization. How can one think of international politics as being any kind of an order at all? The anarchy of politics internationally is often referred to. If structure is an organizational concept, the terms "structure" and "anarchy" seem to be in contradiction. If international politics is "politics in the absence of government," what are we in the presence of? In looking for international structure, one is brought face to face with the invisible, an uncomfortable position to be in.

The problem is this: how to conceive of an order without an orderer and of organizational effects where formal organization is lacking. Because these are difficult questions, I shall answer them through analogy with microeconomic theory. Reasoning by analogy is helpful where one can move from a domain for which theory is well developed to one where it is not. Reasoning by analogy is permissible where different domains are structurally similar.

Classical economic theory, developed by Adam Smith and his followers, is microtheory. Political scientists tend to think that microtheory is theory about small-scale matters, a usage that ill accords with its established meaning. The term "micro" in economic theory indicates the way in which the theory is constructed rather than the scope of the matters it pertains to. Microeconomic theory describes how an order is spontaneously formed from the self-interested acts and interactions of individual units—in this case, persons and firms. The theory then turns upon the two central concepts of the economic units and of the market. Economic units and economic markets are concepts, not descriptive realities or concrete entities. This must be emphasized since from the early eighteenth century to the present, from the sociologist Auguste Comte to the psychologist George Katona, economic theory has been faulted because its assumptions fail to correspond with realities (Martineau 1853, 2:51–53; Katona 1953). Unrealistically, economic theorists conceive of an economy operating in isolation from its society and polity. Unrealistically, economists assume that the economic world is the whole of the world. Unrealistically, economists think of the acting unit, the famous "economic man," as a single-minded profit maximizer. They single out one aspect of man and leave aside the wondrous variety of human life. As any moderately sensible economist knows, "economic man" does not exist. Anyone who asks businessmen how they make their decisions will find that the assumption that men are economic maximizers grossly distorts their characters. The assumption that men behave as economic men, which is known to be false as a descriptive statement, turns out to be useful in the construction of theory.

Markets are the second major concept invented by microeconomic theorists. Two general questions must be asked about markets: How are they formed? How do they work? The answer to the first question is this: The market of a decentralized economy is individualist in origin, spontaneously generated, and unintended. The market arises out of the activities of separate units—persons and firms—whose aims and efforts are directed not toward creating an order but rather toward fulfilling their own internally defined interests by whatever means they can muster. The individual unit acts for itself. From the coaction of like units emerges a structure that affects and constrains all of them. Once formed, a market becomes a force in itself, and a force that the constitutive units acting singly or in small numbers cannot control. Instead, in lesser or greater degree as market conditions vary, the creators become the creatures of the market that their activity gave rise to. Adam Smith's great achievement was to show how self-interested, greed-driven actions may produce good social outcomes if only political and social conditions permit free competition. If a laissez-faire economy is harmonious, it is so because the intentions of actors do *not* correspond with the outcomes their actions produce. What intervenes between the actors and the objects of their action in order to thwart their purposes? To account for the unexpectedly favorable outcomes of selfish acts, the concept of a market is brought into play. Each unit seeks its own good; the result of a number of units simultaneously doing so transcends the motives and the aims of the separate units. Each would like to work less hard and price his product higher. Taken together, all have to work harder and price their products lower. Each firm seeks to increase its profit; the result of many firms doing so drives the profit rate downward. Each man seeks his own end, and, in doing so, produces a result that was no part of his intention. Out of the mean ambition of its members, the greater good of society is produced.

The market is a cause interposed between the economic actors and the results they produce. It conditions their calculations, their behaviors, and their interactions. It is not an agent in the sense of A being the agent that produces outcome X. Rather it is a structural cause. A market constrains the units that comprise it from taking certain actions and disposes them toward taking others. The market, created by self-directed interacting economic units, selects behaviors according to their consequences (cf. article 3, part III). The market rewards some with high profits and assigns others to bankruptcy. Since a market is not an institution or an agent in any concrete or palpable sense, such statements become impressive only if they can be reliably inferred from a theory as part of a set of more elaborate expectations. They can be. Microeconomic theory explains how an economy operates and why certain effects are to be expected. It generates numerous "if-then" statements that can more or less easily be checked. Consider, for example, the following simple but important propositions. If the money demand for a commodity rises, then so will its price. If price rises, then so will profits. If profits rise, then capital will be attracted and production will increase. If production increases, then price will fall to the level that returns profits to the producers of the commodity at the prevailing rate. This sequence of statements could be extended and refined, but to do so would not serve my purpose. I want to point out that although the stated expectations are now commonplace, they could not be arrived at by economists working in a pre-theoretic era. All of the statements are, of course, made at an appropriate level of generality. They require an "other things being equal" stipulation. They apply, as do statements inferred from any theory, only to the extent that the conditions contemplated by the theory obtain. They are idealizations, and so they are never fully borne out in practice. Many things—social customs, political interventions—will in fact interfere with the theoretically predicted outcomes. Though interferences have to be allowed for, it is nevertheless extraordinarily useful to know what to expect in general.

International-political systems, like economic markets, are formed by the coaction of self-regarding units. International structures are defined in terms of the primary political units of an era, be they city states, empires, or nations. Structures emerge from the coexistence of states. No state intends to participate in the formation of a structure by which it and others will be constrained. International-political systems, like economic markets, are individualist in origin, spontaneously generated, and unintended. In both systems, structures are formed by the coaction of their units. Whether those units live, prosper, or die depends on their own efforts. Both systems are formed and maintained on a principle of self-help that applies to the units. To say that the two realms are structurally similar is not to proclaim their identity. Economically, the self-help principle applies within governmentally contrived limits. Market economies are hedged about in ways that channel energies constructively. One may think of pure food-and-drug standards, antitrust laws, securities and exchange regulations, laws against shooting a competitor, and rules forbidding false claims in advertising. International politics is more nearly a realm in which anything goes. International politics is structurally similar to a market economy insofar as the self-help principle is allowed to operate in the latter.

In a microtheory, whether of international politics or of economics, the motivation of the actors is assumed rather than realistically described. I assume that states seek to ensure their survival. The assumption is a radical simplification made for the sake of constructing a theory. The question to ask of the assumption, as ever, is not whether it is true but whether it is the most sensible and useful one that can be made. Whether it is a useful assumption depends on whether a theory based on the assumption can be contrived, a theory from which important consequences not otherwise obvious can be inferred. Whether it is a sensible assumption can be directly discussed.

Beyond the survival motive, the aims of states may be endlessly varied; they may range from the ambition to conquer the world to the desire merely to be left alone. Survival is a prerequisite to achieving any goals that states may have, other than the goal of promoting their own disappearance as political entities. The survival motive is taken as the ground of action in a world where the security of states is not assured, rather than as a realistic description of the impulse that lies behind every act of state. The assumption allows for the fact that no state always acts exclusively to ensure its survival. It allows for the fact that some states may persistently seek goals that they value more highly than survival; they may, for example, prefer amalgamation with other states to their own survival in form. It allows for the fact that in pursuit of its security no state will act with perfect knowledge and wisdom—if indeed we could know what those terms might mean. Some systems have high requirements for their functioning. Traffic will not flow if most, but not all, people drive on the proper side of the road. If necessary, strong measures have to be taken to ensure that everyone does so. Other systems have medium requirements. Elevators in skyscrapers are planned so that they can handle the passenger load if most people take express elevators for the longer runs and locals only for the shorter ones. But if some people choose locals for long runs because the speed of the express makes them dizzy, the system will not break down. To keep it going, most, but not all, people have to act as expected. Some systems, market economies and international politics among them, make still lower demands. Traffic systems are designed on the knowledge that the system's requirements will be enforced. Elevators are planned with extra capacity to allow for human vagaries. Competitive economic and international-political systems work differently. Out of the interactions of their parts they develop structures that reward or punish behavior that conforms more or less nearly to what is required of one who wishes to succeed in the system. Recall my description of the constraints of the British parliamentary system. Why should a would-be Prime Minister not strike out on a bold course of his own? Why not behave in ways markedly different from those of typical British political leaders? Anyone can, of course, and some who aspire to become Prime Ministers do so. They rarely come to the top. Except in deepest crisis, the system selects others to hold the highest office. One may behave as one likes to. Patterns of behavior nevertheless emerge, and they derive from the structural constraints of the system.

Actors may perceive the structure that constrains them and understand how it serves to reward some kinds of behavior and to penalize others. But then again they either may not see it or, seeing it, may for any of many reasons fail to conform their actions to the patterns that are most often rewarded and least often punished. To say that "the structure selects" means simply that those who conform to accepted and successful practices more often rise to the top and are likelier to stay there. The

game one has to win is defined by the structure that determines the
kind of player who is likely to prosper.

Where selection according to behavior occurs, no enforced standard
of behavior is required for the system to operate, although either system
may work better if some standards are enforced or accepted. Internationally, the environment of states' action, or the structure of their system,
is set by the fact that some states prefer survival over other ends ob-
tainable in the short run and act with relative efficiency to achieve that
end. States may alter their behavior because of the structure they form
through interaction with other states. But in what ways and why? To
answer these questions we must complete the definition of international
structure.

2. The Character of the Units

The second term in the definition of domestic political structure specifies
the functions performed by differentiated units. Hierarchy entails relations of super- and subordination among a system's parts, and that
implies their differentiation. In defining domestic political structure the
second term, like the first and third, is needed because each term points
to a possible source of structural variation. The states that are the units
of international-political systems are not formally differentiated by the
functions they perform. Anarchy entails relations of coordination among
a system's units, and that implies their sameness. The second term is
not needed in defining international-political structure, because so long
as anarchy endures, states remain like units. International structures vary
only through a change of organizing principle or, failing that, through
variations in the capabilities of units. Nevertheless I shall discuss these
like units here, because it is by their interactions that international-
political structures are generated.

Two questions arise: Why should states be taken as the units of the
system? Given a wide variety of states, how can one call them "like
units"? Questioning the choice of states as the primary units of international-political systems became popular in the 1960s and '70s as it
was at the turn of the century. Once one understands what is logically
involved, the issue is easily resolved. Those who question the state-centric
view do so for two main reasons. First, states are not the only actors of

importance on the international scene. Second, states are declining in importance, and other actors are gaining, or so it is said. Neither reason is cogent, as the following discussion shows.

States are not and never have been the only international actors. But then structures are defined not by all of the actors that flourish within them but by the major ones. In defining a system's structure one chooses one or some of the infinitely many objects comprising the system and defines its structure in terms of them. For international-political systems, as for any system, one must first decide which units to take as being the parts of the system. Here the economic analogy will help again. The structure of a market is defined by the number of firms competing. If many roughly equal firms contend, a condition of perfect competition is approximated. If a few firms dominate the market, competition is said to be oligopolistic even though many smaller firms may also be in the field. But we are told that definitions of this sort cannot be applied to international politics because of interpenetration of states, because of their inability to control the environment of their action, and because rising multinational corporations and other nonstate actors are difficult to regulate and may rival some states in influence. The importance of nonstate actors and the extent of transnational activities are obvious. The conclusion that the state-centric conception of international politics is made obsolete by them does not follow. That economists and economically minded political scientists have thought that it does is ironic. The irony lies in the fact that all of the reasons given for scrapping the state-centric concept can be restated more strongly and applied to firms. Firms competing with numerous others have no hope of controlling their market, and oligopolistic firms constantly struggle with imperfect success to do so. Firms interpenetrate, merge, and buy each other up at a merry pace. Moreover, firms are constantly threatened and regulated by, shall we say, "nonfirm" actors. Some governments encourage concentration; others work to prevent it. The market structure of parts of an economy may move from a wider to a narrower competition or may move in the opposite direction, but whatever the extent and the frequency of change, market structures, generated by the interaction of firms, are defined in terms of them.

Just as economists define markets in terms of firms, so I define international-political structures in terms of states. If Charles P. Kindleberger were right in saying that "the nation-state is just about through as an economic unit" (1969:207), then the structure of international politics would have to be redefined. That would be necessary because economic capabilities cannot be separated from the other capabilities of states. The distinction frequently drawn between matters of high and low politics is misplaced. States use economic means for military and political ends; and military and political means for the achievement of economic interests.

An amended version of Kindleberger's statement may hold: Some states may be nearly washed up as economic entitites, and others not. That poses no problem for international-political theory since international politics is mostly about inequalities anyway. So long as the major states are the major actors, the structure of international politics is defined in terms of them. That theoretical statement is of course borne out in practice. States set the scene in which they, along with nonstate actors, stage their dramas or carry on their humdrum affairs. Though they may choose to interfere little in the affairs of nonstate actors for long periods of time, states nevertheless set the terms of the intercourse, whether by passively permitting informal rules to develop or by actively intervening to change rules that no longer suit them. When the crunch comes, states remake the rules by which other actors operate. Indeed, one may be struck by the ability of weak states to impede the operation of strong international corporations and by the attention the latter pay to the wishes of the former.

It is important to consider the nature of transnational movements, the extent of their penetration, and the conditions that make it harder or easier for states to control them. But the adequate study of these matters, like others, requires finding or developing an adequate approach to the study of international politics. Two points should be made about latter-day transnational studies. First, students of transnational phenomena have developed no distinct theory of their subject matter or of international politics in general. They have drawn on existing theories, whether economic or political. Second, that they have developed no distinct theory is quite proper, for a theory that denies the central role of states will be needed only if nonstate actors develop to the point of rivaling or surpassing the great powers, not just a few of the minor ones. They show no sign of doing that.

The study of transnational movements deals with important factual questions, which theories can help one to cope with. But the help will not be gained if it is thought that nonstate actors call the state-centric view of the world into question. To say that major states maintain their central importance is not to say that other actors of some importance do not exist. The "state-centric" phrase suggests something about the system's structure. Transnational movements are among the processes that go on within it. That the state-centric view is so often questioned merely reflects the difficulty political scientists have in keeping the distinction between structures and processes clearly and constantly in mind.

States are the units whose interactions form the structure of international-political systems. They will long remain so. The death rate among states is remarkably low. Few states die; many firms do. Who is likely to be around 100 years from now—the United States, the Soviet Union, France, Egypt, Thailand, and Uganda? Or Ford, IBM, Shell, Unilever, and Massey-Ferguson? I would bet on the states, perhaps even on Uganda. But what does it mean to refer to the 150-odd states of today's world, which certainly form a motley collection, as being "like units"? Many students of international politics are bothered by the description. To call states "like units" is to say that each state is like all other states in being an autonomous political unit. It is another way of saying that states are sovereign. But sovereignty is also a bothersome concept. Many believe, as the anthropologist M. G. Smith has said, that "in a system of sovereign states no state is sovereign."[4] The error lies in identifying the sovereignty of states with their ability to do as they wish. To say that states are sovereign is not to say that they can do as they please, that they are free of others' influence, that they are able to get what they want. Sovereign states may be hardpressed all around, constrained to act in ways they would like to avoid, and able to do hardly anything just as they would like to. The sovereignty of states has never entailed their insulation from the effects of other states' actions. To be sovereign and to be dependent are not contradictory conditions. Sovereign states have seldom led free and easy lives. What then is sovereignty? To say that a state is sovereign means that it decides for itself how it will cope with its internal and external problems, including whether or not to seek assistance from others and in doing so to limit its freedom by making commitments to them. States develop their own strategies, chart their own courses, make their own decisions about how to meet whatever needs they experience and whatever desires they develop. It is no more contradictory to say that sovereign states are always constrained and often tightly so than it is to say that free individuals often make decisions under the heavy pressure of events.

Each state, like every other state, is a sovereign political entity. And yet the differences across states, from Costa Rica to the Soviet Union, from Gambia to the United States, are immense. States are alike, and they are also different. So are corporations, apples, universities, and people. Whenever we put two or more objects in the same category, we are saying that they are alike not in all respects but in some. No two objects in this world are identical, yet they can often be usefully compared and combined. "You can't add apples and oranges" is an old saying that seems to be especially popular among salesmen who do not want you to compare their wares with others. But we all know that the trick of adding dissimilar objects is to express the result in terms of a category that comprises them. Three apples plus four oranges equals seven pieces of fruit. The only interesting question is whether the category that classifies objects according to their common qualities is useful. One can add up a large number of widely varied objects and say that one has eight million things, but seldom need one do that.

States vary widely in size, wealth, power, and form. And yet variations in these and in other respects are variations among like units. In what way are they like units? How can they be placed in a single category? States are alike in the tasks that they face, though not in their abilities to perform them. The differences are of capability, not of function. States perform or try to perform tasks, most of which are common to all of them; the ends they aspire to are similar. Each state duplicates the activities of other states at least to a considerable extent. Each state has its agencies for making, executing, and interpreting laws and regulations, for raising revenues, and for defending itself. Each state supplies out of its own resources and by its own means most of the food, clothing, housing, transportation, and amenities consumed and used by its citizens. All states, except the smallest ones, do much more of their business at home than abroad. One has to be impressed with the functional similarity of states and, now more than ever before, with the similar lines their development follows. From the rich to the poor states, from the old to the new ones, nearly all of them take a larger hand in matters of economic regulation, of education, health, and housing, of culture and the arts, and so on almost endlessly. The increase of the activities of states is a strong and strikingly uniform international trend. The functions of states are similar, and distinctions among them arise principally from their varied capabilities. National politics consists of differentiated units performing specified functions. International politics consists of like units duplicating one another's activities.

3. The Distribution of Capabilities

The parts of a hierarchic system are related to one another in ways that are determined both by their functional differentiation and by the extent of their capabilities. The units of an anarchic system are functionally undifferentiated. The units of such an order are then distinguished primarily by their greater or lesser capabilities for performing similar tasks. This states formally what students of international politics have long noticed. The great powers of an era have always been marked off from the others by practitioners and theorists alike. Students of national government make such distinctions as that between parliamentary and presidential systems; governmental systems differ in form. Students of international politics make distinctions between international-political systems only according to the number of their great powers. The structure of a system changes with changes in the distribution of capabilities across the system's units. And changes in structure change expectations about how the units of the system will behave and about the outcomes their interactions will produce. Domestically, the differentiated parts of a system may perform similar tasks. We know from observing the American government that executives sometimes legislate and legislatures sometimes execute. Internationally, like units sometimes perform different tasks. Why they do so, and how the likelihood of their doing so varies with their capabilities, are matters treated at length in the last three chapters [not reprinted here: ed.]. Meanwhile, two problems should be considered.

The first problem is this: Capability tells us something about units. Defining structure partly in terms of the distribution of capabilities seems to violate my instruction to keep unit attributes out of structural definitions. As I remarked earlier, structure is a highly but not entirely abstract concept. The maximum of abstraction allows a minimum of content, and that minimum is what is needed to enable one to say how the units stand in relation to one another. States are differently placed by their power. And yet one may wonder why only *capability* is included in the third part of the definition, and not such characteristics as ideology, form of government, peacefulness, bellicosity, or whatever. The answer is this: Power is estimated by comparing the capabilities of a number of units. Although capabilities are attributes of units, the distribution of capabilities across units is not. The distribution of capabilities is not a unit attribute, but rather a system-wide concept. Again, the parallel with market theory is exact. Both firms and states are like units. Through all of their variations in form, firms share certain qualities: They are self-regarding units that, within governmentally imposed limits, decide for themselves how to cope with their environment and just how to work for their ends. Variation of structure is introduced, not through differences in the character and function of units, but only through distinctions made among them according to their capabilities.

The second problem is this: Though relations defined in terms of interactions must be excluded from structural definitions, relations defined in terms of groupings of states do seem to tell us something about how states are placed in the system. Why not specify how states stand in relation to one another by considering the alliances they form? Would doing so not be comparable to defining national political structures partly in terms of how presidents and prime ministers are related to other political agents? It would not be. Nationally as internationally, structural definitions deal with the relation of agents and agencies in terms of the organization of realms and not in terms of the accommodations and conflicts that may occur within them or the groupings that may now and then form. Parts of a government may draw together or pull apart, may oppose each other or cooperate in greater or lesser degree. These are the relations that form and dissolve within a system rather than structural alterations that mark a change from one system to another. This is made clear by an example that runs nicely parallel to the case of alliances. Distinguishing systems of political parties according to their number is common. A multiparty system changes if, say, eight parties become two, but not if two groupings of the eight form merely for the occasion of fighting an election. By the same logic, an international-political system in which three or more great powers have split into two alliances remains a multipolar system—structurally distinct from a bipolar system, a system in which no third power is able to challenge the top two. In defining market structure, information about the particular quality of firms is not called for, nor is information about their interactions, short of the point at which the formal merger of firms significantly reduces their number. In the definition of market structure, firms are not identified and their interactions are not described. To take the qualities of firms and the nature of their interactions as being parts of market structure would be to say that whether a sector of an economy is oligopolistic or not depends on how the firms are organized internally and how they deal with one another, rather than simply on how many major firms coexist. Market structure is defined by counting firms; international-political structure, by counting states. In the counting, distinctions are made only according to capabilities.

In defining international-political structures we take states with whatever traditions, habits, objectives, desires, and forms of government they may have. We do not ask whether states are revolutionary or legitimate, authoritarian or democratic, ideological or pragmatic. We abstract from every attribute of states except their capabilities. Nor in thinking about structure do we ask about the relations of states—their feelings of friendship and hostility, their diplomatic exchanges, the alliances they form, and the extent of the contacts and exchanges among them. We ask what range of expectations arises merely from looking at the type of order that prevails among them and at the distribution of capabilities within that order. We abstract from any particular qualities of states and from all of their concrete connections. What emerges is a positional picture, a general description of the ordered overall arrangement of a society written in terms of the placement of units rather than in terms of their qualities.

IV

I have now defined the two essential elements of a systems theory of international politics—the structure of the system and its interacting units. In doing so I have broken sharply away from common approaches.

As we have seen, some scholars who attempt systems approaches to international politics conceive of a system as being the product of its interacting parts, but they fail to consider whether anything at the systems level affects those parts. Other systems theorists, like students of international politics in general, mention at times that the effects of the international environment must be allowed for; but they pass over the question of how this is to be done and quickly return their attention to the level of interacting units. Most students, whether or not they claim to follow a systems approach, think of international politics in the way fig. 4.1 suggests. $N_{1,2,3}$ are states internally generating their external effects. $X_{1,2,3}$ are states acting externally and interacting with each other. No systemic force or factor shows up in the picture.

Figure 4.1.

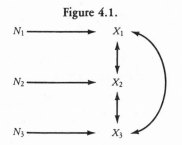

Because systemic effects are evident, international politics should be seen as in fig. 4.2. The circle represents the structure of an international-political system. As the arrows indicate, it affects both the interactions of states and their attributes.[5] Although structure as an organizational concept has proved elusive, its meaning can be explained simply. While states retain their autonomy, each stands in a specifiable relation to the others. They form some sort of an order. We can use the term "organization" to cover this preinstitutional condition if we think of an organization as simply a constraint, in the manner of W. Ross Ashby (1956:131). Because states constrain and limit each other, international politics can be viewed in rudimentary organizational terms. Structure is the concept that makes it possible to say what the expected organizational effects are and how structures and units interact and affect each other.

Thinking of structure as I have defined it solves the problem of separating changes at the level of the units from changes at the level of the system. If one is concerned with the different expected effects of dif-

Figure 4.2.

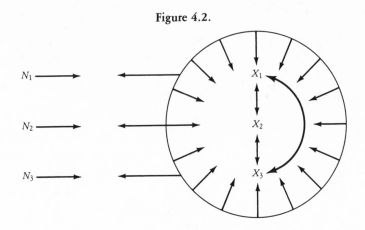

ferent systems, one must be able to distinguish changes of systems from changes within them, something that would-be systems theorists have found exceedingly difficult to do. A three-part definition of structure enables one to discriminate between those types of changes:

- Structures are defined, first, according to the principle by which a system is ordered. Systems are transformed if one ordering principle replaces another. To move from an anarchic to a hierarchic realm is to move from one system to another.
- Structures are defined, second, by the specification of functions of differentiated units. Hierarchic systems change if functions are differently defined and allotted. For anarchic systems, the criterion of systems change derived from the second part of the definition drops out since the system is composed of like units.
- Structures are defined, third, by the distribution of capabilities across units. Changes in this distribution are changes of system whether the system be an anarchic or a hierarchic one.

NOTES

1. The exception, which does not disprove the rule, is Ramsay MacDonald, who, absent from the wartime coalition and with his party not previously in power, had never served in a ministerial position.

2. All calculations as of July 1978.

3. In some respects a century brings little change. Despite the many harsh

comments made about Callaghan by Crossman, Wilson, and others, Crossman thought of him as "easily the most accomplished politician of the Labour Party"; and apparently because of that distinction, Callaghan gained Wilson's help in succeeding him as Prime Minister (1977, 3:627–628 *et passim*).

4. Smith should know better. Translated into terms that he has himself so effectively used, to say that states are sovereign is to say that they are segments of a plural society (1966:122; cf. 1956).

5. No essentials are omitted from fig. 4.2, but some complications are. A full picture would include, for example, coalitions possibly forming on the right-hand side.

FIVE

Anarchic Orders and Balances of Power

KENNETH N. WALTZ

I

1. Violence at Home and Abroad

THE STATE AMONG STATES, it is often said, conducts its affairs in the brooding shadow of violence. Because some states may at any time use force, all states must be prepared to do so—or live at the mercy of their militarily more vigorous neighbors. Among states, the state of nature is a state of war. This is meant not in the sense that war constantly occurs but in the sense that, with each state deciding for itself whether or not to use force, war may break out at any time. Whether in the family, the community, or the world at large, contact without at least occasional conflict is inconceivable; and the hope that in the absence of an agent to manage or to manipulate conflicting parties the use of force will always be avoided cannot be realistically entertained. Among men as among states, anarchy, or the absence of government, is associated with the occurrence of violence.

The threat of violence and the recurrent use of force are said to distinguish international from national affairs. But in the history of the world surely most rulers have had to bear in mind that their subjects might use force to resist or overthrow them. If the absence of government is associated with the threat of violence, so also is its presence. A haphazard list of national tragedies illustrates the point all too well. The most destructive wars of the hundred years following the defeat of Napoleon took place not among states but *within* them. Estimates of deaths in China's Taiping Rebellion, which began in 1851 and lasted 13 years, range as high as 20 million. In the American Civil War some 600,000 people lost their lives. In more recent history, forced collectivization and Stalin's purges eliminated five million Russians, and Hitler exterminated 6 million Jews. In some Latin American countries, coups d'état and rebellions have been normal features of national life. Between 1948 and 1957, for example, 200,000 Colombians were killed in civil strife. In the middle 1970s most inhabitants of Idi Amin's Uganda must have felt their lives becoming nasty, brutish, and short, quite as in Thomas Hobbes's state of nature. If such cases constitute aberrations, they are uncomfortably common ones. We easily lose sight of the fact that struggles to achieve and maintain power, to establish order, and to contrive a kind of justice within states, may be bloodier than wars among them.

If anarchy is identified with chaos, destruction, and death, then the distinction between anarchy and government does not tell us much. Which is more precarious: the life of a state among states, or of a government in relation to its subjects? The answer varies with time and place. Among some states at some times, the actual or expected occurrence of violence is low. Within some states at some times, the actual or expected occurrence of violence is high. The use of force, or the constant fear of its use, is not sufficient grounds for distinguishing international from domestic affairs. If the possible and the actual use of force mark both national and international orders, then no durable distinction between the two realms can be drawn in terms of the use or the nonuse of force. No human order is proof against violence.

To discover qualitative differences between internal and external affairs one must must look for a criterion other than the occurrence of violence. The distinction between international and national realms of politics is not found in the use or the nonuse of force but in their different structures. But if the dangers of being violently attacked are greater, say, in taking an evening stroll through downtown Detroit than they are in picnicking along the French and German border, what practical difference does the difference of structure make? Nationally as internationally, contact generates conflict and at times issues in violence. The difference between national and international politics lies not in the use of force but in the different modes of organization for doing something about it. A government, ruling by some standard of legitimacy, arrogates to itself the right to use force—that is, to apply a variety of sanctions to control the use of force by its subjects. If some use private force, others may appeal to the government. A government has no monopoly on the use of force, as is all too evident. An effective government, however, has a monopoly on the *legitimate* use of force, and legitimate here means that public agents are organized to prevent and to counter the private use of force. Citizens need not prepare to defend themselves. Public agencies do that. A national system is not one of self-help. The international system is.

2. Interdependence and Integration

The political significance of interdependence varies depending on whether a realm is organized, with relations of authority specified and established, or remains formally unorganized. Insofar as a realm is formally organized, its units are free to specialize, to pursue their own interests without concern for developing the means of maintaining their identity and preserving their security in the presence of others. They are free to specialize because they have no reason to fear the increased interdependence that goes with specialization. If those who specialize most benefit most, then competition in specialization ensues. Goods are manufactured, grain is produced, law and order are maintained, commerce is conducted and financial services are provided by people who ever more narrowly specialize. In simple economic terms, the cobbler depends on the tailor for his pants and the tailor on the cobbler for his shoes, and each would be ill-clad without the services of the other. In simple political terms, Kansas depends on Washington for protection and regulation and Washington depends on Kansas for beef and wheat. In saying that in such situations interdependence is close, one need not maintain that the one part could not learn to live without the other. One need only say that the cost of breaking the interdependent relation would be high. Persons and institutions depend heavily on one another because of the different tasks they perform and the different goods they produce and exchange. The parts of a polity binds themselves together by their differences (cf. Durkheim 1893:212).

Differences between national and international structures are reflected in the ways the units of each system define their ends and develop the means for reaching them. In anarchic realms, like units coact. In hierarchic realms, unlike units interact. In an anarchic realm, the units are functionally similar and tend to remain so. Like units work to maintain a measure of independence and may even strive for autarchy. In a hierarchic realm, the units are differentiated, and they tend to increase the extent of their specialization. Differentiated units become closely interdependent, the more closely so as their specialization proceeds. Because of the difference of structure, interdependence within and interdependence among nations are two distinct concepts. So as to follow the logicians' admonition to keep a single meaning for a given term throughout one's discourse, I shall use "integration" to describe the condition within nations and "interdependence" to describe the condition among them.

Although states are like units functionally, they differ vastly in their capabilities. Out of such differences something of a division of labor develops. The division of labor across nations, however, is slight in comparison with the highly articulated division of labor within them. Integration draws the parts of a nation closely together. Interdependence among nations leaves them loosely connected. Although the integration of nations is often talked about, it seldom takes place. Nations could mutually enrich themselves by further dividing not just the labor that goes into the production of goods but also some of the other tasks they perform, such as political management and military defense. Why does their integration not take place? The structure of international politics limits the cooperation of states in two ways.

In a self-help system each of the units spends a portion of its effort, not in forwarding its own good, but in providing the means of protecting itself against others. Specialization in a system of divided labor works to everyone's advantage, though not equally so. Inequality in the expected distribution of the increased product works strongly against extension of the division of labor internationally. When faced with the possibility of cooperating for mutual gain, states that feel insecure must ask how the gain will be divided. They are compelled to ask not "Will both of us gain?" but "Who will gain more?" If an expected gain is to be divided, say, in the ratio of two to one, one state may use its disproportionate gain to implement a policy intended to damage or destroy the other. Even the prospect of large absolute gains for both parties does not elicit their cooperation so long as each fears how the other will use its increased capabilities. Notice that the impediments to collaboration may not lie in the character and the immediate intention of either party. Instead, the condition of insecurity—at the least, the uncertainty of each about the other's future intentions and actions—works against their cooperation.

In any self-help system, units worry about their survival, and the worry conditions their behavior. Oligopolistic markets limits the cooperation of firms in much the way that international-political structures limit the cooperation of states. Within rules laid down by governments, whether firms survive and prosper depends on their own efforts. Firms need not protect themselves physically against assaults from other firms. They are free to concentrate on their economic interests. As economic entities, however, they live in a self-help world. All want to increase profits. If they run undue risks in the effort to do so, they must expect to suffer the consequences. As William Fellner says, it is "impossible to maximize joint gains without the collusive handling of all relevant variables." And this can be accomplished only by "complete disarmament of the firms in relation to each other." But firms cannot sensibly disarm even to increase their profits. This statement qualifies, rather than contradicts, the assumption that firms aim at maximum profits. To maximize profits tomorrow as well as today, firms first have to survive. Pooling all resources implies, again as Fellner puts it, "discounting the future possibilities of all participating firms" (1949:35). But the future cannot be discounted. The relative strength of firms changes over time in ways that cannot be foreseen. Firms are constrained to strike a compromise between maximizing their profits and minimizing the danger of their own demise. Each of two firms may be better off it one of them accepts compensation from the other in return for withdrawing from some part of the market. But a firm that accepts smaller markets in exchange for larger profits will be gravely disadvantaged if, for example, a price war should break out as part of a renewed struggle for markets. If possible, one must resist accepting smaller markets in return for larger profits (pp. 132, 217–218). "It is," Fellner insists, "not advisable to disarm in relation to one's rivals" (p. 199). Why not? Because "the potentiality of renewed warfare always exists" (p. 177). Fellner's reasoning is much like the reasoning that led Lenin to believe that capitalist countries would never be able to cooperate for their mutual enrichment in one vast imperialist enterprise. Like nations, oligopolistic firms must be more concerned with relative strength than with absolute advantage.

A state worries about a division of possible gains that may favor others more than itself. That is the first way in which the structure of international politics limits the cooperation of states. A state also worries lest it become dependent on others through cooperative endeavors and exchanges of goods and services. That is the second way in which the structure of international politics limits the cooperation of states. The more a state specializes, the more it relies on others to supply the materials and goods that it is not producing. The larger a state's imports and exports, the more it depends on others. The world's well-being would be increased if an ever more elaborate division of labor were developed, but states would thereby place themselves in situations of ever closer interdependence. Some states may not resist that. For small and ill-endowed states the costs of doing so are excessively high. But states that can resist becoming ever more enmeshed with others ordinarily do so in either or both of two ways. States that are heavily dependent, or closely interdependent, worry about securing that which they depend on. The high interdependence of states means that the states in question experience, or are subject to, the common vulnerability that high interdependence entails. Like other organizations, states seek to control what they depend on or to lessen the extent of their dependency. This simple thought explains quite a bit of the behavior of states: their imperial thrusts to widen the scope of their control and their autarchic strivings toward greater self-sufficiency.

Structures encourage certain behaviors and penalize those who do not respond to the encouragement. Nationally, many lament the extreme development of the division of labor, a development that results in the allocation of ever narrower tasks to individuals. And yet specialization proceeds, and its extent is a measure of the development of societies. In a formally organized realm a premium is put on each unit's being able to specialize in order to increase its value to others in a system of divided labor. The domestic imperative is "specialize"! Internationally, many lament the resources states spend unproductively for their own defense and the opportunities they miss to enhance the welfare of their people through cooperation with other states. And yet the ways of states change little. In an unorganized realm each unit's incentive is to put itself in a position to be able to take care of itself since no one else can be counted on to do so. The international imperative is "take care of yourself"! Some leaders of nations may understand that the well-being of all of them would increase through their participation in a fuller division of labor. But to act on the idea would be to act on a domestic imperative, an imperative that does not run internationally. What one might want to do in the absence of structural constraints is different from what one is encouraged to do in their presence. States do not willingly place themselves in situations of increased dependence. In a self-help system, considerations of security subordinate economic gain to political interest.

What each state does for itself is much like what all of the others are doing. They are denied the advantages that a full division of labor, political as well as economic, would provide. Defense spending, moreover, is unproductive for all and unavoidable for most. Rather than increased well-being, their reward is in the maintenance of their autonomy. States compete, but not by contributing their individual efforts to the joint production of goods for their mutual benefit.

3. Structures and Strategies

That motives and outcomes may well be disjoined should now be easily seen. Structures cause actions to have consequences they were not intended to have. Surely most of the actors will notice that, and at least some of them will be able to figure out why. They may develop a pretty good sense of just how structures work their effects. Will they not then be able to achieve their original ends by appropriately adjusting their strategies? Unfortunately, they often cannot. To show why this is so I shall give only a few examples; once the point is made, the reader will easily think of others.

If shortage of a commodity is expected, all are collectively better off if they buy less of it in order to moderate price increases and to distribute shortages equitably. But because some will be better off if they lay in extra supplies quickly, all have a strong incentive to do so. If one expects others to make a run on a bank, one's prudent course is to run faster than they do even while knowing that if few others run, the bank will remain solvent, and if many run, it will fail. In such cases, pursuit of individual interest produces collective results that nobody wants, yet individuals by behaving differently will hurt themselves without altering outcomes. These two much used examples establish the main point. Some courses of action I cannot sensibly follow unless you do too, and you and I cannot sensibly follow them unless we are pretty sure that many others will as well. Let us go more deeply into the problem by considering two further examples in some detail.

Each of many persons may choose to drive a private car rather than take a train. Cars offer flexibility in scheduling and in choice of destination; yet at times, in bad weather for example, railway passenger service is a much wanted convenience. Each of many persons may shop in supermarkets rather than at corner grocery stores. The stocks of supermarkets are larger, and their prices lower; yet at times the corner grocery store, offering, say, credit and delivery service, is a much wanted convenience. The result of most people usually driving their own cars and shopping at supermarkets is to reduce passenger service and to decrease the number of corner grocery stores. These results may not be what most people want. They may be willing to pay to prevent services from disappearing. And yet individuals can do nothing to affect the outcomes. Increased patronage *would* do it, but not increased patronage by me and the few others I might persuade to follow my example.

We may well notice that our behavior produces unwanted outcomes, but we are also likely to see that such instances as these are examples of what Alfred E. Kahn describes as "large" changes that are brought about by the accumulation of "small" decisions. In such situations people are victims of the "tyranny of small decisions," a phrase suggesting that "if one hundred consumers choose option x, and this causes the market to make decision X (where X equals 100 x), it is not necessarily true that those same consumers would have voted for that outcome if that large decision had ever been presented for their explicit consideration" (Kahn 1966:523). If the market does not present the large question for decision, then individuals are doomed to making decisions that are sensible within their narrow contexts even though they know all the while that in making such decisions they are bringing about a result that most of them do not want. Either that or they organize to overcome some of the effects of the market by changing its structure—for example, by bringing consumer units roughly up to the size of the units that are making producers' decisions. This nicely makes the point: So long as one leaves the structure unaffected it is not possible for changes in the intentions and the actions of particular actors to produce desirable outcomes or to avoid undesirable ones. Structures may be changed, as just mentioned, by changing the distribution of capabilities across units. Structures may also be changed by imposing requirements where previously people had to decide for themselves. If some merchants sell on Sunday, others may have to do so in order to remain competitive even though most prefer a six-day week. Most are able to do as they please only if all are required to keep comparable hours. The only remedies for strong structural effects are structural changes.

Structural constraints cannot be wished away, although many fail to understand this. In every age and place, the units of self-help systems— nations, corporations, or whatever—are told that the greater good, along with their own, requires them to act for the sake of the system and not for their own narrowly defined advantage. In the 1950s, as fear of the world's destruction in nuclear war grew, some concluded that the alter- native to world destruction was world disarmament. In the 1970s, with the rapid growth of population, poverty, and pollution, some concluded, as one political scientist put it, that "states must meet the needs of the political ecosystem in its global dimensions or court annihilation" (Ster- ling 1974:336). The international interest must be served; and if that means anything at all, it means that national interests are subordinate to it. The problems are found at the global level. Solutions to the problems continue to depend on national policies. What are the conditions that would make nations more or less willing to obey the injunctions that are so often laid on them? How can they resolve the tension between pursuing their own interests and acting for the sake of the system? No one has shown how that can be done, although many wring their hands and plead for rational behavior. The very problem, however, is that rational behavior, given structural constraints, does not lead to the wanted results. With each country constrained to take care of itself, no one can take care of the system.[1]

A strong sense of peril and doom may lead to a clear definition of ends that must be achieved. Their achievement is not thereby made possible. The possibility of effective action depends on the ability to provide necessary means. It depends even more so on the existence of conditions that permit nations and other organizations to follow appro- priate policies and strategies. World-shaking problems cry for global solutions, but there is no global agency to provide them. Necessities do not create possibilities. Wishing that final causes were efficient ones does not make them so.

Great tasks can be accomplished only by agents of great capability. That is why states, and especially the major ones, are called on to do what is necessary for the world's survival. But states have to do whatever they think necessary for their own preservation, since no one can be relied on to do it for them. Why the advice to place the international interest above national interests is meaningless can be explained precisely in terms of the distinction between micro- and macrotheories. Among economists the distinction is well understood. Among political scientists it is not. As I have explained, a microeconomic theory is a theory of the market built up from assumptions about the behavior of individuals. The theory shows how the actions and interactions of the units form and affect the market and how the market in turn affects them. A macro-theory is a theory about the national economy built on supply, income, and demand as systemwide aggregates. The theory shows how these and other aggregates are interconnected and indicates how changes in one or some of them affect others and the performance of the economy. In economics, both micro- and macrotheories deal with large realms. The difference between them is found not in the size of the objects of study, but in the way the objects of study are approached and the theory to explain them is constructed. A macrotheory of international politics would show how the international system is moved by system-wide aggregates. One can imagine what some of them might be—amount of world GNP, amount of world imports and exports, of deaths in war, of everybody's defense spending, and of migration, for example. The theory would look something like a macroeconomic theory in the style of John Maynard Keynes, although it is hard to see how the international aggregates would make much sense and how changes in one or some of them would produce changes in others. I am not saying that such a theory cannot be constructed, but only that I cannot see how to do it in any way that might be useful. The decisive point, anyway, is that a macrotheory of international politics would lack the practical implications of macroeconomic theory. National governments can manipulate system-wide economic variables. No agencies with comparable capabilities exist internationally. Who would act on the possibilities of adjustment that a macrotheory of international politics might reveal? Even were such a theory available, we would still be stuck with nations as the only agents capable of acting to solve global problems. We would still have to revert to a micropolitical approach in order to examine the conditions that make benign and effective action by states separately and collectively more or less likely.

Some have hoped that changes in the awareness and purpose, in the organization and ideology, of states would change the quality of international life. Over the centuries states have changed in many ways, but the quality of international life has remained much the same. States may seek reasonable and worthy ends, but they cannot figure out how to reach them. The problem is not in their stupidity or ill will, although one does not want to claim that those qualities are lacking. The depth of the difficulty is not understood until one realizes that intelligence and goodwill cannot discover and act on adequate programs. Early in this century Winston Churchill observed that the British-German naval race promised disaster *and* that Britain had no realistic choice other than to run it. States facing global problems are like individual consumers trapped by the "tyranny of small decisions." States, like consumers, can get out of the trap only by changing the structure of their field of activity. The message bears repeating: The only remedy for a strong structural effect is a structural change.

4. The Virtues of Anarchy

To achieve their objectives and maintain their security, units in a condition of anarchy—be they people, corporations, states, or whatever—must rely on the means they can generate and the arrangements they can make for themselves. Self-help is necessarily the principle of action in an anarchic order. A self-help situation is one of high risk—of bankruptcy in the economic realm and of war in a world of free states. It is also one in which organizational costs are low. Within an economy or within an international order, risks may be avoided or lessened by moving from a situation of coordinate action to one of super- and subordination, that is, by erecting agencies with effective authority and extending a system of rules. Government emerges where the functions of regulation and management themselves become distinct and specialized tasks. The costs of maintaining a hierarchic order are frequently ignored by those who deplore its absence. Organizations have at least two aims: to get something done and to maintain themselves as organizations. Many of their activities are directed toward the second purpose. The leaders of organizations, and political leaders preeminently, are not masters of the matters their organizations deal with. They have become leaders not by being experts on one thing or another but by excelling in the organizational arts—in maintaining control of a group's members, in eliciting predictable and satisfactory efforts from them, in holding a group together. In making political decisions, the first and most important concern is not to achieve the aims the members of an organization may have but to secure the continuity and health of the organization itself (cf. Diesing 1962:198–204; Downs 1967:262–270).

Along with the advantages of hierarchic orders go the costs. In hierarchic orders, moreover, the means of control become an object of struggle. Substantive issues become entwined with efforts to influence or control the controllers. The hierarchic ordering of politics adds one to the already numerous objects of struggle, and the object added is at a new order of magnitude.

If the risks of war are unbearably high, can they be reduced by organizing to manage the affairs of nations? At a minimum, management requires controlling the military forces that are at the disposal of states. Within nations, organizations have to work to maintain themselves. As organizations, nations, in working to maintain themselves, sometimes have to use force against dissident elements and areas. As hierarchical systems, governments nationally or globally are disrupted by the defection of major parts. In a society of states with little coherence, attempts at world government would founder on the inability of an emerging central authority to mobilize the resources needed to create and maintain the unity of the system by regulating and managing its parts. The prospect of world government would be an invitation to prepare for world civil war. This calls to mind Milovan Djilas's reminiscence of World War II. According to him, he and many Russian soldiers in their wartime discussions came to believe that human struggles would acquire their ultimate bitterness if all men were subject to the same social system, "for the system would be untenable as such and various sects would undertake the reckless destruction of the human race for the sake of its greater 'happiness' "

(1962:50). States cannot entrust managerial powers to a central agency unless that agency is able to protect its client states. The more powerful the clients and the more the power of each of them appears as a threat to the others, the greater the power lodged in the center must be. The greater the power of the center, the stronger the incentive for states to engage in a struggle to control it.

States, like people, are insecure in proportion to the extent of their freedom. If freedom is wanted, insecurity must be accepted. Organizations that establish relations of authority and control may increase security as they decrease freedom. If might does not make right, whether among people or states, then some institution or agency has intervened to lift them out of nature's realm. The more influential the agency, the stronger the desire to control it becomes. In contrast, units in an anarchic order act for their own sakes and not for the sake of preserving an organization and furthering their fortunes within it. Force is used for one's own interest. In the absence of organization, people or states are free to leave one another alone. Even when they do not do so, they are better able, in the absence of the politics of the organization, to concentrate on the politics of the problem and to aim for a minimum agreement that will permit their separate existence rather than a maximum agreement for the sake of maintaining unity. If might decides, then bloody struggles over right can more easily be avoided.

Nationally, the force of a government is exercised in the name of right and justice. Internationally, the force of a state is employed for the sake of its own protection and advantage. Rebels challenge a government's claim to authority; they question the rightfulness of its rule. Wars among states cannot settle questions of authority and right; they can only determine the allocation of gains and losses among contenders and settle for a time the question of who is the stronger. Nationally, relations of authority are established. Internationally, only relations of strength result. Nationally, private force used against a government threatens the political system. Force used by a state—a public body—is, from the international perspective, the private use of force; but there is no government to overthrow and no governmental apparatus to capture. Short of a drive toward world hegemony, the private use of force does not threaten the system of international politics, only some of its members. War pits some states against others in a struggle among similarly constituted entities.

The power of the strong may deter the weak from asserting their claims, not because the weak recognize a kind of rightfulness of rule on the part of the strong, but simply because it is not sensible to tangle with them. Conversely, the weak may enjoy considerable freedom of action if they are so far removed in their capabilities from the strong that the latter are not much bothered by their actions or much concerned by marginal increases in their capabilities.

National politics is the realm of authority, of administration, and of law. International politics is the realm of power, of struggle, and of accommodation. The international realm is preeminently a political one. The national realm is variously described as being hierarchic, vertical, centralized, heterogeneous, directed, and contrived; the international realm, as being anarchic, horizontal, decentralized, homogeneous, undirected, and mutually adaptive. The more centralized the order, the nearer to the top the locus of decisions ascends. Internationally, decisions are made at the bottom level, there being scarcely any other. In the vertical horizontal dichotomy, international structures assume the prone position. Adjustments are made internationally, but they are made without a formal or authoritative adjuster. Adjustment and accommodation proceed by mutual adaptation (cf. Barnard 1948:148–152; Polanyi 1941:428–456). Action and reaction, and reaction to reaction, proceed by a piecemeal process. The parties feel each other out, so to speak, and define a situation simultaneously with its development. Among coordinate units, adjustment is achieved and accommodations arrived at by the exchange of "considerations," in a condition, as Chester Barnard put it, "in which the duty of command and the desire to obey are essentially absent" (pp. 150–151). Where the contest is over considerations, the parties seek to maintain or improve their positions by maneuvering, by bargaining, or by fighting. The manner and intensity of the competition is determined by the desires and the abilities of parties that are at once separate and interacting.

Whether or not by force, each state plots the course it thinks will best serve its interests. If force is used by one state or its use is expected, the recourse of other states is to use force or be prepared to use it singly or in combination. No appeal can be made to a higher entity clothed with the authority and equipped with the ability to act on its own initiative. Under such conditions the possibility that force will be used

by one or another of the parties looms always as a threat in the background. In politics force is said to be the *ultima ratio*. In international
politics force serves, not only as the *ultima ratio,* but indeed as the first
and constant one. To limit force to being the *ultima ratio* of politics implies,
in the words of Ortega y Gasset, "the previous submission of force to
methods of reason" (quoted in Johnson 1966:13). The constant possibility
that force will be used limits manipulations, moderates demands, and
serves as an incentive for the settlement of disputes. One who knows
that pressing too hard may lead to war has strong reason to consider
whether possible gains are worth the risks entailed. The threat of force
internationally is comparable to the role of the strike in labor and management bargaining. "The few strikes that take place are in a sense," as
Livernash has said, "the cost of the strike option which produces set-
tlements in the large mass of negotiations" (1963:430). Even if workers
seldom strike, their doing so is always a possibility. The possibility of
industrial disputes leading to long and costly strikes encourages labor
and management to face difficult issues, to try to understand each other's
problems, and to work hard to find accommodations. The possibility that
conflicts among nations may lead to long and costly wars has similarly
sobering effects.

5. Anarchy and Hierarchy

I have described anarchies and hierarchies as though every political order
were of one type or the other. Many, and I suppose most, political
scientists who write of structures allow for a greater, and sometimes for
a bewildering, variety of types. Anarchy is seen as one end of a continuum
whose other end is marked by the presence of a legitimate and competent
government. International politics is then described as being flecked with
particles of government and alloyed with elements of community—supranational organizations whether universal or regional, alliances, multinational corporations, networks of trade, and what not. International-
political systems are thought of as being more or less anarchic.

Those who view the world as a modified anarchy do so, it seems, for
two reasons. First, anarchy is taken to mean not just the absence of
government but also the presence of disorder and chaos. Since world
politics, although not reliably peaceful, falls short of unrelieved chaos,

students are inclined to see a lessening of anarchy in each outbreak of peace. Since world politics, although not formally organized, is not entirely without institutions and orderly procedures, students are inclined to see a lessening of anarchy when alliances form, when transactions across national borders increase, and when international agencies multiply. Such views confuse structure with process, and I have drawn attention to that error often enough.

Second, the two simple categories of anarchy and hierarchy do not seem to accommodate the infinite social variety our senses record. Why insist on reducing the types of structure to two instead of allowing for a greater variety? Anarchies are ordered by the juxtaposition of similar units, but those similar units are not identical. Some specialization by function develops among them. Hierarchies are ordered by the social division of labor among units specializing in different tasks, but the resemblance of units does not vanish. Much duplication of effort continues. All societies are organized segmentally or hierarchically in greater or lesser degree. Why not, then, define additional social types according to the mixture of organizing principles they embody? One might conceive of some societies approaching the purely anarchic, of others approaching the purely hierarchic, and of still others reflecting specified mixes of the two organizational types. In anarchies the exact likeness of units and the determination of relations by capability alone would describe a realm wholly of politics and power with none of the interaction of units guided by administration and conditioned by authority. In hierarchies the complete differentiation of parts and the full specification of their functions would produce a realm wholly of authority and administration with none of the interaction of parts affected by politics and power. Although such pure orders do not exist, to distinguish realms by their organizing principles is nevertheless proper and important.

Increasing the number of categories would bring the classification of societies closer to reality. But that would be to move away from a theory claiming explanatory power to a less theoretical system promising greater descriptive accuracy. One who wishes to explain rather than to describe should resist moving in that direction if resistance is reasonable. Is it? What does one gain by insisting on two types when admitting three or four would still be to simplify boldly? One gains clarity and economy of concepts. A new concept should be introduced only to cover matters that existing concepts do not reach. If some societies are neither anarchic nor hierarchic, if their structures are defined by some third ordering principle, then we would have to define a third system.[2] All societies are mixed. Elements in them represent both of the ordering principles. That does not mean that some societies are ordered according to a third principle. Usually one can easily identify the principle by which a society is ordered. The appearance of anarchic sectors within hierarchies does not alter and should not obscure the ordering principle of the larger system, for those sectors are anarchic only within limits. The attributes and behavior of the units populating those sectors within the larger system differ, moreover, from what they would be and how they would behave outside of it. Firms in oligopolistic markets again are perfect examples of this. They struggle against one another, but because they need not prepare to defend themselves physically, they can afford to specialize and to participate more fully in the division of economic labor than states can. Nor do the states that populate an anarchic world find it impossible to work with one another, to make agreements limiting their arms, and to cooperate in establishing organizations. Hierarchic elements within international structures limit and restrain the exercise of sovereignty but only in ways strongly conditioned by the anarchy of the larger system. The anarchy of that order strongly affects the likelihood of cooperation, the extent of arms agreements, and the jurisdiction of international organizations.

But what about borderline cases, societies that are neither clearly anarchic nor clearly hierarchic? Do they not represent a third type? To say that there are borderline cases is not to say that at the border a third type of system appears. All categories have borders, and if we have any categories at all, we have borderline cases. Clarity of concepts does not eliminate difficulties of classification. Was China from the 1920s to the 1940s a hierarchic or an an anarchic realm? Nominally a nation, China looked more like a number of separate states existing alongside one another. Mao Tse-tung in 1930, like Bolshevik leaders earlier, thought that striking a revolutionary spark would "start a prairie fire." Revolutionary flames would spread across China, if not throughout the world. Because the interdependence of China's provinces, like the interdependence of nations, was insufficiently close, the flames failed to spread. So nearly autonomous were China's provinces that the effects of war in one part of the country were only weakly registered in other parts. Battles in the Hunan hills, far from sparking a national revolution, were hardly noticed in neighboring provinces. The interaction of largely self-sufficient provinces was slight and sporadic. Dependent neither on one another economically nor on the nation's center politically, they were not subject to the close interdependence characteristic of organized and integrated polities.

As a practical matter, observers may disagree in their answers to such questions as just when did China break down into anarchy, or whether the countries of Western Europe are slowly becoming one state or stubbornly remaining nine. The point of theoretical importance is that our expectations about the fate of those areas differ widely depending on which answer to the structural question becomes the right one. Structures defined according to two distinct ordering principles help to explain important aspects of social and political behavior. That is shown in various ways in the following pages. This section has explained why two, and only two, types of structure are needed to cover societies of all sorts.

II

How can a theory of international politics be constructed? Just as any theory must be. As chapters 1 and 4 [articles 2 and 3 above] explain, first, one must conceive of international politics as a bounded realm or domain; second, one must discover some law-like regularities within it; and third, one must develop a way of explaining the observed regularities. The first of these was accomplished in chapter 5 [article 4]. This chapter so far has shown how political structures account for some recurrent aspects of the behavior of states and for certain repeated and enduring patterns. Wherever agents and agencies are coupled by force and competition rather than by authority and law, we expect to find such behaviors and outcomes. They are closely identified with the approach to politics suggested by the rubric, *Realpolitik*. The elements of *Realpolitik*, exhaustively listed, are these: The ruler's, and later the state's interest provides the spring of action; the necessities of policy arise from the unregulated competition of states; calculation based on these necessities can discover the policies that will best serve a state's interest; success is the ultimate test of policy, and success is defined as preserving and strengthening the state. Ever since Machiavelli, interest and necessity— and *raison d'état,* the phrase that comprehends them—have remained the key concepts of *Realpolitik.* From Machiavelli through Meinecke and Morgenthau the elements of the approach and the reasoning remain constant. Machiavelli stands so clearly as the exponent of *Realpolitik* that one easily slips into thinking that he developed the closely associated idea of balance of power as well. Although he did not, his conviction that politics can be explained in its own terms established the ground on which balance-of-power theory can be built.

Realpolitik indicates the methods by which foreign policy is conducted and provides a rationale for them. Structural constraints explain why the methods are repeatedly used despite differences in the persons and states who use them. Balance-of-power theory purports to explain the result that such methods produce. Rather, that is what the theory should do. If there is any distinctively political theory of international politics, balance-of-power theory is it. And yet one cannot find a statement of the theory that is generally accepted. Carefully surveying the copious balance-of-power literature, Ernst Haas discovered eight distinct meanings of the term, and Martin Wight found nine (1953, 1966). Hans Morgenthau, in his profound historical and analytic treatment of the subject, makes use of four different definitions (1948/1973). Balance of power is seen by some as being akin to a law of nature; by others, as simply an outrage. Some view it as a guide to a statesmen; others as a cloak that disguises their imperialist policies. Some believe that a balance of power is the best guarantee of the security of states and the peace of the world; others, that it has ruined states by causing most of the wars they have fought.[3]

To believe that one can cut through such confusion may seem quixotic. I shall nevertheless try. It will help to hark back to several basic propositions about theory. (1) A theory contains at least one theoretical assumption. Such assumptions are not factual. One therefore cannot legitimately ask if they are true, but only if they are useful. (2) Theories must be evaluated in terms of what they claim to explain. Balance-of-power theory claims to explain the results of states' actions, under given conditions, and those results may not be foreshadowed in any of the actors' motives or be contained as objectives in their policies. (3) Theory, as a general explanatory system, cannot account for particularities.

Most of the confusions in balance-of-power theory, and criticisms of it, derive from misunderstanding these three points. A balance-of-power theory, properly stated, begins with assumptions about states: They are unitary actors who, at a minimum, seek their own preservation and, at a maximum, drive for universal domination. States, or those who act for them, try in more or less sensible ways to use the means available in order to achieve the ends in view. Those means fall into two categories: internal efforts (moves to increase economic capability, to increase military strength, to develop clever strategies) and external efforts (moves to strengthen and enlarge one's own alliance or to weaken and shrink an opposing one). The external game of alignment and realignment requires three or more players, and it is usually said that balance-of-power systems require at least that number. The statement is false, for in a two-power system the politics of balance continue, but the way to compensate for an incipient external disequilibrium is primarily by intensifying one's internal efforts. To the assumptions of the theory we then add the condition for its operation: that two or more states coexist in a self-help system, one with no superior agent to come to the aid of states that may be weakening or to deny to any of them the use of whatever instruments they think will serve their purposes. The theory, then, is built up from the assumed motivations of states and the actions that correspond to them. It describes the constraints that arise from the system that those actions produce, and it indicates the expected outcome: namely, the formation of balances of power. Balance-of-power theory is microtheory precisely in the economist's sense. The system, like a market in economics, is made by the actions and interactions of its units, and the theory is based on assumptions about their behavior.

A self-help system is one in which those who do not help themselves, or who do so less effectively than others, will fail to prosper, will lay themselves open to dangers, will suffer. Fear of such unwanted consequences stimulates states to behave in ways that tend toward the creation of balances of power. Notice that the theory requires no assumptions of rationality or of constancy of will on the part of all of the actors. The theory says simply that if some do relatively well, others will emulate them or fall by the wayside. Obviously, the system won't work if all states lose interest in preserving themselves. It will, however, continue to work if some states do, while others do not, choose to lose their political identities, say, through amalgamation. Nor need it be assumed that all of the competing states are striving relentlessly to increase their power. The possibility that force may be used by some states to weaken or destroy others does, however, make it difficult for them to break out of the competitive system.

The meaning and importance of the theory are made clear by examining prevalent misconceptions that are theoretical, not factual. One of the most common misunderstandings of balance-of-power theory centers on this point. The theory is criticized because its assumptions are erroneous. The following statement can stand for a host of others:

> If nations were in fact unchanging units with no permanent ties to each other, and if all were motivated primarily by a drive to maximize their power, except for a single balancer whose aim was to prevent any nation from achieving preponderant power, a balance of power might in fact result. But we have seen that these assumptions are not correct, and since the assumptions of the theory are wrong, the conclusions are also in error (Organski 1968:292).

The author's incidental error is that he has compounded a sentence some parts of which are loosely stated assumptions of the theory, and other parts not. His basic error lies in misunderstanding what an assumption is. From previous discussion, we know that assumptions are neither true nor false and that they are essential for the construction of theory. We can freely admit that states are in fact not unitary, purposive actors. States pursue many goals, which are often vaguely formulated and inconsistent. They fluctuate with the changing currents of domestic politics, are prey to the vagaries of a shifting cast of political leaders, and are influenced by the outcomes of bureaucratic struggles. But all of this has always been known and it tells us nothing about the merits of balance-of-power theory.

A further confusion relates to our second proposition about theory. Balance-of-power theory claims to explain a result (the recurrent formation of balances of power), which may not accord with the intentions of any of the units whose actions combine to produce that result. To contrive and maintain a balance may be the aim of one or more states, but then again it may not be. According to the theory, balances of power tend to form whether some or all states consciously aim to establish and maintain a balance, or whether some or all states aim for universal domination.[4] Yet many, and perhaps most, statements of balance-of-power theory attribute the maintenance of a balance to the separate states as a motive. David Hume, in his classic essay "Of the Balance of Power," offers "the maxim of preserving the balance of power" as a constant rule of prudent politics (1742:142–144). So it may be, but it has proved to be an unfortunately short step from the belief that a high regard for preserving a balance is at the heart of wise statesmanship to the belief that states must follow the maxim if a balance of power is to be maintained. This is apparent in the first of Morgenthau's four definitions of the term: namely, "a policy aimed at a certain state of affairs." The reasoning then easily becomes tautological. If a balance of power is to be maintained, the policies of states must aim to uphold it. If a balance of power is in fact maintained, we can conclude that their aim was accurate. If a balance of power is not produced, we can say that the theory's assumption is erroneous. Finally, and this completes the drift toward the reification of a concept, if the purpose of states is to uphold a balance, the purpose of the balance is "to maintain the stability of the system without destroying the multiplicity of the elements composing it." Reification has obviously occurred where one reads, for example, of the balance operating "successfully" and of the difficulty that nations have in applying it (1948/1973:167–174, 202–207).

Reification is often merely the loose use of language or the employment of metaphor to make one's prose more pleasing. In this case, however, the theory has been drastically distorted, and not only by introducing the notion that if a balance is to be formed, somebody must want it and must work for it. The further distortion of the theory arises when rules are derived from the results of states' actions and then illogically prescribed to the actors as duties. A possible effect is turned into a necessary cause in the form of a stipulated rule. Thus, it is said, "the balance of power" can "impose its restraints upon the power aspirations of nations" only if they first "restrain themselves by accepting the system of the balance of power as the common framework of their endeavors." Only if states recognize "the same rules of the game" and play "for the same limited stakes" can the balance of power fulfill "its functions for international stability and national independence" (Morgenthau 1948/1973:219–220).

The closely related errors that fall under our second proposition about theory are, as we have seen, twin traits of the field of international politics: namely, to assume a necessary correspondence of motive and result and to infer rules for the actors from the observed results of their action. What has gone wrong can be made clear by recalling the economic analogy (pp. 81–87, above). In a purely competitive economy, everyone's striving to make a profit drives the profit rate downward. Let the competition continue long enough under static conditions, and everyone's profit will be zero. To infer from that result that everyone, or anyone, is seeking to minimize profit, and that the competitors must adopt that goal as a rule in order for the system to work, would be absurd. And yet in international politics one frequently finds that rules inferred from the results of the interactions of states are prescribed to the actors and are said to be a condition of the system's maintenance. Such errors, often made, are also often pointed out, though seemingly to no avail. S. F. Nadel has put the matter simply: "an orderliness abstracted from behaviour cannot guide behaviour" (Nadel 1957:148; cf. Durkheim 1893:366, 418; Shubik 1959:11, 32).

Analytic reasoning applied where a systems approach is needed leads to the laying down of all sorts of conditions as prerequisites to balances of power forming and tending toward equilibrium and as general preconditions of world stability and peace. Some require that the number of great powers exceed two; others that a major power be willing to play the role of balancer. Some require that military technology not change radically or rapidly; others that the major states abide by arbitrarily specified rules. But balances of power form in the absence of the "necessary" conditions, and since 1945 the world has been stable, and the world of major powers remarkably peaceful, even though international conditions have not conformed to theorists' stipulations. Balance-of-power politics prevail wherever two, and only two, requirements are met: that the order be anarchic and that it be populated by units wishing to survive.

For those who believe that if a result is to be produced, someone, or everyone, must want it and must work for it, it follows that explanation turns ultimately on what the separate states are like. If that is true, then theories at the national level, or lower, will sufficiently explain international politics. If, for example, the equilibrium of a balance is maintained through states abiding by rules, then one needs an explanation of how agreement on the rules is achieved and maintained. One does not need a balance-of-power theory, for balances would result from a certain kind of behavior explained perhaps by a theory about national psychology or bureaucratic politics. A balance-of-power theory could not be constructed because it would have nothing to explain. If the good or bad motives of states result in their maintaining balances or disrupting them, then the notion of a balance of power becomes merely a framework organizing one's account of what happened, and that is indeed its customary use. A construction that starts out to be a theory ends up as a set of categories. Categories then multiply rapidly to cover events that the embryo theory had not contemplated. The quest for explanatory power turns into a search for descriptive adequacy.

Finally, and related to our third proposition about theory in general, balance-of-power theory is often criticized because it does not explain the particular policies of states. True, the theory does not tell us why state X made a certain move last Tuesday. To expect it to do so would be like expecting the theory of universal gravitation to explain the wayward path of a falling leaf. A theory at one level of generality cannot answer questions about matters at a different level of generality. Failure to notice this is one error on which the criticism rests. Another is to mistake a theory of international politics for a theory of foreign policy. Confusion about the explanatory claims made by a properly stated balance-of-power theory is rooted in the uncertainty of the distinction drawn between national and international politics or in the denials that the distinction should be made. For those who deny the distinction, for those who devise explanations that are entirely in terms of interacting units, explanations of international politics *are* explanations of foreign policy, and explanations of foreign policy *are* explanations of international politics. Others mix their explanatory claims and confuse the problem of understanding international politics with the problem of understanding foreign policy. Morgenthau, for example, believes that problems of predicting foreign policy and of developing theories about it make international-political theories difficult, if not impossible, to contrive (1970: 253–258). But the difficulties of explaining foreign policy work

against contriving theories of international politics only if the latter reduces to the former. Graham Allison betrays a similar confusion. His
three "models" purport to offer alternative approaches to the study of
international politics. Only model I, however, is an approach to the study
of international politics. Models II and III are approaches to the study of
foreign policy. Offering the bureaucratic-politics approach as an alternative to the state-as-an-actor approach is like saying that a theory of
the firm is an alternative to a theory of the market, a mistake no competent economist would make (1971; cf. Allison and Halperin 1972). If
Morgenthau and Allison were economists and their thinking continued
to follow the same pattern, they would have to argue that the uncer-
tainties of corporate policy work against the development of market
theory. They have confused and merged two quite different matters.[5]

Any theory covers some matters and leaves other matters aside. Balance-of-power theory is a theory about the results produced by the
uncoordinated actions of states. The theory makes assumptions about the
interests and motives of states, rather than explaining them. What it
does explain are the constraints that confine all states. The clear perception of constraints provides many clues to the expected reactions of
states, but by itself the theory cannot explain those reactions. They
depend not only on international constraints but also on the characteristics of states. How will a particular state react? To answer that question
we need not only a theory of the market, so to speak, but also a theory
about the firms that compose it. What will a state have to react to?
Balance-of-power theory can give general and useful answers to that
question. The theory explains why a certain similarity of behavior is
expected from similarly situated states. The expected behavior is similar,
not identical. To explain the expected differences in national responses,
a theory would have to show how the different internal structures of
states affect their external policies and actions. A theory of foreign policy
would not predict the detailed content of policy but instead would lead
to different expectations about the tendencies and styles of different
countries' policies. Because the national and the international levels are
linked, theories of both types, if they are any good, tell us some things,
but not the same things, about behavior and outcomes at both levels (cf.
the second parts of articles 3 and 4 above).

III

In the previous chapter, I constructed a systems theory of international politics. In this chapter, I have stated balance-of-power theory as a further development of that theory. In the next three chapters [not reprinted here: ed.], I shall refine the theory by showing how expectations vary with changes in the structure of international systems. At this point I pause to ask how good the theory so far developed is.

Before subjecting a theory to tests, one asks whether the theory is internally consistent and whether it tells us some things of interest that we would not know in its absence. That the theory meets those requirements does not mean that it can survive tests. Many people prefer tests that, if flunked, falsify a theory. Some people following Karl Popper (1934, ch. 1), insist that theories are tested only by attempting to falsify them. Confirmations do not count because, among other reasons, confirming cases may be offered as proof while consciously or not cases likely to confound the theory are avoided. This difficulty, I suggest later, is lessened by choosing hard cases—situations, for example, in which parties have strong reasons to behave contrary to the predictions of one's theory. Confirmations are also rejected because numerous tests that appear to confirm a theory are negated by one falsifying instance. The conception of theory presented in ch. 1 (article 2 above), however, opens the possibility of devising tests that confirm. If a theory depicts a domain, and displays its organization and the connections among its parts, then we can compare features of the observed domain with the picture the theory has limned (cf. Harris 1970). We can ask whether expected behaviors and outcomes are repeatedly found where the conditions contemplated by the theory obtain.

Structural theories, moreover, gain plausibility if similarities of behavior are observed across realms that are different in substance but similar in structure, and if differences of behavior are observed where realms are similar in substance but different in structure. This special advantage is won: International-political theory gains credibility from the confirmation of certain theories in economics, sociology, anthropology, and other such nonpolitical fields.

Testing theories, of course, always means inferring expectations, or hypotheses, from them and testing those expectations. Testing theories is a difficult and subtle task, made so by the interdependence of fact and theory, by the elusive relation between reality and theory as an instrument for its apprehension. Questions of truth and falsity are somehow involved, but so are questions of usefulness and uselessness. In the end, one sticks with the theory that reveals most, even if its validity is suspect. I shall say more about the acceptance and rejection of theories elsewhere. Here I say only enough to make the relevance of a few examples of theory testing clear. Others can then easily be thought of. Many are provided in the first part of this chapter and in all parts of the next three, although I have not always labeled them as tests or put them in testable form.

Tests are easy to think up, once one has a theory to test, but they are hard to carry through. Given the difficulty of testing any theory, and the added difficulty of testing theories in such nonexperimental fields as international politics, we should exploit all of the ways of testing I have mentioned—by trying to falsify, by devising hard confirmatory tests, by comparing features of the real and the theoretical worlds, by comparing behaviors in realms of similar and of different structure. Any good theory raises many expectations. Multiplying hypotheses and varying tests are all the more important because the results of testing theories are necessarily problematic. That a single hypothesis appears to hold true may not be very impressive. A theory becomes plausible if many hypotheses inferred from it are successfully subjected to tests.

Knowing a little bit more about testing, we can now ask whether expectations drawn from our theory can survive subjection to tests. What will some of the expectations be? Two that are closely related arise in the above discussion. According to the theory, balances of power recurrently form, and states tend to emulate the successful policies of others. Can these expectations be subjected to tests? In principle, the answer is "yes." Within a given arena and over a number of years, we should find the military power of weaker and smaller states or groupings of states growing more rapidly, or shrinking more slowly, than that of stronger and larger ones. And we should find widespread imitation among competing states. In practice, to check such expectations against historical observations is difficult.

Two problems are paramount. First, though balance-of-power theory offers some predictions, the predictions are indeterminate. Because only a loosely defined and inconstant condition of balance is predicted, it is difficult to say that any given distribution of power falsifies the theory. The theory, moreover, does not lead one to expect that emulation among states will proceed to the point where competitors become identical. What will be imitated, and how quickly and closely? Because the theory does not give precise answers, falsification again is difficult. Second, although states may be disposed to react to international constraints and incentives in accordance with the theory's expectations, the policies and actions of states are also shaped by their internal conditions. The failure of balances to form, and the failure of some states to conform to the successful practices of other states, can too easily be explained away by pointing to effects produced by forces that lie outside of the theory's purview.

In the absence of theoretical refinements that fix expectations with certainty and in detail, what can we do? As I have just suggested, and as the sixth rule for testing theories set forth in chapter 1 (article 2 above) urges, we should make tests ever more difficult. If we observe outcomes that the theory leads us to expect even though strong forces work against them, the theory will begin to command belief. To confirm the theory one should not look mainly to the eighteenth-century heyday of the balance of power when great powers in convenient numbers in-teracted and were presumably able to adjust to a shifting distribution of power by changing partners with a grace made possible by the absence of ideological and other cleavages. Instead, one should seek confirmation through observation of difficult cases. One should, for example, look for instances of states allying, in accordance with the expectations the theory gives rise to, even though they have strong reasons not to cooperate with one another. The alliance of France and Russia, made formal in 1894, is one such instance. One should, for example, look for instances of states making internal efforts to strengthen themselves, however distasteful or difficult such efforts might be. The United States and the Soviet Union following World War II provide such instances: the United States by rearming despite having demonstrated a strong wish not to by disman-tling the most powerful military machine the world had ever known; the Soviet Union by maintaining about three million men under arms while striving to acquire a costly new military technology despite the terrible destruction she had suffered in war.

These examples tend to confirm the theory. We find states forming balances of power whether or not they wish to. They also show the difficulties of testing. Germany and Austria-Hungary formed their Dual Alliance in 1879. Since detailed inferences cannot be drawn from the theory, we cannot say just when other states are expected to counter this move. France and Russia waited until 1894. Does this show the theory false by suggesting that states may or may not be brought into balance? We should neither quickly conclude that it does nor lightly chalk the delayed response off to "friction." Instead, we should examine diplomacy and policy in the 15-year interval to see whether the theory serves to explain and broadly predict the actions and reactions of states and to see whether the delay is out of accord with the theory. Careful judgment is needed. For this, historians' accounts serve better than the historical summary I might provide.

The theory leads us to expect states to behave in ways that result in balances forming. To infer that expectation from the theory is not impressive if balancing is a universal pattern of political behavior, as is sometimes claimed. It is not. Whether political actors balance each other or climb on the bandwagon depends on the system's structure. Political parties, when choosing their presidential candidates, dramatically illustrate both points. When nomination time approaches and no one is established as the party's strong favorite, a number of would-be leaders contend. Some of them form coalitions to check the progress of others. The maneuvering and balancing of would-be leaders when the party lacks one is like the external behavior of states. But this is the pattern only during the leaderless period. As soon as someone looks like the winner, nearly all jump on the bandwagon rather than continuing to build coalitions intended to prevent anyone from winning the prize of power. Bandwagoning, not balancing, becomes the characteristic behavior.[6]

Bandwagoning and balancing behavior are in sharp contrast. Internally, losing candidates throw in their lots with the winner. Everyone wants someone to win; the members of a party want a leader established even while they disagree on who it should be. In a competition for the position of leader, bandwagoning is sensible behavior where gains are possible even for the losers and where losing does not place their security in jeopardy. Externally, states work harder to increase their own strength, or they combine with others, if they are falling behind. In a competition for the position of leader, balancing is sensible behavior where the victory of one coalition over another leaves weaker members of the winning coalition at the mercy of the stronger ones. Nobody wants anyone else to win; none of the great powers wants one of their number to emerge as the leader.

If two coalitions form and one of them weakens, perhaps because of the political disorder of a member, we expect the extent of the other coalition's military preparation to slacken or its unity to lessen. The classic example of the latter effect is the breaking apart of a war-winning coalition in or just after the moment of victory. We do not expect the strong to combine with the strong in order to increase the extent of their power over others, but rather to square off and look for allies who might help them. In anarchy, security is the highest end. Only if survival is assured can states safely seek such other goals as tranquility, profit, and power. Because power is a means and not an end, states prefer to join the weaker of two coalitions. They cannot let power, a possibly useful means, become the end they pursue. The goal the system encourages them to seek is security. Increased power may or may not serve that end. Given two coalitions, for example, the greater success of one in drawing members to it may tempt the other to risk preventive war, hoping for victory through surprise before disparities widen. If states wished to maximize power, they would join the stronger side, and we would see not balances forming but a world hegemony forged. This does not happen because balancing, not bandwagoning, is the behavior induced by the system. The first concern of states is not to maximize power but to maintain their positions in the system.

Secondary states, if they are free to choose, flock to the weaker side; for it is the stronger side that threatens them. On the weaker side, they are both more appreciated and safer, provided, of course, that the coalition they join achieves enough defensive or deterrent strength to dissuade adversaries from attacking. Thus Thucydides records that in the Peloponnesian War the lesser city states of Greece cast the stronger Athens as the tyrant and the weaker Sparta as their liberator (circa 400 B.C., Book v, ch. 17). According to Werner Jaeger, Thucydides thought this "perfectly natural in the circumstances," but saw "that the parts of tyrant and liberator did not correspond with any permanent moral quality in these states but were simply masks which would one day be interchanged to the astonishment of the beholder when the balance of power was altered" (1939, 1:397). This shows a nice sense of how the placement of states affects their behavior and even colors their characters. It also supports the proposition that states balance power rather than maximize it. States can seldom afford to make maximizing power their goal. International politics is too serious a business for that.

The theory depicts international politics as a competitive realm. Do states develop the characteristics that competitors are expected to display? The question poses another test for the theory. The fate of each state depends on its responses to what other states do. The possibility that conflict will be conducted by force leads to competition in the arts and the instruments of force. Competition produces a tendency toward the sameness of the competitors. Thus Bismarck's startling victories over Austria in 1866 and over France in 1870 quickly led the major continental powers (and Japan) to imitate the Prussian military staff system, and the failure of Britain and the United States to follow the pattern simply indicated that they were outside the immediate arena of competition. Contending states imitate the military innovations contrived by the country of greatest capability and ingenuity. And so the weapons of major contenders, and even their strategies, begin to look much the same all over the world. Thus at the turn of the century Admiral Alfred von Tirpitz argued successfully for building a battleship fleet on the grounds that Germany could challenge Britain at sea only with a naval doctrine and weapons similar to hers (Art 1973b:16).

The effects of competition are not confined narrowly to the military realm. Socialization to the system should also occur. Does it? Again, because we can almost always find confirming examples if we look hard, we try to find cases that are unlikely to lend credence to the theory. One should look for instances of states conforming to common international practices even though for internal reasons they would prefer not to. The behavior of the Soviet Union in its early years is one such instance. The Bolsheviks in the early years of their power preached international revolution and flouted the conventions of diplomacy. They were saying, in effect, "we will not be socialized to this system." The attitude was well expressed by Trotsky, who, when asked what he would do as foreign minister, replied, "I will issue some revolutionary proclamations to the peoples and then close up the joint" (quoted in Von Laue 1963:235). In a competitive arena, however, one party may need the assistance of others.

Refusal to play the political game may risk one's own destruction. The pressures of competition were rapidly felt and reflected in the Soviet Union's diplomacy. Thus Lenin, sending foreign minister Chicherin to the Genoa Conference of 1922, bade him farewell with this caution: "Avoid big words" (quoted in Moore 1950:204). Chicherin, who personified the carefully tailored traditional diplomat rather than the simply uniformed revolutionary, was to refrain from inflammatory rhetoric for the sake of working deals. These he successfully completed with that other pariah power and ideological enemy, Germany.

The close juxtaposition of states promotes their sameness through the disadvantages that arise from a failure to conform to successful practices. It is this "sameness," an effect of the system, that is so often attributed to the acceptance of so-called rules of state behavior. Chiliastic rulers occasionally come to power. In power, most of them quickly change their ways. They can refuse to do so, and yet hope to survive, only if they rule countries little affected by the competition of states. The socialization of nonconformist states proceeds at a pace that is set by the extent of their involvement in the system. And that is another testable statement.

The theory leads to many expectations about behaviors and outcomes. From the theory, one predicts that states will engage in balancing behavior, whether or not balanced power is the end of their acts. From the theory, one predicts a strong tendency toward balance in the system. The expectation is not that a balance, once achieved, will be maintained, but that a balance, once disrupted, will be restored in one way or another. Balances of power recurrently form. Since the theory depicts international politics as a competitive system, one predicts more specifically that states will display characteristics common to competitors: namely, that they will imitate each other and become socialized to their system. In this chapter, I have suggested ways of making these propositions more specific and concrete so as to test them. In remaining chapters, as the theory is elaborated and refined, additional testable propositions will appear.

NOTES

1. Put differently, states face a "prisoners' dilemma." If each of two parties follows his own interest, both end up worse off than if each acted to achieve joint interests. For thorough examination of the logic of such situations, see Snyder and

Diesing 1977; for brief and suggestive international applications, see Jervis, January 1978.

2. Emile Durkheim's depiction of solidary and mechanical societies still provides the best explication of the two ordering principles, and his logic in limiting the types of society to two continues to be compelling despite the efforts of his many critics to overthrow it (see esp. 1893). I shall discuss the problem at some length in a future work.

3. Along with the explication of balance-of-power theory in the pages that follow, the reader may wish to consult a historical study of balance-of-power politics in practice. The best brief work is Wight (1973).

4. Looking at states over a wide span of time and space, Dowty concludes that in no case were shifts in alliances produced "by considerations of an overall balance of power" (1969:95).

5. The confusion is widespread and runs both ways. Thus Herbert Simon thinks the goal of classical economic theorists is unattainable because he wrongly believes that they were trying "to predict the behavior of rational man without making an empirical investigation of his psychological properties" (1957:199).

6. Stephen Van Evera suggested using "bandwagoning" to serve as the opposite of "balancing."

SIX

Continuity and Transformation in the World Polity:

Toward a Neorealist Synthesis

JOHN GERARD RUGGIE

I

IN *The Rules of Sociological Method,* Emile Durkheim sought to establish the "social milieu," or society itself, "as the determining factor of collective evolution." In turn, he took society to reflect not the mere summation of individuals and their characteristics, but "a specific reality which has its own characteristics." And he attributed this social facticity to "the system formed by [individuals'] association, "by the fact of their combination." Hence, "if the determining condition of social phenomena is, as we have shown, the very fact of association, the phenomena ought to vary with the forms of that association, i.e., according to the ways in which the constituent parts of society are grouped" (Durkheim 1895: 116, 103, xlvii, 112). In sum, the possibilities for individual action in the short run, and collective evolution in the long run, were to be accounted for by the changing forms of social solidarity.[1]

Durkheim's methodological premise was controversial from the start, but over the years its influence has waned and come to be felt largely indirectly, as through the analysis of "primitive social structures" by Claude Lévi-Strauss (1967). Suddenly, it is enjoying a resurgence in the study of a social domain never contemplated by Durkheim: the international system. It is being adopted by the most unlikely of followers: American students of comparative and international politics. And it is as controversial as ever. Adherents share Durkheim's views that social totalities are the appropriate *unit* of analysis for the study of collective phenomena, and forms of association within them the appropriate *level* of analysis. However, they disagree among themselves as to the identity of this totality and its governing structures in the international realm.

One position is represented by Immanuel Wallerstein, himself a sociologist. In his methodological essay, "The Rise and Future Demise of the World Capitalist System: Concepts for Comparative Analysis," he posits that there is no such thing as *national* development in the modern world system, only development *of* the modern world system. "The fundamental error of ahistorical social science (including ahistorical versions of Marxism) is to reify parts of the totality into such [national] units and then to compare these reified structures" (1979:3). Instead, he considers the appropriate focus for comparative analysis to be the world system itself, "which we define quite simply as a unit with a single division of labor and multiple cultural systems" (Wallerstein 1979:5). In the modern world, the capitalist world economy constitutes the appropriate unit of analysis. It is divided into core, periphery, and semi-periphery, which are linked together by unequal exchange and therefore are characterized by unequal development. Onto an ultra-Durkheimian premise, then, Wallerstein grafts his own peculiar brand of Marxism, a structural-functionalist variety in which social relations of production are determined by market exchange rather than the other way round (cf. Brenner 1977), and in which the international polity is at one and the same time an epiphenomenal byproduct of intercapitalist competition and the necessary structural condition for the existence and continued survival of capitalism.[2]

A mirror image of this position is presented in the recent book by Kenneth N. Waltz, *Theory of International Politics*. He has no quarrel with the need to view international phenomena in systemic terms: "Nations change in form and purpose; technological advances are made; weaponry is radically transformed; alliances are forged and disrupted." And yet, "similarity of outcomes prevails despite changes in the agents that produce them." Clearly, "systems-level forces seem to be at work" (Waltz 1979:67, 39). But how should one conceive of international phenomena in systemic terms? Waltz's first answer, taking up roughly one-third of the volume, is: "not in the reductionist manner of the past." He is concerned primarily with the form of reductionism that seeks to know a whole through the study of its parts. This fallacy, he argues, is characteristic of most previous attempts to construct international theory, including self-styled systems theories.[3] For most of the latter, the system is simply an aggregation of pertinent attributes of units and their inter-actions: "the systems level thus becomes all product and is not at all productive" (p. 50). To be productive, the systems level has to express systemic properties and to explain how these act "as a constraining and disposing force on the interacting units within it" (p. 72). For Waltz— in contrast to Wallerstein whom he mentions only in passing—the critical international systemic property is not the hierarchical organization of exchange relations, but the horizontal organization of authority relations, or the international structure of anarchy. Not unequal exchange among economic units, but self-help by political units is the fundamental basis of international association.[4] The other two-thirds of the book are given over to elaborating and illustrating this model.

Wallerstein's efforts at theory construction have recently been re-viewed (Zolberg 1981). The present essay may be taken as a companion piece on Waltz. Other writers have commented on the adequacy and accuracy of various parts of Waltz's theoretical enterprise (Kaplan 1979; Hoffmann 1978; Rosecrance 1981; Fox 1980). My concern here is with the enterprise itself. Accordingly, I first situate Waltz's argument within its selfconsciously Durkheimian problematic.[5] I then assess, modify, and extend it on its own terms, pointing toward the desirability of a more synthetic, neorealist formulation.

II

Waltz starts off by making two important distinctions: between system and unit, and between structure and process. The terms are defined in a somewhat circular manner, but his intention is clear: "A system is composed of a structure and of interacting units. The structure is the system-wide component that makes it possible to think of the system as a whole" (1979:79). Durkheim is helpful in disentangling these notions: "Whenever certain elements combine and thereby produce, by the fact of their combination, new phenomena, it is plain that these new phe-nomena reside not in the original elements, but in the totality formed by their union." A system, then, is this new totality formed by the union of parts, a totality enjoying a "specific reality which has its own char-

acteristics" (Durkheim 1895:xlvii, 103). The structure depicts the organization of a system, or the laws of association by which units are
combined to form the systemic totality. Processes are simply the patterned relations among units that go on within a system—relations that
reflect in varying degrees the constraints imposed by the system's structure.[6]

With these distinctions established, Waltz turns to his central concern:
demonstrating the impact of variations in international structure on international outcomes, and explaining similarities of outcomes over time
by structural continuity. His concept of political structure consists of
three analytical components: (1) the principle according to which the
system is ordered or organized; (2) the differentiation of units and the
specification of their functions; and (3) the degree of concentration or
diffusion of capabilities within the system.

Applying these terms to the international realm, Waltz argues first
that its most important structural feature is the absence of central rule,
or anarchy (1979:88–93). No one by virtue of authority is *entitled* to
command; no one, in turn, is *obligated* to obey. States are the constitutive
units of the system. Waltz advances empirical arguments why this should
be so (pp. 93–95), but it follows logically from his premises: because
legitimate authority is not centralized in the system, states—as the existing repositories of the ultimate arbiter of force—*ipso facto* are its major
units. The desire of these units, at a minimum, to survive is assumed.
And the organizing principle of self-help is postulated: if no one can be
counted on to take care of anyone else, it seems reasonable to infer that
each will try to put itself in a position to be able to take care of itself.

As a result, the international system is formed much like a market: it
is individualistic in origin, and more or less spontaneously generated as
a byproduct of the actions of its constitutive units, "whose aims and
efforts are directed not toward creating an order but rather toward
fulfilling their own internally defined interests by whatever means they
can muster" (p. 90). This situation does not imply the absence of collaboration: collaboration is one of the means that states can muster in
pursuit of their interests, some of which will be shared with others. It
does imply that collaboration occurs "only in ways strongly conditioned
by" the structure of anarchy (p. 116), which is to say that the acceptability
of the means of collaboration takes priority over the desirability of its

ends (pp. 107–110). Once formed, the international system, again like a market, becomes a force that the units may not be able to control; it constrains their behavior and interposes itself between their intentions and the outcomes of their actions (pp. 90–91).

With respect to the second component of international political structure, Waltz contends that, in a system governed by self-help, the units are compelled to try to be functionally alike—alike in the tasks that they pursue. Obviously, they are not alike in their respective capabilities to perform these tasks, but capabilities are the object of the third component of structure, not the second. Accordingly, since no functional differentiation of states exists apart from that imposed by relative capabilities, the second component of political structure is not needed at the international level (pp. 93–97).

The degree of concentration or diffusion of capabilities within the system is the third component of structure. Here Waltz again argues by way of analogy: just as economic outcomes change when the structure of markets shifts from duopoly to oligopoly to perfect competition, so too do international outcomes change depending upon whether two, several, or no preeminent powers inhabit the system. "Market structure is defined by counting firms; international-political structure, by counting states. In the counting, distinctions are made only according to capabilities. ... What emerges is a positional picture, a general description of the ordered overall arrangement of a society written in terms of the placement of units rather than in terms of their qualities" (pp. 98–99).

Care should be taken to understand one extremely subtle but critical point. Waltz strives for a "generative" formulation of structure.[7] He means for the three (or, internationally, two) components of structure to be thought of as successive causal depth levels. Ordering principles constitute the "deep structure" of a system, shaping its fundamental social quality. They are not visible directly, only through their hypothesized effects. Differentiation, where it exists as a structural property, mediates the social effects of the deep structure, but within a context that has already been circumscribed by the deep structure. It is expressed through broad and enduring social institutions, and therefore is more directly accessible to the observer. The distribution of capabilities comes closest to the surface level of visible phenomena, but its impact on outcomes is simply to magnify or modify the opportunities and constraints generated by the other (two) structural level(s). When all is said and done, however, this generative model eludes Waltz, with consequences that we shall explore at the appropriate point.

In conclusion, then, "international structures vary only through a change of organizing principle or, failing that, through variations in the capabilities of units" (p. 93). What outcomes are explained by international structure and structural variation, so defined?

III

"From anarchy one infers broad expectations about the quality of international-political life. Distinguishing between anarchic structures of different type permits somewhat narrower and more precise definitions of expected outcomes" (Waltz 1979:70). Waltz first describes the general consequences of anarchy (ch. 6; article 5 of the present volume), and then stipulates and illustrates more specific expected outcomes in three domains of international relations; the international security order (ch. 8), the international economic order (ch. 7), and the management of "global problems" (ch. 9). In the summary that follows, I combine general and specific consequences.

The Security Order

From the principle of self-help, it will be recalled, one can infer that states will try to put themselves in a position that will enable them to take care of themselves. They have two types of means at their disposal: "internal efforts (moves to increase economic capability, to increase military strength, to develop clever strategies) and external efforts (moves to strengthen one's own alliance or to weaken and shrink an opposing one)." As one or more states successfully undertake nay such measure, however, "others will emulate them or fall by the wayside" (Waltz 1979:118). As other states emulate them, power-balancing ensues. Thus, the international security order is governed by balance-of-power politics. "Balance-of-power politics prevails whenever two, and only two, requirements are met: that the order be anarchic and that it be populated by units wishing to survive" (p. 121).[8]

Though Waltz is careless in maintaining the distinction, it should be noted that the theory predicts balanc*ing*, not balanc*es*, of power, where balances are defined as equivalences. Whether actual balances form, and even more whether any specific configuration or alignment forms, will only in part be determined by positional factors; it will also depend upon information and transaction costs, and a host of unit-level attributes.

Power-balancing can as readily produce war as it can lower its incidence. It is inherently indeterminate. However, its indeterminacy is reduced as the number of great powers in the system diminishes. Here is where the degree of concentration of capabilities becomes an issue. Waltz contends that systemic stability—defined as the absence of systemwide wars—is greatest when the number of great powers is smallest. For then actors exist who have both systemic interests and the unilateral capabilities to manipulate systemic factors—comparable to price-fixing, which becomes easier the smaller the number of firms involved. Barring a universal empire, which would domesticate international politics altogether, the most favorable situation, according to Waltz, is a system dominated by two great powers.[9] World War II produced such an outcome; it transformed a multipolar into a bipolar system, the only war in modern history to have had such a transformational consequence. Waltz's concrete views on the virtues of bipolarity, as well as contrary interpretations, are required reading in introductory courses in international relations, so I will not address them further.[10]

The Economic Order

The principle of self-help also shapes the fundamental contours of the international economic order. In a domestic realm, units are free to pursue economic specialization because the effects of the resultant mutual dependence among them are regulated by the authorities. Economic competition takes place, but it is embedded in a collaborative political framework. As a result, the elaborate division of labor that can evolve among the individual parts becomes a source of strength and welfare for the collectivity as a whole. Internationally, the principle of self-help compels states to try to be functionally alike precisely because mutual dependence remains problematic and therefore is a source of vulnerability to states. Economic collaboration takes place, but it is embedded in a competitive political framework. As a result, the international division of labor is slight in comparison, and reflects the relative strengths of the units and their respective capabilities to provide for their own welfare (Waltz 1979:104–107, 143–44).[11] Hence, "in international relations [economic] interdependence is always a marginal affair" (Waltz 1970:206).[12] This is a general outcome that one expects, given the structure of anarchy.

Structural variation will produce changes in the international economic order. Waltz explores one such change. He contends that systemic interdependence, low to begin with, will be still lower the smaller the number of great powers.[13] The reason is that "size tends to increase as numbers fall," and "the larger a country, the higher the proportion of its business it does at home" (1979:145). Waltz is thereby led to his highly controversial conclusion that international economic interdependence is lower today, in the era of bipolarity, than it was prior to World War I, under multipolarity.[14] To confirm his conclusion, Waltz shows that the external sector "loomed larger" for the great powers prior to World War I than it does today, and that international trade and investment then reflected a greater degree of inter-country specialization than it does today.[15]

What of the internationalization of production and finance and the worldwide integration of markets, of which both liberal and Marxist theorists make so much? Waltz remains unimpressed. These theorists "dwell on the complex ways in which issues, actions, and policies have become intertwined and the difficulty everyone has in influencing or controlling them. They have discovered the complexity of processes and have lost sight of how processes are affected by structure" (p. 145).

Lastly, Waltz is sanguine about this outcome on normative grounds. He believes that "close interdependence means closeness of contact and raises the prospect of occasional conflict," while lower interdependence diminishes this prospect. "If interdependence grows at a pace that exceeds the development of central control, then interdependence hastens the occasion for war" (p. 138). This general premise can be seen to follow from Waltz's theory, though its historical validity is dubious, or at least highly conditioned by unspecified factors.[16]

Managing "Global Problems"

Any political system develops means by which to order relations of force, to organize production and exchange, and to adapt to long-term changes in its environment. The international political system is no exception. The third functional domain, including what Waltz calls "the four p's— pollution, poverty, population, and proliferation" (1979:139)—is discussed under the general rubric of "international management," or the "management of "global problems." It is governed by "the tyranny of small decisions" (p. 108).

The problem is structural. In a domestic society, individual behavior can be constrained by considerations concerning the desirability of the greater social good, as defined by some central agency. But the international system is not an entity that is capable of acting in its own behalf, for the greater social good. Thus, while a growing number of problems may be found at the global level, solutions continue to depend on national policies (p. 109). But national policies are constrained by the structure of self-help. Therefore, the incidence and character of "international management" is determined by the acceptability of the means by which to respond to "global problems," as calculated by the separate units, not by the desirability of the end to be achieved. As a result, international management is likely to be supplied in suboptimal quantities even when all concerned agree that more is necessary. "A strong sense of peril and doom may lead to a clear definition of the ends that must be achieved. Their achievement is not thereby made possible. . . . Necessities do not create possibilities" (p. 109).

To break out of the tyranny of small decisions, "we have to search for a surrogate of government" (p. 196). International organization provides no answer. To manage the system effectively, a central agency would require the means to control and protect its client states, means that it could obtain only from those client states. However, the greater its potential managerial powers, "the stronger the incentives of states to engage in a struggle to control it" (p. 112). The result, far from centralizing authority, would be power-balancing. "The only remedy for a strong structural effect is a structural change" (p. 111). It should come as no surprise, therefore, that for Waltz the likelihood of approximating government is greatest when the number of great powers is smallest. "The smaller the number of great powers, and the wider the disparities between the few most powerful states and the many others, the more likely the former are to act for the sake of the system." (p. 198). Hence, Waltz's overall conclusion that in the world as it exists, not as we might wish it to be, "small is beautiful"—and "smaller is more beautiful than small" (p. 134).

Conclusion to Section III

How durable is this system? Remarkably durable, according to Waltz. There are only two ways to alter it, and neither occurs frequently or rapidly. Within-system change is produced by a shift in the configuration of capabilities. In the history of the modern state system, a multipolar configuration endured for three centuries even though the identity of the great powers changed over time. Bipolarity has lasted for more than three decades, and appears "robust" (Waltz 1979:162). In the foreseeable future, only a united Europe that developed political competence and military power would be a candidate to effect this kind of change, and its prospects for doing so are not bright (p. 180). The other kind of change, a change of system, would be produced if the structure of anarchy were transformed into a hierarchy. In the history of the modern state system, this has never occurred. Indeed, its occurrence has been prevented by the very structure of anarchy. In a hierarchical realm, the emergence of a potentially dominant force (a leading candidate in an election, for example) initially may trigger attempts to balance it, but if its potential for success increases beyond a certain point, there is every likelihood that it will benefit from "bandwagoning," which will assure success. By contrast, in an anarchical realm, the emergence of a potentially dominant force may well be accompanied by bandwagoning *until* it reaches a certain point. Then, if success seems possible, it is likely to result in efforts to balance it (pp. 123–138). Bandwagoning in the one case, and balancing in the other, best secures the position of the constituent units in the respective realms, and serves to maintain the deep structures of the respective realms.[17]

IV

Waltz's views have policy implications that cause displeasure and even distress in a variety of intellectual constituencies most directly concerned with those policy issues: other realists hotly dispute Waltz's benign assessment of recent changes in the correlation of forces between the

United States and the Soviet Union; liberals, his dismissal of the global integration of economic processes; Third World supporters, his stress on the virtues of inequality; and world-order advocates, his general vision of the nature of the international system and the range of possibilities it offers. I make no attempt to recapitulate these debates here, because the various positions are well known. Less well known is the theoretical basis that Waltz invokes to support his views. To be sure, it was signaled in "The Third Image" of *Man, the State and War* (Waltz 1959), but it had never been fleshed out in detail until the present book. Since my concern is the theory, having presented this brief summary sketch, I proceed at the same level of generality.

Insofar as Waltz's theoretical position embodies the mirror image of other and perhaps currently more popular bodies of theory, it is easy enough to reject his interpretations out of hand in favor of some other. Moreover, his own criticisms of contrary positions assume such a tone of *hauteur* and reflect such a sense of certitude as almost to invite this reaction. But that would be a mistake. The volume under discussion is one of the most important contributions to the theory of international relations since *Man, the State and War*; it enhances in a fundamental manner the level of discourse in the field.

The tack I take, therefore, is to ask whether Waltz succeeds on his own terms. I find that he does not do so fully. Part of the reason lies in errors of omission and commission, part is inherent to the enterprise as Waltz conceives of it. Since the chief theoretical aim of his book is to explain systemic continuity in international politics, I will take that to be the focus of my critique of and amendments to the theory.

V

"The texture of international politics remains highly constant, patterns recur, and events repeat themselves endlessly" (Waltz 1979:66). We have seen Waltz's explanation. One problem with it is that it provides no means by which to account for, or even to describe, the most important contextual change in international politics in this *millennium*: the shift from the medieval to the modern international system. The medieval system was, by Waltz's own account (p. 88), an anarchy.[18] Yet the difference between it and the modern international system cannot simply be attributed to differences in the distribution of capabilities among their constituent units. To do so would be historically inaccurate, and nonsensical besides.[19] The problem is that a dimension of change is missing from Waltz's model. It is missing because he drops the second analytical component of political structure, differentiation of units, when discussing international systems. And he drops this component as a result of giving an infelicitous interpretation to the sociological term "differentiation," taking it to mean that which denotes *differences* rather than that which denotes *separateness*. The modern system is distinguished from the medieval not by "sameness" or "differences" of units, but by *the principles on the basis of which the constituent units are separated* from one another. If anarchy tells us *that* the political system is a segmental realm, differentiation tells us *on what basis* the segmentation is determined. The second component of structure, therefore, does *not* drop out; it stays in, and serves as an exceedingly important source of structural variation.

What are these principles of separation or segmentation, and what are their effects? Taking my cue from no less a realist than Meinecke, I refer to the medieval variant of this structural level as a "heteronomous" institutional framework, and to the modern as the institutional framework of "sovereignty."[20]

The feudal state, if the concept makes any sense at all,[21] consisted of chains of lord–vassal relationships. Its basis was the fief, which was an amalgam of conditional property and private authority. Property was conditional in that it carried with it explicit social obligations. And authority was private in that the rights of jurisdiction and administration over the inhabitants of a fiefdom resided personally in the ruler. Moreover, the prevailing concept of usufructure meant that multiple titles to the same landed property were the norm. As a result, the medieval system of rule reflected "a patchwork of overlapping and incomplete rights of government" (Strayer and Munro 1959:115; Strayer 1970), which were "inextricably superimposed and tangled," and in which "different juridical instances were geographically interwoven and stratified, and plural allegiances, asymmetrical suzerainties and anomalous enclaves abounded" (Anderson 1974:37–38).

This system of rule was inherently "international." To begin with, the distinction between "internal" and "external" political realms, separated by clearly demarcated "boundaries," made little sense until late in the day.[22] In addition, it was quite common for rulers in different territorial settings to be one another's feoffor and feoffee for different regions of their respective lands.[23] And the feudal ruling class was mobile in a manner not dreamed of since—able to travel and assume governance from one end of the continent to the other without hesitation or difficulty, because "public territories formed a continuum with private estates" (Anderson 1974:32).[24]

Lastly, the medieval system of rule was legitimated by common bodies of law, religion, and custom that expressed inclusive natural rights pertaining to the social totality formed by the constituent units. These inclusive legitimations posed no threat to the integrity of the constituent units, however, because the units viewed themselves as municipal embodiments of a universal community (Mattingly 1964:41ff.). In sum, this was quintessentially a system of segmental territorial rule; it was an anarchy. But it was a form of segmental territorial rule that had none of the connotations of possessiveness and exclusiveness conveyed by the modern concept of sovereignty. It represented a heteronomous organization of territorial rights and claims—of political space.

As the medieval state represents a fusion of its particular forms of property and authority, so does the modern. The chief characteristic of the modern concept of private property is the right to exclude others from the possession of an object. And the chief characteristic of modern authority is its totalization, the integration into one public realm of parcelized and private authority. "The age in which 'Absolutist' public authority was imposed was also simultaneously the age in which 'absolute' private property was progressively consolidated" (Anderson 1974:428). In contrast to its medieval counterpart, the modern system of rule consists of the institutionalization of public authority within mutually exclusive jurisdictional domains.

The full significance and signification of this shift may best be observed through the lens of legitimation. The concept of sovereignty is critical. Unfortunately, it has become utterly trivialized by recent usage, which treats sovereignty either as a necessary adjunct of anarchy or as a descriptive category expressing unit attributes, roughly synonymous with material autonomy.[25] But sovereignty was not an adjunct of anarchy in the medieval system of rule, as we have seen. And in its proper modern usage, it signifies a form of *legitimation* that pertains to a *system* of relations, as we shall now see.[26]

The rediscovery from Roman law of the concept of absoute private property and the simultaneous emergence of mutually exclusive territorial state formations, which stood in relation to one another much as owners of private estates do,[27] occasioned what we might call a "legitimation crisis" of staggering proportions. How can one justify absolute individuation when one's frame of reference is inclusive natural rights? And if one justifies such individuation, what basis is left for political community? The works we regard today as the modern classics in political theory and international legal thought were produced in direct response to this legitimation crisis. Attempted solutions to the problems were diverse.[28] Of greatest interest for present purposes are the analogous solutions developed by Locke and Vattel, because they came to be the most widely accepted legitimations for their respective realms, bourgeois society, and the interstate system.

Here is how John Locke defined the first of his tasks in resolving the crisis: "I shall endeavour to shew, how Men might come to have a *property* in several parts of that which God gave to Mankind in common."[29] He fulfilled this task by providing a theory of natural individuation of property that obtains "where there is enough, and as good left in common for others" (cited in Tully 1980:129). However, the condition of scarcity ultimately limits such individuation, and its advent is hastened by the introduction of money, which makes possible accumulation beyond what one needs and can use. Covetousness and contention ensue. Therefore, to "avoid these Inconveniences which disorder Mens properties in the state of Nature, Men unite into Societies" (ibid:150–151). As his second task, Locke endeavored to show the basis of the political community so constituted. This he accomplished by establishing a means-ends relation between the public good and the preservation of property: since individual property rights existed prior to the formation of civil society, "the power of Society, or Legislative constituted by them, can never be suppos'd to extend farther than the common good; but is obliged to secure every ones Property by providing against those . . . defects . . . that made the State of Nature so unsafe and uneasie" (ibid:163).[30] In sum, for Locke the purpose of civil society lay in providing a conventional framework within which to protect natural individual property rights that, beyond a certain point in history, could not be vindicated in its absence. And the legitimation for the political community so established derived simply from the minimalist social needs of the separate "proprietors," without recourse to any "standard of right that stood outside and above" these bare facts (Macpherson 1962:80).[31]

Precisely this was also Vattel's accomplishment in international theory. In *Droit des Gens,* published in 1758, Vattel wrote "the international law of political liberty" (Gross 1968:65; Vattel 1916)—the political liberty, that is, of states. This law rested on natural rights doctrines. At the same time, Vattel brought to a successful resolution the floundering efforts of the better part of two centuries to establish a complementarity between the sovereign claims of the separate states and the idea of a community of states, rendered in such a way that the latter was not entirely discarded in favor of the former.[32] In the manner of Locke, Vattel accomplished this by establishing a means-ends relation between the international community and the preservation of the separate existence of its parts. To maintain the order that made this separate existence possible was, for Vattel, the province of the community of states. And the legitimation for the political community consisting of the minimalist social needs of "sovereigns" required no recourse to sources of authority or morality beyond "these bare facts."

In sum, from the vantage point of their respective social totalities—domestic and international systems—private property rights and sovereignty may be viewed as being analogous concepts in three respects. First, they differentiate among units in terms of possession of self and exclusion of others. Second, because *any* mode of differentiation *inherently* entails a corresponding form of sociality, private property rights and sovereignty also establish systems of social relations among their respective units. They give rise to the form of sociality characteristic of "possessive individualists," for whom the social collectivity is merely a conventional contrivance calculated to maintain the basic mode of differentiation and to compensate for the defects of a system so organized by facilitating orderly exchange relations among the separate parts. Third, the most successful theorists of the two realms—as measured by their political impact on bourgeois society and contemporary statesmen, respectively—developed an autonomous legitimation of the political order based simply on the minimalist social needs of its component units. That is to say, they derived an "ought" from an "is," where the "is" was neither transcendental nor purely subjective, but enjoyed an irreducible intersubjective existential quality.[33]

The medieval system differed profoundly in each of these respects. Appropriately, the first specifically modern invention of diplomacy was the principle of extraterritoriality: having so fundamentally redefined and reorganized political space, states "found that they could only communicate with one another by tolerating within themselves little islands of alien sovereignty" (Mattingly 1964:244).[34]

In sum, when the concept "differentiation" is properly defined, the second structural level of Waltz's model does not drop out. It stays in, and serves to depict the kind of institutional transformation illustrated by the shift from the medieval to the modern international system; by extension of the argument, it serves as a dimension of possible future transformation, from the modern to a postmodern international system. Its inclusion has a number of more specific consequences, which I will simply enumerate:

1. This structural level gives greater determinate content to the general constraints of anarchy deduced by Waltz. One illustration will suffice to make the point. According to Waltz, the constitutive element of collaboration in an anarchical realm is "the exchange of considerations" (Waltz 1979:113). Neither he nor Chester I. Barnard (1948:151), whom he follows on this point, defines the term "considerations." And from anarchy alone one *cannot* infer a definition. We do discover more of the meaning, however, by looking at the institutional frameworks of heteronomy and sovereignty. In the medieval system, the exchange of considerations was calculated *intuitu personae,* that is, taking into account the "majesty," "dignity," and other such individual and subjective attributes of the status and wealth of the parties to the exchange (Mattingly 1964). This is as foreign to the modern mind as is Aristotle's effort to calculate a just price for exchange by taking into account the social standing of the parties to it (cf. Polanyi 1957a), but it represents no less an "exchange of considerations" for it. In the framework of sovereignty characteristic of "possessive individualists," we know that "considerations" translates as rough quantitative equivalency—which, of course, is what Waltz mistakenly thinks he is deducing from anarchy.

2. This structural level provides the basis for a more refined and

compelling response than Waltz is able to give to liberal interdependence theorists who argue that *because* sovereignty (erroneously defined as unit autonomy) is becoming "relatively irrelevant," realism no longer offers an appropriate explanation of international outcomes. All that Waltz can, and does, say is that this is a unit-level issue which has no place in systemic theory. However, in view of the analogous relationship established above between private property rights and sovereignty, those who would dispense with the concept of sovereignty on the grounds of growing international interdependence must first show why the idea of private property rights should not have been dispensed with long ago in the capitalist societies, where they are continuously invaded and interfered with by the actions of the state. Yet we know that, at a minimum, the structure of private property rights will influence *when* the state intervenes; usually it also affects *how* the state intervenes. If this concept still has utility domestically, in the face of definitive state action, then its international analogue ought, if anything, to be even more relevant. The reason for the continued significance of the concepts is that they are not simply descriptive categories. Rather, they are components of generative structures: they shape, condition, and constrain social behavior.

3. This structural level allows us to reach beyond the confines of conventional realist analysis, to incorporate factors and address issues not normally considered by it—without, however, violating its basic premises. One illustration will again suffice. The institutional framework of sovereignty differentiates units in terms of juridically mutually exclusive and morally self-entailed domains. However, the *scope* of these domains is defined not only territorially but also functionally, depending upon the range and depth of state intervention in domestic social and economic affairs. It follows that the functional scope of the international system will also vary, depending upon the hegemonic form of state/society relations that prevails internationally at any given time. Therefore, the hegemonic form of state/society relations, or a lack thereof, constitutes an attribute of the international system and can be used as a systems-level explanatory factor. And a good thing that it can be so used; for despite his best efforts, Waltz cannot explain the qualitative differences in economic interdependence between the late nineteenth century and the post-World War II period simply by the facts of multipolarity then and bipolarity now. The differences stem from the respective hegemonic

forms of state/society relations prevailing in the two eras—"laissez-faire liberalism" then and "embedded liberalism" now.[35]

4. Lastly, this structural level provides a basis from which to fashion a more comprehensive view of the "world system," including both its political and economic dimensions. I share Waltz's view on the priority of the states system, so long as the deep structure of anarchy prevails. Nevertheless, it is clear from the above discussion that the early modern redefinition of property rights and reorganization of political space unleashed both interstate political relations and capitalist production relations. The two systems, then, have similar structural roots. They gave rise to similar forms of sociality in their respective realms. They are reproduced by analogous mechanisms. And the evolution of these systems, at least in part, is "co-determined."[36] A properly augmented realist model ought to be able gradually to generate an explanation of this more comprehensive social formation.

VI

There is not only a *dimension* of change missing from Waltz's model. If he takes his Durkheimian premises seriously, then a *determinant* of change is missing as well. According to Durkheim, "growth in the volume and dynamic density of societies modifies profoundly the fundamental conditions of collective existence." (1895:115). Both are capable of altering "social facts." By volume, Durkheim means the number of socially relevant units, which Waltz includes in his model by counting the number of great powers. But what of dynamic density? By this, Durkheim understands the quantity, velocity, and diversity of transactions that go on within society. But Waltz, as we have seen, banishes such factors to the level of process, shaped by structure but not in turn affecting structure in any manner depicted by his model. Why this departure from Durkheim's framework, when it is followed closely in other respects? Waltz's neglect of "dynamic density" results, in my view, from three limitations of his model.

The first is simply the missing dimension of change that we have just discussed. It is the case, both on logical and historical grounds, that the pressure of what Durkheim calls dynamic density is exerted most directly on prevailing property rights within a society. Formal theories of property rights, for example, routinely invoke such factors as crowding, the existence of externalities, and the incentives of optimal scale to explain and justify the reordering of individual property rights (cf. Furubotn and Pejovich 1974). Lacking this dimension of structure, Waltz rejects the phenomenon as not having anything to do with structure. True, the only relevant question for Waltz's purposes is whether the pressure of dynamic density is ever *so* great as to trigger a change not simply in *individual* property rights, but in the basic *structure* of property rights that characterizes an entire social formation. It happens that the shift from the medieval to the modern international system represents one such instance. And it is not an unreasonable hypothesis that any transformation beyond the modern international system will represent a similar instance.

In their enormously ambitious and provocative analytical economic history of the rise of the West from 1300 to 1700, North and Thomas (1973) discuss the medieval-to-modern shift in the following terms.[37]

Self-sustained economic growth in the West was made possible by the instituting of efficient economic organization. Efficient economic organization in turn entailed a societal restructuring of property rights that reduced the discrepancy between private and social rates of return. This restructuring of property rights was produced by a combination of diminishing returns to land, resulting from population pressures; a widening of markets, resulting from migration patterns; and an expansion of the institutions providing justice and protection to achieve a more optimal size for commerce and warfare, as well as their reorganization to eliminate domestic competitors. The transformation of the state was driven on the supply side by rulers' pursuit of revenues; where the particular fiscal interests of state actors coincided with an economically efficient structure of property rights—as they did in the Netherlands and Britain—successful economic growth ensued; others became also-rans. In this instance, then, Durkheim's notion of dynamic density *can* be linked to a societal restructuring of property rights and political organization, which had the domestic and international consequences that we examined in the previous section. North and Thomas's model, even if it were without problems on its own terms, cannot simply be extended into the future of the international system. For one thing (as the authors themselves point out), from the seventeenth century on, differences in the efficiency of economic organization have become a major determinant of the consequences of the "natural" forces that they examine, so that the phenomenon of dynamic density today is infinitely more complex. For another, the restructuring of property rights and political organization that they describe were in large measure instituted from the top down by rulers gaining control of the emerging state formations; no analogue exists in the contemporary international system. However, neither of these qualifications warrants neglecting dynamic density as a possible determinant of future systemic change; they merely suggest that its manifestations and effects are likely to be different, and that indicators designed to detect them will have to reflect these differences.[38]

A second reason for Waltz's neglect of dynamic density as a possible source of change reflects an error of commission rather than of omission. I mentioned earlier that Waltz strives for, but fails fully to achieve, a generative formulation of international political structure. As a result of this failure, one circuit through which the effects of dynamic density could register at the systems level is severed. In a generative structure, it will be recalled, the deeper structural levels have causal priority, and the structural levels closer to the surface of visible phenomena take effect only within a context that is already "prestructured" by the deeper levels. For example, we ask of the distribution of capabilities within the international system *what difference it makes* for the realization of the general organizational effects of the deep structure of anarchy, as mediated by the more specific organizational effects of the institutional framework of sovereignty. That is how we determine the *systemic effects* of changes in the distribution of capabilities. We then go on to ask how these systemic effects in turn *condition* and *constrain* international outcomes.

However, when assessing possible sources of change, Waltz shortcircuits his own model: he shifts from a generative to a descriptive conception of structure. For example, in the face of demographic trends, quantitative and qualitative changes in industrial production and location as well as in technologies, ecological and resource constraints, and shifts in the international balance of forces—some of which surely could be coded as measures of systemic dynamic density—Waltz tends to conclude: yes, but the United States and the Soviet Union still are relatively better off than anybody else, and the United States is relatively better off than the Soviet Union; therefore these changes have no systemic effects, and remain of no concern to systemic theory.[39] Whether or not Waltz's specific empirical assessments are correct has been widely contested.[40] But let us grant, for the sake of the argument, that bipolarity remains intact. A more fundamental problem stems from the fact that, in linking theory to real-world outcomes, Waltz has abandoned his generative model of structure at this critical juncture. The question that Waltz *should* be asking is whether any of these changes, singly or in some combination, make any difference not simply for the *relative* positions of the superpowers, but for the *absolute* capacity of bipolarity to *mute* the underlying deleterious organizational effects of anarchy and sovereignty. The answer to *this* question provides the basis for predicting the constraining and conditioning consequences of structure, within which individual states, including the United States and the Soviet Union, must find their way. A generative model demands this chain of reasoning, as Waltz himself makes clear in his abstract description of it.[41] I, for one, would be surprised to learn that some of the changes alluded to above do not adversely affect the managerial capacity of bipolarity and, thereby, alter systemic outcomes.

There is a third and final reason why Waltz neglects dynamic density as a potential source of systemic change, and why he discounts the very possibility of systemic change more generally. Waltz reacts strongly against what he calls the reductionist tendencies in international relations theory. In the conventional usage, as noted above, he finds that the system is all product and is not at all productive. He takes pains to rectify this imbalance. He goes too far, however. In his conception of systemic theory, *unit-level processes* become all product and are not at all productive.[42] Hence, what Anthony Giddens says of Durkheim is said even more appropriately of Waltz: he adopts what is supposed to be a methodological principle, and turns it into an ontological one (Giddens 1978:126).[43] In consequence, while his model in the end may *reflect* changes in its own parameters, it lacks any basis on which to *predict* them.

In Waltz's model of the system, as we have seen, structural features are sharply differentiated from unit-level processes, and structure is the productive agency that operates at the level of system. Accordingly, only structural change can produce systemic change. Waltz's posture in this regard is a welcome antidote to the prevailing superficiality of the proliferating literature on international transformation, in which the sheer momentum of processes sweeps the international polity along toward its next encounter with destiny. The problem with Waltz's posture is that, in any social system, structural change itself ultimately has no source *other than* unit-level processes. By banishing these from the domain of systemic theory, Waltz also exogenizes the ultimate source of systemic change.[44] By means of the concept of dynamic density, Durkheim at least in part endogenized change of society into his theory of society.[45] Not so Waltz. As a result, Waltz's theory of "society" contains only a reproductive logic, but no transformational logic.

In sum, I have made no concerted attempt to show that Waltz is substantively mistaken in his expectation about future continuity in the international system. My purpose has been to demonstrate that in his model, continuity—at least in part—is a product of premise even before it is hypothesized as an outcome. Despite its defects, Waltz's model is powerful and elegant. And, as I have suggested, its defects can be compensated for in a suitably amended and augmented neorealist formulation. Such a formulation would also go some way toward subsuming the major competing systemic theories. How far the "perfect" realist model would take us in understanding and shaping continuity and transformation in the world polity is a question for another occasion.

NOTES

1. Cf. Durkheim (1893) wherein this model was first developed. It should be noted that for Durkheim the designation "social fact" does not refer to all phenomena that take place within society, but only to those that exist exterior to individuals, are not subject to modification by a simple effort of will on the part of individuals, and function as a constraint on individual behavior (cf. 1895:ch. 1).

2. "Capitalism has been able to flourish precisely because the world economy has had within its bounds not one but a multiplicity of political systems" (Wallerstein 1974:348); this structure in turn is maintained by the functional needs of capitalism, specifically the high economic costs of political imperium (Wallerstein 1979:32) and the tendency of capitalists to resort to the instrumentalities of their respective states so as to enhance their international competitive position (ibid:19–20).

3. Waltz's critical review of the literature has generated a sizable secondary literature of rejoinders and counteroffensives, of which the most offensive no doubt is by Morton A. Kaplan (1979). More generous readings may be found in Stanley Hoffmann (1978:146–147), and Richard Rosecrance (1981).

4. Waltz acknowledges that Wallerstein has also developed a systemic theory,

but rejects Wallerstein's claims for its logical priority (Waltz 1979:38). In principle, Waltz allows for the possibility of co-equality, but in deed he argues for the priority of the international polity, as we shall see below.

5. Durkheim is referenced four times in the index of Waltz's book; in a footnote (1979:115), Waltz promises to elaborate on Durkheim's typology of social ordering principles in a future work.

6. There has been inordinate confusion about these distinctions, stemming largely from the way in which the so-called levels-of-analysis problem is usually interpreted. As originally defined, it simply says that the international system and national states constitute two different levels of analysis in the study of international relations (Singer 1961). But that isn't the whole of it. The two terms, international and system, are frequently conjoined, and the assumption is made that any model expressing *international* factors is automatically a *systemic* model. However, as Waltz shows (1979: chs. 3–4), the norm—even when systems language is employed—is to explain international phenomena in terms of units and their interactions, not in terms of systems as ontologically distinct totalities.

7. The distinction here is between generative and descriptive structures. Descriptive structures are simply abstract summaries of patterned interactions within a system. For example, national capabilities are measured, and hierarchies of state power are depicted. Trade and capital flows are measured, and hierarchies of economic power are adduced. Most uses of the concept of structure in international relations theory employ this meaning; the structural theories of Stephen Krasner and Johan Galtung offer a representative sampling. In the realm of generative structures, the concern is "with principles, not things" (Leach 1961:7). The object is to discover the underlying principles that govern the patterning of interactions, to infer their syntax. Saussurean lingustics probably was the first self-conscious expression of generative structralism in the social sciences, which has transformed the study of linguistics and cultural anthropology. For useful surveys, see Glucksman (1974) and Kurzweil (1980).

8. Waltz thus rejects the conventional view that a balance-of-power system requires a minimum number of effective actors larger than two—preferably five, so that one can act as balancer. This, he points out, "is more a historical generalization than a theoretical concept" (1979:164). In fact, balancing takes place in a bipolar world no less than in a multipolar world, except that the methods of balancing are largely internal rather than external.

9. The relationship between number and stability is not perfectly continuous, since, *ceteris paribus,* a world of three great powers is thought to be less stable than a world of four, though it may be *so* unstable that it inevitably resolves into bipolarity in any case (Waltz 1979:163). Note also that the emergence of two opposing alliances in a multipolar world does *not* transform it into bipolarity; polarity is a structural attribute of systems, measured by the number of great powers, whereas alliances are process-level phenomena that serve as one of the means by which states pursue their interests (pp. 169–170). By the same token, the loss of an ally in a bipolar system does *not* transform it into multipolarity.

10. One vexing problem does require special mention, however. The absence of system-wide wars is not the only definition of stability employed by Waltz. He also uses the term in the economists' sense—of the system returning to a prior or

corresponding point of equilibrium after a disturbance. Confusion ensues because *either* bipolarity *or* multipolarity comes out being *more* stable, depending upon the definition of stability, and Waltz is inconsistent and often unclear in his usage. As I understand him, multipolarity is more stable in the dynamic equilibrium sense (see p. 162 on the relative durability of the multipolar era in the modern state system), and bipolarity is more stable in the sense of the absence of system-wide wars (pp. 170–176); and Waltz 1964). But it remains to be seen whether the current bipolarity will do as well at averting system-wide wars as the nineteenth-century multipolarity did after 1815.

11. These notions closely parallel Durkheim's distinction between organic solidarity, linking highly differentiated units in a complex society, and mechanical solidarity, linking like units in a segmental society. Organic solidarity represents a qualitatively higher form and quantitatively greater extent of interdependence (Durkheim 1893).

12. Waltz means international system-level interdependence (see below) relative to domestic system-level interdependence.

13. Waltz is quite explicit in denouncing what he calls unit-level measures of interdependence, but much less clear in defining what he means by systems-level interdependence. I infer from the Durkheimian inspiration and from the kind of evidence that Waltz presents that he defines it in terms of two factors: (1) the relative size of the external sector, and (2) the degree of national specialization reflected in international transactions. Both of these factors are expected to co-vary with the number of great powers. Matters are muddled further, however, because Waltz insists that in measuring systemic interdependence we take into account only "the relatively high or low level of dependence of the great powers" (1979:145). But to do so is to employ the same indicator for both independent and dependent variables! The number of great powers is a structural attribute used to *predict* systemic outcomes; surely, in order to *describe* these outcomes, we need some aggregate measure that will include, but not be limited to, the economic activities accounted for by the great powers.

14. Waltz's original argument was with Richard N. Cooper (1968). Cooper shows, among other things, that the price sensitivity of factors is much higher today than in the pre-World War I period. That may be economically a more interesting form of interdependence, Waltz maintains, but it is politically less important. The quick reallocation of factors of production in response to relatively small margins of advantage demonstrates that those ties do not *need* to be maintained, that they do not reflect mutual dependence stemming from functional differentiation (1979:141–142). The debate concerning these two positions is ably conceptualized and summarized by Robert O. Keohane and Joseph S. Nye (1977 ch. 1).

15. Economists would point out that intrasectoral trade, which accounts for an ever-increasing share of total world trade, also reflects an international specialization of labor. Waltz's response would be that this increases interdependence at the level of the *firm,* while it decreases it for the *state* compared to what it would be given an equivalent level of intersectoral trade.

16. Waltz might be inclined to discuss the origins of World War I in this fashion, for instance, but then we would also need to have an explanation for the preceding "Hundred Years' Peace."

17. Cf. Ludwig Dehio (1962), to whom Waltz, curiously, makes no reference.

18. Anarchy, recall, is defined as the absence of central rule. On the concept of "feudal anarchy," see Gianfranco Poggi (1978:31): "It arose from the fact that the system of rule relied, both for order-keeping and for the enforcement of rights and the redress of wrongs, on self-activated coercion exercised by a small, privileged class of warriors and rentiers in their own interest." Moreover, any standard text will document that neither the papacy nor the empire constituted agents of centralized political authority; see, for example, Strayer and Munro (1959). Strayer (1970) demonstrates nicely the balancing consequences triggered by threats of supranationality from the papacy, most profoundly in this instance: "the Gregorian concept of the Church almost demanded the invention of the concept of the state" (p. 22).

19. Such an attribution would be historically inaccurate because there is a good deal of continuity in the "core units," if these are identified retrospectively as the units that would become the major European nation-states. But the exercise is nonsensical because, as Hedley Bull has pointed out, contemporaries found it impossible to enunciate a "fundamental constitutive principle or criterion of membership" in the international system. The major units were known as *civitates, principes, regni, gentes* and *respublicae,* the common element among them, the idea of statehood, not yet having taken hold (Bull 1977:29). To these must be added cities, associations of trades, commercial leagues, and even universities, not to mention the papacy and empire—all of which, for some purposes, were considered to be legitimate political actors, though of course they varied in scope and importance. For example, the right of embassy could be granted or denied to any of them, depending upon the social status of the parties involved and the business at hand (Mattingly 1964).

20. Meinecke (1957) spoke of the "heteronomous shackles" of the Middle Ages, referring to the lattice-like network of authority relations.

21. Poggi refers to a protracted dispute over whether this designation is appropriate (1978:26 n.11). The end of the feudal period does not end the cause of the dispute: see Chabod (1964).

22. For instance, the lines between France, England, and Spain did not harden until the early thirteenth century. "It was at this period that not only were the boundary lines decided but, even more important, it was decided that there would be boundary lines. This is what Edouard Perroy calls the 'fundamental change' in the political structure of Europe" (Wallerstein 1974:32). But the story does not end there. As late as 1547, when Francis I reformed the apparatus of the French state, he fixed the number of *secrétaires d'État* at four; but the conception of "internal" and "external" was still so blurred that, rather than separating their duties according to it, each of the four supervised the affairs of one quadrant of France *and* the relations with contiguous and outlying states (Mattingly 1964:195).

23. Strayer (1970:83) relates the hypothetical example of a king of France, who "might send letters on the same day to the count of Flanders, who was definitely his vassal, but a very independent and unruly one, to the count of Luxembourg, who was a prince of the Empire but who held a money-fief (a regular, annual pension) of the king of France, and to the king of Sicily, who was certainly a ruler of a sovereign state but also a prince of the French royal house."

24. "Angevin lineages could rule indifferently in Hungary, England or Naples; Norman in Antioch, Sicily or England; Burgundian in Portugal or Zeeland; Luxemburger in the Rhineland or Bohemia; Flemish in Artois ro Byzantium; Hapsburg in Austria, the Netherlands or Spain" (Anderson 1974:32).

25. It is quite common, particularly in liberal writings on interdependence, to read of "the relative irrelevance of sovereignty" in the contemporary world wherein all states "are subject to diverse internal and external conditioning factors that induce and constrain their behavior," and in which some states apparently are "more 'sovereign' than others." The cited snippets are from Mansbach et al. (1976:20–22). Waltz's definition of sovereignty is not helpful either: "To say that states are sovereign is not to say that they can do as they please. . . . To say that a state is sovereign means that it decides for itself how it will cope with its internal and external problems." (1979:96). If sovereignty meant no more than this, then I would agree with Ernst Haas, who once declared categorically: "I do not use the concept at all and see no need to" (1969:70).

26. More precisely, the internal side of sovereignty had to do with sovereignty as a legitimation for central state authority vis-à-vis competing domestic claimants. That was Bodin's concern. My discussion addresses only the external side, which dealt with sovereignty as a legitimation for the interstate order.

27. " 'Private,' to put it another way, refers not so much to the *nature* of the entity that owns, but to the fact that it is an entity, a unit whose ownership of nature . . . signifies the *exclusion* of others from this ownership" (Berki 1971:99, emphasis added).

28. Neo-Thomists like Vitoria and Suarez sought to adapt both inclusive property rights and natural law to the new circumstances, without abandoning either. Filmer and Hobbes abandoned both, arguing—on Adamite and utilitarian grounds, respectively—for the necessity of absolutist arrangements internally and, in the case of Hobbes, for the inevitability of the state of war externally. Grotius and Pufendorf developed mixed solutions that pointed the way toward the future. Both accepted the idea of exclusive property rights. Grotius allowed for some natural rights in things while Pufendorf argued that these rights must be conventional. But, critically, both defined the only remaining natural rights basis for sociableness or community negatively, in terms of the duty to abstain from that which belongs to another. Liberal theories of social order followed directly from this premise. A good summary, on which this characterization has drawn, may be found in Tully (1980 chs. 3–5). For a brief and useful overview of the international side, see Gross (1968).

29. As cited in Tully (1980:95); the quotation is from the chapter in Locke's *Second Treatise of Government* entitled on "On Property," emphasis in original. Tully tries to debunk the notion that Locke was an apologist for absolute private property and emergent capitalist relations of production, as argued most forcefully by C. B. Macpherson (1962); but he seems to me to go too far in the opposite direction.

30. Note, however, that Locke defined property very broadly here, to include that in which individuals have rights, including life, liberty, and possessions.

31. Macpherson (1962:80). Macpherson develops this point in his discussion of Hobbes, but subsequently applies it to Locke as well.

32. Cf. Hinsley (1967:242–252, 245): "It was a condition of the discovery of the international version of sovereignty that the notion of Christendom be replaced by

a different understanding of international society—one that was compatible, as the medieval understanding was not, with belief in the sovereignty of the state. . . . there could be no successful international application of the theory until the notion of the sovereign power of the individual state had been reconciled with the ethical principles and the political needs of an international community consisting of independent states."

33. Macpherson (1962, ch. 6). Autonomy, then, which is so often confused with the very term sovereignty, characterizes the ontological basis of the legitimation expressed by sovereignty.

34. See also Bozeman (1960 ch. 13), where the origin, generalization, and acceptance of this "necessity" is traced.

35. At least, that is what I have attempted to show in Ruggie (1982).

36. The term is Zolberg's (1981).

37. My summary perforce is a highly stylized rendering of what is already fairly stylized historical work.

38. For a preliminary and still largely descriptive effort in this direction, see Ruggie (1980). My tentative conclusion in that paper is that greater global dynamic density has produced change in the international framework of states' "private property rights," but that to date this change continues to reflect an underlying determining logic that has not itself changed. Thus far, therefore, it represents an adaptive redeployment of this structural level, not a fundamental rupture in it.

39. This mode of reasoning permeates the last three chapters of Waltz (1979); but see especially pp. 146–160.

40. See, most recently, Rosecrance (1981).

41. Constructing and then adhering to generative structural models are extremely difficult intellectual exercises. Perhaps it is some consolation to know that, according to Lévi-Strauss (1946:528), Durkheim failed too, as a result of which "he oscillates between a dull empiricism and a prioristic frenzy." Waltz's empiricism is never dull.

42. Waltz imputes this unidirectional causality to the structural mode of explanation: "Structural thought conceives of actions simultaneously taking place within a matrix. Change the matrix—the structure of the system—and expected actions and outcomes are altered." Waltz (1982b:35). In point of fact, structural explanations in the social sciences are far more complex, and sometimes even dialectical, as the surveys in Glucksman (1974) and Kurzweil (1980) testify.

43. To avoid any possible misunderstanding, let me add that Waltz does not argue that unit-level phenomena are important for nothing, but that they have no place in systemic theory. In international relations, according to Waltz, they belong to the realm of foreign policy. See his exchange with Richard Rosecrance (Waltz 1982a).

44. For a structural model of international systemic continuity/transformation which stresses the concatenation of "synchronic articulations" and "diachronic processes," and which I find more satisfactory than either Waltz's model or the prevailing alternatives, see Anderson (1974:419–431).

45. For Durkheim, the notion of dynamic density at one and the same time reflected structural effects and aggregated unit-level processes into a systemic variable that in turn affected structure.

SEVEN

Theory of World Politics:
Structural Realism and Beyond

ROBERT O. KEOHANE

FOR OVER 2000 years, what Hans J. Morgenthau dubbed "Political Realism" has constituted the principal tradition for the analysis of international relations in Europe and its offshoots in the New World (Morgenthau 1966). Writers of the Italian Renaissance, balance of power theorists, and later adherents of the school of *Machtpolitik* all fit under a loose version of the Realist rubric. Periodic attacks on Realism have taken place; yet the very focus of these critiques seems only to reconfirm the centrality of Realist thinking in the international political thought of the West.[1]

Realism has been criticized frequently during the last few years, and demands for a "new paradigm" have been made. Joseph S. Nye and I called for a "world politics paradigm" a decade ago, and Richard Mansbach and John A. Vasquez have recently proposed a "new paradigm for global politics." In both these works, the new paradigm that was envisaged entailed adopting additional concepts—for instance, "transnational relations," or "issue phases" (Keohane and Nye 1972, esp. 379–386; Mansbach and Vasquez 1981, ch. 4). Yet for these concepts to be useful as part of a satisfactory general theory of world politics, a theory of state action—which is what Realism purports to provide—is necessary.

I am grateful to Raymond Hopkins for inviting me to prepare the original version of this paper for the American Political Science Association Annual Meeting in Denver, September 1982. A number of ideas presented here were developed with the help of discussions in the graduate international relations field seminar at Brandeis University during the spring semester, 1982, which I taught with my colleague, Robert J. Art. I have also received extremely valuable comments from a number of friends and colleagues on an earlier draft of this paper, in particular from Vinod Aggarwal, David Baldwin, Seyom Brown, Ben Dickinson, Alexander George, Robert Gilpin, Ernst Haas, Thomas Ilgen, Robert Jervis, Peter Katzenstein, Stephen Krasner, Timothy McKeown, Helen Milner, Joseph Nye, and Kenneth Waltz.

Understanding the general principles of state action and the practices of governments is a necessary basis for attempts to refine theory or to extend the analysis to non-state actors. Approaches using new concepts may be able to supplement, enrich, or extend a basic theory of state action, but they cannot substitute for it.[2]

The fixation of critics and reformers on the Realist theory of state action reflects the importance of this research tradition. In my view, there is good reason for this. Realism is a necessary component in a coherent analysis of world politics because its focus on power, interests, and rationality is crucial to any understanding of the subject. Thus any approach to international relations has to incorporate, or at least come to grips with, key elements of Realist thinking. Even writers who are concerned principally with international institutions and rules, or analysts in the Marxist tradition, make use of some Realist premises. Since Realism builds on fundamental insights about world politics and state action, progress in the study of international relations requires that we seek to build on this core.

Yet as we shall see, Realism does not provide a satisfactory theory of world politics, if we require of an adequate theory that it provide a set of plausible and testable answers to questions about state behavior under specified conditions. Realism is particularly weak in accounting for change, especially where the sources of that change lie in the world political economy or in the domestic structures of states. Realism, viewed dogmatically as a set of answers, would be worse than useless. As a sophisticated framework of questions and initial hypotheses, however, it is extremely valuable.[3]

Since Realism constitutes the central tradition in the study of world politics, an analysis, like this one, of the current state of the field must evaluate the viability of Realism in the penultimate decade of the twentieth century. Doing this requires constructing a rather elaborate argument of my own, precluding a comprehensive review of the whole literature of international relations. I have therefore selected for discussion a relatively small number of works that fit my theme, ignoring entire areas of research, much of it innovative.[4] Within the sphere of work dealing with Realism and its limitations, I have focused attention on several especially interesting and valuable contributions. My intention is to point out promising lines of research rather than to engage in what

Stanley Hoffmann once called a "wrecking operation" (Hoffmann 1960:171).

Since I have written on the subject of Realism in the past, I owe the reader an explanation of where I think my views have changed, and where I am only restating, in different ways, opinions that I have expressed before. This chapter deals more systematically and more sympathetically with Realism than does my previous work. Yet its fundamental argument is consistent with that of *Power and Interdependence*. In that book Nye and I relied on Realist theory as a basis for our structural models of international regime change (Keohane and Nye 1977:42–46). We viewed our structural models as attempts to improve the ability of Realist or neo-Realist analysis to account for international regime change: we saw ourselves as adapting Realism, and attempting to go beyond it, rather than rejecting it.

Admittedly, chapter 2 of *Power and Interdependence* characterized Realism as a descriptive ideal type rather than a research program in which explanatory theories could be embedded. Realist and Complex Interdependence ideal types were used to help specify the conditions under which overall structure explanations of change would or would not be valid; the term "Realist" was used to refer to conditions under which states are the dominant actors, hierarchies of issues exist, and force is usable as an instrument of policy (Keohane and Nye 1977:23–29. Taken as a full characterization of the Realist tradition this would have been unfair, and it seems to have led readers concerned with our view of Realism to focus excessively on chapter 2 and too little on the attempt, which draws on what I here call structural realism, to account for regime change (chapters 3–6).[5]

To provide criteria for the evaluation of theoretical work in international politics—Structural Realism, in particular—I employ the conception of a "scientific research programme" explicated in 1970 by the philosopher of science Imre Lakatos (1970). Lakatos developed this concept as a tool for the comparative evaluation of scientific theories, and in response to what he regarded as the absence of standards for evaluation in Thomas Kuhn's (1962) notion of a paradigm.[6] Theories are embedded in research programs. These programs contain inviolable assumptions (the "hard core") and initial conditions, defining their scope. For Lakatos, they also include two other very important elements: auxiliary, or observational, hypotheses, and a "positive heuristic," which tells the scientist what sorts of additional hypotheses to entertain and how to go about conducting research. In short, a research program is a set of methodological rules telling us what paths of research to avoid and what paths to follow.

Consider a research program, with a set of observational hypotheses, a "hard core" of irrefutable assumptions, and a set of scope conditions. In the course of research, anomalies are bound to appear sooner or later: predictions of the theory will seem to be falsified. For Lakatos, the reaction of scientists developing the research program is to protect the hard core by constructing auxiliary hypotheses that will explain the anomalies. Yet any research program, good or bad, can invent such auxiliary hypotheses on an *ad hoc* basis. The key test for Lakatos of the value of a research program is whether these auxiliary hypotheses are "progressive," that is, whether their invention leads to the discovery of *new facts* (other than the anomalous facts that they were designed to explain). Progressive research programs display "continuous growth": their auxiliary hypotheses increase our capacity to understand reality (Lakatos 1970:116–122, 132–138, 173–180).

Lakatos developed this conception to assess developments in the natural sciences, particularly physics. If we took literally the requirements that he laid down for "progressive" research programs, all actual theories of international politics—and perhaps all conceivable theories—would fail the test. Indeed, it has been argued that much of economics, including oligopoly theory (heavily relied upon by Structural Realists), fails to meet this standard (Latsis 1976). Nevertheless, Lakatos's conception has the great merit of providing clear and sensible criteria for the evaluation of scientific traditions, and of asking penetrating questions that may help us to see Realism in a revealing light. Lakatos's questions are relevant, even if applying them without modification could lead to premature rejection not only of Realism, but of our whole field, or even the entire discipline of political science![7]

The stringency of Lakatos's standards suggests that we should supplement this test with a "softer," more interpretive one. That is, how much insight does Realism provide into contemporary world politics?

For this line of evaluation we can draw inspiration from Clifford Geertz's discussion of the role of theory in anthropology. Geertz argues that culture "is not a power, something to which social events, behaviors, institutions, or processes can be causally attributed; it is a context—something within which they can be intelligibly—that is, thickly—described" (1973:14). The role of theory, he claims, is "not to codify abstract regularities but to make thick description possible, not to generalize across cases but to generalize within them" (ibid., p. 26). This conception is the virtual antithesis of the standards erected by Lakatos, and could all too easily serve as a rationalization for the proliferation of atheoretical case studies. Nevertheless, culture as discussed by Geertz has something in common with the international system as discussed by students of world politics. It is difficult to generalize across systems. We are continually bedeviled by the paucity of comparable cases, particularly when making systemic statements—for example, about the operation of balances of power. Much of what students of world politics do, and what Classical Realism in particular aspires to, is to make the actions of states understandable (despite obfuscatory statements by their spokesmen): that is, in Geertz's words, to provide "a context within which they can be intelligibly described." For example, Morgenthau's discussion of the concept of interest defined in terms of power, quoted at length below, reflects this objective more than the goal of arriving at testable generalizations.

This essay is divided into four major sections. The first of these seeks to establish the basis for a dual evaluation of Realism: as a source of interpretive insights into the operation of world politics, and as a scientific research program that enables the investigator to discover new facts. I examine the argument of Thucydides and Morgenthau to extract the key assumptions of Classical Realism. Then I discuss recent work by Kenneth N. Waltz, whom I regard as the most systematic spokesman for contemporary Structural Realism.

Section II addresses the question of interpretation and puzzle-solving within the Realist tradition. How successful are Realist thinkers in making new contributions to our understanding of world politics? In Section III, I consider the shortcomings of Realism when judged by the standards that Lakatos establishes, or even when evaluated by less rigorous criteria, and begin to ask whether a modified version of Structural Realism could correct some of these faults. Section IV carries this theme further by attempting to outline how a multidimensional research program, including a modified structural theory, might be devised; what its limitations would be; and how it could be relevant, in particular, to problems of peaceful change.

The conclusion emphasizes the issue of peaceful change as both a theoretical and a practical problem. Realism raises the question of how peaceful change could be achieved, but does not resolve it. Understanding the conditions under which peaceful change would be facilitated remains, in my view, the most urgent task facing students of world politics.

I. STRUCTURAL REALISM AS RESEARCH PROGRAM

To explicate the research program of Realism, I begin with two classic works, one ancient, the other modern: *The Peloponnesian War,* by Thucydides, and *Politics Among Nations,* by Morgenthau.[8] The three most fundamental Realist assumptions are evident in these books: that the most important actors in world politics are territorially organized entities (city-states or modern states); that state behavior can be explained rationally; and that states seek power and calculate their interests in terms of power, relative to the nature of the international system that they face.

The Peloponnesian War was written in an attempt to explain the causes of the great war of the Fifth Century B.C. between the coalition led by Athens and its adversaries, led by Sparta. Thucydides assumes that to achieve this purpose, he must explain the behavior of the major city-states involved in the conflict. Likewise, Morgenthau assumes that the subject of a science of international politics is the behavior of states. Realism is "state-centric."[9]

Both authors also believed that observers of world politics could understand events by imagining themselves, as rational individuals, in authoritative positions, and reflecting on what they would do if faced with the problems encountered by the actual decisionmakers. They both, therefore, employ the method of *rational reconstruction.* Thucydides admits that he does not have transcripts of all the major speeches given during the war, but he is undaunted:

> It was in all cases difficult to carry [the speeches] word for word in one's memory, so my habit has been to make the speakers say what was in my opinion demanded of them by the various occasions, of course adhering as closely as possible to the general sense of what they really

said. (Thucydides, Book I, paragraph 23 [Chapter I, Modern Library edition, p. 14])

Morgenthau argues that in trying to understand foreign policy,

> We put ourselves in the position of a statesman who must meet a certain problem of foreign policy under certain circumstances, and we ask ourselves what the rational alternatives are from which a statesman may choose . . . and which of these rational alternatives this particular statesman, acting under these circumstances, is likely to choose. It is the testing of this rational hypothesis against the actual facts and their consequences that gives meaning to the facts of international politics and makes a theory of politics possible. (Morgenthau 1966:5)

In reconstructing state calculations, Thucydides and Morgenthau both assume that states will act to protect their power positions, perhaps even to the point of seeking to maximize their power. Thucydides seeks to go beneath the surface of events to the power realities that are fundamental to state action:

> The real cause [of the war] I consider to be the one which was formally most kept out of sight. *The growth in the power of Athens, and the alarm which this inspired in Lacedemon, made war inevitable* (Thucydides, Book I, paragraph 24 [Chapter I, Modern Library edition, p. 15]).[10]

Morgenthau is even more blunt: "International politics, like all politics, is a struggle for power" (1966:25; see also Morgenthau 1946). Political Realism, he argues, understands international politics through the concept of "interest defined as power":

> We assume that statesmen think and act in terms of interest defined as power, and the evidence of history bears that assumption out. That assumption allows us to retrace and anticipate, as it were, the steps a statesman—past, present, or future—has taken or will take on the political scene. We look over his shoulder when he writes his dispatches; we listen in on his conversation with other statesmen; we read and anticipate his very thoughts. (1966:5)

The three assumptions just reviewed define the hard core of the Classical Realist research program:

(1) The *state-centric assumption*: states are the most important actors in world politics;

(2) The *rationality assumption*: world politics can be analyzed as if states were unitary rational actors, carefully calculating costs of alternative courses of action and seeking to maximize their expected utility, although doing so under conditions of uncertainty and without necessarily having sufficient information about alternatives or resources (time or otherwise) to conduct a full review of all possible courses of action;[11]

(3) The *power assumption*: states seek power (both the ability to influence others and resources that can be used to exercise influence); and they calculate their interests in terms of power, whether as end or as necessary means to a variety of other ends.

More recently, Kenneth N. Waltz (1959) has attempted to reformulate and systematize Realism on the basis of what he called, in *Man, the State and War*, a "third image" perspective. This form of Realism does not rest on the presumed iniquity of the human race—original sin in one form or another—but on the nature of world politics as an anarchic realm:

> Each state pursues its own interests, however defined, in ways it judges best. Force is a means of achieving the external ends of states because there exists no consistent, reliable process of reconciling the conflicts of interests that inevitably arise among similar units in a condition of anarchy. (p. 238)[12]

Even well-intentioned statesmen find that they must use or threaten force to attain their objectives.

Since the actions of states are conceived of as resulting from the nature of international politics, the paramount theoretical task for Realists is to create a *systemic* explanation of international politics. In a systemic theory, as Waltz explains it, the propositions of the theory specify relationships between certain aspects of the system and actor behavior (1979:67–73). Waltz's third-image Realism, for instance, draws connections between the distribution of power in a system and the actions of states: small countries will behave differently than large ones, and in a balance of power system, alliances can be expected to shift in response to changes in power relationships. Any theory will, of course, take into account the attributes of actors, as well as features of the system itself. But the key distinguishing characteristic of a systemic theory is that *the internal attributes of actors are given by assumption rather than treated as variables.* Changes in actor behavior, and system outcomes, are explained not on the basis of variations in these actor characteristics, but on the basis of changes in the attributes of the system itself. A good example of such a systemic theory is microeconomic theory in its standard form. It posits the existence of business firms, with given utility functions (such as profit maximization), and attempts to explain their behavior on the basis of environmental factors such as the competitiveness of markets. It is systemic because its propositions about variations in behavior depend on variations in characteristics of the system, not of the units (Waltz 1979:89–91, 93–95, 98).

To develop a systemic analysis, abstraction is necessary: one has to avoid being distracted by the details and vagaries of domestic politics and other variables at the level of the acting unit. To reconstruct a systemic research program, therefore, Structural Realists must devide a way to explain state behavior on the basis of systemic characteristics, and to account for outcomes in the same manner. This needs to be a coherent explanation, although it need not tell us everything we would like to know about world politics.

Waltz's formulation of Structural Realism as a systemic theory seeks to do this by developing a concept not explicitly used by Morgenthau or Thucydides: the *structure* of the international system. Two elements of international structure are constants: (1) the international system is anarchic rather than hierarchic, and (2) it is characterized by interaction among units with similar functions. These are such enduring background characteristics that they are constitutive of what we mean by "international politics."[14] The third element of structure, the distribution of capabilities across the states in the system, varies from system to system, and over time. Since it is a variable, this element—the distribution of "power"—takes on particular importance in the theory. The most significant capabilities are those of the most powerful actors. Structures "are defined not by all of the actors that flourish within them but by the major ones" (Waltz 1979:93).

According to Waltz, structure is the principal determinant of outcomes at the systems level: structure encourages certain actions and discourages others. It may also lead to unintended consequences, as the ability of states to obtain their objectives is constrained by the power of others (1979:104–111).

For Waltz, understanding the structure of an international system allows us to explain patterns of state behavior, since states determine their interests and strategies on the basis of calculations about their own positions in the system. The link between system structure and actor behavior is forged by the rationality assumption, which enables the theorist to predict that leaders will respond to the incentives and constraints imposed by their environments. Taking rationality as a constant permits one to attribute variations in state behavior to variations in characteristics of the international system. Otherwise, state behavior might have to be accounted for by variations in the calculating ability of states; in that case, the systemic focus of Structural Realism (and much of its explanatory power) would be lost. Thus the rationality assumption—as we will see in examining Waltz's balance of power theory—is essential to the theoretical claims of Structural Realism.[15]

The most parsimonious version of a structural theory would hold that any international system has a single structure of power. In such a conceptualization, power resources are homogeneous and fungible: they can be used to achieve results on any of a variety of issues without significant loss of efficacy. Power in politics becomes like money in economics: "in many respects, power and influence play the same role in international politics as money does in a market economy" (Wolfers 1962:105).

In its strong form, the Structural Realist research program is similar to that of microeconomics. Both use the rationality assumption to permit inferences about actor behavior to be made from system structure. The Realist definition of interests in terms of power and position is like the economist's assumption that firms seek to maximize profits: it provides the utility function of the actor. Through these assumptions, actor characteristics become constant rather than variable, and systemic theory becomes possible.[16] The additional assumption of power fungibility simplifies the theory further: on the basis of a *single* characteristic of the international system (overall power capabilities), *multiple* inferences can be drawn about actor behavior and outcomes. "Foreknowledge"—that aspiration of all theory—is thereby attained (Eckstein 1975:88–89). As we will see below, pure Structural Realism provides an insufficient basis for explaining state interests and behavior, even when the rationality assumption is accepted; and the fungibility assumption is highly questionable. Yet the Structural Realist research program is an impressive intellectual achievement: an elegant, parsimonious, deductively rigorous instrument for scientific discovery. The anomalies that it generates are more interesting than its own predictions; but as Lakatos emphasizes, it is the exploration of anomalies that moves science forward.

Richard K. Ashley has recently argued that Structural Realism—which he calls "technical realism"—actually represents a regression from the classical Realism of Herz or Morgenthau.[17] In his view, contemporary Realist thinkers have forgotten the importance of subjective self-reflection, and the dialectic between subjectivity and objectivity, which are so important in the writings of "practical," or "classical" realists such as Thucydides and Morgenthau. Classical Realism for Ashley is interpretive: "a practical tradition of statesmen is the real subject whose language of experience the interpreter tries to make his own" (1981:221). It is self-reflective and nondeterministic. It treats the concept of balance of power as a dialectical relation: not merely as an objective characterization of the international system but also as a collectively recognized orienting scheme for strategic action. Classical Realism encompasses the unity of opposites, and draws interpetive insight from recognizing the dialectical quality of human experience. Thus its proponents understand that the state system is problematic, and that "strategic artistry" is required to keep it in existence (Ashley 1982:22).

The problem with Classical Realism is that it is difficult to distinguish what Ashley praises as dialectical insight from a refusal to define concepts clearly and consistently, or to develop a systematic set of propositions that could be subjected to empirical tests. Structural Realism seeks to correct these flaws, and thus to construct a more rigorous theoretical framework for the study of world politics, while drawing on the concepts and insights of the older Realism. Structural Realism, as embodied particularly in the work of Waltz, is more systematic and logically more coherent than that of its Classical Realist predecessors. By its own standards, Structural Realism is, in Ashley's words, "a progressive scientific redemption of classical realism" (Ashley 1982:25). That is, it sees itself, and Classical Realism, as elements of a continuous research tradition.

Ashley complains that this form of Realism objectifies reality, and that in particular it regards the state as unproblematic. This leads, in his view, to some pernicious implications: that the interests expressed by dominant elites must be viewed as legitimate, that economic rationality is the highest form of thought, and that individuals are not responsible for the production of insecurity (1982:34–41). But Structural Realists need not make any of these claims. It is true that Structural Realism seeks to understand the limits of, and constraints on, human action in world politics. It emphasizes the strength of these constraints, and in that sense could be considered "conservative." But an analysis of constraints, far from implying an acceptance of the *status quo,* should be seen as a precondition to sensible attempts to change the world. To be self-reflective, human action must take place with an understanding of the context within which it occurs. Structural Realists can be criticized, as we will see, for paying insufficient attention to norms, institutions, and change. But this represents less a fault of Structural Realism as such than a failure of some of its advocates to transcend its categories. Structural Realism's focus on systemic constraints does not contradict classical Realism's concern with action and choice. On the contrary, Classical Realism's emphasis on *praxis* helps us to understand the origins of Structural Realism's search for systematic understanding, and—far from negating the importance of this search—makes it seem all the more important.

I have argued thus far that Structural Realism is at the center of contemporary international relations theory in the United States; that it constitutes an attempt to systematize Classical Realism; and that its degree of success as a theory can be legitimately evaluated in part according to standards such as those laid down by Lakatos, and in part through evaluation of its capacity to generate insightful interpretations of international political behavior. Two distinct tests, each reflecting one aspect of this dualistic evaluative standard, can be devised to evaluate Structural Realism as a research program for international relations:

(1) How "fruitful" is the Realist paradigm for puzzle-solving and interpretation of world politics (Toulmin 1963)? That is, does current work in the Realist tradition make us see issues more clearly, or provide answers to formerly unsolved puzzles? Realism was designed to provide insights into such issues, and if it remains a live tradition, should continue to do so.

(2) Does Realism meet the standards of a scientific research program as enunciated by Lakatos? To answer this question, it is important to remind ourselves that the hard core of a research program is irrefutable within the terms of the paradigm. When anomalies arise that appear to challenge Realist assumptions, the task of Realist analysts is to create

auxiliary theories that defend them. These theories permit explanation of anomalies consistent with Realist assumptions. For Lakatos, the key question about a research program concerns whether the auxiliary hypotheses of Realism are "progressive." That is, do they generate new insights, or predict new facts? If not, they are merely exercises in "patching up" gaps or errors on an ad hoc basis, and the research program is degenerative.

Realism cannot be judged fairly on the basis of only one set of standards. Section II addresses the question of fruitfulness by examining works in the central area of Realist theory: the study of conflict, bargaining, and war. Section II then judges Realism by the more difficult test of Lakatos, which (as noted above) is better at asking trenchant questions than at defining a set of standards appropriate to social science. We will see that in one sense Realism survives these tests, since it still appears as a good starting point for analysis. But it does not emerge either as a comprehensive theory or as a progressive research program in the sense employed by Lakatos. Furthermore, it has difficulty interpreting issues, and linkages among issues, outside of the security sphere: it can even be misleading when applied to these issues without sufficient qualification. It also has little to say about the crucially important question of peaceful change. The achievements of Realism, and the prospect that it can be modified further to make it even more useful, should help students of world politics to avoid unnecessary self-deprecation. Yet they certainly do not justify complacency.

II. PROGRESS WITHIN THE REALISM PARADIGM: THREE ACHIEVEMENTS

The fruitfulness of contemporary Realist analysis is best evaluated by considering some of the finest work in the genre. Poor scholarship can derive from even the best research program; only the most insightful work reveals the strengths as well as the limits of a theoretical approach. In this section I will consider three outstanding examples of works that begin, at least, from Realist concerns and assumptions: Waltz's construction of balance of power theory in *Theory of International Politics* (1979); the attempt by Glenn Snyder and Paul Diesing in *Conflict Among Nations*

(1977) to apply formal game-theoretic models of bargaining to sixteen case studies of major-power crises during the seventy-five years between Fashoda and the Yom Kippur "alert crisis" of 1973; and Robert Gilpin's fine recent work, *War and Change in World Politics* (1981). These works are chosen to provide us with one systematic attempt to develop structural Realist theory, one study of bargaining in specific cases, and one effort to understand broad patterns of international political change. Other recent works could have been chosen instead, such as three books on international conflict and crises published in 1980 or 1981 (Brecher 1980; Bueno de Mesquita 1981; Lebow 1981), or the well-known works by Nazli Choucri and Robert C. North (1975) or by Alexander George and Richard Smoke (1974). But there are limits on what can be done in a single chapter of limited size.

Balance of Power Theory: Waltz

Waltz has explicated balance of power theory as a central element in his Structural Realist synthesis: "If there is any distinctively political theory of international politics, balance of power theory is it" (1979:117). The realization that balances of power periodically form in world politics, is an old one, as are attempts to theorize about it. The puzzle that Waltz addresses is how to "cut through such confusion" as has existed about it: that is, in Kuhn's words, how to "achieve the anticipated in a new way" (1962:36).

Waltz attacks this problem by using the concept of structure, which he has carefully developed earlier in the book, and which he also employs to account for the dreary persistence of patterns of international action (1979:66–72). Balance of power theory applies to "anarchic" realms, which are formally unorganized and in which, therefore, units have to worry about their survival: "Self-help is necessarily the principle of action in an anarchic order" (p. 111). In Waltz's system, states (which are similar to one another in function) are the relevant actors; they use external as well as internal means to achieve their goals. Relative capabilities are (as we saw above) the variable element of structure; as they change, we expect coalitional patterns or patterns of internal effort to be altered as well. From his assumptions, given the condition for the theory's operation (self-help), Waltz deduces "the expected outcome; namely, the formation of balances of power" (p. 118). His solution to the puzzle that he has set for himself is carefully formulated and ingenious.

Nevertheless, Waltz's theory of the balance of power encounters some difficulties. First, it is difficult for him to state precisely the conditions under which coalitions will change. He only forecasts that balances of power will periodically recur. Indeed, his theory is so general that it hardly meets the difficult tests that he himself establishes for theory. In chapter 1 we are told that to test a theory, one must "device a number of distinct and demanding tests" (1979:13). But such tests are not proposed for balance of power theory: "Because only a loosely defined and inconstant condition of balance is predicted, it is difficult to say that any given distribution of power falsifies the theory" (p. 124). Thus rather than applying demanding tests, Waltz advises that we "should seek *confirmation* through observation of difficult cases" (p. 125, emphasis added). In other words, he counsels that we should search through history to find examples that conform to the predictions of the theory; he then proclaims that "these examples tend to confirm the theory" (p. 125). Two pages later, Waltz appears to change his view, admitting that "we can almost always find confirming cases if we look hard." We should correct for this by looking "for instances of states conforming to common international practices even though for internal reasons they would prefer not to" (p. 127). But Waltz is again making an error against which he warns us. He is not examining a universe of cases, in all of which states would prefer not to conform to "international practice," and asking how often they nevertheless do conform. Instead, he is looking only at the latter cases, chosen *because* they are consistent with his theory. Building grand theory that meets Popperian standards of scientific practice is inherently difficult; even the best scholars, such as Waltz, have trouble simultaneously saying what they want to say and abiding by their canons of scientific practice.

Waltz's theory is also ambiguous with respect to the status of three assumptions that are necessary to a strong form of Structural Realism. I have already mentioned the difficult problem of whether a structural theory must (implausibly) assume fungibility of power resources. Since this problem is less serious with respect to balance of power theory than in a broader context, I will not pursue it here, but will return to it in

Section III. Yet Waltz is also, in his discussion of balances of power, unclear on the questions of rationality and interests.

Waltz argues that his assumptions do not include the rationality postulate: "The theory says simply that if some do relatively well, others will emulate them or fall by the wayside" (p. 118). This evolutionary principle, however, can hold only for systems with many actors, experiencing such severe pressure on resources that many will disappear over time. Waltz undermines this argument by pointing out later (p. 137) that "the death rate for states is remarkably low." Furthermore, he relies explicitly on the rationality principle to show that bipolar balances must be stable. "Internal balancing," he says, "is more reliable and precise than external balancing. States are less likely to misjudge their relative strengths than they are to misjudge the strength and reliability of opposing coalitions" (p. 168). I conclude that Waltz does rely on the rationality argument, despite his earlier statement to the contrary.

The other ambiguity in Waltz's balance of power theory has to do with the interests, or motivations, of states. Waltz recognizes that any theory of state behavior must ascribe (by assumption) some motivations to states, just as microeconomic theory ascribes motivations to firms. It is not reductionist to do so as long as these motivations are not taken as varying from state to state as a result of their internal characteristics. Waltz specifies such motivations: states "at a minimum, seek their own preservation, and at a maximum, drive for universal domination" (p. 118).

For his balance of power theory to work, Waltz needs to assume that states seek self-preservation, since if at least some major states did not do so, there would be no reason to expect that roughly equivalent coalitions (i.e., "balances of power") would regularly form. The desire for self-preservation makes states that are behind in a struggle for power try harder, according to Waltz and leads states allied to a potential hegemon to switch coalitions in order to construct balances of power. Neither of these processes on which Waltz relies to maintain a balance— intensified effort by the weaker country in a bipolar system and coalition formation against potentially dominant states in a multipolar system— could operate reliably without this motivation.

The other aspect of Waltz's motivational assumption—that states "at a maximum, drive for universal domination," is reminiscent of the implication of Realists such as Morgenthau that states seek to "maximize power." For a third-image Realist theory such as Waltz's, such an assumption is unnecessary. Waltz's defense of it is that the balance of power depends on the possibility that force may be used. But this possibility is an attribute of the self-help international system, for Waltz, rather than a reflection of the actors' characteristics. That some states seek universal domination is not a necessary condition for force to be used.

This ambiguity in Waltz's analysis points toward a broader ambiguity in Realist thinking: *Balance of power theory is inconsistent with the assumption frequently made by Realists that states "maximize power,"* if power is taken to refer to tangible resources that can be used to induce other actors to do what they would not otherwise do, through the threat or infliction of deprivations.[18] States concerned with self-preservation do not seek to maximize their power when they are not in danger. On the contrary, they recognize a trade-off between aggrandizement and self-preservation; they realize that a relentless search for universal domination may jeopardize their own autonomy. Thus they moderate their efforts when their positions are secure. Conversely, they intensify their efforts when danger arises, which assumes that they were not maximizing them under more benign conditions.

One might have thought that Realists would readily recognize this point, yet they seem drawn against their better judgment to the "power maximization" or "universal domination" hypotheses. In part, this may be due to their anxiety to emphasize the significance of force in world politics. Yet there may be theoretical as well as rhetorical reasons for their ambivalence. The assumption of power maximization makes possible strong inferences about behavior that would be impossible if we assumed only that states "sometimes" or "often" sought to aggrandize themselves. In that case, we would have to ask about competing goals, some of which would be generated by the internal social, political, and economic characteristics of the countries concerned. Taking into account these competing goals relegates Structural Realism to the status of partial, incomplete theory.

Waltz's contribution to the study of world politics is conceptual. He helps us think more clearly about the role of systemic theory, the explanatory power of structural models, and how to account deductively for the recurrent formation of balances of power. He shows that the international system shapes state behavior as well as vice versa. These are major contributions. But Waltz does not point out "new ways of seeing" international relations that point toward major novelties. He reformulates and systematizes Realism, and thus develops what I have called Structural Realism, consistently with the fundamental assumptions of his classical predecessors.

Game Theory, Structure, and Bargaining: Snyder and Diesing

Game theory has yielded some insights into issues of negotiations, crises, and limited war, most notably in the early works of Thomas Schelling (1960). Snyder and Diesing's contribution to this line of analysis, as they put it, is to "distinguish and analyze nine different kinds of bargaining situations, each one a unique combination of power and interest relations between the bargainers, each therefore having its own dynamics and problems" (1977:181–182). They employ their game-theoretic formulations of these nine situations, within an explicit structural context, to analyze sixteen historical cases.

This research design is consistent with the hard core of Realism. Attention is concentrated on the behavior of states. In the initial statement of the problem, the rationality assumption, in suitably modest form, is retained: each actor attempts "to maximize expected value across a given set of consistently ordered objectives, given the information actually available to the actor or which he could reasonably acquire in the time available for decision" (p. 181). Interests are defined to a considerable extent in terms of power: that is, power factors are built into the game structure. In the game of "Protector," for instance, the more powerful state can afford to "go it alone" without its ally, and thus has an interest in doing so under certain conditions, whereas its weaker partner cannot (pp. 145–147). Faced with the game matrix, states, as rational actors, calculate their interests and act accordingly. The structure of world politics, as Waltz defines it, is reflected in the matrices and becomes the basis for action.

If structural Realism formed a sufficient basis for the understanding of international crises, we could fill in the entries in the matrices solely on the basis of states' positions in the international system, given our knowledge of the fact that they perform "similar functions," including the need to survive as autonomous entities. Interests would indeed be defined in terms of power. This would make game theory a powerful analytic tool, which could even help us predict certain outcomes. Where the game had no unique solution (because of strategic indeterminacy), complete predictability of outcomes could not be achieved, but our expectations about the range of likely action would have been narrowed.

Yet Snyder and Diesing find that even knowledge of the values and goals of top leaders could not permit them to determine the interests of about half the decision-making units in their cases. In the other cases, one needed to understand intragovernmental politics, even when one ignored the impact of wider domestic political factors (pp. 510–511). The "internal-external interaction" is a key to the understanding of crisis bargaining.

As Snyder and Diesing make their analytical framework more complex and move into detailed investigation of their cases, their focus shifts toward concern with cognition and with the effects on policy of ignorance, misperception, and misinformation. In my view, the most creative and insightful of their chapters use ideas developed largely by Robert Jervis (1976) to analyze information processing and decision-making. These chapters shift the focus of attention away from the systemic-level factors reflected in the game-theoretic matrices, toward problems of perception, personal bias, and group decision-making (Snyder and Diesing 1977, chapters 4 and 5).

Thus Snyder and Diesing begin with the hard core of Realism, but their most important contributions depend on their willingness to depart from these assumptions. They are dissatisfied with their initial game-theoretic classificatory scheme. They prefer to explore information processing and decision-making, without a firm deductive theory on which to base their arguments, rather than merely to elucidate neat logical typologies.

Is the work of Snyder and Diesing a triumph of Realism or a defeat? At this point in the argument, perhaps the most that can be said is that it indicates that work in the Realist tradition, analyzing conflict and bargaining with the concepts of interests and power, continues to be fruitful, but it does not give reason for much confidence that adhering strictly to Realist assumptions will lead to important advances in the field.

Cycles of Hegemony and War: Gilpin

In *War and Change in World Politics,* Gilpin uses Realist assumptions to reinterpret the last 2400 years of Western history. Gilpin assumes that states, as the principal actors in world politics, make cost-benefit calculations about alternative courses of action. For instance, states attempt to change the international system as the expected benefits of so doing exceed the costs. Thus, the rationality assumption is applied explicitly, in a strong form, although it is relaxed toward the end of the book (1981b:77, 202). Furthermore, considerations of power, relative to the structure of the international system, are at the core of the calculations made by Gilpin's states: "the distribution of power among states constitutes the principal form of control in every international system" (p. 29). Thus Gilpin accepts the entire hard core of the classical Realist research program as I have defined it.[19]

Gilpin sees world history as an unending series of cycles: "The conclusion of one hegemonic war is the beginning of another cycle of growth, expansion, and eventual decline" (p. 210). As power is redistributed, power relations become inconsistent with the rules governing the system and, in particular, the hierarchy of prestige; war establishes the new hierarchy of prestige and "thereby determines which states will in effect govern the international system" (p. 33).

The view that the rules of a system, and the hierarchy of prestige, must be consistent with underlying power realities is a fundamental proposition of Realism, which follows from its three core assumptions. If states, as the central actors of international relations, calculate their interests in terms of power, they will seek international rules and institutions that are consistent with these interests by maintaining their power. Waltz's conception of structure helps to systematize this argument, but it is essentially static. What Gilpin adds is a proposed solution to the anomalies (for static Realism) that institutions and rules can become inconsistent with power realities over time, and that hegemonic states eventually decline. If, as Realists argue, "the strong do what they can and the weak suffer what they must" (Thucydides, Book V, paragraph 90 [Chapter XVII, Modern Library Edition, p. 331]), why should hegemons ever lose their power? We know that rules do not always reinforce the power of the strong and that hegemons do sometimes lose their hold, but static Realist theory cannot explain this.

In his attempt to explain hegemonic decline, Gilpin formulates a "law of uneven growth":

> According to Realism, the fundamental cause of wars among states and changes in international systems is the uneven growth of power among states. Realist writers from Thucydides and MacKinder to present-day scholars have attributed the dynamics of international relations to the fact that the distribution of power in an international system shifts over a period of time; this shift results in profound changes in the relationships among the states and eventually changes in the nature of the international system itself. (p. 94)

This law, however, restates the problem without resolving it. In accounting for this pattern, Gilpin relies on three sets of processes. One has to do with increasing, and then diminishing, marginal returns from empire. As empires grew, "the economic surplus had to increase faster than cost of war" (p. 115). Yet sooner or later, diminishing returns set in: "the law of diminishing returns has universal applicability and causes the growth of every society to describe an S-shaped curve" (p. 159). Secondly, hegemonic states tend increasingly to consume more and invest less; Gilpin follows the lead of Carlo Cipolla in viewing this as a general pattern in history (Cipolla 1970). Finally, hegemonic states decline because of a process of diffusion of technology to others. In *U.S. Power and Multinational Corporation* (1975), Gilpin emphasized this process as contributing first to the decline of Britain, then in the 1970s to that of the United States. In *War and Change* he makes the argument more general:

> Through a process of diffusion to other states, the dominant power loses the advantage on which its political, military, or economic success has been based. Thus, by example, and frequently in more direct fashion, the dominant power helps to create challenging powers. (p. 176)

This third argument is systemic, and, therefore, fully consistent with Waltz's Structural Realism. The other two processes, however, reflect the operation of forces within the society as well as international forces. A hegemonic power may suffer diminishing returns as a result of the expansion of its defense perimeter and the increased military costs that result (Gilpin 1981b:191; Luttwak 1976). But whether diminishing returns set in also depends on internal factors such as technological inventiveness of members of the society and the institutions that affect incentives for innovation (North 1981). The tendency of hegemonic states to consume more and invest less is also, in part, a function of their dominant positions in the world system: they can force costs of adjustment to change onto others, at least for some time. But it would be hard to deny that the character of the society affects popular tastes for luxury, and, therefore, the tradeoffs between guns and butter that are made. Eighteenth-century Saxony and Prussia were different in this regard; so are contemporary America and Japan. In Gilpin's argument as in Snyder and Diesing's, the "external-internal interaction" becomes a crucial factor in explaining state action, and change.

Gilpin explicitly acknowledges his debt to Classical Realism: "In honesty, one must inquire whether or not twentieth-century students of international relations know anything that Thucydides and his fifth-century compatriots did not know about the behavior of states" (p. 227). For Gilpin as for Thucydides, changes in power lead to changes in relations among states: the *real* cause of the Peloponnesian War, for Thucydides, was the rise of the power of Athens and the fear this evoked in the Spartans and their allies. Gilpin has generalized the theory put forward by Thucydides to explain the Peloponnesian War, and has applied it to the whole course of world history:

> Disequilibrium replaces equilibrium, and the world moves toward a new round of hegemonic conflict. It has always been thus and always will be, until men either destroy themselves or learn to develop an effective mechanism of peaceful change. (p. 210)

This Thucydides-Gilpin theory is a systemic theory of change only in a limited sense. It explains the *reaction* to change systematically, in a rationalistic, equilibrium model. Yet at a more fundamental level, it does not account fully for the sources of change. As we saw above, although it is insightful about systemic factors to hegemonic decline, it also has to rely on internal processes to explain the observed effects. Furthermore, it does not account well for the rise of hegemons in the first place, or for the fact that certain contenders emerge rather than others.[20] Gilpin's systemic theory does not account for the extraordinary bursts of energy that occasionally catapult particular countries into dominant positions on the world scene. Why were the Athenians, in words that Thucydides attributes to Corinthian envoys to Sparta, "addicted to innovation," whereas the Spartans were allegedly characterized by a "total want of invention" (Thucydides, Book I, paragraph 70 [Chapter III, Modern Library edition, p. 40])? Like other structural theories, Gilpin's theory underpredicts outcomes. It contributes to our understanding but (as its author recognizes) does not explain change.

This is particularly true of peaceful change, which Gilpin identifies as a crucial issue: "The fundamental problem of international relations in the contemporary world is the problem of peaceful adjustment to the consequences of the uneven growth of power among states, just as it was in the past" (p. 230).

Gilpin's book, like much contemporary American work on international politics, is informed and propelled by concern with peaceful change under conditions of declining hegemony. Gilpin sympathetically discusses E. H. Carr's "defense of peaceful change as the solution to the problem of hegemonic war," written just before World War II (Gilpin, p. 206; Carr 1939/1946). Yet peaceful change does not fit easily into Gilpin's analytical framework, since it falls, by and large, into the category of "interactions change," which does not entail alteration in the overall hierarchy of power and prestige in a system, and Gilpin deliberately avoids focusing on interactions change (p. 44). Yet after one puts down *War and Change,* the question of how institutions and rules can be developed *within* a given international system, to reduce the probability of war and promote peaceful change, looms even larger than it did before.

Thus Gilpin's sophisticated adaptation of Classical Realism turns us away from Realism. Classical Realism, with its philosophical roots in a tragic conception of the human condition, directs our attention in the twentieth century to the existential situation of modern humanity, doomed apparently to recurrent conflict in a world with weapons that could destroy life on our planet. But Realism, whether classical or structural, has little to say about how to deal with that situation, since it offers few insights into the international rules and institutions that people invent to reduce risk and uncertainty in world affairs, in the hope of ameliorating the security dilemma.[21] Morgenthau put his hopes in diplomacy (1966 ch. 32). This is a practical art, far removed from the abstractions of structural Realism. But diplomacy takes place within a context of international rules, institutions, and practices, which affect the incentives of the actors (Keohane 1982b). Gilpin realizes this, and his gloomy argument—hardly alleviated by a more optimistic epilogue—helps us to understand their importance, although it does not contribute to an explanation of their creation or demise.

Conclusions

Realism, as developed through a long tradition dating from Thucydides, continues to provide the basis for valuable research in international relations. This point has been made by looking at writers who explicitly draw on the Realist tradition, and it can be reinforced by briefly examining some works of Marxist scholars. If they incorporate elements of Realism despite their general antipathy to its viewpoint, our conclusion that Realism reflects enduring realities of world politics will be reinforced.

For Marxists, the fundamental forces affecting world politics are those of class struggle and uneven development. International history is dynamic and dialectical rather than cyclical. The maneuvers of states, on which Realism focuses, reflect the stages of capitalist development and the contradictions of that development. Nevertheless, in analyzing the surface manifestations of world politics under capitalism, Marxists adopt similar categories to those of Realists. Power is crucial; world systems are periodically dominated by hegemonic powers wielding both economic and military resources.

Lenin defined imperialism differently than do the Realists, but he analyzed its operation in part as a Realist would, arguing that "there can be *no* other conceivable basis under capitalism for the division of spheres of influence, of interests, of colonies, etc. than a calculation of the *strength* of the participants in the division." (Lenin 1916/1939:119).

Immanuel Wallerstein provides another example of my point. He goes to some effort to stress that modern world history should be seen as the history of capitalism as a world system. Apart from "relatively minor accidents" provided by geography, peculiarities of history, or luck—which give one country an edge over over others at crucial historical junctures—

"it is the operations of the world-market forces which accentuate the differences, institutionalize them, and make them impossible to surmount over the long run" (1979:21). Nevertheless, when his attention turns to particular epochs, Wallerstein emphasizes hegemony and the role of military force. Dutch economic hegemony in the seventeenth century was destroyed, in quintessential Realist fashion, not by the operation of the world-market system, but by the force of British and French arms (Wallerstein 1980:38–39).

The insights of Realism are enduring. They cross ideological lines. Its best contemporary exponents use Realism in insightful ways. Waltz has systematized the basic assumptions of Classical Realism in what I have called Structural Realism. Snyder and Diesing have employed this framework for the analysis of bargaining; Gilpin has used the classical arguments of Thucydides to explore problems of international change. For all of these writers, Realism fruitfully focuses attention on fundamental issues of power, interests, and rationality. But as we have seen, many of the most interesting questions raised by these authors cannot be answered within the Realist framework.

III. EXPLANATIONS OF OUTCOMES FROM POWER: HYPOTHESES AND ANOMALIES

A Structural Realist theory of interests could be used both for explanation and for prescription. If we could deduce a state's interests from its position in the system, via the rationality assumption, its behavior could be explained on the basis of systemic analysis. Efforts to define the national interest on an a priori basis, however, or to use the concept for prediction and explanation, have been unsuccessful. We saw above that the inability to define interests independently of observed state behavior robbed Snyder and Diesing's game-theoretical matrices of predictive power. More generally, efforts to show that external considerations of power and position play a dominant role in determining the "national interest" have failed. Even an analyst as sympathetic to Realism as Stephen D. Krasner has concluded, in studying American foreign economic policy, that the United States was "capable of defining its own autonomous goals" in a nonlogical manner (1978a:333). That is, the systemic constraints emphasized by Structural Realism were not binding on the American government during the first thirty years after the Second World War.

Sophisticated contemporary thinkers in the Realist tradition, such as Gilpin, Krasner, and Waltz, understand that interests cannot be derived, simply on the basis of rational calculation, from the external positions of states, and that this is particularly true for great powers, on which, ironically, Structural Realism focuses its principal attentions (Gilpin 1975; Waltz 1967). Realist analysis has to retreat to a "fall-back position": that, *given state interests,* whose origins are not predicted by the theory, patterns of outcomes in world politics will be determined by the overall distribution of power among states. This represents a major concession for systemically oriented analysts, which it is important not to forget. Sensible Realists are highly cognizant of the role of domestic politics and of actor choices within the constraints and incentives provided by the system. Since systemic theory cannot predict state interests, it cannot support deterministic conclusions (Sprout and Sprout 1971:73–77). This limitation makes it both less powerful as a theory, and less dangerous as an ideology.[22] Despite its importance, it cannot stand alone.

When realist theorists say that, given interests, patterns of outcomes will be determined by the overall distribution of power among states, they are using "power" to refer to resources that can be used to induce other actors to do what they would not otherwise do, in accordance with the desires of the power-wielder. "Outcomes" refer principally to two sets of patterns: (1) the results of conflicts, diplomatic or military, that take place between states; and (2) changes in the rules and institutions that regulate relations among governments in world politics. This section focuses on conflicts, since they pose the central puzzles that Realism seeks to explain. Section IV and the Conclusion consider explanations of changes in rules and institutions.

Recent quantitative work seems to confirm that power capabilities (measured not only in terms of economic resources but with political variables added) are rather good predictors of the outcomes of wars. Bueno de Mesquita finds, for example, that countries with what he calls positive "expected utility" (a measure that uses composite capabilities but adjusts them for distance, alliance relationships, and uncertainty) won 179 conflicts while losing only 54 between 1816 and 1974, for a success ratio of over 75 percent (1981, especially p. 151; Organski and Kugler 1980, ch. 2).

The question of the fungibility of power poses a more troublesome issue. As I have noted earlier (see note 19), Structural Realism is ambiguous on this point; the desire for parsimonious theory impels Realists toward a unitary notion of power as homogeneous and usable for a variety of purposes, but close examination of the complexities of world politics induces caution about such an approach. In his discussion of system structure, for instance, Waltz holds that "the units of an anarchic system are distinguished primarily by their greater or lesser capabilities for performing similar tasks," and that the distribution of capabilities across a system is the principal characteristic differentiating international-political structures from one another (1979:97, 99). Thus each international political system has one structure. Yet in emphasizing the continued role of military power, Waltz admits that military power is not perfectly fungible: "Differences in strength do matter, *although not for every conceivable purpose*"; "military power no longer brings political control, but then it never did" (1979:189, 191, emphasis added). This seems to imply that any given international system is likely to have *several* structures, differing by issue-areas and according to the resources that can be used to affect outcomes. Different sets of capabilities will qualify as "power resources" under different conditions. This leads to a much less parsimonious theory and a much more highly differentiated view of the world, in which what Nye and I called "issue-structure" theories play a major role, and in which military force, although still important, is no longer assumed to be at the top of a hierarchy of power resources (Keohane and Nye 1977, chs. 3 and 6).

The status in a Structural Realist theory of the fungibility assumption affects both its power and the incidence of anomalies. A strong version of Structural Realism that assumed full fungibility of power across issues would predict that when issues arise between great powers and smaller states, the great powers should prevail. This has the advantage of generating a clear prediction and the liability of being wrong much of the time. Certainly it does not fit the American experience of the last two decades. The United States lost a war in Vietnam and was for more than a year unable to secure the return of its diplomats held hostage in Iran.

Small allies such as Israel, heavily dependent on the United States, have displayed considerable freedom of action. In the U.S.-Canadian relationship of the 1950s and 1960s, which was virtually free of threats of force, outcomes of conflicts as often favored the Canadian as the American position, although this was not true for relations between Australia and the United States (Keohane and Nye 1977, ch. 7).

In view of power theory in social science, the existence of these anomalies is not surprising. As James G. March observes, "there appears to be general consensus that either potential power is different from actually exerted power or that actually exerted power is variable" (1966:57). That is, what March calls "basic force models," which rely, like Realist theory, on measurable indices of power, are inadequate tools for either prediction or explanation. They are often valuable in suggesting long-term trends and patterns, but they do not account well for specific outcomes: the more that is demanded of them, the less well they are likely to perform.

Lakatos's discussion of scientific research programs leads us to expect that, when confronted with anomalies, theorists will create auxiliary theories that preserve the credibility of their fundamental assumptions. Thus it is not surprising that Realists committed to the fungibility assumption have devised auxiliary hypotheses to protect its "hard core" against challenge. One of these is what David Baldwin calls the "conversion-process explanation" of unanticipated outcomes: "The would-be wielder of power is described as lacking in skill and/or the 'will' to use his power resources effectively: 'The Arabs had the tanks but didn't know how to use them.' 'The Americans had the bombs but lacked the will to use them.' " (1979:163–164)

The conversion-process explanation is a classic auxiliary hypothesis, since it is designed to protect the assumption that power resources are homogeneous and fungible. If we were to accept the conversion-process account, we could continue to believe in a single structure of power, even if outcomes do not favor the "stronger" party. This line of argument encounters serious problems, however, when it tries to account for the discrepancy between anticipated and actual outcomes by the impact of intangible resources (such as intelligence, training, organization, foresight) not recognized until after the fact. The problem with this argument lies in its post hoc quality. It is theoretically degenerate in Lakatos's sense, since it does not add any explanatory power to structural Realist theory, but merely "explains away" uncomfortable facts.

Thus what March says about "force activation models" applies to Structural Realist theories when the conversion-process explanation relies upon sources of power that can be observed only after the events to be explained have taken place:

> If we observe that power exists and is stable and if we observe that sometimes weak people seem to triumph over strong people, we are tempted to rely on an activation hypothesis to explain the discrepancy. But if we then try to use the activation hypothesis to predict the results of social-choice procedures, we discover that the data requirements of 'plausible' activation models are quite substantial. As a result, we retreat to what are essentially degenerate forms of the activation model—retaining some of the form but little of the substance. This puts us back where we started, looking for some device to explain our failures in prediction. (1966:61).

A second auxiliary hypothesis designed to protect the fungibility assumption must be taken more seriously: that discrepancies between power resources and outcomes are explained by an asymmetry of motivation in favor of the objectively weaker party. Following this logic, John Harsanyi has proposed the notion of power "in a schedule sense," describing how various resources can be translated into social power. An actor with intense preferences on an issue may be willing to use more resources to attain a high probability of a favorable result, than an actor with more resources but lower intensity. As a result, outcomes may not accurately reflect underlying power resources (Harsanyi 1962).

To use this insight progressively rather than in a degenerate way, Realist theory needs to develop indices of intensity of motivation that can be measured independently of the behavior that theorists are trying to explain. Russett, George, and Bueno de Mesquita are among the authors who have attempted, with some success, to do this (Russett 1963; George et al. 1971; Bueno de Mesquita 1981). Insofar as motivation is taken simply as a control, allowing us to test the impact of varying power configurations more successfully, Harsanyi's insights can be incorporated into structural Realist theory. If it became a key variable, however, the effect could be to transform a systemic theory into a decision-making one.

An alternative approach to relying on such auxiliary hypotheses is to relax the fungibility assumption itself. Failures of great powers to control smaller ones could be explained on the basis of independent evidence that in the relevant issue-areas, the states that are weaker on an overall basis have more power resources than their stronger partners, and that the use of power derived from one area of activity to affect outcomes in other areas (through "linkages") is difficult. Thus Saudi Arabia can be expected to have more impact on world energy issues than on questions of strategic arms control; Israel more influence over the creation of a Palestinian state than on the reconstruction of the international financial and debt regime.

Emphasizing the problematic nature of power fungibility might help to create more discriminating power models, but it will not resolve the inherent problems of power models, as identified by March and others. Furthermore, at the limit, to deny fungibility entirely risks a complete disintegration of predictive power. Baldwin comes close to this when he argues that what he calls the "policy-contingency framework" of an influence attempt must be specified before power explanations are employed. If we defined each issue as existing within a unique "policy-contingency framework," no generalizations would be possible. Waltz could reply, if he accepted Baldwin's view of power, that all of world politics should be considered a single policy-contingency framework, characterized by anarchy and self-help.[23] According to this argument, the parsimony gained by assuming the fungibility of power would compensate for the marginal mispredictions of such a theory.

This is a crucial theoretical issue, which should be addressed more explicitly by theorists of world politics. In my view, the dispute cannot be resolved a priori. The degree to which power resources have to be disaggregated in a structural theory depends both on the purposes of the theory and on the degree to which behavior on distinct issues is linked together through the exercise of influence by actors. The larger the domain of a theory, the less accuracy of detail we expect. Since balance of power theory seeks to explain large-scale patterns of state action over long periods of time, we could hardly expect the precision from it that we demand from theories whose domains have been narrowed.

This assertion suggests that grand systemic theory can be very useful as a basis for further theoretical development in international relations, even if the theory is lacking in precision, and it therefore comprises part of my defense of the Realist research program as a foundation on which scholars should build. Yet this argument needs immediate qualification.

Even if a large-scale theory can be developed and appropriately tested, its predictions will be rather gross. To achieve a more finely tuned understanding of how resources affect behavior in particular situations, one needs to specify the policy-contingency framework more precisely. The domain of theory is narrowed to achieve greater precision. Thus the debate between advocates of parsimony and proponents of contextual subtlety resolves itself into a question of *stages,* rather than an either/or choice. We should seek parsimony first, then add complexity while monitoring the adverse effects that this has on the predictive power of our theory: its ability to make significant inferences on the basis of limited information.

To introduce greater complexity into an initially spare theoretical structure, the conception of an issue-area, developed many years ago by Robert A. Dahl (1961) and adapted for use in international relations by James N. Rosenau (1966), is a useful device. Having tentatively selected an area of activity to investigate, the analyst needs to delineate issue-areas at various levels of aggregation. Initial explanations should seek to account for the main features of behavior at a high level of aggregation— such as the international system as a whole—while subsequent hypotheses are designed to apply only to certain issue-areas.

In some cases, more specific issue-areas are "nested" within larger ones (Aggarwal 1981; Snidal 1981). For instance, North Atlantic fisheries issues constitute a subset of fisheries issues in general, which comprise part of the whole area of oceans policy, or "law of the sea." In other cases, specific issues may belong to two or more broader issues: the question of passage through straits, for example, involves questions of military security as well as the law of the sea.

Definitions of issue-areas depend on the beliefs of participants, as well as on the purposes of the investigator. In general, however, definitions of issue-areas should be made on the basis of empirical judgments about the extent to which governments regard sets of issues as closely inter-dependent and treat them collectively. Decisions made on one issue must affect others in the issue-area, either through functional links or through regular patterns of bargaining. These relationships of interdependence among issues may change. Some issue-areas, such as international financial relations, have remained fairly closely linked for decades; others, such as oceans, have changed drastically over the past 35 years (Keohane and Nye 1977, ch. 4, especially pp. 64–65; Simon 1969; Haas 1980).

When a hierarchy of issue-areas has been identified, power-structure models employing more highly aggregated measures of power resources can be compared with models that disaggregate resources by issue-areas. How much accuracy is gained, and how much parsimony lost, by each step in the disaggregation process? In my view, a variegated analysis, which takes some specific "snapshots" by issue-area as well as looking at the broader picture, is superior to either monistic strategy, whether assuming perfect fungibility or none at all.

This approach represents an adaptation of Realism. It preserves the basic emphasis on power resources as a source of outcomes in general, but it unambiguously jettisons the assumption that power is fungible across all of world politics. Disaggregated power models are less parsi-monious than more aggregated ones, and they remain open to the ob-jections to power models articulated by March and others. But in one important sense disaggregation is progressive rather than degenerative. Disaggregated models call attention to linkages among issue-areas, and raise the question: under what conditions, and with what effects, will such linkages arise? Current research suggests that understanding linkages systematically, rather than merely describing them on an ad hoc basis, will add significantly to our comprehension of world politics (Oye 1979, 1983; Stein 1980; Tollison and Willett 1979). It would seem worthwhile, in addition, for more empirical work to be done on this subject, since we know so little about when, and how, linkages are made.

Conclusions

Structural Realism is a good starting-point for explaining the outcomes of conflicts, since it directs attention to fundamental questions of interest and power within a logically coherent and parsimonious theoretical framework. Yet the ambitious attempt of Structural Realist theory to deduce national interests from system structure via the rationality postulate has been unsuccessful. Even if interests are taken as given, the attempt to predict outcomes from interests and power leads to ambiguities and incorrect predictions. The auxiliary theory attributing this failure to conversion-processes often entails unfalsifiable tautology rather than genuine explanation. Ambiguity prevails on the question of the fungibility of power: whether there is a single structure of the international system or several. Thus the research program of Realism reveals signs of degeneration. It certainly does not meet Lakatos's tough standards for progressiveness.

More attention to developing independent measures of intensity of motivation, and greater precision about the concept of power and its relationship to the context of action, may help to correct some of these faults. Careful disaggregation of power-resources by issue-area may help to improve the predictive capability of structural models, at the risk of reducing theoretical parsimony. As I argue in the next section, modified structural models, indebted to Realism although perhaps too different to be considered Realist themselves, may be valuable elements in a multi-level framework for understanding world politics.

Yet to some extent the difficulties encountered by Structural Realism reflect the inherent limitations of structural models, which will not be corrected by mere modifications or the relaxation of assumptions. Domestic politics and decision-making, Snyder and Diesing's "internal-external interactions," and the workings of international institutions all play a role, along with international political structure, in affecting state behavior and outcomes. Merely to catalog these factors, however, is not to contribute to theory but rather to compound the descriptive anarchy that already afflicts the field, with too many independent variables, exogenously determined, chasing too few cases. As Waltz emphasizes, the role of unit-level forces can be properly understood only if we comprehend the structure of the international system within which they operate.

IV. BEYOND STRUCTURAL REALISM

Structural Realism helps us to understand world politics as in part a systemic phenomenon, and provides us with a logically coherent theory that establishes the context for state action. This theory, because it is relatively simple and clear, can be modified progressively to attain closer correspondence with reality. Realism's focus on interests and power is central to an understanding of how nations deal with each other. Its adherents have understood that a systemic theory of international relations must account for state behavior by examining the constraints and incentives provided by the system; for this purpose to be accomplished, an assumption of rationality (although not of perfect information) must be made. The rationality assumption allows inferences about state behavior to be drawn solely from knowledge of the structure of the system.

Unfortunately, such predictions are often wrong. The concept of power is difficult to measure validly a priori; interests are underspecified by examining the nature of the international system and the position of various states in it; the view of power resources implied by overall structure theories is overaggregated, exaggerating the extent to which power is like money. The problem that students of international politics face is how to construct theories that draw on Realism's strengths without partaking fully of its weaknesses.

To do this we need a multidimensional approach to world politics that incorporates several analytical frameworks or research programs. One of these should be that of Structural Realism, which has the virtues of parsimony and clarity, although the range of phenomena that it encompasses is limited. Another, in my view, should be a modified structural research program, which relaxes some of the assumptions of Structural Realism but retains enough of the hard core to generate a priori predictions on the basis of information about the international environment. Finally, we need better theories of domestic politics, decisionmaking, and information processing, so that the gap between the external and internal environments can be bridged in a systematic way, rather than by simply adding catalogs of exogenously determined foreign policy facts to theoretically more rigorous structural models. That is, we need more attention to the "internal-external interactions" discussed by Snyder and Diesing.

Too much work in this last category is being done for me to review it in detail here. Mention should be made, however, of some highlights. Peter J. Katzenstein, Peter Gourevitch, and others have done pioneering work on the relationship between domestic political structure and political coalitions, on the one hand, and foreign economic policies, on the other (Katzenstein 1978; Gourevitch 1978). This line of analysis, which draws heavily on the work of Alexander Gerschenkron (1962) and Barrington Moore (1966), argues that the different domestic structures characteristic of various advanced industrialized countries result from different historical patterns of development; in particular, whether development came early or late, and what the position of the country was in the international political system at the time of its economic development (Kurth 1979). Thus it attempts to draw connections both between international and domestic levels of analysis, and across historical time. This research does not provide deductive explanatory models, and it does not account systematically for changes in established structures after the formative developmental period, but its concept of domestic structure brings order into the cacophony of domestic political and economic variables that could affect foreign policy, and therefore suggests the possibility of eventual integration of theories relying on international structure with those focusing on domestic structure.

Katzenstein and his associates focus on broad political, economic, and social patterns within countries, and their relationship to the international division of labor and the world political structure. Fruitful analysis can also be done at the more narrowly intragovernmental level, as Snyder and Diesing show. An emphasis on bureaucratic politics was particularly evident in the 1960s and early 1970s, although Robert J. Art has pointed out in detail a number of difficulties, weaknesses, and contradictions in this literature (1973). At the level of the individual decisionmaker, insights can be gained by combining theories of cognitive psychology with a rich knowledge of diplomatic history, as in Jervis's work, as long as the investigator understands the systemic and domestic-structural context within which decicionmakers operate.[24] This research program has made decided progress, from the simple-minded notions criticized by Waltz (1959) to the work of Alexander and Juliette George (1964), Alexander George (1980), Ole Holsti (1976) and Jervis (1976).[25]

Despite the importance of this work at the levels of domestic structure, intragovernmental politics, and individual cognition, the rest of my analysis will continue to focus on the concept of international political structure and its relevance to the study of world politics. I will argue that progress could be made by constructing a modified structural research program, retaining some of the parsimony characteristic of Structural

Realism and its emphasis on the incentives and constraints of the world system, while adapting it to fit contemporary reality better. Like Realism, this research program would be based on microeconomic theory, particularly oligopoly theory. It would seek to explain actor behavior by specifying a priori utility functions for actors, using the rationality principle as a "trivial animating law" in Popper's sense (Latsis 1976:21), and deducing behavior from the constraints of the system as modeled in the theory.

Developing such a theory would only be worthwhile if there were something particularly satisfactory both about systemic explanations and about the structural forms of such explanations. I believe that this is the case, for two sets of reasons.

First, systemic theory is important because we must understand the context of action before we can understand the action itself. As Waltz (1979) has emphasized, theories of world politics that fail to incorporate a sophisticated understanding of the operation of the system—that is, how systemic attributes affect behavior—are bad theories. Theoretical analysis of the characteristics of an international system is as important for understanding foreign policy as understanding European history is for understanding the history of Germany.

Second, structure theory is important because it provides an irreplaceable *component* for a thorough analysis of action, by states or non-state actors, in world politics. A good structural theory generates testable implications about behavior on an a priori basis, and, therefore, comes closer than interpretive description to meeting the requirements for scientific knowledge of neopositivist philosophers of science such as Lakatos. This does not mean, of course, that explanation and rich interpretation—Geertz's "thick description" (1973)—are in any way antithetical to one another. A good analysis of a given problem will include both.[26]

The assumptions of a modified structural research program can be compared to Realist assumptions as follows:

(1) The assumption that the principal actors in world politics are states would remain the same, although more emphasis would be placed on nonstate actors, intergovernmental organizations, and transnational and transgovernmental relations than is the case in Realist analysis (Keohane and Nye 1972).

(2) The rationality assumption would be retained, since without it, as

we have seen, inferences from structure to behavior become impossible without heroic assumptions about evolutionary processes or other forces that compel actors to adapt their behavior to their environments. It should be kept in mind, however, as is made clear by sophisticated Realists, that the rationality postulate only assumes that actors make calculations "so as to maximize expected value across a given set of consistently ordered objectives" (Snyder and Diesing 1977:81). It does not assume perfect information, consideration of all possible alternatives, or unchanging actor preferences.

(3) The assumption that states seek power, and calculate their interests, accordingly, would be qualified severely. Power and influence would still be regarded as important state interests (as ends or necessary means), but the implication that the search for power constitutes an overriding interest in all cases, or that is always takes the same form, would be rejected. Under different systemic conditions states will define their self-interests differently. For instance, where survival is at stake efforts to maintain autonomy may take precedence over all other activities, but where the environment is relatively benign energies will also be directed to fulfilling other goals. Indeed, over the long run, whether an environment is malign or benign can alter the standard operating procedures and sense of identity of the actors themselves.[27]

In addition, this modified structural approach would explicitly modify the assumption of fungibility lurking behind unitary conceptions of "international structure." It would be assumed that the value of power resources for influencing behavior in world politics depends on the goals sought. Power resources that are well-suited to achieve certain purposes are less effective when used for other objectives. Thus power resources are differentially effective across issue-areas, and the usability of a given set of power resources depends on the "policy-contingency frameworks" within which it must be employed.

This research program would pay much more attention to the roles of institutions and rules than does Structural Realism. Indeed, a structural interpretation of the emergence of international rules and procedures, and of obedience to them by states, is one of the rewards that could be expected from this modified structural research program (Krasner 1982; Keohane 1982b; Stein 1982).

This research program would contain a valuable positive heuristic—

a set of suggestions about what research should be done and what questions should initially be asked—which would include the following pieces of advice:

(1) When trying to explain a set of outcomes in world politics, always consider the hypothesis that the outcomes reflect underlying power resources, without being limited to it;

(2) When considering different patterns of outcomes in different relationships, or issue-areas, entertain the hypothesis that power resources are differently distributed in these issue-areas, and investigate ways in which these differences promote or constrain actor attempts to link issue-areas in order to use power-resources from one area to affect results in another;

(3) When considering how states define their self-interests, explore the effects of international structure on self-interests, as well as the effects of other international factors and of domestic structure.

Such a modified structural research program could begin to help generate theories that are more discriminating, with respect to the sources of power, than is Structural Realism. It would be less oriented toward reaffirming the orthodox verities of world politics and more inclined to explain variations in patterns of rules and institutions. Its concern with international institutions would facilitate insights into processes of peaceful change. This research program would not solve all of the problems of Realist theory, but it would be a valuable basis for interpreting contemporary world politics.

Yet this form of structural theory still has the weaknesses associated with power analysis. The essential problem is that from a purely systemic point of view, situations of strategic interdependence do not have determinate solutions. No matter how carefully power resources are defined, no power model will be able accurately to predict outcomes under such conditions.[28]

One way to alleviate this problem without moving immediately to the domestic level of analysis (and thus sacrificing the advantages of systemic theory), is to recognize that what it is rational for states to do, and what states' interests are, depend on the institutional context of action as well as on the underlying power realities and state position upon which Realist thought concentrates. Structural approaches should be seen as only a basis for further systemic analysis. They vary the power condition in the system, but they are silent on variations in the frequency of mutual interactions in the system or in the level of information.

The importance of these non-power factors is demonstrated by some recent work on cooperation. In particular, Robert Axelrod has shown that cooperation can emerge among egoists under conditions of strategic interdependence as modeled by the game of prisoners' dilemma. Such a result requires, however, that these egoists expect to continue to interact with each other for the indefinite future, and that these expectations of future interactions be given sufficient weight in their calculations (Axelrod 1981). This argument reinforces the practical wisdom of diplomats and arms controllers, who assume that state strategies, and the degree of eventual cooperation, will depend significantly on expectations about the future. The "double-cross" strategy, for instance, is more attractive when it is expected to lead to a final, winning move, than when a continuing series of actions and reactions is anticipated.

High levels of uncertainty reduce the confidence with which expectations are held, and may therefore lead governments to discount the future heavily. As Axelrod shows, this can inhibit the evolution of cooperation through reciprocity. It can also reduce the ability of actors to make mutually beneficial agreements at any given time, quite apart from their expectations about whether future interactions will occur. That is, it can lead to a form of "political market failure" (Keohane 1982b).

Information that reduces uncertainty is therefore an important factor in world politics. But information is not a systemic constant. Some international systems are rich in institutions and processes that provide information to governments and other actors; in other systems, information is scarce or of low quality. Given a certain distribution of power (Waltz's "international structure"), variations in information may be important in influencing state behavior. If international institutions can evolve that improve the quality of information and reduce uncertainty, they may profoundly affect international political behavior even in the absence of changes either in international structure (defined in terms of the distribution of power) or in the preference functions of actors.

Taking information seriously at the systemic level could stimulate a new look at theories of information-processing within governments, such as those of Axelrod (1976), George (1980), Jervis (1976), and Holsti (1976). It could also help us, however, to understand a dimension of the concept of complex interdependence (Keohane and Nye 1977) that has been largely ignored. Complex interdependence can be seen as a condition under which it is not only difficult to use conventional power resources for certain purposes, but under which information levels are relatively high due to the existence of multiple channels of contact among states. If we focus exclusively on questions of power, the most important feature of complex interdependence—almost its *only* important feature— is the ineffectiveness of military force and the constraints that this implies on fungibility of power across issue-areas. Sensitizing ourselves to the role of information, and information-provision, at the international level brings another aspect of complex interdependence—the presence of multiple channels of contact among societies—back into the picture. Actors behave differently in information-rich environments than in information-poor ones where uncertainty prevails.

This is not a subject that can be explored in depth here.[29] I raise it, however, to clarify the nature of the multidimensional network of theories and research programs that I advocate for the study of world politics. We need both spare, logically tight theories, such as Structural Realism, and rich interpretations, such as those of the historically oriented students of domestic structure and foreign policy. But we also need something in-between: systemic theories that retain some of the parsimony of Structural Realism, but that are able to deal better with differences between issue-areas, with institutions, and with change. Such theories could be developed on the basis of variations in power (as in Structural Realism), but they could also focus on variations in other systemic characteristics, such as levels and quality of information.

CONCLUSION:
WORLD POLITICS AND PEACEFUL CHANGE

As Gilpin points out, the problem of peaceful change is fundamental to world politics. Thermonuclear weapons have made it even more urgent than it was in the past. Realism demonstrates that peaceful change is more difficult to achieve in international politics than within well-ordered domestic societies, but it does not offer a theory of peaceful change.[30] Nor is such a theory available from other research traditions. The question remains for us to grapple with: Under what conditions will adaptations to shifts in power, in available technologies, or in fundamental economic relationships take place without severe economic disruption or warfare?

Recent work on "international regimes" has been addressed to this question, which is part of the broader issue of order in world politics (*International Organization,* Spring 1982). Structural Realist approaches to understanding the origins and maintenance of international regimes are useful (Krasner 1982), but since they ignore cognitive issues and questions of information, they comprise only part of the story (Haas 1982).

Realism, furthermore, is better at telling us why we are in such trouble than how to get out of it. It argues that order can be created from anarchy by the exercise of superordinate power: periods of peace follow establishment of dominance in Gilpin's "hegemonic wars." Realism sometimes seems to imply, pessimistically, that order can *only* be created by hegemony. If the latter conclusion were correct, not only would the world economy soon become chaotic (barring a sudden resurgence of American power), but at some time in the foreseeable future, global nuclear war would ensue.

Complacency in the face of this prospect is morally unacceptable. No serious thinker could, therefore, be satisfied with Realism as the correct theory of world politics, even if the scientific status of the theory were stronger than it is. Our concern for humanity requires us to do what Gilpin does in the epilogue to *War and Change* (1981), where he holds out the hope of a "new and more stable international order" in the final decades of the twentieth century, despite his theory's contention that such a benign outcome is highly unlikely. Although Gilpin could be criticized for inconsistency, this would be beside the point: the conditions of terror under which we live compel us to search for a way out of the trap.

The need to find a way out of the trap means that international relations must be a policy science as well as a theoretical activity.[31] We should be seeking to link theory with practice, bringing insights from Structural Realism, modified structural theories, other systemic approaches, and actor-level analyses to bear on contemporary issues in a sophisticated way. This does not mean that the social scientist should adopt the policymaker's framework, much less his normative values or blinders about the range of available alternatives. On the contrary, independent observers often do their most valuable work when they reject the normative or analytic framework of those in power, and the best theorists may be those who maintain their distance from those at the center of events. Nevertheless, foreign policy and world politics are too important to be left to bureaucrats, generals, and lawyers—or even to journalists and clergymen.

Realism helps us determine the strength of the trap, but does not give us much assistance in seeking to escape. If we are to promote peaceful change, we need to focus not only on basic long-term forces that determine the shape of world politics independently of the actions of particular decision-makers, but also on variables that to some extent can be manipulated by human action. Since international institutions, rules, and patterns of cooperation can affect calculations of interest, and can also be affected incrementally by contemporary political action, they provide a natural focus for scholarly attention as well as policy concern.[32] Unlike Realism, theories that attempt to explain rules, norms, and institutions help us to understand how to create patterns of cooperation that could be essential to our survival. We need to respond to the questions that Realism poses but fails to answer: How can order be created out of anarchy *without* superordinate power; how can peaceful change occur?

To be reminded of the significance of international relations as policy analysis, and the pressing problem of order, is to recall the tradition of Classical Realism. Classical Realism, as epitomized by the work of John Herz (1981), has recognized that no matter how deterministic our theoretical aspirations may be, there remains a human interest in autonomy and self-reflection. As Ashley puts it, the Realism of a thinker such as Herz is committed to an "emancipatory cognitive interest—an interest in securing freedom from unacknowledged constraints, relations of domination, and conditions of distorted communication and understanding that deny humans the capacity to make their future with full will and consciousness" (1981:227).[33] We think about world politics not because it is aesthetically beautiful, because we believe that it is governed by simple, knowable laws, or because it provides rich, easily accessible data for the testing of empirical hypotheses. Were those concerns paramount, we would look elsewhere. We study world politics because we think it will determine the fate of the earth (Schell 1982). Realism makes us aware of the odds against us. What we need to do now is to understand peaceful change by combining multidimensional scholarly analysis with more visionary ways of seeing the future.

NOTES

1. An unfortunate limitation of this chapter is that its scope is restricted to work published in English, principally in the United States. I recognize that this reflects the Americanocentrism of scholarship in the United States, and I regret it. But I am not sufficiently well-read in works published elsewhere to comment intelligently on them. For recent discussions of the distinctively American stamp that has been placed on the international relations field see Hoffmann (1977) and Lyons (1982).

2. Nye and I, in effect, conceded this in our later work, which was more cautious about the drawbacks of conventional "state-centric" theory (see Keohane and Nye 1977).

3. For a discussion of "theory as a set of questions," see Hoffmann (1960:1–12).

4. For a complementary account of developments in international relations theory, which originally appeared in the same volume as this essay, see Bruce Russett, "International Interactions and Processes: The Internal versus External Debate Revisited," in Finifter (1983):541–568.

5. Stanley J. Michalak, Jr. pointed out correctly that our characterization of Realism in *Power and Interdependence* was unfair when taken literally, although he also seems to me to have missed the Realist basis of our structural models. (See Michalak 1979).

6. It has often been noted that Kuhn's definition of a paradigm was vague: one sympathetic critic identified 21 distinct meanings of the term in Kuhn's relatively brief book (Masterman 1970). But Lakatos particularly objected to what he regarded as Kuhn's relativism, which in his view interpreted major changes in science as the result of essentially irrational forces. (See Lakatos 1970:178).

7. Lakatos's comments on Marxism and psychology were biting, and a colleague of his reports that he doubted the applicability of the methodology of scientific research programs to the social sciences. (See Latsis 1976:2).

8. Robert Jervis and Ann Tickner have both reminded me that Morgenthau and John H. Herz, another major proponent of Realist views in the 1950s, later severely qualified their adherence to what has generally been taken as Realist doctrine. (See Herz 1981, and Boyle 1980:218). I am particularly grateful to Dr. Tickner for obtaining a copy of the relevant pages of the latter article for me.

9. For commentary on this assumption, see Keohane and Nye (1972), and Mansbach, Ferguson, and Lampert (1976). In *Power and Interdependence,* Nye and I were less critical than we had been earlier of the state-centric assumption. In view of the continued importance of governments in world affairs, for many purposes it seems justified on grounds of parsimony. Waltz's rather acerbic critique of our earlier position seems to me essentially correct (see Waltz 1979:7).

10. Emphasis added. Thucydides also follows this "positive heuristic" of looking for underlying power realities in discussions of the Athenian-Corcyrean alliance (chapter II), the decision of the Lacedemonians to vote that Athens had broken the treaty between them (chapter III), and Pericles' Funeral Oration (chapter IV). In the Modern Library edition, the passages in question are on pp. 28, 49–50, and 83.

11. Bruce Bueno de Mesquita (1981:29–33) has an excellent discussion of the rationality assumption as used in the study of world politics.

12. As Waltz points out, Morgenthau's writings reflect the "first image" Realist view that the evil inherent in man is at the root of war and conflict.

13. Sustained earlier critiques of the fungibility assumption can be found in Keohane and Nye (1977:49–52) and in Baldwin (1979).

14. In an illuminating recent review essay, John Gerard Ruggie has criticized Waltz's assumption that the second dimension of structure, referring to the degree of differentiation of units, can be regarded as a constant (undifferentiated units with similar functions) in world politics. Ruggie argues that "when the concept 'differentiation' is properly defined, the second structural level of Waltz's model . . . serves to depict the kind of institutional transformation illustrated by the shift from the medieval to the modern international system." See Ruggie (1983:279), this volume, p. 146.

15. Waltz denies that he relies on the rationality assumption; but I argue in section II that he requires it for his theory of the balance of power to hold.

16. For a brilliant discussion of this theoretical strategy in microeconomics, see Latsis (1976 esp. pp. 16–23).

17. Since the principal purpose of Realist analysis in the hands of Waltz and others is to develop an explanation of international political reality, rather than to offer specific advice to those in power, the label "technical realism" seems too narrow. It also carries a pejorative intent that I do not share. "Structural Realism" captures the focus on explanation through an examination of the structure of the international system. Capitalization is used to indicate that Realism is a specific school, and that it would be possible to be a realist—in the sense of examining reality as it really is—without subscribing to Realist assumptions. For a good discussion, see Krasner (1982).

18. This is the commonsense view of power, as discussed, for example, by Arnold Wolfers (1962:103). As indicated in section III, any such definition conceals a large number of conceptual problems.

19. My reading of Gilpin's argument on pp. 29–34 led me originally to believe that he also accepted the notion that power is fungible, since he argues that hegemonic war creates a hierarchy of prestige in an international system, which is based on the hegemon's "demonstrated ability to enforce its will on other states" (p. 34), and which appears to imply that a single structure of power resources exists, usable for a wide variety of issues. But in letters sent to the author commenting on an earlier draft of this paper, both Gilpin and Waltz explicitly disavowed the assumption that power resources are necessarily fungible. In *War and Change*, Gilpin is very careful to disclaim the notion, which he ascribes to Political Realists but which I have not included in the hard core of Realism, that states seek to maximize their power: "Acquisition of power entails an opportunity cost to a society; some other desired good must be abandoned" (p. 5).

20. A similar issue is posed in chapter 3 of part II of *Lineages of the Absolutist State* (1974). Its author, Perry Anderson, addresses the puzzle of why it was Prussia, rather than Bavaria or Saxony, that eventually gained predominance in Germany. Despite his inclinations, Anderson has to rely on a variety of conjunctural, if not accidental, factors to account for the observed result.

21. For a lucid discussion of the security dilemma, see Jervis (1978).

22. The fact that sensitive Realists are aware of the limitations of Realism makes me less worried than Ashley about the policy consequences of Realist analysis. (See above, pp. 168–169).

23. Waltz does not accept Baldwin's (and Dahl's) definition of power in terms of causality, arguing that "power is one cause among others, from which it cannot be isolated." But this makes it impossible to falsify any power theory; one can always claim that other factors (not specified a priori) were at work. Waltz's discussion of power (1979:191–192) does not separate power-as-outcome properly from power-as-resources; it does not distinguish between resources that the observer can assess a priori from those only assessable post hoc; it does not relate probabilistic thinking properly to power theory; and it takes refuge in a notion of power as "affecting others more than they affect him," which would result (if taken literally) in the absurdity of attributing maximum power to the person or government that is least responsive to outside stimuli, regardless of its ability to achieve its purposes.

24. Jervis (1976, ch. 1) has an excellent discussion of levels of analysis and the relationship between perceptual theories and other theories of international relations. Snyder and Diesing discuss similar issues in chapter 6 on "Crises and International Systems" (1977).

25. Waltz commented perceptively in *Man, the State and War* that contributions of behavioral scientists had often been "rendered ineffective by a failure to comprehend the significance of the political framework of international action" (1959:78).

26. Thorough description—what Alexander George has called "process-tracing"—may be necessary to evaluate a structural explanation, since correlations are not reliable where only a small number of comparable cases is involved. (See George 1979).

27. I am indebted for this point to a conversation with Hayward Alker.

28. Latsis (1976) discusses the difference between "single-exit" and "multiple-exit" situations in his critique of oligopoly theory. What he calls the research program of "situational determinism"—structural theory, in my terms—works well for single-exit situations, where only one sensible course of action is possible. (The building is burning down and there is only one way out: regardless of my personal characteristics, one can expect that I will leave through that exit.) It does not apply to multiple-exit situations, where more than one plausible choice can be made. (The building is burning, but I have to choose between trying the smoky stairs or jumping into a fireman's net: my choice may depend on deep-seated personal fears.) In foreign policy, the prevalence of multiple-exit situations reinforces the importance of decision-making analysis at the national level.

29. For a more detailed discussion of some aspects of this notion, and for citations to some of the literature in economics on which my thinking is based, see

Keohane (1982b). Discussions with Vinod Aggarwal have been important in formulating some of the points in the previous two paragraphs.

30. Morgenthau devotes a chapter of *Politics Among Nations* to peaceful change, but after a review of the reasons why legalistic approaches will not succeed, he eschews general statements for descriptions of a number of United Nations actions affecting peace and security. No theory of peaceful change is put forward. In *Politics Among Nations* Morgenthau put whatever faith he had in diplomacy. The chapter on peaceful change is chapter 26 of the fourth edition (1966).

31. For a suggestive discussion of international relations as policy science, see George and Smoke (1974), Appendix, "Theory for Policy in International Relations," pp. 616–642.

32. Recall Weber's aphorism in "Politics as a Vocation": "Politics is the strong and slow boring of hard boards." Although much of Weber's work analyzed broad historical forces beyond the control of single individuals or groups, he remained acutely aware of "the truth that man would not have attained the possible unless time and again he had reached out for the impossible" (Gerth and Mills 1958:128). For a visionary, value-laden discourse on future international politics by a scholar "reaching out for the impossible," see North (1976, ch. 7).

33. Ernst B. Haas, who has studied how political actors learn throughout his distinguished career, makes a similar point in a recent essay, where he espouses a "cognitive-evolutionary view" of change and argues that such a view "cannot settle for a concept of hegemony imposed by the analyst. . . . It makes fewer claims about basic directions, purposes, laws and trends than do other lines of thought. It is agnostic about the finality of social laws" (1982:242–243). The difference between Haas and me is that he seems to reject structural analysis in favor of an emphasis on cognitive evolution and learning, whereas I believe that modified structural analysis (more modest in its claims than Structural Realism) can provide a context within which analysis of cognition is politically more meaningful.

EIGHT

Social Forces, States and World Orders:

Beyond International Relations Theory

ROBERT W. COX

A CADEMIC CONVENTIONS divide up the seamless web of the real social world into separate spheres, each with its own theorizing; this is a necessary and practical way of gaining understanding. Contemplation of undivided totality may lead to profound abstractions or mystical revelations, but practical knowledge (that which can be put to work through action) is always partial or fragmentary in origin. Whether the parts remain as limited, separated objects of knowledge, or become the basis for constructing a structured and dynamic view of larger wholes, is a major question of method and purpose. Either way, the starting point is some initial subdivision of reality, usually dictated by convention.

It is wise to to bear in mind that such a conventional cutting up of reality is at best just a convenience of the mind. The segments which result, however, derive indirectly from reality insofar as they are the result of practices, that is to say, the responses of consciousness to the pressures of reality. Subdivisions of social knowledge thus may roughly correspond to the ways in which human affairs are organized in particular times and places. They may, accordingly, appear to be increasingly arbitrary when practices change.

International relations is a case in point. It is an area of study concerned with the interrelationships among states in an epoch in which states, and most commonly nation-states, are the principal aggregations of political power. It is concerned with the outcomes of war and peace and thus has obvious practical importance. Changing practice has, however, generated confusion as to the nature of the actors involved (different kinds of state, and non-state entities), extended the range of stakes (low as well as high politics), introduced a greater diversity of goals pursued, and produced a greater complexity in the modes of interaction and the institutions within which action takes place.

One old intellectual convention which contributed to the definition of international relations is the distinction between state and civil society. This distinction made practical sense in the eighteenth and early nineteenth centuries when it corresponded to two more or less distinct spheres of human activity or practice: to an emergent society of individuals based on contract and market relations which replaced a status-based society, on the one hand, and a state with functions limited to maintaining internal peace, external defense and the requisite conditions for markets, on the other. Traditional international relations theory maintains the distinctness of the two spheres, with foreign policy appearing as the pure expression of state interests. Today, however, state and civil society are so interpenetrated that the concepts have become almost purely analytical (referring to difficult-to-define aspects of a complex reality) and are only very vaguely and imprecisely indicative of distinct spheres of activity.

One recent trend in theory has undermined the conceptual unity of the state by perceiving it as the arena of competing bureaucratic entities, while another has reduced the relative importance of the state by introducing a range of private transnational activity and transgovernmental networks of relationships among fragments of state bureaucracies. The state, which remained as the focus of international relations thinking, was still a singular concept: a state was a state was a state. There has been little attempt within the bounds of international relations theory to consider the state/society complex as the basic entity of international relations. As a consequence, the prospect that there exist a plurality of forms of state, expressing different configurations of state/society complexes, remains very largely unexplored, at least in connection with the study of international relations.

The Marxist revival of interest in the state might have been expected to help fill this gap by broadening and diversifying the notion of state and, in particular, by amplifying its social dimensions. Some of the foremost products of this revival, however, either have been of an entirely abstract character, defining the state as a "region" of a singularly conceived capitalist mode of production (Althusser, Poulantzas), or else have shifted attention away from the state and class conflict toward a motivational crisis in culture and ideology (Habermas). Neither goes very far toward exploring the actual or historical differences among forms of state, or considering the implications of the differences for international behavior.

Some historians, both Marxist and non-Marxist, quite independently of theorizing about either international relations or the state, have contributed in a practical way toward filling the gap. E. H. Carr and Eric Hobsbawm have both been sensitive to the continuities between social forces, the changing nature of the state and global relationships. In France, Fernand Braudel (1979) has portrayed these interrelationships in the sixteenth and seventeenth centuries on a vast canvas of the whole world. Inspired by Braudel's work a group led by Immanuel Wallerstein (1974 and 1979) has proposed a theory of world systems defined essentially in terms of social relations: the exploitative exchange relations between a developed core and an underdeveloped periphery, to which correspond different forms of labor control, for example, free labor in the core areas, coerced labor in the peripheries, with intermediate forms in what are called semi-peripheries. Though it offers the most radical alternative to conventional international relations theory, the world systems approach has been criticized on two main grounds: first, for its tendency to undervalue the state by considering the state as merely derivative from its position in the world system (strong states in the core, weak states in the periphery); second, for its alleged, though unintended, system-maintenance bias. Like structural-functional sociology, the approach is better at accounting for forces that maintain or restore a system's equilibrium than identifying contradictions which can lead to a system's transformation.[1]

The above comments are not, however, the central focus of this essay but warnings prior to the following attempt to sketch a method for understanding global power relations: look at the problem of world order in the whole, but beware of reifying a world system.[2] Beware of underrating state power, but in addition give proper attention to social forces and processes and see how they relate to the development of states and world orders. Above all, do not base theory on theory but rather on changing practice and empirical-historical study, which are a proving ground for concepts and hypotheses.

On Perspectives and Purposes

Theory is always *for* someone and *for* some purpose. All theories have a perspective. Perspectives derive from a position in time and space, specifically social and political time and space. The world is seen from a standpoint definable in terms of nation or social class, of dominance or subordination, of rising or declining power, of a sense of immobility or of present crisis, of past experience, and of hopes and expectations for the future. Of course, sophisticated theory is never just the expression of a perspective. The more sophisticated a theory is, the more it reflects upon and transcends its own perspective; but the initial perspective is always contained within a theory and is relevant to its explication. There is, accordingly, no such thing as theory in itself, divorced from a standpoint in time and space. When any theory so represents itself, it is the more important to examine it as ideology, and to lay bare its concealed perspective.

To each such perspective the enveloping world raises a number of issues; the pressures of social reality present themselves to consciousness as problems. A primary task of theory is to become clearly aware of these problems, to enable the mind to come to grips with the reality it confronts. Thus, as reality changes, old concepts have to be adjusted or rejected and new concepts forged in an initial dialogue between the theorist and the particular world he tries to comprehend. This initial dialogue concerns the *problematic* proper to a particular perspective. Social and political theory is history-bound at its origin, since it is always traceable to a historically conditioned awareness of certain problems and issues, a problematic, while at the same time it attempts to transcend the particularity of its historical origins in order to place them within the framework of some general propositions or laws.

Beginning with its problematic, theory can serve two distinct purposes. One is a simple, direct response: to be a guide to help solve the problems posed within the terms of the particular perspective which was the point of departure. The other is more reflective upon the process of theorizing itself: to become clearly aware of the perspective which gives rise to theorizing, and its relation to other perspectives (to achieve a perspective on perspectives); and to open up the possibility of choosing a different valid perspective from which the problematic becomes one of creating an alternative world. Each of these purposes gives rise to a different kind of theory.

The first purpose gives rise to *problem-solving theory*. It takes the world as it finds it, with the prevailing social and power relationships and the institutions into which they are organized, as the given framework for action. The general aim of problem-solving is to make these relationships and institutions work smoothly by dealing effectively with particular sources of trouble. Since the general pattern of institutions and relationships is not called into question, particular problems can be considered in relation to the specialized areas of activity in which they arise. Problem-solving theories are thus fragmented among a multiplicity of spheres or aspects of action, each of which assumes a certain stability in the other spheres (which enables them in practice to be ignored) when confronting a problem arising within its own. The strength of the problem-solving approach lies in its ability to fix limits or parameters to a problem area and to reduce the statement of a particular problem to a limited number of variables which are amenable to relatively close and precise examination. The *ceteris paribus* assumption, upon which such theorizing is based, makes it possible to arrive at statements of laws or regularities which appear to have general validity but which imply, of course, the institutional and relational parameters assumed in the problem-solving approach.

The second purpose leads to *critical theory*. It is critical in the sense that it stands apart from the prevailing order of the world and asks how that order came about. Critical theory, unlike problem-solving theory, does not take institutions and social and power relations for granted but calls them into question by concerning itself with their origins and how and whether they might be in the process of changing. It is directed toward an appraisal of the very framework for action, or problematic, which problem-solving theory accepts as its parameters. Critical theory is directed to the social and political complex as a whole rather than to the separate parts. As a matter of practice, critical theory, like problem-solving theory, takes as its starting point some aspect or particular sphere of human activity. But whereas the problem-solving approach leads to further analytical subdivision and limitation of the issue to be dealt with, the critical approach leads toward the construction of a larger picture of the whole of which the initially contemplated part is just one component, and seeks to understand the processes of change in which both parts and whole are involved.

Critical theory is theory of history in the sense of being concerned not just with the past but with a continuing process of historical change. Problem-solving theory is nonhistorical or ahistorical, since it, in effect, posits a continuing present (the permanence of the institutions and power relations which constitute its parameters). The strength of the one is the weakness of the other. Because it deals with a changing reality, critical theory must continually adjust its concepts to the changing object it seeks to understand and explain.[3] These concepts and the accompanying methods of inquiry seem to lack the precision that can be achieved by problem-solving theory, which posits a fixed order as its point of reference. This relative strength of problem-solving theory, however, rests upon a false premise, since the social and political order is not fixed but (at least in a long-range perspective) is changing. Moreover, the assumption of fixity is not merely a convenience of method, but also an ideological bias. Problem-solving theories can be represented, in the broader perspective of critical theory, as serving particular national, sectional, or class interests, which are comfortable within the given order. Indeed, the purpose served by problem-solving theory is conservative, since it aims to solve the problems arising in various parts of a complex whole in order to smooth the functioning of the whole. This aim rather belies the frequent claim of problem-solving theory to be value-free. It is methodologically value-free insofar as it treats the variables it considers as objects (as the chemist treats molecules or the physicist forces and motion); but it is value-bound by virtue of the fact that it implicitly accepts the prevailing order as its own framework. Critical theory contains problem-solving theories within itself, but contains them in the form of identifiable ideologies, thereby pointing to their conservative consequences, not to their usefulness as guides to action. Problem-solving theory stakes its claims on its greater precision and, to the extent that it recognizes critical theory at all, challenges the possibility of achieving any scientific knowledge of historical processes.

Critical theory is, of course, not unconcerned with the problems of the real world. Its aims are just as practical as those of problem-solving theory, but it approaches practice from a perspective which transcends that of the existing order, which problem-solving theory takes as its starting point. Critical theory allows for a normative choice in favor of a social and political order different from the prevailing order, but it limits the range of choice to alternative orders which are feasible transformations of the existing world. A principal objective of critical theory, therefore, is to clarify this range of possible alternatives. Critical theory thus contains an element of utopianism in the sense that it can represent a coherent picture of an alternative order, but its utopianism is constrained by its comprehension of historical processes. It must reject improbable alternatives just as it rejects the permanency of the existing order. In this way critical theory can be a guide to strategic action for bringing about an alternative order, whereas problem-solving theory is a guide to tactical actions which, intended or unintended, sustain the existing order.

The perspectives of different historical periods favor one or the other kind of theory. Periods of apparent stability or fixity in power relations favor the problem-solving approach. The Cold War was one such period. In international relations, it fostered a concentration upon the problems of how to manage an apparently enduring relationship between two superpowers. However, a condition of uncertainty in power relations beckons to critical theory as people seek to understand the opportunities and risks of change. Thus the events of the 1970s generated a sense of greater fluidity in power relationships, of a many-faceted crisis, crossing the threshold of uncertainty and opening the opportunity for a new development of critical theory directed to the problems of world order. To reason about possible future world orders now, however, requires a broadening of our inquiry beyond conventional international relations, so as to encompass basic processes at work in the development of social forces and forms of state, and in the structure of global political economy. Such, at least, is the central argument of this essay.

Realism, Marxism, and an Approach to a Critical Theory of World Order

Currents of theory which include works of sophistication usually share some of the features of both problem-solving and critical theory but tend to emphasize one approach over the other. Two currents which have had something important to say about interstate relations and world orders—realism and Marxism—are considered here as a preliminary to an attempted development of the critical approach.

The realist theory of international relations had its origin in a historical mode of thought. Friedrich Meinecke (1957), in his study on *raison d'état,* traced it to the political theory of Machiavelli and the diplomacy of Renaissance Italian city-states quite distinct from the general norms propagated by the ideologically dominant institution of medieval society, the Christian church. In perceiving the doctrines and principles underlying the conduct of states as a reaction to specific historical circumstances, Meinecke's interpretation of *raison d'état* is a contribution to critical theory. Other scholars associated with the realist tradition, such as E. H. Carr and Ludwig Dehio, have continued this historical mode of thought, delineating the particular configurations of forces which fixed the framework of international behavior in different periods and trying to understand institutions, theories and events within their historical contexts.

Since the Second World War, some American scholars, notably Hans Morgenthau and Kenneth Waltz, have transformed realism into a form of problem-solving theory. Though individuals of considerable historical learning, they have tended to adopt the fixed ahistorical view of the framework for action characteristic of problem-solving theory, rather than standing back from this framework, in the manner of E. H. Carr, and treating it as historically conditioned and thus susceptible to change. It is no accident that this tendency in theory coincided with the Cold War, which imposed the category of bipolarity upon international relations, and an overriding concern for the defense of American power as a bulwark of the maintenance of order.

The generalized form of the framework for action postulated by this new American realism (which we shall henceforth call neorealism, which is the ideological form abstracted from the real historical framework imposed by the Cold War) is characterized by three levels, each of which can be understood in terms of what classical philosophers would call substances or essences, that is, fundamental and unchanging substrata of changing and accidental manifestations or phenomena. These basic realities were conceived as: (1) the nature of man, understood in terms of Augustinian original sin or the Hobbesian "perpetual and restless desire for power after power that ceaseth only in death" (Hobbes 16: part I, ch. xi); (2) the nature of states, which differ in their domestic cor :i-tutions and in their capabilities for mobilizing strength, but are similar in their fixation with a particular concept of national interest (a Leibnizian *monad*) as a guide to their actions; and (3) the nature of the state system, which places rational constraints upon the unbridled pursuit of rival national interests through the mechanism of the balance of power.

Having arrived at this view of underlying substances, history becomes for neorealists a quarry providing materials with which to illustrate variations on always recurrent themes. The mode of thought ceases to be historical even though the materials used are derived from history. Moreover, this mode of reasoning dictates that, with respect to essentials, the future will always be like the past.[4]

In addition, this core of neorealist theory has extended itself into such areas as game theory, in which the notion of substance at the level of human nature is presented as a rationality assumed to be common to the competing actors who appraise the stakes at issue, the alternative strategies, and the respective payoffs in a similar manner. This idea of a common rationality reinforces the nonhistorical mode of thinking. Other modes of thought are to be castigated as inapt; and there is no attempt to understand them in their own terms (which makes it difficult to account for the irruption into international affairs of a phenomenon like Islamic integralism for instance).

The "common rationality" of neorealism arises from its polemic with liberal internationalism. For neorealism, this rationality is the one appropriate response to a postulated anarchic state system. Morality is effective only to the extent that it is enforced by physical power. This has given neorealism the appearance of being a non-normative theory. It is "value-free" in its exclusion of moral goals (wherein it sees the weakness of liberal internationalism) and in its reduction of problems to their physical power relations. This non-normative quality is, however, only superficial. There is a latent normative element which derives from the assumptions of neorealist theory: security within the postulated interstate system depends upon each of the major actors understanding this system in the same way, that is to say, upon each of them adopting neorealist rationality as a guide to action. Neorealist theory derives from its foundations the prediction that the actors, from their experiences within the system, will tend to think in this way; but the theory also performs a proselytising function as the advocate of this form of rationality. To the neorealist theorist, this proselytising function (wherein lies the normative role of neorealism) is particularly urgent in states which have attained power in excess of that required to balance rivals, since such states may be tempted to discard the rationality of neorealism and try to impose their own moral sense of order, particularly if, as in the case of the United States, cultural tradition has encouraged more optimistic and moralistic views of the nature of man, the state and world order.[5]

The debate between neorealist and liberal internationalists reproduces, with up-to-date materials, the seventeenth-century challenge presented by the civil philosophy of Hobbes to the natural-law theory of Grotius. Each of the arguments is grounded in different views of the essences of man, the state and the interstate system. An alternative which offered the possibility of getting beyond this opposition of mutually exclusive concepts was pointed out by the eighteenth-century Neapolitan Giambattista Vico, for whom the nature of man and of human institutions (among which must be included the state and the interstate system) should not be thought of in terms of unchanging substances but rather as a continuing creation of new forms. In the duality of continuity and change, where neorealism stresses continuity, the Vichian perspective stresses change; as Vico wrote (1744/1970: para. 349), ". . . this world of nations has certainly been made by men, and its guise must therefore be found within the modifications of our own human mind."

This should not be taken as a statement of radical idealism, (that is, that the world is a creation of mind). For Vico, everchanging forms of mind were shaped by the complex of social relations in the genesis of which class struggle played the principal role, as it later did for Marx. Mind is, however, the thread connecting the present with the past, a means of access to a knowledge of these changing modes of social reality. Human nature (the modifications of mind) and human institutions are identical with human history; they are to be understood in genetic and not in essentialist terms (as in neorealism) or in teleological terms (as in functionalism). One cannot, in this Vichian perspective, properly abstract man and the state from history so as to define their substances or essences as *prior to* history, history being but the record of interactions of manifestations of these substances. A proper study of human affairs should

be able to reveal both the coherence of minds and institutions characteristic of different ages, and the process whereby one such coherent
pattern—which we can call a historical structure—succeeds another.
Vico's project, which we would now call social science, was to arrive at
a "mental dictionary," or set of common concepts, with which one is
able to comprehend the process of "ideal eternal history," or what is
most general and common in the sequence of changes undergone by
human nature and institutions (paras. 35, 145, 161, 349). The error
which Vico criticized as the "conceit of scholars," who will have it that
"what they know is as old as the world," consists in taking a form of
thought derived from a particular phase of history (and thus from a
particular structure of social relations) and assuming it to be universally
valid [para. 127]. This is an error of neorealism and more generally, the
flawed foundation of all problem-solving theory. It does not, of course,
negate the practical utility of neorealism and problem-solving theories
within their ideological limits. The Vichian approach, by contrast, is that
of critical theory.

How does Marxism relate to this method or approach to a theory of
world order? In the first place, it is impossible, without grave risk of
confusion, to consider Marxism as a single current of thought. For our
purposes, it is necessary to distinguish two divergent Marxist currents,
analogous to the bifurcation between the old realism and the new. There
is a Marxism which reasons historically and seeks to explain, as well as
to promote, changes in social relations; there is also a Marxism, designed
as a framework for the analysis of the capitalist state and society, which
turns its back on historical knowledge in favor of a more static and
abstract conceptualization of the mode of production. The first we may
call by the name under which it recognizes itself: historical materialism.
It is evident in the historical works of Marx, in those of present-day
Marxist historians such as Eric Hobsbawm, and in the thought of Gramsci. It has also influenced some who would not be considered (or consider
themselves) Marxist in any strict sense, such as many of the French
historians associated with the *Annales*. The second is represented by the
so-called structural Marxism of Althusser and Poulantzas ("so-called" in
order to distinguish their use of "structure" from the concept of historical structure in this essay) and most commonly takes the form of an
exegesis of *Capital* and other sacred texts. Structural Marxism shares

some of the features of the neorealist problem-solving approach such as its ahistorical, essentialist epistemology, though not its precision in handling data nor, since it has remained very largely a study in abstractions, its practical applicability to concrete problems. To this extent it does not concern us here. Historical materialism is, however, a foremost source of critical theory and it corrects neorealism in four important respects.

The first concerns dialectic, a term which, like Marxism, has been appropriated to express a variety of not always compatible meanings, so its usage requires some definition. It is used here at two levels: the level of logic and the level of real history. At the level of logic, it means a dialogue seeking truth through the explorations of contradictions.[6] One aspect of this is the continual confrontation of concepts with the reality they are supposed to represent and their adjustment to this reality as it continually changes. Another aspect, which is part of the method of adjusting concepts, is the knowledge that each assertion concerning reality contains implicitly its opposite and that both assertion and opposite are not mutually exclusive but share some measure of the truth sought, a truth, moreover, that is always in motion, never to be encapsulated in some definitive form. At the level of real history, dialectic is the potential for alternative forms of development arising from the confrontation of opposed social forces in any concrete historical situation.

Both realism and historical materialism direct attention to conflict. Neorealism sees conflict as inherent in the human condition, a constant factor flowing directly from the power-seeking essence of human nature and taking the political form of a continual reshuffling of power among the players in a zero-sum game, which is always played according to its own innate rules. Historical materialism sees in conflict the process of a continual remaking of human nature and the creation of new patterns of social relations which change the rules of the game and out of which— if historical materialism remains true to its own logic and method—new forms of conflict may be expected ultimately to arise. In other words, neorealism sees conflict as a recurrent consequence of a continuing structure, whereas historical materialism sees conflict as a possible cause of structural change.

Second, by its focus on imperialism, historical materialism adds a vertical dimension of power to the horizontal dimension of rivalry among the most powerful states, which draws the almost exclusive attention of neorealism. This dimension is the dominance and subordination of metropole over hinterland, center over periphery, in a world political economy.

Third, historical materialism enlarges the realist perspective through its concern with the relationship between the state and civil society. Marxists, like non-Marxists, are divided between those who see the state as the mere expression of the particular interests in civil society and those who see the state as an autonomous force expressing some kind of general interest. This, for Marxists, would be the general interest of capitalism as distinct from the particular interests of capitalists. Gramsci (1971:158–168) contrasted historical materialism, which recognizes the efficacy of ethical and cultural sources of political action (though always relating them with the economic sphere), with what he called historical economism or the reduction of everything to technological and material interests. Neorealist theory in the United States has returned to the state/civil society relationship, though it has treated civil society as a constraint upon the state and a limitation imposed by particular interests upon *raison d'état,* which is conceived of, and defined as, independent of civil society.[7] The sense of a reciprocal relationship between structure (economic relations) and superstructure (the ethico-political sphere) in Gramsci's thinking contains the potential for considering state/society complexes as the constituent entities of a world order and for exploring the particular historical forms taken by these complexes.[8]

Fourth, historical materialism focuses upon the production process as a critical element in the explanation of the particular historical form taken by a state/society complex. The production of goods and services, which creates both the wealth of a society and the basis for a state's ability to mobilize power behind its foreign policy, takes place through a power relationship between those who control and those who execute the tasks of production. Political conflict and the action of the state either maintain, or bring about changes in, these power relations of production. Historical materialism examines the connections between power in production, power in the state, and power in international relations. Neorealism has, by contrast, virtually ignored the production process. This is the point on which the problem-solving bias of neorealism is most clearly to be distinguished from the critical approach of historical materialism. Neorealism implicitly takes the production process and the power relations inherent in it as a given element of the national interest, and therefore as part of its parameters. Historical materialism is sensitive to the dialectical possibilities of change in the sphere of production which could affect the other spheres, such as those of the state and world order.

This discussion has distinguished two kinds of theorizing as a preliminary to proposing a critical approach to a theory of world order. Some of the basic premises for such a critical theory can now be restated:

(1) An awareness that action is never absolutely free but takes place within a framework for action which constitutes its problematic. Critical theory would start with this framework, which means starting with historical inquiry or an appreciation of the human experience that gives rise to the need for theory;[9]

(2) A realization that not only action but also theory is shaped by the problematic. Critical theory is conscious of its own relativity but through this consciousness can achieve a broader time-perspective and become less relative than problem-solving theory. It knows that the task of theorizing can never be finished in an enclosed system but must continually be begun anew;

(3) The framework for action changes over time and a principal goal of critical theory is to understand these changes;

(4) This framework has the form of a historical structure, a particular combination of thought patterns, material conditions and human institutions which has a certain coherence among its elements. These structures do not determine people's actions in any mechanical sense but constitute the context of habits, pressures, expectations and constraints within which action takes place;

(5) The framework or structure within which action takes place is to be viewed, not from the top in terms of the requisites for its equilibrium or reproduction (which would quickly lead back to problem-solving), but rather from the bottom or from outside in terms of the conflicts which arise within it and open the possibility of its transformation.[10]

Frameworks for Action: Historical Structures

As its most abstract, the notion of a framework for action or historical structure is a picture of a particular configuration of forces. This configuration does not determine actions in any direct, mechanical way but imposes pressures and constraints. Individuals and groups may move with the pressures or resist and oppose them, but they cannot ignore them. To the extent that they do successfully resist a prevailing historical structure, they buttress their actions with an alternative, emerging configuration of forces, a rival structure.

Three categories of forces (expressed as potentials) interact in a structure: material capabilities, ideas and institutions (see fig. 8.1). No one-way determinism need be assumed among these three; the relationships can be assumed to be reciprocal. The question of which way the lines of force run is always a historical question to be answered by a study of the particular case.

Figure 8.1..

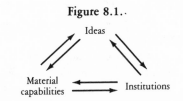

Material capabilities are productive and destructive potentials. In their dynamic form these exist as technological and organizational capabilities, and in their accumulated forms as natural resources which technology can transform, stocks of equipment (for example, industries and armaments), and the wealth which can command these.

Ideas are broadly of two kinds. One kind consists of intersubjective meanings, or those shared notions of the nature of social relations which tend to perpetuate habits and expectations of behavior (Taylor 1965). Examples of intersubjective meanings in contemporary world politics are the notions that people are organized and commanded by states which have authority over defined territories; that states relate to one another through diplomatic agents; that certain rules apply for the protection of diplomatic agents as being in the common interest of all states; and that certain kinds of behavior are to be expected when conflict arises between states, such as negotiation, confrontation, or war. These notions, though durable over long periods of time, are historically conditioned. The realities of world politics have not always been represented in precisely this way and may not be in the future. It is possible to trace the origins of such ideas and also to detect signs of a weakening of some of them.[11]

The other kind of ideas relevant to a historical structure are collective images of social order held by different groups of people. These are differing views as to both the nature and the legitimacy of prevailing power relations, the meanings of justice and public good, and so forth. Whereas intersubjective meanings are broadly common throughout a particular historical structure and constitute the common ground of social discourse (including conflict), collective images may be several and opposed.[12] The clash of rival collective images provides evidence of the potential for alternative paths of development and raises questions as to the possible material and institutional basis for the emergence of an alternative structure.

Institutionalization is a means of stabilizing and perpetuating a particular order. Institutions reflect the power relations prevailing at their point of origin and tend, at least initially, to encourage collective images consistent with these power relations. Eventually, institutions take on their own life; they can become a battleground of opposing tendencies, or rival institutions may reflect different tendencies. Institutions are particular amalgams of ideas and material power which in turn influence the development of ideas and material capabilities.

There is a close connection between institutionalization and what Gramsci called hegemony. Institutions provide ways of dealing with conflicts so as to minimize the use of force. There is an enforcement potential in the material power relations underlying any structure, in that the strong can clobber the weak if they think it necessary. But force will not have to be used in order to ensure the dominance of the strong to the extent that the weak accept the prevailing power relations as legitimate. This the weak may do if the strong see their mission as hegemonic and not merely dominant or dictatorial, that is, if they are willing to make concessions that will secure the weak's acquiescence in their leadership and if they can express this leadership in terms of universal or general interests, rather than just as serving their own particular interests.[13] Institutions may become the anchor for such a hegemonic strategy since they lend themselves both to the representations of diverse interests and to the universalization of policy.

It is convenient to be able to distinguish between hegemonic and nonhegemonic structures, that is to say between those in which the power basis of the structure tends to recede into the background of consciousness, and those in which the management of power relations is always in the forefront. Hegemony cannot, however, be reduced to an

institutional dimension. One must beware of allowing a focus upon institutions to obscure either changes in the relationship of material forces,
or the emergence of ideological challenge to an erstwhile prevailing order.
Institutions may be out of phase with these other aspects of reality and
their efficacy as a means of regulating conflict (and thus their hegemonic
function) thereby undermined. They may be an expression of hegemony
but cannot be taken as identical to hegemony.

The method of historical structures is one of representing what can
be called limited totalities. The historical structure does not represent
the whole world but rather a particular sphere of human activity in its
historically located totality. The *ceteris paribus* problem, which falsifies
problem-solving theory by leading to an assumption of total stasis, is
avoided by juxtaposing and connecting historical structures in related
spheres of action. Dialectic is introduced, first, by deriving the definition
of a particular structure, not from some abstract model of a social system
or mode of production, but from a study of the historical situation to
which it relates, and second, by looking for the emergence of rival
structures expressing alternative possibilities of development. The three
sets of forces indicated in figure 8.1 are a heuristic device, not categories
with a predetermined hierarchy of relationships. Historical structures are
contrast models: like ideal types they provide, in a logically coherent
form, a simplified representation of a complex reality and an expression
of tendencies, limited in their applicability in time and space, rather than
fully realized developments.

For the purpose of the present discussion, the method of historical
structures is applied to the three levels, or spheres of activity: (1) organization of production, more particularly with regard to the *social forces*
engendered by the production process; (2) *forms of state* as derived from
a study of state/society complexes; and (3) *world orders,* that is, the particular configurations of forces which successively define the problematic
of war or peace for the ensemble of states. Each of these levels can be
studied as a succession of dominant and emergent rival structures.

The three levels are interrelated. Changes in the organization of production generate new social forces which, in turn, bring about changes
in the structure of states; and the generalization of changes in the structure of states alters the problematic of world order. For instance, as E. H.
Carr (1945) argued, the incorporation of the industrial workers (a new

social force) as participants within western states from the late nine-teeenth century, accentuated the movement of these states toward eco-nomic nationalism and imperialism (a new form of state), which brought about a fragmentation of the world economy and a more conflictual phase of international relations (the new structure of world order).

The relationship among the three levels is not, however, simply uni-linear. Transnational social forces have influenced states through the world structure, as evidenced by the effect of expansive nineteenth-century capitalism, *les bourgeois conquérants* (Morazé 1957), upon the development of state structures in both core and periphery. Particular structures of world order exert influence over the forms which states take: Stalinism was, at least in part, a response to a sense of threat to the existence of the Soviet state from a hostile world order; the military-industrial com-plex in core countries, justifies its influence today by pointing to the conflictual condition of world order; and the prevalence of repressive militarism in periphery countries can be explained by the external sup-port of imperialism as well as by a particular conjunction of internal forces. Forms of state also affect the development of social forces through the kinds of domination they exert, for example, by advancing one class interest and thwarting others.[14]

Considered separately, social forces, forms of state, and world orders can be represented in a preliminary approximation as particular config-urations of material capabilities, ideas and institutions (as indicated in figure 8.1). Considered in relation to each other, and thus moving toward a fuller representation of historical process, each will be seen as con-taining, as well as bearing the impact of, the others (as in figure 8.2).[15]

Figure 8.2.

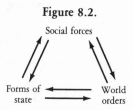

Hegemony and World Orders

How are these reciprocal relationships to be read in the present historical conjuncture? Which of the several relationships will tell us the most? A sense of the historicity of concepts suggests that the critical relationships may not be the same in successive historical periods, even within the post-Westphalian era for which the term "state system" has particular meaning. The approach to a critical theory of world order, adumbrated here, takes the form of an interconnected series of historical hypotheses.

Neo-realism puts the accent on states reduced to their dimension of material force and similarly reduces the structure of world order to the balance of power as a configuration of material forces. Neorealism, which generally dismisses social forces as irrelevant, is not much concerned with differentiating forms of state (except insofar as "strong societies" in liberal democratic polities may hamper the use of force by the state or advance particular interests over the national interest), and tends to place a low value on the normative and institutional aspects of world order.

One effort to broaden the realist perspective to include variations in the authority of international norms and institutions is the theory of "hegemonic stability" which, as stated by Robert Keohane (1980), "holds that hegemonic structures of power, dominated by a single country, are most conducive to the development of strong international regimes, whose rules are relatively precise and well-obeyed."[16] The classic illustrations of the theory discussed by Keohane are the *pax britannica* of the mid-nineteenth century and the *pax americana* of the years following the Second World War. The theory appears to be confirmed by the decline in observance of the norms of the nineteenth-century order which accompanied Britain's relative decline in state power from the late-nineteenth century. Exponents of the theory see a similar decline, since the early 1970s, in the observance of norms of the postwar order, relating it to a relative decline in U.S. power. Robert Keohane has tested the theory in particular issue areas (energy, money and trade) on the grounds that power is not a fungible asset, but has to be differentiated according to the contexts in which a state tried to be influential. He finds that, particularly in the areas of trade and money, changes in U.S. power are insufficient to explain the changes that have occurred and need to be supplemented by the introduction of domestic political, economic and cultural factors.

An alternative approach might start by redefining what it is that is to be explained, namely, the relative stability of successive world orders. This can be done by equating stability with a concept of hegemony that is based on a coherent conjunction or fit between a configuration of material power, the prevalent collective image of world order (including certain norms) and a set of institutions which administer the order with a certain semblance of universality (that is, not just as the overt instruments of a particular state's dominance). In this formulation, state power ceases to be the sole explanatory factor and becomes part of what is to be explained. This rephrasing of the question addresses a major difficulty in the neorealist version signalled by Keohane and others, namely, how to explain the failure of the United States to establish a stable world order in the interwar period despite its preponderance of power. If the dominance of a single state coincides with a stable order on some occasions but not on others, then there may be some merit in looking more closely at what is meant by stability and more broadly at what may be its sufficient conditions. Dominance by a powerful state may be a necessary but not a sufficient condition of hegemony.

The two periods of the *pax britannica* and the *pax americana* also satisfy the reformulated definition of hegemony. In the mid-nineteenth century, Britain's world supremacy was founded on its sea power, which remained free from challenge by a continental state as a result of Britain's ability to play the role of balancer in a relatively fluid balance of power in Europe. The norms of liberal economics (free trade, the gold standard, free movement of capital and persons) gained widespread acceptance with the spread of British prestige, providing a universalistic ideology which represented these norms as the basis of a harmony of interests. While there were no formal international institutions, the ideological separation of economics from politics meant that the City could appear as administrator and regulator according to these universal rules, with British sea power remaining in the background as potential enforcer.

The historical structure was transformed in its three dimensions during the period running from the last quarter of the nineteenth century through the Second World War. During this period British power declined relatively, losing its undisputed supremacy at sea, first with the German challenge and then with the rise of U.S. power; economic liberalism foundered with the rise of protectionism, the new imperialisms and ultimately the end of the gold standard; and the belated and abortive attempt at international institutionalization through the League of Nations, unsustained either by a dominant power or a widely accepted ideology, collapsed in a world increasingly organized into rival power blocs.

The power configuration of the *pax americana* was more rigid than that of the earlier hegemony, taking the form of alliances (all hinging on U.S. power) created in order to contain the Soviet Union. The stabilization of this power configuration created the conditions for the unfolding of a global economy in which the United States played a role similar to that of Britain and mid-nineteenth century. The United States rarely needed to intervene directly in support of specific national economic interests; by maintaining the rules of an international economic order according to the revised liberalism of Bretton Woods, the strength of U.S. corporations engaged in the pursuit of profits was sufficient to ensure continuing national power. The *pax americana* produced a greater number of formal international institutions than the earlier hegemony. The nineteenth-century separation of politics and eocnomics had been blurred by the experience of the Great Depression and the rise of Keynesian doctrines. Since states now had a legitimate and necessary overt role in national economic management, it became necessary both to multilateralize the administrative management of the international economy and to give it an intergovernmental quality.

The notion of hegemony as a fit between power, ideas and institutions makes it possible to deal with some of the problems in the theory of state dominance as the necessary condition for a stable international order; it allows for lags and leads in hegemony. For example, so appealing was the nostalgia for the nineteenth-century hegemony that the ideological dimension of the *pax brittanica* flourished long after the power configuration that supported it had vanished. Sustained, and utlimately futile, efforts were made to revive a liberal world economy along with the gold standard in the interwar period. Even in the postwar period, British policy continued to give precedence to balance of payments problems over national industrial development and employment considerations.[17] A "lead" case is that of the United States, where the growth indicators of material power during the interwar period were insufficient predictors of a new hegemony. It was necessary that U.S. leaders should come to see themselves in ideological terms as the necessary guarantors of a new world order. The Roosevelt era made this transition, including both the conscious rejection of the old hegemony (e.g., by torpedoing the world economic conference in 1933 and abandoning the gold standard) and the gradual incorporation of New-Deal principles into the ideological basis of the new world order. There followed U.S. initiative to create the institutions to administer this order.[18] Neomercantilists in the United States now warn against a danger of repeating the British error, urging U.S. policymakers not to continue to operate according to doctrines appropriate to the *pax americana* when the United States can no longer afford to act as guarantor for a universalist world order. Their persuasive efforts underline the point that in these matters ideology is a determining sphere of action which has to be understood in its connections with material power relations.

Social Forces, Hegemony and Imperialism

Represented as a fit between material power, ideology and institutions, hegemony may seem to lend itself to a cyclical theory of history; the three dimensions fitting together in certain times and places and coming apart in others. This is reminiscent of earlier notions of *virtù*, or of the *weltgeist* migrating from people to people. The analogy merely points to something which remains unexplained. What is missing is some theory as to how and why the fit comes about and comes apart. It is my contention that the explanation may be sought in the realm of social forces shaped by production relations.

Social forces are not to be thought of as existing exclusively within states. Particular social forces may overflow state boundaries, and world structures can be described in terms of social forces just as they can be described as configurations of state power. The world can be represented as a pattern of interacting social forces in which states play an inter-mediate though autonomous role between the global structure of social forces and local configurations of social forces within particular countries. This may be called a political economy perspective of the world: power is seen as *emerging* from social processes rather than taken as given in the form of accumulated material capabilities, that is as the result of these processes. (Paraphrasing Marx, one could describe the latter, neo-realist view as the "fetishism of power.")[19] In reaching for a political economy perspective, we move from identifying the structural charac-teristics of world orders as configurations of material capabilities, ideas and institutions (fig. 8.1) to explaining their origins, growth and demise in terms of the interrelationships of the three levels of structures (fig. 8.2).

It is, of course, no great discovery to find that, viewed in the political economy perspective, the *pax britannica* was based both on the ascendancy of manufacturing capitalism in the international exchange economy, of which Britain was the center, and on the social and ideological power, in Britain and other parts of northwest Europe, of the class which drew its wealth from manufacturing. The new bourgeoisie did not need to control states directly; its social power became the premise of state politics.[20]

The demise of this hegemonic order can also be explained by the development of social forces. Capitalism mobilized an industrial labor force in the most advanced countries, and from the last quarter of the nineteenth century industrial workers had an impact on the structure of the state in these countries. The incorporation of the industrial workers, the new social force called into existence by manufacturing capitalism, into the nation involved an extension in the range of state action in the form of economic intervention and social policy. This in turn brought the factor of domestic welfare (i.e., the social minimum required to maintain the allegiance of the workers) into the realm of foreign policy. The claims of welfare competed with the exigencies of liberal internationalism within the management of states; as the former gained ground, protectionism, the new imperialism and ultimately the end of the gold standard marked the long decline of liberal internationalism.[21] The liberal form of state was slowly replaced by the welfare nationalist form of state.

The spread of industrialization, and the mobilization of social classes it brought about, not only changed the nature of states but also altered the international configuration of state power as new rivals overtook Britain's lead. Protectionism, as the means of building economic power comparable to Britain's, was for these new industrial countries more convincing than the liberal theory of comparative advantage. The new imperialisms of the major industrial powers were a projection abroad of the welfare nationalist consensus among social forces sought or achieved within the nations. As both the material predominance of the British economy and the appeal of the hegemonic ideology weakened, the hegemonic world order of the mid-nineteenth century gave place to a non-hegemonic configuration of rival power blocs.

Imperialism is a rather loose concept which in practice has to be newly defined with reference to each historical period. There is little point in looking for any "essence" of imperialism beyond the forms which dominance and subordination take in different successive world order structures. The actual form, whether activated by states, by social forces (e.g., the managements of multinational corporations), or some combination of both, and whether domination is primarily political or economic, is to be determined by historical analysis, and not by deductive reasoning.

The expansive capitalism of the mid-nineteenth century brought most of the world into the exchange relations of an international economy centered in London. The liberal imperialism of this phase was largely indifferent as to whether or not peripheral countries were formally independent or under the political-administrative control of a colonial power, provided that the rules of the international economy were observed.[22] Canada and Argentina, for example, had similar positions in real terms, though one had colonial and the other independent status. In the phase of liberal imperialism, local authorities, who were often precapitalist in their relationship to the production process (e.g., traditional agrarian-based rulers), kept their countries in the commercial system. During the second phase, that of the so-called new imperialism following the 1870s, direct state control began to supplant the less formal patterns of the commercial period. Capitalist production relations under this political aegis penetrated the periphery more thoroughly, notably in the extraction of raw materials and the building of the infrastructure (roads, railways, ports, and commercial and governmental administrations) required to link the colonies more closely with the metropole.

Capitalist production relations generated new social forces in the periphery. Outsiders came to play important roles in the local society, some as agents of the colonial administration and of big capital from the metropole, others in smaller businesses, filling the interstices between big capital and traditional local production (for example, the Chinese in southeast Asia, the Indians in east Africa or the Lebanese in west Africa). A local workforce often numerically small and materially better off than the majority of the population, was drawn into capitalist production. This politically strategic group was opposed to capital on wage and labor issues but aligned with it as regards the development of the capitalist production sector. An indigenous petty bourgeoisie also grew up, occupying the subordinate positions in colonial administration and metropole-based enterprises, as well as in local small business. A local state apparatus emerged under colonial tutelage, encouraging the new production relations by methods ranging from the introduction of compulsory labor or a head tax as a means of generating a labor force, to reproducing, in the colonial context, some of the institutions and procedures of the industrial relations of the metropole.

The existence in the colonial territory of these new social forces, labor and the petty bourgeoisie, which could agree on a nationalist political program, together with the introduction by the colonial administration of the elements of a modern state apparatus (control of which could be the aim of this program) laid the basis for the anticolonial revolt which swept the colonial world after the Second World War. This movement reacted against administrative control from the metropole, but not continued involvement in capitalist production and exchange relations. The anti-imperialist label on the forces which replaced the structures created by the second phase or new imperialism obscured their role in ushering in yet a third phase of imperialism.

James Petras (1980), in his use of the concept of an imperial state system, has posed a number of questions concerning the structural characteristics of states in the present world order. The dominant imperial state and subordinate collaborator states differ in structure and have complementary functions in the imperial system; they are not just more and less powerful units of the same kind, as might be represented in a simple neorealist model. A striking feature in his framework is that the imperial state he analyzes is not the whole U.S. government; it is "those executive bodies within the 'government' which are charged with promoting and protecting the expansion of capital across state boundaries." The imperial system is at once more than and less than the state. It is more than the state in that it is a transnational structure with a dominant core and dependent periphery. This part of the U.S. government is at the system's core, together (and here we may presume to enlarge upon Petras' indications) with interstate institutions such as the IMF and the World Bank symbiotically related to expansive capital, and with collaborator governments (or at any rate parts of them linked to the system) in the system's periphery. It is less than the state in the sense that nonimperial, or even anti-imperial, forces may be present in other parts of both core and periphery states. The unity of the state, posited by neorealism, is fragmented in this image, and the struggle for and against the imperial system may go on within the state structures at both core and periphery as well as among social forces ranged in support and opposition to the system. The state is thus a necessary but insufficient category to account for the imperial system. The imperial system itself becomes the starting point of inquiry.

The imperial system is a world order structure drawing support from a particular configuration of social forces, national and transnational, and of core and periphery states. One must beware of slipping into the language of reification when speaking of structures; they are constraints on action, not actors. The imperial system includes some formal and less formal organizations at the system level through which pressures on states can be exerted without these system-level organizations actually usurping state power. The behavior of particular states or of organized economic and social interests, however, finds its meaning in the larger totality of the imperial system. Actions are shaped either directly by pressures projected through the system or indirectly by the subjective awareness on the part of actors of the constraints imposed by the system. Thus one cannot hope to understand the imperial system by identifying imperialism with actors, be they states or multinationals; these are both dominant elements in the system, but the system as a structure is more than their sum. Furthermore, one must beware of ignoring the principle of dialectic by overemphasizing the power and coherence of a structure, even a very dominant one. Where a structure is manifestly dominant, critical theory leads one to look for a counterstructure, even a latent one, by seeking out its possible bases of support and elements of cohesion.

At this point, it is preferable to revert to the earlier terminology which referred to hegemonic and nonhegemonic world order structures. To introduce the term "imperial" with reference to the *pax americana* risks both obscuring the important difference between hegemonic and non-hegemonic world orders and confusing structurally different kinds of imperialism (e.g., liberal imperialism, the new or colonial imperialism, and the imperial system just outlined). The contention here is that the *pax americana* was hegemonic: it commanded a wide measure of consent among states outside the the Soviet sphere and was able to provide sufficient benefits to the associated and subordinate elements in order to maintain their acquiescence. Of course, consent wore thin as one approached the periphery where the element of force was always apparent, and it was in the periphery that the challenge to the imperial system first became manifest.

It was suggested above how the particular fit between power, ideology, and institutions constituting the *pax americana* came into being. Since the practical issue at the present is whether or not the *pax americana* has irretrievably come apart and if so what may replace it, two specific questions deserving attention are: (1) what are the mechanisms for maintaining hegemony in this particular historical structure? and (2) what social forces and/or forms of state have been generated within it which could oppose and ultimately bring about a transformation of the structure?

The Internationalization of the State

A partial answer to the first question concerns the internationalization of the state. The basic principles of the *pax americana* were similar to those of the *pax britannica*—relatively free movement of goods, capital and technology and a reasonable degree of predictability in exchange rates. Cordell Hull's conviction that an open trading world was a necessary condition of peace could be taken as its ideological text, supplemented by confidence in economic growth and ever-rising productivity as the basis for moderating and controlling conflict. The postwar hegemony was, however, more fully institutionalized than the *pax britannica* and the main function of its institutions was to reconcile domestic social pressures with the requirements of a world economy. The International Monetary Fund was set up to provide loans to countries with balance of payments deficits in order to provide time in which they could make adjustments, and to avoid the sharp deflationary consequences of an automatic gold standard. The World Bank was to be a vehicle for longer term financial assistance. Economically weak countries were to be given assistance by the system itself, either directly through the system's institutions or by other states after the system's institutions had certified their conformity to the system's norms. These institutions incorporated mechanisms to supervise the application of the system's norms and to make financial assistance effectively conditional upon reasonable evidence of intent to live up to the norms.

This machinery of surveillance was, in the case of the western allies and subsequently of all industrialized capitalist countries, supplemented by elaborate machinery for the harmonization of national policies. Such procedures began with the mutual criticism of reconstruction plans in western European countries (the U.S. condition for Marshall aid funds), continued with the development of annual review procedure in NATO (which dealt with defense and defense support programs), and became an acquired habit of mutual consultation and mutual review of national policies (through the OECD and other agencies).

The notion of international obligation moved beyond a few basic commitments, such as observance of the most favored nation principle or maintenance of an agreed exchange rate, to a general recognition that measures of national economic policy affect other countries and that such consequences should be taken into account before national policies are adopted. Conversely, other countries should be sufficiently understanding of one country's difficulties to acquiesce in short-term exceptions. Adjustments are thus perceived as responding to the needs of the system as a whole and not to the will of dominant countries. External pressures upon national policies were accordingly internationalized.

Of course, such an internationalized policy process presupposed a power structure, one in which central agencies of the U.S. government were in a dominant position. But it was not necessarily an entirely hierarchical power structure with lines of force running exclusively from the top down, nor was it one in which the units of interaction were whole nation-states. It was a power structure seeking to maintain consensus through bargaining and one in which the bargaining units were fragments of states. The power behind the negotiation was tacitly taken into account by the parties.

The practice of policy harmonization became such a powerful habit that when the basic norms of international economic behavior no longer seemed valid, as became the case during the 1970s, procedures for mutual adjustment of national economic policies were, if anything, reinforced. In the absence of clear norms, the need for mutual adjustment appeared the greater.[23]

State structures appropriate to this process of policy harmonization can be contrasted with those of the welfare nationalist state of the preceding period. Welfare nationalism took the form of economic planning at the national level and the attempt to control external economic impacts upon the national economy. To make national planning effective, corporative structures grew up in most industrially advanced countries for the purpose of bringing industry, and also organized labor, into consultation with the government in the formulation and implementation of policy. National and industrial corporative structures can raise protectionist or restrictive obstacles to the adjustments required for adaptation of national economies to the world economy in a hegemonic system. Corporatism at the national level was a response to the conditions of the interwar period; it became institutionally consolidated in western Europe just as the world structure was changing into something for which national corporatism was ill-suited.

The internationalization of the state gives precedence to certain state agencies—notably ministries of finance and prime ministers' offices—which are key points in the adjustment of domestic to international economic policy. Ministries of industries, labor ministries, planning offices, which had been built up in the context of national corporatism, tended to be subordinated to the central organs of internationalized public policy. As national economies became more integrated in the world economy, it was the larger and more technologically advanced enterprises that adapted best to the new opportunities. A new axis of influence linked international policy networks with the key central agencies of government and with big business. This new informal corporative structure overshadowed the older more formalized national corporatism and reflected the dominance of the sector oriented to the world economy over the more nationally oriented sector of a country's economy.[24]

The internationalization of the state is not, of course, limited to advanced capitalist core countries. It would not be difficult to make a catalogue of recent cases in peripheral countries where institutions of the world economy, usually as a condition for debt renewal, have dictated policies which could only be sustained by a coalition of conservative forces. Turkey, Peru, and Portugal are among those recently affected. As for Zaire, a conference of creditors laid down the condition that officials of the IMF be placed within the key ministries of the state to oversee the fulfillment of the conditions of debt renewal.[25]

The Internationalization of Production

The internationalization of the state is associated with the expansion of international production. This signifies the integration of production processes on a transnational scale, with different phases of a single process being carried out in different countries. International production currently plays the formative role in relation to the structure of states and world order that national manufacturing and commercial capital played in the mid-nineteenth century.

International production expands through direct investment, whereas the rentier imperialism, of which Hobson and Lenin wrote, primarily took the form of portfolio investment. With portfolio investment, control over the productive resources financed by the transaction passed with ownership to the borrower. With direct investment, control is inherent in the production process itself and remains with the originator of the investment. The essential feature of direct investment is possession, not of money, but of knowledge—in the form of technology and especially in the capacity to continue to develop new technology. The financial arrangements for direct investment may vary greatly, but all are subordinated to this crucial factor of technical control. The arrangements may take the form of wholly owned subsidiaries, joint ventures with local capital sometimes put up by the state in host countries, management contracts with state-owned enterprises, or compensation agreements with socialist enterprises whereby, in return for the provision of technology, these enterprises become suppliers of elements to a globally organized production process planned and controlled by the source of the technology. Formal ownership is less important than the manner in which various elements are integrated into the production system.

Direct investment seems to suggest the dominance of industrial capital over finance capital. The big multinational corporations which expand by direct investment are, to some degree, self-financing and to the extent that they are not they seem capable of mobilizing money capital in a number of ways, such as through local capital markets (where their credit is better than that of national entrepreneurs), through the Euro-currency markets, through infusions of capital from other multinationals linked to technology and production agreements, through state subsidies, and so forth. And yet, particularly since the 1970s, finance capital seems to be returning to prominence through the operations of the multinational banks, not only in the old form of rentier imperialism administering loans to peripheral states, but also as a network of control and private planning for the world economy of international production. This network assesses and collectivizes investment risks and allocates investment opportunities among the participants in the expansion of international production, that is, it performs the function of Lenin's collective capitalist in the conditions of late-twentieth-century production relations.

International Production and Class Structure

International production is mobilizing social forces, and it is through these forces that its major political consequences vis-à-vis the nature of states and future world orders may be anticipated. Hitherto, social classes have been found to exist within nationally defined social formations, despite rhetorical appeals to the international solidarity of workers. Now, as a consequence of international production, it becomes increasingly pertinent to think in terms of a global class structure alongside or superimposed upon national class structures.

At the apex of an emerging global class structure is the transnational managerial class. Having its own ideology, strategy and institutions of collective action, it is a class both in itself and for itself. Its focal points of organization, the Trilateral Commission, World Bank, IMF and OECD, develop both a framework of thought and guidelines for policies. From these points, class action penetrates countries through the process of internationalization of the state. The members of this transnational class are not limited to those who carry out functions at the global level, such as executives of multinational corporations or as senior officials of international agencies, but include those who manage the internationally oriented sectors within countries, the finance ministry officials, local managers of enterprises linked into international production systems, and so on.[26]

National capitalists are to be distinguished from the transnational class. The natural reflex of national capital faced with the challenge of international production is protectionism. It is torn between the desire to use the state as a bulwark of an independent national economy and the opportunity of filling niches left by international production in a sub-ordinate symbiotic relationship with the latter.

Industrial workers have been doubly fragmented. One line of cleavage is between established and nonestablished labor. Established workers are those who have attained a status of relative security and stability in their jobs and have some prospects of career advancement. Generally they are relatively skilled, work for larger enterprises, and have effective trade unions. Nonestablished workers, by contrast, have insecure employment, have no prospect of career advancement, are relatively less skilled, and confront great obstacles in developing effective trade unions. Frequently, the nonestablished are disproportionately drawn from lower-status ethnic minorities, immigrants and women. The institutions of working class action have privileged established workers. Only when the ideology of class solidarity remains powerful, which usually means only in conditions of high ideological polarization and social and political conflict, do or-ganizations controlled by established workers (unions and political par-ties) attempt to rally and act for nonestablished workers as well.

The second line of cleavage among industrial workers is brought about by the division between national and international capital (i.e., that en-gaged in international production). The established workers in the sector of international production are potential allies of international capital. This is not to say that those workers have no conflict with international capital, only that international capital has the resources to resolve these conflicts and to isolate them from conflicts involving other labor groups by creating an enterprise corporatism in which both parties perceive their interest as lying in the continuing expansion of international pro-duction.

Established workers in the sector of national capital are more suscep-tible to the appeal of protectionism and national (rather than enterprise) corporatism in which the defense of national capital, of jobs and of the workers' acquired status in industrial relations institutions, are perceived to be interconnected.[27]

Nonestablished labor has become of particular importance in the ex-pansion of international production. Production systems are being de-signed so as to make use of an increasing proportion of semi-skilled (and therefore frequently nonestablished) in relation to skilled (and established) labor.[28] This tendency in production organization makes it possible for the center to decentralize the actual physical production of goods to peripheral locations in which an abundant supply of relatively cheap nonestablished labor is to be found, and to retain control of the process and of the research and development upon which its future depends.

As a nonestablished workforce is mobilized in Third-World countries by international production, governments in these countries have very frequently sought to preempt the possibility of this new social force developing its own class-conscious organizations by imposing upon it structures of state corporatism in the form of unions set up and controlled by the government or the dominant political party. This also gives local governments, through their control over local labor, additional leverage with international capital regarding the terms of direct investment. If industrial workers in Third-World countries have thus sometimes been reduced to political and social quiescence, state corporatism may prove to be a stage delaying, but in the long run not eliminating, a more articulate self-consciousness.[29]

Even if industry were to move rapidly into the Third World and local governments were, by and large, able to keep control over their industrial workforces, most of the populations of these countries may see no improvement, but probably a deterioration, in their conditions. New industrial jobs lag far behind increases in the labor force, while changes in agriculture dispossess many in the rural population. No matter how fast international production spreads, a very large part of the world's population in the poorest areas remains marginal to the world economy, having no employment or income, or the purchasing power derived from it. A major problem for international capital in its aspiration for hegemony is how to neutralize the effect of this marginalization of perhaps one-third of the world's population so as to prevent its poverty from fueling revolt.[30]

Social Forces, State Structures, and Future World Order Prospects

It would, of course, be logically inadmissible, as well as imprudent, to base predictions of future world order upon the foregoing considerations. Their utility is rather in drawing attention to factors which could incline an emerging world order in one direction or another. The social forces generated by changing production processes are the starting point for thinking about possible futures. These forces may combine in different configurations, and as an exercise one could consider the hypothetical configurations most likely to lead to three different outcomes as to the future of the state system. The focus on these three outcomes is not, of course, to imply that no other outcomes or configurations of social forces are possible.

First, is the prospect for a new hegemony being based upon the global structure of social power generated by the internationalizing of production. This would require a consolidation of two presently powerful and related tendencies: the continuing dominance of international over national capital within the major countries, and the continuing internationalization of the state. Implicit in such an outcome is a continuance of monetarism as the orthodoxy of economic policy, emphasizing the stabilization of the world economy (antiinflationary policies and stable exchange rates) over the fulfillment of domestic sociopolitical demands (the reduction of unemployment and the maintenance of real-wage levels).

The interstate power configuration which could maintain such a world order, provided its member states conformed to this model, is a coalition centering upon the United States, the Federal Republic of Germany, and Japan, with the support of other OECD states, the co-optation of a few of the more industrialized Third-World countries, such as Brazil, and of leading conservative OPEC countries, and the possibility of revived détente allowing for a greater linkage of the Soviet sphere into the world economy of international production. The new international division of labor, brought about through the progressive decentralization of manufacturing into the Third World by international capital, would satisfy demands for industrialization from those countries. Social conflict in the core countries would be combated through enterprise corporatism, though many would be left unprotected by this method, particularly the nonestablished workers. In the periphercal countries, social conflict would be contained through a combination of state corporatism and repression.

The social forces opposed to this configuration have been noted above. National capital, those sections of established labor linked to national capital, newly mobilized nonestablished workers in the Third World, and social marginals in the poor countries are all in some way or another potentially opposed to international capital, and to the state and world order structures most congenial to international capital. These forces do not, however, have any natural cohesion, and might be dealt with separately, or neutralized, by an effective hegemony. If they did come together under particular circumstances in a particular country, precipitating a change of regime, then that country might be dealt with in isolation through the world structure. In other words, where hegemony failed within a particular country, it could reassert itself through the world structure.

A second possible outcome is a nonhegemonic world structure of conflicting power centers. Perhaps the most likely way for this to evolve would be through the ascendancy in several core countries of neomercantilist coalitions which linked national capital and established labor, and were determined to opt out of arrangements designed to promote international capital and to organize their own power and welfare on a national or sphere-of-influence basis. The continuing pursuit of monetarist policies may be the single most likely cause of neomercantilist reaction. Legitimated as antiinflationary, monetarist policies have been perceived as hindering national capital (because of high interest rates), generating unemployment (through planned recession), and adversely affecting relatively deprived social groups and regions dependent upon government services and transfer payments (because of budget-balancing cuts in state expenditures). An opposing coalition would attack monetarism for subordinating national welfare to external forces, and for showing an illusory faith in the markets (which are perceived to be manipulated by corporate-administered pricing). The likely structural form of neomercantilism within core states would be industry-level and national-level corporatism, bringing national capital and organized labor into a relationship with the government for the purpose of making and implementing of state policy. Peripheral states would have much the same structure as in the first outcome, but would be more closely linked to one or another of the core-country economies.

A third and more remotely possible outcome would be the development of a counter-hegemony based on a Third-World coalition against core-country dominance and aiming toward the autonomous development of peripheral countries and the termination of the core-periphery relationship. A counterhegemony would consist of a coherent view of an alternative world order, backed by a concentration of power sufficient to maintain a challenge to core countries. While this outcome is foreshadowed by the demand for a New International Economic Order, the prevailing consensus behind this demand lacks a sufficiently clear view of an alternative world political economy to constitute counterhegemony. The prospects of counterhegemony lies very largely in the future development of state structures in the Third World.

The controlling social force in these countries is, typically, what has been called a "state class,"[31] a combination of party, bureaucratic and military personnel and union leaders, mostly petty-bourgeois in origin, which controls the state apparatus and through it attempts to gain greater control over the productive apparatus in the country. The state class can be understood as a local response to the forces generated by the internationalizing of production, and an attempt to gain some local control over these forces. The orientation of the state class is indeterminate. It can be either conservative or radical. It may either bargain for a better deal within the world economy of international production, or it may seek to overcome the unequal internal development generated by international capital.

State classes of the first orientation are susceptible to incorporation into a new hegemonic world economy, and to the maintenance of state corporatist structures as the domestic counterpart to international capital. The second orientation could provide the backing for counterhegemony. However, a state class is only likely to maintain the second and more radical orientation if it is supported from below in the form of a genuine populism (and not just a populism manipulated by political leaders). One may speculate that this could come about through the unfolding social consequences of international production, such as the mobilization of a new nonestablished labor force coupled with the marginalization of an increasing part of the urban population. The radical alternative could be the form of response to international capital in Third-World countries, just as neomercantilism could be the response in richer countries. Each projects a particular state structure and vision of world order.

POSTSCRIPT 1985

Robert Keohane's proposal to include my article published in *Millennium* in the summer of 1981 in this collection of readings is a challenge to define my position in relation to the other texts selected. These other texts are all part of a single debate stimulated by recent works by Waltz and Gilpin. My article stems from a different—and very largely idiosyncratic—intellectual process. It does, however, touch upon themes that emerged in this debate, making of me a Monsieur Jourdain, writing prose without having been aware of the fact.

I have deliberately refrained from revising my text and have made only some strictly stylistic and editorial changes to the 1981 version so as to adapt it to the present volume. Once placed before the public, a text is entitled to respect for its own integrity. It has a life of its own, rich or poor. The author too is entitled to assume a certain independence of the text. My own views (as I hope those of most authors) have evolved since 1981. Accordingly, I prefer to try to make the link with the other readings through this postscript.

In the range of their different arguments, I find myself in agreement and in disagreement with aspects of each of the other authors' texts. I am, however, left with the general impression that this is a specifically American debate even though it is couched in terms of international or world systems. Stanley Hoffmann (1977) put it that international relations is an *American* social science. This is not (on my part any more than on Hoffmann's) to suggest that American thought is cast in a single mold. (I protest in advance my innocence of Robert Gilpin's strictures against lumping together authors whose views differ in important respects.) What is common, it seems to me, is (1) the perspective of the United States as the preponderant of the two major powers in the system and consequently the sharing of a certain measure of responsibility for U.S. policy, and (2) the organization of argument around certain obligatory themes of debates, notably those of power versus morality and of science versus tradition. The first of these is, to employ Waltz's language, a systemic conditioning of American thought. The second derives more from an explicitly American cultural process. One aspect of this process was the intellectual conversion of U.S. policymakers to the use of the accumulated physical power of the United States for the performance of a world system-creating and system-maintaining role. Important influences in this conversion were European-formed thinkers like Reinhold Niebuhr and Hans Morgenthau who introduced a more pessimistic and power-oriented view of mankind into an American milieu conditioned by eighteenth-century optimism and nineteenth-century belief in progress. Another aspect was the need to legitimate this newfound realism in "scientific" terms. The second aspect can be read as the revenge of eighteenth-century natural-law thinking for the loss of innocence implicit in the first. Richard Ashley has well recounted the socializing process through which successive cohorts of American (and by assimilation Canadian) graduate students have been brought into this stream of thinking.

At this point, following Gilpin's example, an autobiographical reference is in order: The reader should know that this author did not experience the abovementioned process of intellectual formation. His introduction to international political processes came through practice as an "empathetic neutral" (Cox and Jacobson 1977) in his role of international official in one of the less salient spheres of policy. His only formal academic training was in the study of history. Accordingly, he never shared a sense of responsibility for nor aspired to influence U.S. policy or that of any other country, though he has been well aware that his destiny, like that of the rest of mankind, is profoundly shaped by what he cannot influence. These circumstances have inclined him toward an initial acceptance of the realist position. The political world is at the outset a *given* world. Men make history, as Marx wrote, but not in conditions of their own choosing. To have any influence over events, or at the very least to forestall the worst eventualities, it is necessary to begin with an understanding of the conditions not chosen by oneself in which action is possible.

The intellectual influences that contributed to the formation of this idiosyncratic view share with realism a common source in Machiavelli. They diverge in having followed a historicist current, through Giambattista Vico to Georges Sorel and, above all, Antonio Gramsci. These thinkers were not concerned primarily with international relations; they addressed the problem of knowledge about society and social transformations. Historians provided the more specific light on international structures—to some extent the twentieth-century British Marxist historians, and more particularly Fernand Braudel and the French *Annales* school. Intellectual points of contact with influences upon other contributors to this volume include E. H. Carr (especially with Gilpin), Friedrich Meinecke, Ludwig Dehio, and Karl Polanyi (especially with Ruggie). So much for autobiography: the point is that the itinerary to the *Millennium* article did not pass through neorealism; it contemplates neorealism from the destination reached.

To change the world, we have to begin with an understanding of the world as it is, which means the structures of reality that surround us. "Understanding" is the key word here. The issues in the confrontation of approaches are linked to different modes of knowledge: positivism and historicism. Since these two terms have been used in contradictory ways in different texts included in this book, I reiterate my own usage here.

By "positivism" I mean the effort to conceive social science on the model of physics (or more particularly, physics as it was known in the eighteenth and nineteenth centuries before it had assimilated the principles of relativity and uncertainty). This involves positing a separation of subject and object. The data of politics are externally perceived events brought about by the interaction of actors in a field. The field itself, being an arrangement of actors, has certain properties of its own which can be called "systemic." The concept of "cause" is applicable within such a framework of forces. Powerful actors are "causes" of change in the behavior of less powerful ones, and the structure of the system "causes" certain forms of behavior on the part of actors.

I use "historicism" to mean a quite different approach to knowledge about society which was well defined by Giambattista Vico (1774/1970) and has continued as a distinctive tradition to the present. In this approach, human institutions are made by people—not by the individual gestures of "actors" but by collective responses to a collectively perceived problematic that produce certain practices. Institutions and practices are therefore to be understood through the changing mental processes of their makers. There is, in this perspective, an identity of subject and object. The objective realities that this approach encompasses—the state, social classes, the conflict groups that Robert Gilpin (following Ralf Dahrendorf) refers to and their practices—are constituted by intersubjective ideas. As Gilpin says, none of these realities exist in the same way that individuals exist, but individuals act *as though* these other realities exist, and by so acting they reproduce them. Social and political institutions are thus seen as collective responses to the physical material context (natural nature) in which human aggregates find themselves. They in turn form part of the social material framework (artificial nature or the network of social relations) in which historical action takes place. Historicism thus understood is the same as historical materialism. The method of historical materialism—or, in Robert Keohane's term, its research program—is to find the connections between the mental schema through which people conceive action and the material world which constrains both what people can do and how they can think about doing it.

The two approaches—positivist and historicist—yield quite different versions of the task of science. There can be no dispute about Kenneth Waltz's adherence to the positivist approach and he lays out clearly the tasks of a positivist science: to find laws (which are regularities in human activity stateable in the form of "if A, then B"); and to develop theories which explain why observable laws hold within specific spheres of activity. Laws and theories advance knowledge beyond what would otherwise be "mere description," i.e., the cataloguing of externally observed events.[32]

Insofar as this approach aspires to a general science of society, it cannot discriminate between times and places. All human activity is its province (though this activity is arbitrarily divided among a priori categories of activity of which international relations is one), all of it treated as raw material for the finding of laws and the development of theories. I believe this to be the root of the major defect in Waltz's approach pointed to by his critics (see especially Keohane and Ruggie): the inability of his theory to account for or to explain structural transformation. A general (read: universally applicable) science of society can allow for variations in technologies and in the relative capabilities of actors, but not in either the basic nature of the actors (power-seeking) or in their mode of interaction (power-balancing). The universality of these basic attributes of the social system comes to be perceived as standing outside of and prior to history. History becomes but a mine of data illustrating the permutations and combinations that are possible within an essentially unchanging human story. Despite his wide historical learning, Waltz's work is fundamentally ahistorical. The elegance he achieves in the clarity of his theoretical statement comes at the price of an unconvincing mode of historical understanding.

The historicist approach to social science does not envisage any general or universally valid laws which can be explained by the development of appropriate generally applicable theories. For historicism, both human nature and the structures of human interaction change, if only very slowly. History is the process of their changing. One cannot therefore speak of "laws" in any generally valid sense transcending historical eras, nor of structures as outside of or prior to history.[33] Regularities in human activities may indeed be observed within particular eras, and thus the positivist approach can be fruitful within defined historical limits, though not with the universal pretensions it aspires to. The research program of historicism is to reveal the historical structures characteristic of particular eras within which such regularities prevail. Even more important, this research program is to explain transformations from one structure to another. If elegance is what Robert Keohane writes of as "spare, logically tight" theory (p. 197), then the historicist approach does not lead to elegance. It may, however, lead to better appraisal of historically specific conjunctures. One person's elegance is another's oversimplification.

In choosing between the two approaches, much depends upon one's idea of what theory is for. I have suggested two broad purposes corresponding to the two approaches: a problem-solving purpose, i.e., tacitly assuming the permanency of existing structures, which is served by the positivist approach; and a critical purpose envisaging the possibilities of structural transformation which is served by the historicist approach. The usefulness of all theory, whether problem-solving or critical, is in its applicability to particular situations. But whereas problem-solving theory assimilates particular situations to general rules, providing a kind of programmed method for dealing with them, critical theory seeks out the developmental potential within the particular.

Developmental potential signifies a possible change of structure. It can be grasped by understanding the contradictions and sources of conflict within existing structures; and this task may be aided by an understanding of how structural transformations have come about in the past.[34] Thus the determination of breaking points between successive structures—those points at which transformations take place—becomes a major problem of method. John Ruggie raised this issue in pointing to the structural disjuncture between the medieval and modern world system, and to the inability of Waltz's structural realism to even consider let alone explain this transformation. The case is extremely important, since it contrasts two worlds constituted by quite distinct intersubjectivities. The entities as well as the modes of relations among them are of different orders.

This case of transformation can be contrasted to the frequent invocations of Thucydides in neorealist literature in support of the contention that a balance-of-power system is the universal condition. What these invocations do establish is that there have been other periods in history where structures analogous to the balance of power of the modern states system have appeared. They do not consider that there have likewise been otherwise-constituted historical structures of which the medieval order of European Christendom was one. The instinct of structural realism may be to reduce the medieval order to its power model; but if so that would be to reject an opportunity for scientific exploration.

Ruggie suspects—and I share his suspicions—that the transformation from the medieval to the modern order cannot be understood solely in terms of a general international-systems theory (indeed, one could point out that the very term "international," derived from modern practice, is inapposite to the medieval world) but probably has also to be explained in terms of changing state structures and changing modes of production. This joins the substantive point of my argument: I have tried to sketch out a research program that would examine the linkage between changes in production, in forms of state and in world orders.

The relevancy of such a research program is strictly practical. It flows from the question whether the present age is one of those historical breaking points between world-order structures, whether the present world situation contains the development potential of a different world order. If this were to be the case, what then would be the range of future structural possibilities? What social and political forces would have to be mobilized in order to bring about one or another of feasible outcomes? The practical use of political theory should be to help answer such questions. That they are present in the minds of the contributors to this volume is clear—for instance in Keohane's primary concern to discover the means of bringing about peaceful change, and Gilpin's with the problems of change under conditions of declining hegemony. Neither of these authors sees clearly how structural realism can be a guide to the answers. My suggestion is that the approach of historical structures would be more apposite.

For Fernand Braudel (1958), a historical structure is the *longue durée*, the enduring practices evolved by people for dealing with the recurrent necessities of social and political life and which come by them to be regarded as fixed attributes of human nature and social intercourse. But, particularly with regard to the world system, how long is the *longue durée*? Ruggie pointed to the breaking point between medieval and modern world orders, but have there been other breaking points since then? What is the proper periodization of world orders? I am inclined to answer that yes, there have been further breaking points, and to suggest a succession of mercantilist, liberal (*pax britannica*), neoimperialist, and neo-liberal (*pax americana*) orders. At the same time, I would not want to give the impression that this was in some manner the uncovering of an ontological substratum of world history, that these successive world orders were real entities fixed in order of time within some immutable world-historic plan. This periodizing is an intellectual construct pertinent to the present and useful for the purpose of understanding how changes in economic and political practices and in the relations of social groups contribute to the genesis of new world orders. The approach is not reductionist in the sense of making one single factor or set of factors the explanation of all changes. It is grounded in the notion of reciprocal relationships among basic forces shaping social and political practice.[35]

Ruggie made another point in suggesting that Waltz's exclusive stress on power capabilities precludes consideration of other significant factors differentiating international systems, in particular the presence or absence of hegemony. Indeed, in neorealist discourse the term "hegemony" is reduced to the single dimension of dominance, i.e., a physical capabilities relationship among states. The Gramscian meaning of hegemony which I have used (see also Cox 1983), and which is important in distinguishing the *pax britannica* and *pax americana* from the other world orders of the sequence suggested above, joins an ideological and intersubjective element to the brute power relationship. In a hegemonic order, the dominant power makes certain concessions or compromises to secure the acqui-escence of lesser powers to an order that can be expressed in terms of a general interest. It is important, in appraising a hegemonic order, to know both (a) that it functions mainly by consent in accordance with universalist principles, and (b) that it rests upon a certain structure of power and serves to maintain that structure. The consensual element distinguishes hegemonic from nonhegemonic world orders. It also tends to mystify the power relations upon which the order ultimately rests.

The hegemonic concept has analytical applicability at the national as well as the international level (indeed, Gramsci developed it for application at the national level). I would differ from Gilpin when he (and Stephen Krasner 1978a, in line with him) suggests that it is possible to distinguish a national interest from the welter of particular interests, if they mean that such a general will exists as some form of objective reality. I can accept their proposition if national interest is understood in a hegemonic sense, i.e., as the way in which the dominant groups in the state have been able—through concessions to the claims of subordinate groups— to evolve a broadly accepted mode of thinking about general or national interests. Unfortunately, Gilpin (and Krasner) end their inquiry with the identification of national interests. When the concept of hegemony is introduced, it becomes necessary to ask what is the form of power that underlies the state and produces this particular understanding of national interest, this particular *raison d'état*—or in Gramscian terms, what is the configuration of the historic bloc?

Finally, there is the troublesome question of the ideological nature of thought—troublesome insofar as the imputation of ideology may appear to be insulting to the positivist who draws a line between his science and another's ideology. I should make it clear that I do not draw such a line; I accept that my own thought is grounded in a particular perspective; and I mean no offense in pointing to what appears to be a similar grounding in other people's thought. Science, for me, is a matter of rigor in the development of concepts and in the appraisal of evidence. There is an inevitable ideological element in science which lies in the choice of subject and the purposes to which analysis is put. The troublesome part comes when some scientific enterprise claims to transcend history and to propound some universally valid form of knowledge. Positivism, by its pretensions to escape from history, runs the greater risk of falling into the trap of unconscious ideology.

There are two opposed concepts of history, each of which is intellectually grounded in the separation of subject and object. One is a methodological separation wherein events are conceived as an infinite series of objectified data. This approach seeks universal laws of behavior. Structural realism, as noted, is one of its manifestations. The other sees the subjectivity of historical action as determined by an objectified historical process. It seeks to discover the "laws of motion" of history. Both of these concepts of history lend themselves readily to ideology: the one becoming an ideology reifying the status quo; the other an ideology underpinning revolution by revealing the certainty of a particular future. Both remove the element of uncertainty inherent in the historicist expectation of dialectical development arising out of the contradictions of existing forces—a conception in which, as argued above, subject and object are united.

Neorealism, both in its Waltzian structuralist form and in its game-theoretic interactionist form, appear ideologically to be a science at the service of big-power management of the international system. There is an unmistakably Panglossian quality to a theory published in the late 1970s which concludes that a bipolar system is the best of all possible worlds. The historical moment has left its indelible mark upon this purportedly universalist science.

To the American social science of international relations, Marxism is the great "other," the ideology supportive of the rival superpower. It is also that most readily associated with the alternative mode of separation of subject and object. In the works of this American social science, Marxism is politely recognized but usually reduced to a few simple propositions which do not impinge upon its own discourse. If there is any dialogue between the American science of international relations and Marxism, it is a *dialogue de sourds*. Gilpin was justified in protesting the richness and diversity of realist thought, but it is at least as justifiable to point to the diversity of Marxist thought. It cuts across all the epistemological distinctions discussed above. There is a structuralist Marxism which, as Richard Ashley has indicated, has analogies to structural realism, not in the use to which theory is put but in its conception of the nature of knowledge. There is a determinist tradition (perhaps less evident at present) which purports to reveal the laws of motion of history. And there is a historicist Marxism that rejects the notion of objective laws of history and focuses upon class struggle as the heuristic model for the understanding of structural change. It is obviously in the last of these Marxist currents that this writer feels most comfortable. Were it not for the contradictory diversity of Marxist thought, he would be glad to acknowledge himself (in a parody of Reaganite rhetoric) as your friendly neighborhood Marxist-Leninst subversive. But as things stand in the complex world of Marxism, he prefers to be identified simply as a historical materialist.

NOTES

1. Among critics of the world systems approach, note especially Skocpol (1977 and 1979) and Brenner (1977).

2. I use the term "world order" in preference to "interstate system," as it is relevant to all historical periods (and not only those in which states have been the component entities) and in preference to "world system" as it is more indicative of a structure having only a certain duration in time and avoiding the equilibrium connotations of "system." "World" designates the relevant totality, geographically limited by the range of probable interactions (some past "worlds" being limited to the Mediterranean, to Europe, to China, etc.). "Order" is used in the sense of the way things usually happen (*not* the absence of turbulence); thus disorder is included in the concept of order. An interstate system is one historical form of world order. The term is used in the plural to indicate that particular patterns of power relationships which have endured in time can be contrasted in terms of their principal characteristics as distinctive world orders.

3. E. P. Thompson (1978:231–242) argues that historical concepts must often "display extreme elasticity and allow for great irregularity."

4. Kenneth Waltz (1980) asked the question "will the future be like the past?," which he answered affirmatively—not only was the same pattern of relationships likely to prevail but it would be for the good of all that this should be so. It should be noted that the future contemplated by Waltz was the next decade or so.

5. A recent example of this argument is Stephen Krasner (1978). The normative intent of the new realism is most apparent as a polemic response to liberal moralism. This was also the case for E. H. Carr (1946), who offered a "scientific" mode of thinking about international relations in opposition to the "utopianism" of the supporters of the League of Nations in Britain. Dean Acheson and George Kennan, in laying the foundations of U.S. Cold War policy, acknowledged their debt to Reinhold Niebuhr, whose revival of a pessimistic Augustinian view of human nature challenged the optimistic Lockean view native to American culture. Krasner's chosen target is "Lockean liberalism," which he sees as having undermined the rational defense of U.S. national interests.

6. See, for instance, R. G. Collingwood's (1942) distinction between dialectical and eristical reasoning. Collingwood takes dialectic back to its Greek origins and spares us the assertions of theological Marxism concerning "Diamat."

7. As in Krasner (1978b) and Katzenstein (1978). The United States is represented by these authors as a state which is weak in relation to the strength of civil society (or more particularly of interests in civil society), whereas other states—

e.g., Japan or France—are stronger in relation to their societies. Civil society is thus seen in the U.S. case as limiting the effectiveness of the state.

8. Gramsci saw ideas, politics, and economics as reciprocally related, convertible into each other and bound together in a *blocco storico*. "Historical materialism" he wrote, "is in a certain sense a reform and development of Hegelianism. It is philosophy freed from unilateral ideological elements, the full consciousness of the contradictions of philosophy" (1975:471, my rough translation).

9. The notion of a framework for action recalls what Machiavelli (1531/ 1970:105–106) called *necessità*, a sense that the conditions of existence require action to create or sustain a form of social order. *Necessità* engenders both the possibility of a new order and all the risks inherent in changing the existing order. "Few men ever welcome new laws setting up a new order in the state unless necessity makes it clear to them that there is a need for such laws; and since such a necessity cannot arise without danger, the state may easily be ruined before the new order has been brought to completion."

10. In this regard, Stanley Hoffmann (1977) has written: "Born and raised in America, the discipline of international relations is, so to speak, too close to the fire. It needs triple distance: it should move away from the contemporary world toward the past; from the perspective of a superpower (and a highly conservative one), toward that of the weak and the revolutionary—away from the impossible quest for stability; from the glide into policy science, back to the steep ascent toward the peaks which the questions raised by traditional political philosophy represent (p. 59).

11. Taylor (1965) points out that expectations with regard to negotiating behavior are culturally differentiated in the present world. Garrett Mattingly (1955) studied the origin of the ideas outlined in this paragraph which are implicit in the modern state system.

12. Collective images are not aggregations of fragmented opinions of individuals such as are compiled through surveys; they are coherent mental types expressive of the world views of specific groups such as may be reconstructed through the work of historians and sociologists—.e.g., Max Weber's reconstructions of forms of religious consciousness.

13. Gramsci's principal application of the concept of hegemony was to the relations among social classes—e.g., in explaining the inability of the Italian industrial bourgeoisie to establish its hegemony after the unification of Italy and in examining the prospects of the Italian industrial workers establishing their class hegemony over peasantry and petty bourgeoisie so as to create a new *blocc storico* (historic bloc)—a term which in Gramsci's work corresponds roughly to the notion of historic structure in this essay. The term "hegemony" in Gramsci's work is linked to debates in the international Communist movement concerning revolutionary strategy and in this connection its application is specifically to classes. The form of the concept, however, draws upon his reading of Machiavelli and is not restricted to class relations; it has a broader potential applicability. Gramsci's adjustment of Machiavellian ideas to the realities of the world he knew was an exercise in dialectic in the sense defined above. It is an appropriate continuation of his method to perceive the applicability of the concept to world order structures as suggested here. For Gramsci, as for Machiavelli, the general question involved in hegemony is

the nature of power, and power is a centaur, part man, part beast, a combination of force and consent. See Machiavelli (1513/1977:149–150) and Gramsci (1971:169–170).

14. A recent discussion of the reciprocal character of these relations is in Gourevitch (1978).

15. I have been engaged with Jeffrey Harrod in a study of production relations on a world scale which begins with an examination of distinctive patterns of power relations in the production process as separate historical structures and which then leads to a consideration of different forms of state and global political economy. Bringing in these last two levels is necessary to an understanding of the existence of the different patterns of production relations and the hierarchy of relationships among them. One could equally well adopt forms of state or world orders at the point of departure and ultimately be required to bring the other levels in to explain the historical process.

16. Keohane cites as others who have contributed to this theory Charles Kindleberger, Robert Gilpin, and Stephen Krasner. "Hegemony" is used by Keohane here in the limited sense of dominance by a state. This meaning is to be distinguished from its meaning in this article, which is derived from Gramsci—i.e., hegemony as a structure of dominance, leaving open the question of whether the dominant power is a state or a group of states or some combination of state and private power, which is sustained by broadly based consent through acceptance of an ideology and of institutions consistent with this structure. Thus a hegemonic structure of world order is one in which power takes a primarily consensual form, as distinguished from a nonhegemonic order in which there are manifestly rival powers and no power has been able to establish the legitimacy of its dominance. There can be dominance without hegemony; hegemony is one possible form dominance may take. Institutionalized hegemony, as used in this essay, corresponds to what Keohane calls a "strong international regime." His theory can be restated in our terms as: dominance by a powerful state is most conducive to the development of hegemony. In this present text, the term "hegemony" is reserved for a consensual order and "dominance" refers only to a preponderance of material power. Keohane's discussion of hegemony is developed in his later work (1984) but without affecting the distinction made here.

17. Two classic studies relevant particularly to the interwar period are Karl Polanyi (1957b) and E. H. Carr (1946). Stephen Blank (1978) comments on postwar British economic policy; as does Stephen Krasner (1976). Also see R. F. Harrod (1951).

18. The international implications of the New Deal are dealt with in several passages in Arthur M. Schlesinger, Jr. (1960: vol. 2). Charles Maier (1978) discusses the relationship between the New Deal and the postwar ideology of world order. Richard Gardner (1956) shows the link between New Deal ideas and the institutions of world economy set up after World War II in the Bretton Woods negotiations.

19. The basic point I am making here is suggested by a passage from Gramsci (1971:176–177; 1975:1562) which reads: "Do international relations precede or follow (logically) fundamental social relations? There can be no doubt but that they follow. Any organic innovation in the social structure, through its technical-military expressions, modifies organically absolute and relative relations in the international

field too." Gramsci used the term "organic" to refer to relatively long-term and permanent changes, as opposed to "conjunctural."

20. E. J. Hobsbawm (1977:15) writes: "The men who officially presided over the affairs of the victorious bourgeois order in its moment of triumph were a deeply reactionary country nobleman from Prussia, an imitation emperor in France and a succession of aristocratic landowners in Britain."

21. Among analysts who concur in this are Karl Polanyi (1957b); Gunnar Myrdal (1960); and Geoffrey Barraclough (1968).

22. George Lichtheim (1971) has proposed a periodization of imperialisms, and I have taken the term "liberal imperialism" from him.

23. Max Beloff (1961) was perhaps the first to point to the mechanisms whereby participation in international organizations altered the internal policymaking practices of states. R. W. Cox and H. K. Jacobson et al. (1972) represented the political systems of international organizations as including segments of states. R. O. Keohane and J. S. Nye (1974) pointed to the processes whereby coalitions are formed among segments of the apparatuses of different states and the ways in which international institutions facilitate such coalitions. These various works, while they point to the existence of mechanisms for policy coordination among states and for penetration of external influences within states, do not discuss the implications of these mechanisms for the structure of power within states. It is this structural aspect I wish to designate by the term "internationalization of the state." Christian Palloix (1975:82) refers to "internationalisation de l'appareil de l'Etat national, de certains lieux de cet appareil d'Etat" by which he designates those segments of national states which serve as policy supports for the internationalization of production. He thus raises the question of structural changes in the state, though he does not enlarge upon the point. Keohane and Nye (1977) linked the transgovernmental mechanism to the concept of "interdependence." I find this concept tends to obscure the power relationships involved in structural changes in both state and world order and prefer not to use it for that reason. Gourevitch (1978) does retain the concept of interdependence while insisting that it be linked with power struggles among social forces within states.

24. There is, of course, a whole literature implicit in the argument of this paragraph. Some sketchy references may be useful. Andrew Shonfield (1965) illustrated the development of corporative-type structures of the kind I associate with the welfare-nationalist state. The shift from industry-level corporatism to an enterprise-based corporatism led by the big public and private corporations has been noted in some industrial relations works, particularly those concerned with the emergence of a "new working class," e.g., Serge Mallet (1963), but the industrial relations literature has generally not linked what I have elsewhere called enterprise corporatism to the broader framework suggested here (R. W. Cox 1977). Erhard Friedberg (1974:94–108) discusses the subordination of the old corporatism to the new. The shift in terminology from planning to industrial policy is related to the internationalizing of state and economy. Industrial policy has become a matter of interest to global economic policymakers (see William Diebold 1980, and John Pinder, Takashi Hosomi and William Diebold, for the Trilateral Commission, 1979). If planning evokes the specter of economic nationalism, industrial policy, as the Trilateral Commission study points out, can be looked upon with favor from a world

economy perspective as a necessary aspect of policy harmonization: "We have argued that industrial policies are needed to deal with structural problems in the modern economies. Thus, international action should not aim to dismantle these policies. The pressure should, rather, be toward positive and adaptive industrial policies, whether on the part of single countries or groups of countries combined. Far from being protectionist, industrial policy can help them to remove a cause of protectionism, by making the process of adjustment less painful" (p. 50). It may be objected that the argument and references presented here are more valid for Europe than for the United States, and that, indeed, the very concept of corporatism is alien to U.S. ideology. To this it can be replied that since the principal levers of the world economy are in the United States, the U.S. economy adjusts less than those of European countries and peripheral countries, and the insitutionalization of adjustment mechanisms is accordingly less developed. Structural analyses of the U.S. economy have, however, pointed to a distinction between a corporate internationally oriented sector and a medium and small business nationally oriented sector, and to the different segments of the state and different policy orientations associated with each. Cf. John Kenneth Galbraith (1974) and James O'Connor (1973). Historians point to the elements of corporatism in the New Deal, e.g., Schlesinger (1960).

25. The Zaire case recalls the arrangements imposed by western powers on the Ottoman Empire and Egypt in the late nineteenth century, effectively attaching certain revenues for the service of foreign debt. See Herbert Feis (1961:332–342, 384–397).

26. The evidence for the existence of a transnational managerial class lies in actual forms of organization, the elaboration of ideology, financial supports, and the behavior of individuals. Other structures stand as rival tendencies—e.g., national capital and its interests sustained by a whole other structure of loyalties, agencies, etc. Individuals or firms and state agencies may in some phases of their activity be caught up now in one, now in another, tendency. Thus the membership of the class may be continually shifting though the structure remains. It is sometimes argued that this is merely a case of U.S. capitalists giving themselves a hegemonic aura, an argument that by implication makes of imperialism a purely national phenomenon. There is no doubting the U.S. origin of the values carried and propagated by this class, but neither is there any doubt that many non-U.S. citizens and agencies also participate in it nor that its world view is global and distinguishable from the purely national capitalisms which exist alongside it. Through the transnational managerial class American culture, or a certain American business culture, has become globally hegemonic. Of course, should neomercantilist tendencies come to prevail in international economic relations, this transnational class structure would wither.

27. Some industries appear as ambiguously astride the two tendencies—e.g., the automobile industry. During a period of economic expansion, the international aspect of this industry dominated in the United States, and the United Auto Workers union took the lead in creating world councils for the major international auto firms with a view to inaugurating mutlinational bargaining. As the industry was hit by recession, protectionism came to the fore.

28. See Cox (1978). This tendency can be seen as the continuation of a long-term direction of production organization of which Taylorism was an early stage, in which control over the work process is progressively wrested from workers and

separated out from the actual performance of tasks so as to be concentrated with management. See Harry Braverman (1974).

29. Recent news from Brazil indicates restiveness on the part of São Paulo workers whose unions have been subjected to a state corporatist structure since the time of President Vargas.

30. The World Bank promotes rural development and birth control. The concept of "self-reliance," once a slogan of anti-imperialism meaning "decoupling" from the imperial system, has been co-opted by the imperial system to mean self-help among populations becoming marginalized—a do-it-yourself welfare program.

31. I have borrowed the term from Hartmut Elsenhans (n.d.)

32. The term "description" as used in positivist discourse (often preceded by "mere") is meaningless in historicist discourse. Description, for the historicist, is inseparable from interpretation or understanding—i.e., the appraisal of a unique fact through the medium of an explanatory hypothesis. The task of theory is to develop such hypotheses and the concepts of limited historical applicability in which they are expressed—i.e., concepts like mercantilism, capitalism, fascism, etc. The difference between "description" (positivist) and "understanding" (historicist) is reflected in the words used to denote the object of study: datum (positivist) versus fact (historicist). The distinction is less self-evident in English than in Latin languages, where the corresponding words are past participles of the verbs "to give" and "to make." Positivism deals with externally perceived givens; historicism with events or institutions that are "made"—i.e., that have to be understood through the subjectivity of the makers as well as in terms of the objective consequences that flow from their existence.

33. Nor can one speak of "cause" in historicist discourse, except in a most trivial sense. The "cause" of a murder is the contraction of the murderer's finger on a trigger which detonates a charge in a cartridge, sending a bullet into the vital parts of the victim. Explanation is the purpose of historicist inquiry. It is much more complex, requiring an assembling of individual motivations and social structures to be connected by explanatory hypotheses.

34. This does not imply the presumption that the future will be like the past. But there can be (in the historicist approach) no complete separation between past and and future. The practical utility of knowledge about the past is in the development of explanatory hypotheses about change. Fernand Braudel (1958) employed the metaphor of a ship for such hypotheses. The hypothesis sails well in certain waters under a range of conditions; it remains becalmed or it founders in others. The task of theory is to explore the limits of validity of particular hypotheses and to devise new hypotheses to explain those cases in which they fail.

35. Waltz writes of reductionism and reification in a curious way in saying that systems are reified by political scientists when they reduce them to their interacting parts (p. 61). In my reading of his work, Waltz comes close to the opposite of this position, reifying the international system by treating it not as an intellectual construct but as a "cause," and deriving the behavior of its parts, i.e., states, from the system itself; thus international relations is reduced to the workings of a reified system.

NINE

The Poverty of Neorealism

RICHARD K. ASHLEY

The theory of knowledge is a dimension of political theory because the specifically symbolic power to impose the principles of the construction of reality—in particular, social reality—is a major dimension of political power.

Pierre Bourdieu

It is a dangerous thing to be a Machiavelli. It is a disastrous thing to be a Machiavelli without *virtu*.

Hans Morgenthau

SOME TIME AGO, E. P. Thompson fixed his critical sights across the English Channel and let fly with a lengthy polemic entitled *The Poverty of Theory* (1978; see also Anderson, 1980). Thompson's immediate target was Louis Althusser. His strategic objective was to rebut the emergent Continental orthodoxy that Althusser championed: structural Marxism, a self-consciously scientific perspective aiming to employ Marxian categories within a structuralist framework to produce theoretical knowledge of the objective structures of capitalist reality.

The charges Thompson hurled defy brief summary, but some key themes can be quickly recalled. Althusser and the structuralists, Thompson contended, were guilty of an egregiously selective, hopelessly one-sided representation of the Marxian legacy they claimed to carry forward. In the name of science, Althusser had purged the legacy of its rich dialectical content while imposing a deadening ahistorical finality upon categories stolen from Marx's work. To produce this backhanded hagiography, Thompson charged, Althusser had superimposed a positivist understanding of science upon Marx even as he claimed to surpass the limits of positivism. What is worse, his structural Marxism had to ignore the historical context of Marx's work, subordinate the dialectical "Young Marx" to the objectivist "Mature Marx" of the *Grundrisse,* cast disrespect on Old Engels, "the clown," and systematically forget much of the Marxist literature since Marx, including Lenin. In Thompson's view, this reading of Marx produced a mechanistic theory of capitalist society—a machine-like model consisting of self-contained, complete entities or parts connected, activated, and synchronized by all manner of apparatuses. It was, Thompson complained, "an orrery of errors."[1]

Thompson's attack was by no means a plea for fidelity to Marx's original texts. Rather, it was primarily concerned with restoring a respect for practice in history. In Thompson's view, structural Marxism had abolished the role of practice in the constitution of history, including the historical making of social structures. It had produced an ahistorical and depoliticized understanding of politics in which women and men are the objects, but not the makers, of their circumstances. Ultimately, it presented a totalitarian project, a totalizing antihistorical structure, which defeats the Marxian project for change by replicating the positivist tendency to unversalize and naturalize the given order.

Repeated in the context of current European and Latin American social theory, non-Marxist as well as Marxist, Thompson's assault might today seem anachronistic. The fortress he attacked is already in ruins. In Europe, at least, the unquestioned intellectual paramountcy of structuralism has seen its day. True, European social theory remains very much indebted to structuralist thought—that set of principles and problematics differently reflected in, say, Saussure's linguistics, Durkheim's sociology, Lévi-Strauss's cultural anthropology, or Piaget's developmental psychology. Yet today, that debt is honored not by uncritical adherence to structuralist principles but by the post structuralist questioning of their limits.

On this side of the Atlantic, however, the themes of Thompson's attack are still worth recalling. For just as the dominance of structuralist thought is waning elsewhere, North American theorists of international and comparative politics claim to be at last escaping the limits of what Piaget called "atomistic empiricism." Just as the United States' position of hegemony in the world economy is called into question, North American theorists of international relations are proudly proclaiming their own belated "structuralist turn." The proponents of this North American structuralism include some of the last two generations' most distinguished and productive theorists of international relations and comparative politics: Kenneth Waltz, Robert Keohane, Stephen Krasner, Robert

Gilpin, Robert Tucker, George Modelski, and Charles Kindleberger, among many others. The movement they represent is known by many names: modern realism, new realism, and structural realism, to name a few. Let us call it "neorealism."[2]

Like Althusser and other proponents of structural Marxism, North American proponents of neorealism claim to carry forward a rich intellectual tradition of long standing. The neorealist typically defines his or her heritage, as the name implies, in the Europe-born tradition of "classical realism"—the tradition associated in the United States with Morgenthau, Niebuhr, Herz, and Kissinger. Like Althusser's structuralism, too, neorealist structuralism claims to surpass its predecessors by offering a "truly scientific" rendering of its subject matter—an objective, theoretical rendering, which breaks radically with its predecessors' allegedly commonsensical, subjectivist, atomistic, and empiricist understandings. Like Althusser's structuralism, neorealism claims to grasp a structural totality that constrains, disposes, and finally limits political practice. Like Althusser's structuralism, neorealism has achieved consensus about the categories defining the dominant structures of the totality examined: in the case of neorealism, these categories refer not to social classes and the arenas and instruments of class struggle but to modern states, their struggles for hegemony, and the instruments by which and arenas in which they wage it. And like Althusser's structural Marxism, neorealism has very quickly become a dominant orthodoxy. In France of the late 1960s and 1970s, Althusserian structuralism provided the pivotal text upon which the intellectual development of a generation of radical philosophers would turn. In the United States of the 1980s, neorealism and its structural theory of hegemony frames the measured discourse and ritual of a generation of graduate students in international politics.

It is time for another polemic. Setting my sights on neorealist structuralism, I offer an argument whose main themes closely parallel Thompson's attack on structural Marxism. I want to challenge not individual neorealists but the neorealist movement *as a whole.*[3] Like Thompson's critique, my argument has both negative and positive aspects: both its critical attack and its implications for an approach that would do better. In spirit with Thompson, let me phrase key themes of that critique in deliberately exaggerated terms.

On the negative side, I shall contend that neorealism is itself an "orrery of errors," a self-enclosed, self-affirming joining of statist, utilitarian, positivist, and structuralist commitments. Although it claims to side with the victors in two American revolutions—the realist revolution against idealism, and the scientific revolution against traditionalism—it in fact betrays both. It betrays the former's commitment to political autonomy by reducing political practice to an economic logic, and it neuters the critical faculties of the latter by swallowing methodological rules that render science a purely technical enterprise. From realism it learns only an interest in power, from science it takes only an interest in expanding the reach of control, and from this selective borrowing it creates a theoretical perspective that parades the possibility of a rational power that need never acknowledge power's limits. What emerges is a positivist structuralism that treats the given order as the natural order, limits rather than expands political discourse, negates or trivializes the significance of variety across time and place, subordinates all practice to an interest in control, bows to the ideal of a social power beyond responsibility, and thereby deprives political interaction of those practical capacities which make social learning and creative change possible. What emerges is an ideology that anticipates, legitimizes, and orients a totalitarian project of global proportions: the rationalization of global politics.[4]

On the positive side, I shall suggest that theoretical alternatives are not exhausted by the false choice between neorealism's "progressive" structuralism and a "regression" to atomistic, behavioralist, or, in Waltz's terms, "reductionist" perspectives on international politics. This dichotomy of wholes and parts, often invoked by neorealist orthodoxy, obscures another cleavage of at least equal importance. This is a cleavage that pits early structuralist "compliance models" of action and social reality (physicalistic models as seen in early Durkheim, for instance) against dialectical "competence models" (as seen in poststructuralist thought over the last few decades).[5] Against the neorealist tendency to march triumphantly backward to compliance models of the nineteenth century, I shall be suggesting that the rudiments of an alternative competence model of international politics, a model more responsive to contemporary arguments in social theory, are already present in classical realist scholarship. Drawing especially upon the work of Pierre Bourdieu, I shall suggest that a *dialectical* competence model would allow us to grasp all that neorealism can claim to comprehend while also recovering from classical realism those insights into political practice which neorealism threatens to purge. Such a model, fully developed, would reinstate the theoretical role of practice. It would sharpen the depiction of the current world crisis, including dilemmas of hegemonic leadership. And it would shed light on the role and limits of knowledge, including neorealism, in the production, rationalization, and possible transformation of the current order.

A critique of this breadth necessarily finds its inspiration in several quarters. In addition to Thompson, I should single out two poststructuralist sources, one French and one German. The French source of inspiration, as indicated, is primarily Bourdieu's dialectical *Outline of a Theory of Practice* (1977; see also Foucault, 1970, 1972, 1977, 1980). The German source of inspiration is the critical theory of Jurgen Habermas and more distantly, the whole tradition of the Frankfurt School (see Habermas 1971, 1974, 1979). Habermas's theme of the "scientization of politics" is more than faintly echoed in my critique of neorealism. His diagnosis of a "legitimation crisis" in advanced capitalist society complements my discussion of the historical conditions of neorealist orthodoxy.[6]

At the same time, the studied parochialism of American international political discourse would make it too easy to deploy alien concepts from European social theory to outflank, pummel, and overwhelm that discourse. Such a strategy would be self-defeating given my intentions. My arguments here, intentionally phrased in provocative terms, are like warning shots, meant to provoke a discussion, not destroy an alleged enemy. I feel an obligation to present my position in "familiar" terms, that is, in a way that makes reference to the collective experiences of North American students of international relations. As it turns out, this is not so hard to do. For those experiences are not nearly so impoverished as the keepers of neorealist lore would make them seem.

1. THE LORE OF NEOREALISM

Every great scholarly movement has its own lore, its own collectively recalled creation myths, its ritualized understandings of the titanic struggles fought and challenges still to be overcome in establishing and maintaining its paramountcy. The importance of this lore must not be underestimated: to a very considerable degree, the solidarity of a movement depends upon the members' abilities to recount this lore and locate their every pratice in its terms. Small wonder, therefore, that rites of passage, such as oral qualifying examinations, put so much stress on the student's ability to offer a satisfying reconstruction of the movement's lore and to identify the ongoing struggles that the student, in turn, will continue to wage. Two generations ago, aspiring North American students of international relations had to show themselves ready to continue classical realism's noble war against an entrenched American idealism. A generation ago, they had to internalize another lore: they had to sing the battle hymns of behavioral science triumphant against traditionalism. Today, thanks to the emergence of a neorealist orthodoxy, students must prepare themselves to retell and carry forward yet another lore.

a. The Triumph of Scientific Realism

The lore of neorealism might be retold in several ways, and each telling might stress different heroes; but a central theme is likely to remain the same. Neorealism, according to this theme, is a progressive scientific redemption of classical realist scholarship. It serves the interests of classical realism under new and challenging circumstances and as advantaged by a clearer grasp of objective science's demands and potentialities. As such, neorealism is twice blessed. It is heir to and carries forward both of the great revolutions that preceded it: realism against idealism, and science against traditionalist thought.

A fuller recounting of the lore would begin by diagnosing some lapses in the classical realist scholarship of, say, Morgenthau, Kissinger, and Herz. In neorealist eyes, and for reasons considered below, these and other classical realists were quite correct in their emphasis on power, national interest, and the historically effective political agency of the state. Unfortunately, when held up to modern *scientific* standards of theory, these classical realist scholars seemed to fall woefully short. Four lapses in the classical heritage might be stressed.

First, classical realist concepts, arguments, and knowledge claims might be said to be too fuzzy, too slippery, too resistant to consistent operational formulation, and, in application, too dependent upon the artful sensitivity of the historically minded and context-sensitive scholar. Somehow, classical realist concepts and knowledge claims never quite ascend to Popper's "third world of objective knowledge," because classical realists hold that the truth of these concepts and claims is to be found only through the situation-bound interpretations of the analyst or statesman.[7]

Second, and closely related, classical realists might be said to distinguish insufficiently between subjective and objective aspects of international political life, thereby undermining the building of theory. Such a concern is to be found, for example, in Waltz's complaints about Morgenthau's and Kissinger's understandings of the international system. They are, for Waltz, "reductionist" because they tend to accord to the "attribute" of actors' subjective perceptions an important role in constituting and reproducing the "system." They thereby deny the system a life of its own as an objective social fact to be grasped by theory (Waltz 1979:62–64).

Third, it might be claimed that, in Gilpin's words, classical realist scholarship "is not well grounded in social theory" (Gilpin 1981a:3). For all its strengths, classical realism could be claimed to exhibit a lamentable lack of learning from the insights of economics, psychology, or sociology.

The fourth lapse, however, is the most salient from the neorealist point of view, for it marks both a failure of realist nerve and a point of considerable vulnerability in the defense of a key realist principle: the principle of "the autonomy of political sphere." Classical realists limited themselves to the domain of political-military relations, where balance of power could be granted the status of a core concept. As a result, realism was naïve with respect to economic processes and relations; it left them to the power-blind eyes of liberal interdependence thinkers and the questioning eyes of radical theorists of dependency and imperialism. As neorealists see it, this was not just a matter of rivalry between scholarly paradigms. Since economic processes and relations have definite power-political ramifications over the longer term, and since these same processes are badly described by reference to balance-of-power logics, classical realism's blindness with respect to economics had several related effects: it situated interstate politics in a reactive "superstructural" pose vis-à-vis economic dynamics, rendered classical realism incapable of grasping political-economic dilemmas, and limited realism's capacity to guide state practice amidst these dilemmas. Given all of this, and given a period of world economic crisis that increasingly calls into question states' capacities to justify themselves as managers of economic dysfunctions, realism was in danger of failing in one of its foremost functions: as a framework that could be deployed to legitimize and orient the state.

This situation and the neorealist can be phrased in more definite terms. In a period of world economic crisis, welling transnational outcries against the limits of the realist vision, and evidently politicized developments that realism could not comprehend, the classical realist tradition and its key concepts suffered a crisis of legitimacy, especially in the United States. Sensing this crisis, a number of American scholars, most of whom are relatively young and very few of whom are steeped in the classical tradition, more or less independently undertook to respond in a distinctly American fashion; that is, *scientifically*.[8] They set out to develop and to corroborate historically scientific theories that would portray or assume a fixed structure of international anarchy;[9] trim away the balance-of-power concept's scientifically inscrutable ideological connotations; reduce balance of power's scientific status to that of a systemic property or a situational logic undertaken by rational, calculating, self-interested states; and, most importantly, disclose the power-political struggle for hegemony behind the economic dynamics that liberal and radical analysts had too falsely treated in isolation from interstate politics.[10] More than that, they set out to construct theories that would lay bare the structural relations—the causal connections between means and ends—that give form to the dynamics of hegemonic rise and decline and in light of which a hegemon might orient its efforts both to secure its hegemony and to preserve cooperative economic and ecological regimes. Political-economic order follows from the concentration of political-economic power, say these theories. Power begets order. Order requires power. The realist emphasis on the role of state power had been saved.

According to neorealist lore, this rescue of realist power politics was by no means a paltry act. It was, if anything, heroic. For it depended, above all, upon one bold move: a move of cunning and daring against stiff odds and in opposition to the mass of sedimented social-scientific habits. In order to bring science to bear in saving and extending realism, neorealists had first to escape the limits of logical atomism, then pre-

vailing among "scientific" approaches to the study of international relations. To do this, they adopted a critical stance with respect to
"reductionist" arguments, arguments that would reduce "systems" to
the interactions among distinct parts. In their place, neorealists erected
what have come to be called "systemic," "holistic," or "structuralist"
arguments.

For the neorealist rescue of realist power politics, this structuralist
move was decisive. By appeal to objective structures, which are said to
dispose and limit practices among states (most especially, the anarchic
structure of the modern states system), neorealists seemed to cut through
the subjectivist veils and dark metaphysics of classical realist thought.
Dispensing with the normatively laden metaphysics of fallen man, they
seemed to root realist power politics, including concepts of power and
national interest, securely in the scientifically defensible terrain of objective necessity. Thus rooted, realist power politics could be scientifically
defended against modernist and radical critics. Without necessarily denying such tendencies as economic interdependence or uneven development, neorealists could argue that power-politics structures would refract
and limit the effects of these tendencies in ways securing the structures
themselves.

Such is the stuff of legends. Even in neorealist lore, to be sure, this
revolutionary structuralist turn is only part of neorealism's story. The
graduate student going through neorealist rites of passage would have to
grasp a good deal more. As will become clear later, the aspiring student
would also have to come to grips with neorealist perspectives on international collaboration and the role of regimes, on the role and limits of
ideology, and on the dynamics of hegemonic succession and "system
change." Most of all, he or she would have to demonstrate an ability to
interpret state practices in neorealist terms, which is to say as calculating,
"economically" rational behaviors under constraints. Still, it is the structuralist turn that is decisive, the sine qua non of neorealism's triumph.
Let us take a closer look at this vaunted structuralist aspect.

b. The Structuralist Promise

As John Ruggie has been among the first to point out, the promise of
neorealism, like the promise of Immanuel Wallerstein's world systems

perspective, is in very large measure attributable to its structuralist aspect (Ruggie 1983:261–264). Ruggie is right. There are indeed isomorphisms between aspects of neorealist argument and elements of structuralist argument (as seen in the work, say, Saussure, Durkheim, Lévi-Strauss, and Althusser). Noting the isomorphisms, one can let neorealism back in the reflected glory of yesteryear's structuralist triumphs in fields such as linguistics, sociology, anthropology, and philosophy. One can say that structuralism's successes in other fields suggest neorealism's promise for the study of international relations. (See Culler 1975; Kurzweil 1980; Giddens 1979; Ricoeur 1974; and Glucksman 1974).

At the risk of oversimplification, it is possible to abstract a number of more or less continuous "elements" of structuralist thought. Five of these elements—overlapping aspects, really—are especially important for my present purposes. They suggest some of the parallels between neorealist argument and structuralist argument in general.

1. Wherever it has emerged, structuralist argument has taken form in reaction against phenomenological knowledge and speculative, evolutionary thought (Giddens 1979:9). Structuralist thought breaks radically with the former because of phenomenology's debt to a conscious subjectivity that, in structuralist eyes, is always suspect. It poses precisely the question that phenomenological knowledge excludes: how is this familiar apprehension of the given order, and hence the community itself, possible? Structuralism also breaks with speculative, evolutionary thought, regarding it as nothing more than the "other side" of phenomenology. Evolutionary thought too often fails to see that what pretends to promise change is but an expression of continuity in the deeper order of things.

2. Structuralist argument aims to construct the objective relations (linguistic, economic, political, or social) that structure practice and representations of practice, including primary knowledge of the familiar world (Bourdieu 1977:3). Human conduct, including human beings' own understandings, is interpreted as *surface* practice generated by a deeper, independently existing logic or structure. In striving to comprehend this deeper logic, structuralism breaks with individualist perspectives or social subjectivity, as in the Cartesian *cogito*. In the same stroke, it attempts to transcend the subject/object dualism. For structuralism, to simplify, social consciousness is not "transparent to itself." It is generated by a deep social intersubjectivity—linguistic rules, for example—which

is itself regarded as the objective structure of society. In Paul Ricoeur's words, "Structuralism is predicated on a Kantian rather than a Freudian unconscious, on structural imperatives that constitute the logical geography of mind" (Ricoeur 1974:79).

3. Thus, structuralism shifts toward the interpretation of practice from a social, totalizing, or "systemic" point of view. Ferdinand de Saussure's distinction between speech and language (*parole et lange*) is paradigmatic; what concerned him was not speech per se but the logical conditions of its intelligibility (an inherently social or "systemic" concern) (Bourdieu 1977:23–24). What concerns structuralists in general is not practice per se but the logical conditions that account for the significance and signification of practice within a community (again, a social or "systemic" relation). Saussure located his logical preconditions for the intelligibility of speech in language: speech becomes the product of language. Structuralists in general locate their explanations in deep social structures: practice becomes the product of structure. For Saussure, language contained possible speech, that is, speech that will be understood within the language community. For structuralists more generally, structure is a system of constitutive rules "which do not regulate behavior so much as create the possibility of particular forms of behavior."

4. Consistent with its totalizing inclinations, structuralism presupposes not only the priority of structure over practice but also the "absolute predominance of the whole over the parts" (Ollman 1976:266). Structuralists emphasize the "system" not only in contrast to but also as *constitutive of* the elements that compose it. The overall structure exists autonomously, independent of the parts or actors, and the identities of the constituent elements are attributed not to intrinsic qualities or contents of the elements themselves but to the differentiation among them supplied or determined by the overall structure. Thus, the units have no identity independent of the structural whole. Saussure's position is again exemplary: "In language," he wrote "there are only differences. . . . [A] difference generally implies positive terms between which the difference is set up; but in language there are only differences without *positive* terms" (quoted in Giddens 1979:12).

5. In their treatments of time and change, structuralist arguments tend to presuppose an absolute distinction between synchronic (static) and diachronic (dynamic) viewpoints, and they tend to accentuate the one-way dependence of diachrony (dynamics) upon synchrony (statics) (Giddens 1979:46). Change, for the structuralist, is always to be grasped in the context of a model of structure—an elaborated model whose elements

are taken to be fixed and immutable in the face of the changes it conditions and limits.

Cursory though it is, this listing suggests some obvious correspon-
dences between neorealist argument and some of the fundamentals of
structuralism. Consider the first "element": neorealism's criticism of
classical realism's subjectivist tendencies (the tendencies of Morgenthau
and Kissinger, among others, to adopt the posture of an ethnomethod-
ologist of a diplomatic community) closely parallels structuralism's reaction against phenomenological knowledge. The neorealist reaction to
the writings of transnationalists and modernists similarly parallels structuralism's attitudes with respect to speculative, evolutionary thought.
The shallow analysis behind such writings, neorealists tend to feel, mis-
takes the ephemeral for the eternal and too eagerly seizes upon epiphenomenal change as evidence of system change.

The second, third, and fourth "elements" are equally suggestive of
parallels. It might be argued, for example, that the central importance
of Waltz's well-known work lies in its attempt to realize these "elements"
for the study of international politics. Waltz's argument against "attribute
theories" and on behalf of "systemic" theories might seem to locate the
proper object of theory not in "parts," and not in external relations
among them, but in independently existing objective "wholes," which,
as ordering and orientating properties of a system, constitute parts and
generate relations among them. His argument clearly adopts a totalizing
stance in that he focuses not on explaining the variety of foreign-policy
behavior per se (such behavior remains indeterminate) but on uncovering
the objective structures that determine the significance of practice within
the context of an overall system. And while Waltz allows that there may
be considerable variety among "actors," only those forms of differentiation
significant within the overall structure, namely distributions of capabilities, are of concern to his theory.

Finally, the fifth "element" of structuralist argument, having to do
with time and change, finds expression in neorealism: Robert Gilpin's
recent *War and Change in World Politics* offers one example, George Modelski's important "long-cycle" argument another (Gilpin 1981b; Modelski
1978). Indeed, the preoccupation with cycles of hegemonic rise and
decline would seem near-perfectly to illustrate the structuralist tendency

to emphasize synchrony over diachrony. As in structuralist thought, dynamics of change are of concern to neorealists primarily insofar as their structural determinants can be theoretically grasped.

In view of these isomorphisms, it is easy to see why neorealism might be viewed as a "welcome antidote" to the "prevailing superficiality" of much international relations discourse. If nothing else, neorealists, like Wallersteinians, have illustrated that scientific international relations discourse can entertain structuralist arguments, can transcend empiricist fixations, and can in principle escape the limits of logical atomism. At least, research programs now purport to try. In turn, the field is encouraged to recognize that reality is not all "on the surface," that it has, or might have, depth levels, that an adequate social or political analysis cannot be reduced to a concatenation of commonsense appearances, and that one can look for a unity behind and generating evident differences. Herein is the neorealist promise.

If neorealism is to bathe in the glow of structuralist accomplishments, however, it must also be prepared to suffer criticisms as to structuralism's limits. Above all, such critiques stress the troubling consequences of structuralism's tendency to "put at a distance, to objectify, to separate out from the personal equation of the investigator the structure of an institution, a myth, a rite" (Paul Ricoeur, as quoted in Rabinow and Sullivan 1979:10–11). In trying to avoid "the shop-girl's web of subjectivity" or "the swamps of experience," to use Lévi-Strauss's words, structuralists adopt a posture that denies the role of practice in the making and possible transformation of social order. In part, of course, such critiques are animated by revulsion at structuralism's "scandalous anti-humanism" (Giddens 1979:38). But in part, also, they are animated by a concern for the disastrous consequences for political theory and the possibly dangerous consequences for political practice. An adequate critique of neorealism must develop these themes.

2. THE STRUCTURE OF NEOREALIST STRUCTURALISM: AN ORRERY OF ERRORS

I am, however, a step or two ahead of myself. I have so far spoken only of the neorealist lore, including the structuralist promise neorealism often purports to bear. I have tried to assay that promise by drawing out parallels between neorealist argument and the now classic positions of structuralism. Still, such comparisons are more than a trifle misleading. For there is at once more and less to neorealism than might be inferred from its isomorphisms with structuralist argument. There is *more* to neorealism in that it exhibits three further commitments: statist, utilitarian, and positivist. There is *less* to neorealism in that, thanks to the priority given to these commitments, neorealist "structuralism" takes a shallow, physicalistic form—a form that exacerbates the dangers while negating the promise of structuralism.

Within neorealism, I suggest, structuralism, statism, utilitarianism, and positivism are bound together in machine-like, self-enclosing unity. This machine-like joining of commitments appears as if designed to defy criticism or to draw all opposition into its own self-centered arc. Herein is neorealism's answer to Althusser's "orrery"—an orrery of errors. Far from questioning commonsense appearances, the neorealist orrery hypostatizes them. Far from expanding international political discourse, the neorealist orrery excludes all standpoints that would expose the limits of the given order of things. Before returning to the matter of neorealist "structuralism," let me take up each of the other elements of this orrery—neorealism's statist, utilitarian, and positivist commitments—in turn.

a. Statism

Neorealism is bound to the state. Neorealist theory is "state centric" or "statist," as Krasner has labeled the position (Krasner 1978a). It offers a "state-as-actor" model of the world. So long as one proposes to be understood among neorealists, one must work within this model. At a minimum, this means that for purposes of theory, one must view the state as an entity capable of having certain objectives or interests and of deciding among and deploying alternative means in this service. Thus, for purposes of theory, the state must be treated as an unproblematic unity: an entity whose existence, boundaries, identifying structures, constituencies, legitimations, interests, and capacities to make self-regarding decisions can be treated as given, independent of transnational class and human interests, and undisputed (except, perhaps, by other states). In all of these respects, the state is regarded as the stuff of theorists' unexamined assumptions—a matter upon which theorists will consensually agree, and not as a problematic relation whose consensual acceptance needs explanation. The proposition that the state might be *essentially* problematic or contested is excluded from neorealist theory. Indeed, neorealist theory is prepared to acknowledge problems of the state only to the extent that the state itself, within the framework of its own legitimations, might be prepared to recognize problems and mobilize resources toward their solution.

True, individual neorealists sometimes allow that the theoretical commitment to the state-as-actor construct involves a distortion of sorts. Waltz, for instance, writes that he "can freely admit that states are in fact not unitary, purposive actors" (Waltz 1979:91). Gilpin can acknowledge that, "strictly speaking, states as such, have no interests, or what economists call 'utility functions,' nor do bureaucracies, interest groups, or so-called transnational actors, for that matter." He can even go on to say that "the state may be conceived as a coalition whose objectives and interests result from the powers and bargaining among the several coalitions comprising the larger society and political elite" (Gilpin 1981b:18). And Keohane, as coauthor of *Power and Interdependence,* can certainly recognize that the conditions of "complex interdependence," including the fact of transnational and transgovernmental relations, fall well short of the "realist" assumption that states are "coherent units" with sharp boundaries separating them from their external environments (Keohane and Nye 1977, esp. ch. 2).

The issue, however, is the theoretical discourse of neorealism as a movement, not the protective clauses that individual neorealists deploy to preempt or deflect criticisms of that discourse's limits. Once one enters this theoretical discourse among neorealists, the state-as-actor model needs no defense. It stands without challenge. Like Waltz (1979:91), one simply *assumes* that states have the status of unitary actors. Or like Gilpin (1981b:19), one refuses to be deterred by the mountainous inconsistencies between the state as a coalition of coalitions (presumably in opposition to the losing coalitions against which the winning coalition is formed) and the state as a provider of public goods, protector of citizens' welfare, and solver of the free-rider problem in the name of winners and losers alike. Knowing that the "objectives and foreign policies of states are determined primarily by the interests of their dominant members or ruling coalitions," one nonetheless simply joins the victors in proclaiming the state a singular actor with a unified set of objectives in the name of the collective good. This proclamation is the starting point of theoretical discourse, one of the unexamined assumptions from which theoretical discourse proceeds.

In short, the state-as-actor assumption is a metaphysical commitment prior to science and exempted from scientific criticism. Despite neorealism's much ballyhooed emphasis on the role of hard falsifying tests as the measure of theoretical progress, neorealism immunizes its statist commitments from any form of falsification. Excluded, for instance, is the historically testable hypothesis that the state-as-actor construct might be not a first-order given of international political life but part of a historical justificatory framework by which dominant coalitions legitimize and secure consent for their precarious conditions of rule.

Two implications of this "state-centricity," itself an ontological principle of neorealist theorizing, deserve emphasis. The first is obvious. As a framework for the interpretation of international politics, neorealist theory cannot accord recognition to—it cannot even comprehend—those global collectivist concepts that are irreducible to logical combinations of state-bounded relations. In other words, global collectivist concepts— concepts of transnational class relations, say, or the interests of human-kind—can be granted an objective status only to the extent that they can be interpreted as *aggregations* of relations and interests having logically and historically prior roots within state-bounded societies. Much as the "individual" is a prism through which methodological individualists comprehend collectivist concepts as aggregations of individual wants, needs, beliefs, and actions, so also does the neorealist refract all global collectivist concepts through the prism of the state.[11] Importantly, this means that neorealist theory implicitly takes a side amidst contending political interests. Whatever the personal commitments of individual neorealists might be, neorealist theory allies with, accords recognition to, and gives expression to those class and sectoral interests (the apexes of Waltz's domestic hierarchies or Gilpin's victorious coalitions of coalitions) that are actually or potentially congruent with state interests and legitimations. It implicitly opposes and denies recognition to those class and human interests which cannot be reduced to concatenations of state interests or transnational coalitions of domestic interests.

The second implication takes longer to spell out, for it relates to neorealist "structuralism"—the neorealist position with respect to structures of the international system. Reflecting on the fourth element of structuralist argument presented above, one might expect the neorealist to accord to the structure of the international system an identity independent of the parts or units (states-as-actors in this case); the identities of the units would be supplied via differentation. The neorealist orrery disappoints these expectations, however. For the neorealist, the state is *ontologically prior* to the international system. The system's structure is produced by defining states as individual unities and *then* by noting properties that emerge when several such unities are brought into mutual reference. For the neorealist, it is impossible to describe international structures without first fashioning a concept of the state-as-actor.

The proper analogy, as Waltz points out, is classical economic theory—microtheory, not macrotheory. As Waltz puts it, "international-political systems, like economic markets, are formed by the coaction of self-regarding units." They "are individualist in origin, spontaneously generated, and unintended" (Waltz 1979:91). Other neorealists would agree. Gilpin, for example, follows economists Robert Mundell and Alexander Swoboda in defining a system as "an aggregate of diverse entities united by regular interaction according to a form of control" (Mundell and Swoboda 1969:343; Gilpin 1981b:26). He then names states as "the principal entities or actors," and he asserts that control over or governance of the international system is a function of three factors, all of which are understood to have their logical and historical roots in the capabilities, interests, and interactions of states: the distribution of power among states, the hierarchy of prestige among states, and rights and rules that have their "primary foundation . . . in the power and interests of the dominant groups or states in a social system" (Gilpin 1981b:25). For Gilpin, as for other neorealists, the structure of international politics, far from being an autonomous and absolute whole that expresses itself in the constitution of acting units, is an emergent property produced by the joining of units having a prior existence.

Ruggie's recent review of Waltz's *Theory of International Politics* brings this point home by diagnosing a lapse in Waltz's "structuralism." Informed by structuralist literatures, Ruggie considers the three analytical components (or "depth levels") of Waltz's political structure—organizational principle, differentiation of units, and concentration or diffusion of capabilities—and pinpoints what he takes to be a problem:

> A dimension of change is missing from Waltz's model. It is missing because he drops the second analytical component of political structure, differentiation of units, when discussing international systems. And he drops this component as a result of giving an infelicitous interpretation to the sociological term "differentiation," taking it to mean that which denotes *differences* rather than that which denotes *separateness* (Ruggie 1983:273–274).

The alleged problem, in other words, is that Waltz has misunderstood the structuralist position on identity and difference (the fourth element presented above). Ruggie moves to put it right by restoring the second "depth level" of political structure, now as principles of differentation that tell us "on what basis" acting units are individuated. Specifically, he contents that there are contrasting medieval and modern variants of the second depth level of structure: a "heteronomous" institutional framework for the medieval versus the modern institutional framework of "sovereignty." Ruggie's argument is important. From a genuine structuralist point of view, it is indispensable.

Ruggie introduces his argument as a contribution to a "neorealist synthesis," it is true, and he couches it in an extremely generous interpretation of Waltz's theory. By posing and trying to repair the problem of differentiation in Waltz's theory, however, Ruggie indirectly issues what is so far the strongest critique of the structuralist pretensions in Waltz's neorealism. By posing the problem of differentation from a structuralist standpoint, Ruggie invites us to wonder why neorealists, most especially Waltz, had not considered the problem before. The answer is simple: neorealism is statist before it is structuralist. From a neorealist point of view, Ruggie's argument is simply superfluous because it treats as problematic, and hence in need of a structural accounting, what neorealists insist on treating as unproblematic—the identity of the state.

In neorealist eyes, there is nothing "infelicitous" about Waltz's interpretation of differentiation. When Waltz (1979:93) takes differentiation to refer to specification of the "functions performed by differentiated units," he is giving the only interpretation possible from a neorealist standpoint. There is no need to decide the basis upon which units are individuated, because the essential individuality of states is already taken for granted. It is embedded in a definition of sovereignty that neorealists accord to states independent of the system. For Waltz (1979:96), "to say that a state is sovereign means that it decides for itself how it will cope with its internal and external problems." For Gilpin (1981b:17), "the state is sovereign in that it must answer to no higher authority in the international sphere." Whether it is one state in the lone isolation of universal dominion or many interacting, the definition is the same.

Ruggie's critique of Waltz has a familiar ring. His position vis-à-vis Waltz is not unlike the critique of "utilitarian individualism" in the work of Durkheim, upon whom Ruggie draws. "The clincher in Durkheim's argument," writes John O'Neill (1972:195–196), "is his demonstration that modern individualism[,] so far from creating industrial society[,] presupposes its differentiation of the sociopsychic space which creates the concepts of personality and autonomy." The clincher in Ruggie's argument is his attempt to show that the sovereign state, so far from creating modern international society, presupposes international society's production of the sociopolitical space within which sovereignty could flourish as the modern concept of international political identity and liberty.

b. Utilitarianism

The aptness of the analogy is no accident. For if neorealism's first commitment is statism, its second commitment is to a utilitarian perspective on action, social order, and institutional change. By utilitarianism I do not mean the moral philosophy often associated with Bentham and Mill—a philosophy that holds, for example, that the proper measure of the moral worth of acts and policies is to be found in the value of their consequences. My usage of the term is broader, much more in the sociological sense employed by Durkheim, Polanyi (1957b, 1977), Parsons (1937), and, more recently, Brian Barry (1970), Charles Camic (1979), and Michael Hechter (1981). As these people have made clear, sociological and utilitarian positions stand sharply opposed. As Camic (1979) argues, modern sociology emerged as the critique of utilitarianism. Still, the utilitarian position has refused to die. Indeed, the utilitarian perspective—first outlined by Hobbes and Mandeville, evolving through the classical political economists, and finding more recent expression in the writings of von Mises and Hayek—has "been making steady inroads into the territory that sociology had traditionally staked out as its own." Today it finds expression in the form of microeconomic theories of politics, game theory, exchange theory, and rational choice theory. Today, Hechter can argue that, "if current social science can boast anything remotely resembling a paradigm, then utilitarianism is its leading candidate (Hechter 1981:399). Neorealism shares in the "paradigm."

Broadly construed, utilitarianism is characterized by its individualist and rationalist premises. Its individualism stipulates the theoretical primacy of individual actors rather than of social collectives. The individual acting unit is taken to be essentially private. It exists prior to and independent of larger social institutions and is understood as the autonomous generator of its own ends. Social reality is understood as made up of many such individual actors, inhabiting a world characterized by scarcity—a world in which not all goals can be equally realized and, hence, choices have to be made. Utilitarian rationalism defines rationality in means-ends or instrumental terms: efficient action in the service of established ends whose value or truth is properly the province of the individual actor and cannot be held to account in public terms. Economic rationality is the archetype, the ideal form. What Weber called "substantive rationality" and Habermas called "practical reason" (both of which can pass judgment on ends as well as means) are excluded from the utilitarian notion of rationality. Indeed, insofar as substantive rationality and practical reason presuppose normative structures transcending and irreducible to individual wants and needs, the utilitarian would hold them to be scientifically indefensible metaphysical notions.

Upon these premises, utilitarians found their theories of action, interaction, order, and change. Utilitarian theories of *action* hold that actors behave rationally, in the narrow instrumental sense. Actors strive to serve their intrinsic (biologically or psychologically produced) desires or ends in the most efficient means possible. Social *interaction* is interpretable, by direct extension, as instrumental coaction or exchange among individual actors, each party regarded as an external object or instrument in the eyes of the rationally acting other. Utilitarian theories also hold that, at base, *social order* is a derivative relation. It derives entirely from equilibria (dynamic or static, stable or unstable) in the instrumental relations and mutual expectations among rational egoistic individuals. Social institutions are taken to be the consequence of the regularization of mutual expectations. As for its theory of *institutional change,* utilitarianism proposes that changes occur spontaneously, as a consequence of relative changes in the competing demands and capabilities of individual actors. Social order being a consequence of instrumental relations among individual actors, changes in actors' interests and means give rise to demands for change and, among other things, new coalitions.

It is important to add that such modes of action, interaction, order, and change are deemed instrinsically objective, in need neither of normative defense nor of historical accounting. Their realization in practice, while not always to be observed historically, is taken to be an essential, objective, and progressive tendency of history. It follows that, for the utilitarian, modes of action following the logic of economic rationality are inherently objective: the existence of an economy of universal and objective truths existing independent of any social-normative basis. Hence, for the utilitarian, the market presents itself as an ideal model of rational, objective action, interaction, order, and change—a framework for the interpretation of political as well as economic life.

Neorealism approaches the international system from a utilitarian point of view. The major difference, of course, stems from the neorealist's statism. For the neorealist, states are the rational individual actors whose interests and calculating actions and coactions give form and moment to the international system. Such a position could easily provoke lengthy critical analysis. For the present purposes, I shall confine myself to a brief, two-step commentary.

The first step is simply to note that the utilitarian model is indeed the effective model of international politics in neorealist research programs. This is not to say that neorealists systematically exclude insights or hypotheses from other points of view. Among neorealism's noteworthy traits is an unexcelled eclecticism: many neorealists will *use* an argument, a clause, a phrase from almost any source if it suits their purposes.[12] The point, rather, is that utilitarian premises together with statist commitments establish the anchoring "purposes" that all these borrowings serve. To use Imre Lakatos's familiar terminology, utilitarian statism is the "hard core" of the neorealist "scientific research program." Around this hard core, neorealists develop a "protective belt" of "auxiliary hypotheses" derived from many sources (Lakatos 1970).

This claim, which goes to the orienting structure or "grammar" of neorealist practice, cannot be demonstrated in a few pages. Two examples will have to suffice. The first is the neorealist treatment of power. In neorealism, there is no concept of social power behind or constitutive of states and their interests. Rather, power is generally regarded in terms of capabilities that are said to be distributed, possessed, and potentially used *among* states-as-actors. They are said to exist independent of the actors' knowing or will. They are regarded as finally collapsible, in principle, into a unique, objective measure of a singular systemic distribution (as if there were one uniquely true point of view from which the distribution could be measured). Waltz puts it this way: "To be politically pertinent, power has to be defined in terms of the distribution of capabilities [among agents or actors]; the extent of one's power cannot be inferred from the results one may not get. . . . an agent is powerful to the extent that he effects others more than they effect him" (1979:192). Gilpin's understanding is not dissimilar. Power, he writes, "refers simply to the military, economic, and technological capabilities of states." As he is quick to add, "This definition obviously leaves out important and intangible elements that affect outcomes of political actions, such as public morale, qualities of leadership, and situational factors. It also excludes what E. H. Carr called 'power over opinion.' These psychological and frequently incalculable aspects of power and international relations are more closely associated with the concept of prestige." (Gilpin 1981b:13–14). Such understandings of power are rooted in a utilitarian understanding of international society: an understanding in which (a) there exists no form of sociality, no intersubjective consensual basis, prior to or constitutive of individual actors or their private ends, and hence (b) the *essential* determinants of actors' relative effects on one another will be found in the capabilities they respectively control. Only within such a conception could one believe, as Waltz believes, that "power provides the means of maintaining one's autonomy." Only within such a framework is one inclined to join Gilpin in reducing matters of morale, leadership, and power over opinion to "psychological" factors.

The second is the neorealist conception of international order. For the neorealist, there are no rules, norms, mutual expectations, or principles of practice prior to or independent of actors, their essential ends, and their capabilities. In the last analysis, if not immediately, the evolution of all rules follows from the regularization and breakdown of mutual expectations in accordance with the vectoring of power and interest among states-as-actors. It follows that, for the neorealist, a world of a multiplicity of actors having relatively equal power is a formula for chaos. The potentiality for order increases as the hierarchical concentration of power steepens. For Waltz, who is concerned lest the envisioned concentration reduce to a single dominant state, thereby overturning the fundamental organizational principle of international politics, the optimal concentration is with two states. For other neorealists, who somehow manage to ignore Waltz's concerns while citing his "structuralist" authority, the condition of maximal order is a hierarchy centering power within the grasp of a singular hegemon, a state, in Keohane and Nye's words, that is "powerful enough to maintain the essential rules governing interstate relations, and willing to do so" (Keohane and Nye 1977, ch. 3; see also, Keohane 1980 and 1982a). Even in the analysis of international regimes, this emphasis persists. As Krasner puts it, "The most common proposition [among neorealists] is that hegemonic distributions of power lead to stable, open economic regimes because it is in the interest of a hegemonic state to pursue such a policy and because the hegemon has the resources to provide the collective goods needed to make such a system function effectively."[13] In short, neorealism regards international order entirely as a derivative relation. Deriving from the rational coactions of individual actors, order is taken to be finally dependent upon their respective interests and relative means of influencing one another.[14]

The second step in this two-step commentary is to consider some of the objections with which neorealism, as an instance of utilitarian thought, must contend. Three established criticisms of utilitarian thought, all centering on the utilitarian conception of order, deserve mention. As will be seen, the objections suggest a contradiction in neorealist thought, one that threatens to fracture the statist pillars of neorealist international political theory.

The three objections can be briefly summarized. The first objection has its roots in sociology. It is found in Talcott Parsons' diagnosis (informed by Durkheim and Weber) of the so-called Hobbesian problem: in the absence of a framework of norms consensually accepted by its members, it might be possible momentarily to establish an orderly social aggregate (a "social contract," for example) among instrumentally rational individuals. Except under conditions of absolute stasis, however, it cannot be maintained. The second objection to the utilitarian conception of order is developed within the utilitarian framework itself. This is Mancur Olson's (1965) critique. As aptly summarized by Hechter:

> Rational self-interest actors will not join large organizations to pursue collective goods when they can reap the benefit of other people's activity to pursue those ends. This means that the rational actor in the utilitarian model will always be a free rider whenever given the opportunity. Thus, according to utilitarian behavioral premises, social organization is unlikely to arise even among those individuals who have a strong personal interest in reaping the benefits that such organization provides" (Hechter 1981:403, n. 6).

The third objection, and no doubt the most important, is Marx's. Anticipating the broad outlines of both Parsons' and Olson's arguments, Marx went beyond them to try to draw out what utilitarians must presuppose if they are to hold to their "contractarian" (i.e., instrumentalist or exchange-based) understandings of order in society. Marx argued convincingly that the myth of the contract, put into practice, depends upon a dominant class's ability to externalize the costs of keeping promises onto a class that lacks the freedom to contract; the Hobbesian "state of war" is thus held in check through one-sided power in a "class war" (O'Neill 1972). Utilitarian order thus presupposes class relations (and associated political, legal and institutional relations), which its conscious individualist premises prohibit it from confronting, comprehending, or explaining.

How do neorealists deal with these objections? The answer, quite simply, is that they finesse them. In a bold stroke, neorealism embraces these objections as articles of faith. Turning problems of utilitarian analysis into virtues, neorealism redefines the Hobbesian problem of order as an "ordering principle" of international politics. Struggles for power among states become the normal process of orderly change and succession. The free-rider problem among states becomes a global "sociological" legitimation for hegemonic states, whose private interests define the public "good" and whose preponderant capabilities see to it that more "good" gets done. As for the Marxian critique, it is accepted, albeit with a twist. It is accepted not as global class analysis per se but in the idea that order among the great powers, the great *states,* is ever dependent on the perpetuation of a hierarchy of domination among great and small states. Inequality, Waltz says, has its virtues. Order is among them (Waltz 1979:131–132).

One has to have some grudging admiration for theorists who would make such a move. They must have enormous courage, and not just because such positions expose neorealists to a lot of self-righteous moralizing. Neorealists must be courageous because their attempt to finesse objections to utilitarian accounts of order involves a bluff of sorts. It counts on our failure to notice that, at a certain moment in making their move, neorealists are suspended in thin idealist air.

That moment comes when, conceding objections to utilitarian accounts, the neorealist embraces them to describe international order *among states* at the "level" of the international system. The rhetorical force of this concession, ironically, is to divert the critic of utilitarian conceptions of order into momentary complicity with the neorealist's own statism, a statism that would collapse on its face if the critic were to raise the same objections at the level of the state. That is to say, the neorealist counts on our being so awestruck by the Hobbesian and free-rider dilemmas we confront at the "international level" that we shall join in neglecting the same dilemmas at the level of the state. The neorealist counts on our failure to notice that the objections accepted at the level of the international system can equally well be turned against the metaphysical prop upon which depends the reification of an international political system analytically distinguishable from domestic and transnational relations: the conception of the state-as-actor.

The neorealist move is, in short, a sleight of hand. For despite its statism, neorealism can produce no theory of the state capable of satisfying the state-as-actor premises of its international political theory. On the contrary, by adopting a utilitarian theory of action, order, and change, neorealists implicitly give the lie to their *idée fixe,* the ideal of the state-as-actor upon which their distinction among "levels" and their whole theory of international politics depend.

c. Positivism

I am being unfair. To suggest, as I have, that neorealists play a trick of sorts is to imply some kind of intentional duping of an innocent audience. This is surely wrong. It is wrong because neorealists are as much victims as perpetrators. And it is wrong because, in truth, the bedazzled audience is far from innocent. We already share complicity in the illusion. Neither neorealists nor we, the fawning audience, can imagine seeing the world in any other way.

Why should this be so? Why, for example, is it so difficult to see that the utilitarian perspective neorealists embrace at the "international level" undermines the state-as-actor notion upon which their whole theoretical edifice, including the distinction between levels, depends? The history of utilitarian thought is, after all, largely the story of philosophical *opposition* to the "personalist" concept of state required by neorealism's international political theory. In part, surely, this refusal to see is due to the blinding light of the halo surrounding the state in neorealist thought. But in part, too, this blindness is due to the third commitment of the neorealist orrery. Neorealist theory is theory of, by, and for positivists. It secures instantaneous recognition, I want to suggest, because it merely projects onto the place of explicit theory certain metatheoretical commitments that have long been implicit in the habits of positivist method. It tells us what, hidden in our method, we have known all along.

Born in struggle, "positivism" is of course a disputed term. Many American political scientists are unaware of its rich currents of meaning in recent European, Latin American, and North American sociology, philosophy, and anthropology. Many trivialize and thus evade the term by misequating positivism with "mindless number crunching," brute empiricism, inductivist logic, or the narrow logical positivism of the Vienna Circle. And the term has suffered at the hands of a number of silly or naïve who, having encountered Lenin's indictment, use the term as a synonym for regime-supporting scholarship or bourgeois social science. Many of these radicals are positivists themselves.[15]

At the very minimum, positivism means two contemporary things. In its most general meaning, positivism refers to the so-called "received model" of *natural* science (Giddens 1979:257). At the same time, and apropos the subject-object, man-nature dualisms implicit in this "received model," one can follow Michel Foucault in distinguishing positivist from eschatalogical discourse. For eschatological discourse (evident in phenomenology, ethnomethodology, and some hermeneutical sciences) the objective truth of the discourse lies within and is produced by the discourse itself. By contrast, for positivist discourse, with its naturalistic bias, the truth of discourse lies in the external object (Foucault 1970).

In general, positivist discourse holds to four expectations. The first is that scientific knowledge aims to grasp a reality that exists in accord with certain fixed structural or causal relations which are independent of human subjectivity (hence their objectivity) and internally harmonious or contradiction-free (as if authored from a single point of view). The second is that science seeks to formulate technically useful knowledge, knowledge that enhances human capacities to make predictions, orient efficient action, and exert control in the service of given human values. The third is that sought-after knowledge is value-neutral. The fourth, consistent with the first three, holds that the truth of claims and concepts is to be tested by their correspondence to a field of external experience as read via (problematic) instruments or interpretative rules (Giddens 1974, ch. 1; cf. Alker 1982).

When one turns to positive *social* science, at least one other expectation needs to be added to the list. This is the expectation that "the phenomena of human subjectivity . . . do not offer any particular barriers to the treatment of social conduct as an 'object' on a par with objects in the natural world" (Giddens 1974:4). Obviously, this is a most troublesome expectation. Making good on it requires that one overcome a double problem inherent in human subjectivity. On the one side, human subjectivity raises a problem from the perspective of social actors: the problem of meaningful, value-laden social action. On the other side, there is a problem from the analyst's point of view: the analyst's own norms, values, and understandings potentially negate the analyst's ability to detach himself or herself from the social world, to treat it, on a par with nature, as an external, objective, "dumb generality." Positivist social science has had to "solve" this double problem.

As it turns out, the "solutions" are worth a few moments of our time. For it is in these solutions that we encounter the *social-theoretical* commitments embedded within dominant conceptions of social science itself. In particular, I have in mind positivist solutions to the problem of human subjectivity anchored in an unquestioned commitment to the objective, historical force of instrumental or technical rationality. Let me briefly describe this commitment and then consider its role in "solutions" to the dual problem of subjectivity in positivist social science. As I shall indicate, the result is a metatheoretical outlook implicit in positivist method, which circumscribes scientific criticism and limits the range of theories about society that can be scientifically entertained. As I shall also suggest, these limits establish among positivists an uncritical receptivity to neorealists' conceptions of the international system.

Again, the commitment in question is a commitment to the essential objectivity of technical rationality. According to this (typically unspoken) commitment, which also appears at the center of utilitarian thought, means-ends rationality is inherently objective, value-neutral, void of normative or substantive content. Technical rationality is said to inhabit the domain of the "is" rather than the domain of the "ought," and hence its truth requires no normative defense. Indeed, as exemplified by Max Weber's resignation to the world historical "rationalization" of all modes of life, technical rationality is taken to be a *necessary* progressive force in history. Rationalization involves the breaking down of traditional limits and the progressive absorption of all institutions of life within a mode of thought that aims to reduce all aspects of human action to matters of purposive-rational action—efficiency in the service of pregiven ends. For Weber, this tendency was inexorable, its outcome inevitable: the "iron cage" of a totally bureaucratized life (Weber 1972; see also Marcuse 1968, Habermas 1971, and Giddens 1972). Science, committed to the objectivity of technical reason, is on the side of this necessary historical tendency. It is at the leading edge.

Immediately one can see that this commitment replicates in a novel way the classical justification of positivist science as a critical, even revolutionary force, a force that demystifies all forms of romanticism, dispenses with atavistic myth, and establishes the "end of ideology." What may be harder to see, especially for positivists, is that this commitment ties positivism to an ideology of its own. It endorses a metahistorical faith in scientific-technical progress that positivist science itself cannot question. Insofar as the commitment affords "solutions" to the dual problem of human subjectivity, it justifies itself in its own technical terms, enriching the theoretical content of positivist method qua political ideology. Having mentioned Weber's position as exemplary, it is appropriate to consider the role of this commitment in Weber's own (now conventional) solutions to the two sides of the problem.

In Weber, the first side of the problem, the side concerned with the meaningful character of social action, could be reduced to this: how can there be a naturalistic social science, one that produces objective knowledge capable of calculating and predicting social outcomes, given that human action is necessarily "subjective" in character? Weber confronted this problem in the specific context of the German historical school (Giddens 1974). Authors like Roscher and Knies had concluded that, given the subjective quality of human action, human action has an "irrational" quality (Weber 1974). In Weber's view, this conflation of "subjectivism" and "irrationalism" presented a serious obstacle to the reconciliation of naturalism and sociological and historical method. He thus set out the classic synthesis to which much of modern positivist social science is indebted.

Premised on the inherent objectivity of technical rationality, the synthesis was this; if we abstract and regard as objectively given an agent's substantively empty logic of technical reason, then in interpreting the agent's action we can assume that, from this objective standpoint, society will appear to the individual agent as a subjectless set of external constraints, a *meaningless* second nature. We shall then be able to say that meaning enters society primarily through the autonomously generated ends of individual acting agents: meaningful action is merely *motivated* action. With that, we have objective, naturalistic social science. For with knowledge of an agent's pregiven ends and "meaningless" social constraints, "meaningful" and "rational" subjective relations become calculable, predictable, and susceptible to causal accounts (Weber 1974).

For most North American theorists of international and comparative politics, Weber's solution is a "methodological principle" whose obviousness precludes any need for justification. Yet as recollection of the Weberian moment makes clear, the methodological principle implicit in this solution restricts us to a particular conception of society. We may call this conception an *actor model*. Upon commencing any analysis of a social system, the habit-born principle predisposes the positivist to identify the irreducible actors whose rational decisions will mediate the entry of meaning into social reality. Thanks to this "principle," the committed positivist knows almost "instinctively" that all explanations of social action must ultimately come to rest with the interpretation of some frozen set of actors, their values, and their ends. All analysis comes to rest with actors who are capable of exercising technical rationality; whose ends, values, and boundaries separating one another are taken to be given and independent of communication and interaction among the several; who accordingly must appear to one another, individually and in aggregates, as external constraints; and who must relate to one another, in the last analysis, in strictly instrumental terms.[16]

Weber's solution to the *second side* of the problem of human subjectivity is equally important. The problem, seen from the second side, is the possible confounding of scientific detachment and objectivity owing to the fact that the social scientist's own norms, values, and understandings implicate him or her in the social world examined. As Weber recognized, even one's categories of analysis and the meanings one attaches to them depend upon normative commitments that bind one to the social world. All knowledge has its socially rooted presuppositions.

Weber's solution to this second side of the problem is also anchored in a commitment to the essential objectivity of technical rationality. The solution involves radicalizing the separation between the process by which the validity of scientific concepts and knowledge claims may be scientifically decided and the process by which scientists take interest in, generate, or come to recognize as meaningful their concepts and knowledge claims. In Weber's view, social scientific discourse would center on the former process—a process whose objectivity would be assured because it could and should be monopolized by the logic of technical rationality. It would concentrate on issues decidable within technical rationality's own inherently objective terms (Shapiro 1981).

Thus, while individual scientists' norms, values, and socially established understandings may help decide the direction in which the scientific beacon will cast its light, science *as an enterprise* cannot pass judgment on the truth of values, ethics, ends, or understandings, including those at work in scientists' choices of what to study. Scientific discourse cannot critically examine the meaning structures at work in and accounting for scientists' mutual recognition of the concepts they deploy. Scientific discourse can speak decisively only to the efficiency of means. In sum, science *as an enterprise* preserves its objectivity by excluding from its terrain all questions that cannot be formulated and solved within the allegedly objective logic of technical rationality.

This solution, like the first, is now widely taken for granted as one of science's delimiting features. Like the first, too, it buttresses the commitment of positivist science to an actor model. It does so primarily by limiting the range of scientific criticism. In particular, it excludes discussion of forms of social consensus that might themselves be value-laden, that might be historically contingent and susceptible to change, and that might nonetheless coordinate human practices and distributions of resources in ways that produce and accord recognition to the consensually recognized actors (including their boundaries and ends) which positivists take as the irreducible elements of analyses.

Taken together, then, the two solutions establish a methodological predisposition that is anything but neutral with respect to social ordering possibilities. On the contrary, they implicate and profoundly limit the range of possibilities that theory can contemplate if it is to find acceptance as objective scientific theory. Even before the first self-consciously theoretical word passes anyone's lips, a theoretical picture worth a thousand words is already etched in the minds of positivist speakers and hearers. Born of long practice conforming to the solutions just described, this picture, a kind of scheme, orders and limits expectations about what explicit theoretical discourse can do and say. In particular, it commits scientific discourse to an "actor model" of social reality—a model within which science itself is incapable of questioning the historical *constitution* of social actors, cannot question their ends, but can only advise them as the efficiency of means.

Here in this theory-masked-as-method we find a partial explanation of the ease with which neorealists are able to delude themselves as well as us, their admiring audience. Despite the contradiction between neo-realists' utilitarian conception of politics and their statist commitments, neorealists are able to perpetuate the state-as-actor illusion in their conception of the international system. They are able to do so because, as positivists, we are methodologically predisposed to look for precisely the kind of model they "reveal." Without an actor model, we somehow sense, we shall lack any scientific point of entry into a *meaningful understanding* of the international system; the system will appear to us, we worry, as a meaningless swirl of "disembodied forces." They are further able to do so because, as positivists, we join them in excluding from the realm of proper scientific discourse precisely those modes of criticism that would allow us to unmask the move for what it is. At the very moment we begin to question this state-as-actor conception, we are given to feel that we have stumbled beyond the legitimate grounds of science, into the realm of personal ethics, values, loyalties, or ends. We are given to feel that our complaints have no scientific standing. And so as scientists, we swallow our questions. We adopt the posture of Waltz's utter detachment, Gilpin's fatalism, Krasner's wonderment, or Keohane's Weberian resignation with respect to the powers that be. We might not like it, we say, but this is the world that is. As scientists, we think, we cannot say otherwise.

d. Structuralism

There is more to the story of neorealism's success than this, however. As noted earlier, the decisive moment in neorealism's triumph was its celebrated structuralist turn. As also noted, this structuralist turn would appear to hold out a promise for a deepening of international political discourse. Now, having examined the other three aspects of the neorealist orrery, we can return at last to neorealist structuralism and consider once again its attractions. We can listen as it explodes the one-time limits of international political discourse. We can look to see how it penetrates beneath commonsense appearances of the given order. We can sift through the arguments to find the many ways in which structuralism transcends the confines of utilitarianism, statism, and positivism—perhaps enriching them by disclosing their deeper historical significance. We can listen, look, and sift some more. And what do we find? Disappointment, primarily.

The reason is now beginning to become clear: neorealists slide all too easily between two concepts of the whole, one structuralist in the sense described earlier and one atomist and physicalist. The structuralist posits the possibility of a structural whole—a deep social subjectivity—having an autonomous existence independent of, prior to, and constitutive of the elements. From a structuralist point of view, a structural whole cannot be described by starting with the parts as abstract, already defined entities, taking note of their external joining, and describing emergent properties among them. The standpoint of the structural whole affords the only objective perspective. By contrast, the atomist conception describes the whole precisely in terms of the external joinings of the elements, including emergent properties produced by the joinings and potentially limiting further movement or relations among the elements. Clearly, in this conception, the whole has no existence independent of the parts taken together. But it may be possible that, from the point of view of any one part (a point of view that remains legitimate within an atomist perspective), the whole may exist independent of that part of its possible movements. From this standpoint, the standpoint of the single part, the whole is an external physical relation—a "second nature" to be dealt with, in the last analysis, only physically or instrumentally. It cannot be otherwise, for no prior intersubjective unity joins part and whole (see Ollman 1976, Appendix 2).

Neorealism has managed to conflate these two concepts of the whole. Consider the one position, the misnamed "sociological position," that many neorealists take to be exemplary: Waltz's position. As noted earlier, Waltz understands "international structure" not as a deep, internal relation prior to and constitutive of social actors but as an external joining of states-as-actors who have precisely the boundaries, ends, and self-understandings that theorists accord to them on the basis of unexamined common sense. In turn—and here is the coup—Waltz grants this structure a life of its own independent of the parts, the states-as-actors; and he shows in countless ways how this structure limits and disposes action on the part of states such that, on balance, the structure is reproduced and actors are drawn into conformity with its requisites. But how is the independence of this structural whole established? It is not established independent of the parts taken together, for it is never anything more than the logical consequence of the parts taken together. Nor is it established by anchoring it in any deep intersubjective structure of the state-systemic whole. Indeed, Waltz systematically purges from the realist legacy all hints that subjective relations might be, in his terminology, "systemic"; true to Waltz's atomism, all subjective relations are interpreted as psychological relations, and propositions that refer to them are thus banished as "reductionist."

Rather, Waltz establishes the independence of the structured whole from the idealized point of view of the lone, isolated state-as-actor, which cannot alone alter the whole and cannot rely on others to aid it in bringing about change in the whole's deepest structures. We are encouraged to glimpse and authenticate the independence of this structure, in other words, from the standpoint of a frozen abstraction: the point of view of the single state-as-actor, or the point of view of any number of states-as-actors, one at a time. These, though, are precisely the states-as-actors (or, more correctly, this is the same fixed, abstract state-as-actor category) with which the theorist began. The autonomy of the neorealist whole is established precisely from the hypostatized point of view of the idealized parts whose appearances are independent entities provided the starting point of the analysis, the basic material, the props without which the whole physical structure could never have been erected. From start to finish, we never escape or penetrate these appearances. From start to finish, Waltz's is an atomist conception of the international system.

At the same time, once neorealists do arrive at their physicalistic notion of structure, they do attribute to it some of the qualities of structure in structuralist thought. Neorealists do tend to grant to the international political system "absolute predominance over the parts." In neorealism, as in structuralism, diachrony is subordinated to synchrony, and change is interpretable solely within the fixed logic of the system. And neorealists, like structuralists, do tend to regard the structure that they describe in the singular. Thus, as noted earlier, there *are* definite isomorphisms between aspects of neorealist thought and structuralist principles.

This, however, is no compliment. For what it means is that neorealism gives us the worst of two worlds. In neorealism we have atomism's superficiality combined with structuralism's closure such that, once we are drawn into the neorealist circle, we are condemned to circulate entirely at the surface-level of appearances. And what an idealist circle it is! What we have in neorealism's so-called structuralism is the commonsense idealism of the powerful, projected onto the whole in a way that at once necessitates and forgives that power. It is the statist idealism developed from the point of view of the one state (or, more properly, the dominant coalition) that can afford the illusion that it is a finished state-as-actor because, for a time, it is positioned such that the whole world pays the price of its illusions.

With apologies to E. P. Thompson, I would suggest that there is a certain "snake-like" quality to neorealist structuralism. The head of the snake is an unreflective state-as-actor, which knows itself only to rely on itself and which will not recognize its own limits or dependence upon the world beyond its skin. It slithers around hissing "self-help" and projecting its own unreflectivity onto the world. Finding its own unreflectivity clearly reflected in others, it gets its own tail into its mouth, and the system is thus defined. Asked to describe the system so defined, the snake says it reproduces itself, and it swallows more of its tail. What, though, of the values or norms of this system? The values and norms, the snake answers, are those that reflect the power and interests of the powerful and interested. What, then, of power? The snake—or what is left of it, for it is now a wriggling knot—has an answer for this, too. Power is rooted in those capabilities which provide a basis for the state-as-actor's autonomy. And what of autonomy? In a final gulp, the snake answers. Autonomy is the state-as-actor's privilege of not having to reflect because the whole world bends to its unreflected projections of itself. "Plop! The snake has disappeared into total theoretical vacuity" (Thompson 1978:77).

As Thompson says of another structuralism: "It is, of course, a highly conservative vacuity; what is governs what is whose first function is to preserve the integrity of is-ness; what dominates has the functional imperative of preserving its own dominance." Thompson's words are apt. Neorealist structuralism lends itself wonderfully well to becoming an apologia for the status quo, an excuse for domination, and "an invective against 'utopian' and 'maladjusted' heretics" who would question the givenness of the dominant order (1978:77, 73).

In The Poverty of Historicism, Karl Popper (1961) concerned himself with the totalitarian implications of certain progressivist versions of structuralism to which he gave the label "historicism." What we find in neorealist structuralism is a historicism of stasis. It is a historicism that freezes the political institutions of the current world order while at the same time rendering absolute the autonomy of technical rationality as the organ of social progress to which all aspects of this order, including states-as-actors, must bow. It is a historicism that almost perfectly mirrors Hans Morgenthau's understanding of the "totalitarian state of mind."[17]

Whereas perfectionism creates an abstract ideal to which it tries to elevate political life through force or exhortation or reform, totalitarianism, that is, the totalitarian state of mind, identifies the ideal with the facts of political life. What is, is good because it is, and power is to the totalitarian not only a fact of social life with which one must come to terms but also the ultimate standard for judging human affairs and the ideal source of all human values. He says "Yes" to his lust for power, and he recognizes no transcendent standard, no spiritual concept which might tame and restrain the lust for power by confronting it with an ideal alien and hostile to political domination. (Morgenthau 1958:244–245)

Of course, neorealism's totalitarian implications are only partly to be discovered in its celebration of power before order. They are also present in neorealism's silences, in those aspects of history neorealism denies, omits, or represses. As Aldous Huxley (1952:14) reminds us, the greatest triumph of totalitarian propaganda have been accomplished "not by doing something, but by refraining from doing. Great is the truth, but still greater, from a practical point of view, is silence about truth." Neorealist structuralism is silent about four dimensions of history. I will call these the "four p's": process, practice, power, and politics.

First, neorealist structuralism denies *history as process*. Like other static structuralisms, neorealist theory has two characteristics. One is a "fixity of theoretical categories" such that each is a category of stasis even when it is set in motion among other moving parts. The other characteristic is that all movement is confined within a closed field whose limits are defined by the pregiven structure. Thompson very clearly articulates the consequences of such a conception: "History *as process,* as open ended indeterminate eventuation—but not for that reason devoid of rational *logic* or of determining *pressures*—in which categories are defined in particular contexts but are continuously undergoing historical redefinition, and whose structure is not pre-given but protean, continually changing in form and in articulation—all of this . . . must be denied" (1978:83–84).

Second, neorealism joins all modes of historicism in denying the historical significance of *practice,* the moment at which men and women enter with greater or lesser degrees of consciousness into the making of their world. For the neorealist intellectual, men and women, statesmen and entrepreneurs, appear as mere supports for the social process that produces their will and the logics by which they serve it. In particular, people are reduced to some idealized *Homo oeconomicus,* able only to carry out, but never to reflect critically on, the limited rational logic that the system demands of them. They are reduced in the last analysis to mere objects who must participate in reproducing the whole or, as the enlightened intellectual knows, fall by the wayside of history. True, neorealists would never admit that theory is without "practical relevance." But for them, relevance finds its measure only in terms of the technical adequacy of the theorists' advice to agents of power, and technical adequacy consists solely in the enhancement of the efficiency of means under objective structural constraints. Nowhere in neorealist categories do we find room for the idea that men and women who are the objects of theory can themselves theorize about their lives; are in fact engaged in a continuing struggle to shape and redefine their understandings of themselves, their circumstances, their agencies of collective action, and the very categories of social existence; do indeed orient their practices in light of their understandings; and, thanks to all of this, do give form and motion to the open-ended processes by which the material conditions of their practices are made, reproduced, and transformed. Neorealist structuralism cannot allow this to be so. For to do so would mean that neorealist theory would itself be a mere part of history, and not the intellectual master of history it aspires to be.

Third, for all its emphasis on "power politics," neorealism has no comprehension of, and in fact denies, the social basis and social limits of *power.* For the neorealist, as we have seen, power must ultimately be reducible to a matter of capabilities, or means, under the control of the unreflective actor whose status as an actor is given from the start. No other position on power could possibly be compatible with neorealism's atomistic and utilitarian conceptions of international order. Yet such a position strictly rules out a *competence model* of social action. According to a competence model, the power of an actor, and even its status as an agent competent to act, is not in any sense attributable to the inherent qualities or possessions of a given entity. Rather, the power and status of an actor depends on and is limited by the conditions of its *recognition* within a community as a whole. To have power, an agent must first secure its recognition as an agent capable of having power, and, to do that, it must first demonstrate its competence in terms of the collective and coreflective structures (that is, the practical cognitive schemes and history of experience) by which the community confers meaning and organizes collective expectations. It is always by way of performance in reference to such collectively "known" (but not necessarily intellectually accessible) generative schemes that actors gain recognition and are *empowered*. Thus, according to a competence model, building power always has a community-reflective performative aspect. Thus, too, the power of an actor always has its limits. Although an actor can play creatively off of given practical schemes, and although an actor can sometimes offer up virtuoso improvisations that elicit novel orchestrated responses to new circumstances, the actor can never exceed the limits of recognition (see especially Bourdieu 1977, ch. 4). The author of the "Melian Dialogues" understood this dialectic of power and recognition. Neorealists have forgotten what Thucydides knew, in favor of a notion of power wedded to the Industrial Revolution's faith in humankind's limitless expansion of control over nature.

Fourth, despite its spirited posturing on behalf of political autonomy and in opposition to the alleged economism of other traditions, neorealist historicism denies *politics*. More correctly, neorealism reduces politics to those aspects which lend themselves to interpretation exclusively within a framework of economic action under structural constraints. In so doing, neorealism both immunizes that economic framework from criticism as to its implicit political content and strips politics of any practical basis for the autonomous reflection on and resistance to strictly economic demands. It thereby implicitly allies with those segments of society that benefit from the hegemony of economic logic in concert with the state. Politics in neorealism becomes pure technique: the efficient achievement of whatever goals are set before the political actor. Political strategy is deprived of its artful and performative aspect, becoming instead the mere calculation of instruments of control. Absent from neorealist categories is any hint of politics as a creative, critical enterprise, an enterprise by which men and women might reflect on their goals and strive to shape freely their collective will.

Taken together, reflections on these "four p's" suggest that neorealist structuralism represents anything but the profound broadening and deepening of international political discourse it is often claimed to be. Far from expanding discourse, this so-called structuralism encloses it by equating structure with external relations among powerful entities as they would have themselves be known. Far from penetrating the surface of appearances, this so-called structuralism's fixed categories freeze given order, reducing the history and future of social evolution to an expression of those interests which can be mediated by the vectoring of power among competing states-as-actors.[18] Far from presenting a structuralism that envisions political learning on a transnational scale, neorealism presents a structure in which political learning is reduced to the consequence to instrumental coaction among dumb, unreflective, technical-rational unities that are barraged and buffeted by technological and economic changes they are powerless to control.

Again, though, none of this is to say that neorealist "structuralism" is without its attractions. For one thing, and most generally, there is something remarkably congenial about a structuralism that pretends to a commanding, objective portrait of the whole while at the same time leaving undisturbed, even confirming, our commonsense views of the world and ourselves. Compared to Wallerstein's conception of the modern world system, for instance, neorealist structuralism is far more reassuring as to the objective *necessity* of the state-as-unit-of-analysis convention among students of politics.[19] It thus relieves this particular niche in the academic division of responsibility for reflection on its own historicity. Its pose of Weberian detachment can be preserved.

For another thing, this strange structuralism finds much of its appeal in the fact that it complements and reinforces the other three commitments of the neorealist orrery. As already noted, neorealism's atomistic understanding of structure gives priority to—and then reconfirms—the commitment to the state-as-actor. One might also note that neorealism employs the only form of structuralism that could possibly be consistent with its utilitarian and positivist conceptions of international society. Anchored as they are in the ideal of rational individual action under meaningless, quasinatural constraints, these conceptions would be radically challenged by modes of structuralism that question the dualism of subject and object and thus highlight the deep intersubjective constitution of objective international structures. Neorealism is able to avoid this radical challenge. It is able to do so by restricting its conception of structure to the physicalist form of a clockwork, the philosophical *mechanism* so dear to the heart of the Industrial Revolution's intelligentsia.

3. ELEMENTS OF A DIALECTICAL COMPETENCE MODEL

[*Editor's Note*: Professor Ashley goes on to compare neorealism to the classical realism of Hans J. Morgenthau and Martin Wight. Despite neorealism's
critique of classical realism as unscientific, Ashley regards classical realism
as richer with insights into political practice and "far truer to the traditional practice of world politics" (p. 275). Nevertheless, like neorealism,
classical realism is a closed system of thought. Ashley seeks to correct this,
but also to build on the "generative potential" of classical realism in developing a dialectical explanation of world politics. To think of classical realism in this way, he argues, "is to anticipate the development of a *dialectical
competence model.*" He proceeds by listing the virtues of such a model.]

First, such a model would be developed to account for the emergence,
reproduction, and possible transformation of a world-dominant public
political apparatus: a tradition of regime anchored in the balance-of-
power scheme and constitutive of the modern states system. The regime
should not be construed to organize and regulate behaviors among states-
as-actors. It instead *produces* sovereign states who, as condition of their
sovereignty, embody the regime. So deeply is this regime bound within
the identities of the participant states that their observations of its rules
and expectations become acts not of conscious obedience to something
external but of self-realization, of survival as what they have become (see
Ashley 1980). We may refer to this regime as a balance-of-power regime.
We may understand it to be the tradition of statecraft interpreted by
classical realism. Classical realists are the "organic intellectuals" of this
regime, the reigning intelligentsia of the worldwide public sphere of
modern global life.

Second, such a model would situate this balance-of-power regime in
terms of the conditions making it possible: the social, economic, and
environmental conditions upon which its practical efficacy depends. One
such condition can be inferred from classical realists' notorious silence
on economic processes and their power-political ramifications. As Hedley
Bull says of Martin Wight, so can it be said of classical realists and
regime-bound statecraft: they are "not much interested in the economic
dimension of the subject" (Bull 1976:108). How is it possible for the
balance-of-power regime to maintain such a silence? Under what historical, social, economic, and environmental conditions is it possible for the

balance-of-power regime, as the public political sphere of world society, to maintain silence on matters economic while at the same time coordinating and orienting practices in ways reaffirming the regime itself? One possible answer is that the regime presupposes capitalist relations of production and exchange. It presupposes a deep consensus granting control over production to a sphere of "private" decisions that are themselves immunized from public responsibility—a practical consensus that thereby produces a sphere of "economy" operating according to the technical rational logics of action. In turn, such a consensus further presupposes capitalist labor and property relations. This consensus, together with the worldwide power bloc whose dominance it signifies and secures, might be called the *modern global hegemony*. The balance-of-power regime is its public political fare. The silences of regime on matters economic at once reflect and reinforce the dominant power bloc's control over production independent of public responsibility.

Third, such a model would necessarily account for the balance-of-power regime's orientation and coordination of political practices such that, on balance (and as an unintended consequence), they tend to direct commitments of resources and the development of ideological legitimations in ways securing the possibility conditions of the regime. The model might show, for example, how the competent statesman's interest in accumulating symbolic capital, or symbolic power, by playing off the balance-of-power scheme, effects a "double standard" of political action. That double standard, in turn, secures the political preconditions of global domination on the part of a transnational capitalist coalition, the dominant power bloc of the modern global hegemony.

Fourth, such a model would explore the learning potential of the balance-of-power regime. In particular, along the lines of Pierre Bourdieu's (1977) argument, it might further develop its specifications of the process of symbolic capital accumulation. It might explore how symbolic capital, accumulated through the ambiguous and "disinterested" performances of competent hegemonic statesmen, provides a kind of "creative reserve," a basis in authority, for the exercise of leadership in the orchestration of collective improvisations in response to crisis.

Fifth, such a model would offer an account of crisis. It would specify the tendencies threatening to undermine or transform the conditions upon which the practical efficacy of the balance-of-power regime depends. It might specifically consider those tendencies that threaten to eradicate the statesman's latitude for ambiguous, intrinsically equivocal political performances honoring the balance-of-power scheme and not immediately reducible to expressions of economic interests.[20] Owing to this loss of latitude for ambiguous performances, it might be shown, the competent statesman is deprived of the ability to accumulate symbolic capital and, with it, a reserve capacity for learning and change in response to system crisis. Such reasoning would suggest the possibility of a world crisis—not just one more cyclical economic crisis, but an epochal crisis of world political authority, a crisis involving a degeneration in the learning capacity of the regime and, consequently, a loss of political control. Understood in the context of the modern global hegemony, such a crisis might be expected to be marked by the economization of politics and the resulting loss of political autonomy vis-à-vis economic and technological change. As if international politics were the last frontier of the progressive world rationalization tendency delineated by Weber, hegemonic pratice might come under increasing pressures to find its rationale not by playing equivocally off the balance-of-power scheme, but by measuring every gesture in terms of the ultrarationalistic logic of economy.

Sixth, such a model would not view the modern global hegemony in isolation. Nor would it mistake it for *the* whole of world politics (Ashley 1980; Alker in progress). It would instead regard it as the dominant world order among a multiplicity of mutually interpenetrating and opposed world orders, some of which might escape the logic of the modern global hegemony and assert alternative structuring possibilities under circumstances and by way of oppositional strategies that can in principle be specified. For example, the modern global hegemony might be understood to contest with—and, as a kind of "pluralistic insecurity community," to contain—totalitarian communist, collectivist self-reliance, Euro-communist, Muslim transnationalist, and corporatist authoritarian world order alternatives (Alker 1981). Developing such a model would involve exploring the strategies by which oppositional movements representing these and other alternatives might take advantage of the indeterminate and ambiguous qualities of regime-bound statecraft, while exploiting its traditional silences, to transform its conditions of dominance, produce the conditions of their own self-realization, and secure the widening recognition of their own ordering principles as the active principles of practice.[21]

These anticipations of theory are, of course, rudimentary at best. They do, however, suggest some possibilities for the development of a model that would preserve classical realism's rich insights into international political practice while at the same time exposing the conditions, limits, and potential for change of the tradition in which classical realism is immersed. Fully developed, such a model would more than surpass neo-realism. It would offer an interpretation of neorealism, finding in it a historically specific reaction to crisis that refuses to comprehend that crisis because it cannot acknowledge the richness of the tradition that is endangered. It would interpret neorealism, in other words, as an ideo-logical move toward the economization of politics. And it would under-score the possibly dangerous consequences should this move succeed. For from the point of view of such a model, the economization of international politics can only mean the purging to international politics of those reflective capacities which, however limited, make global learning and creative change possible. It can only mean the impoverishment of political imagination and the reduction of international politics to a bat-tleground for the self-blind strategic clash of technical reason against technical reason in the service of unquestioned ends.

NOTES

1. Also called a "planetarium," an orrery is a mechanical device used to illustrate with balls of various sizes the relative motions and positions of the bodies in a solar system. It takes its name from Charles Boyle, the Earl of Orrery, for whom one was made.

2. In speaking of a "neorealism movement," it is necessary to confront several issues. First, the name "neorealism" is not universally recognized by those I am calling neorealists. Some no doubt assume that their work reflects no larger move-ment or trend they themselves did not consciously set into motion; they thus reject the application of general labels to their own work. Second, I recognize that the scholars here regarded as neorealist have many serious differences and quarrels among themselves. Third, I stress that my treatment here is with respect to the structure of an overall movement in its context and not the expressed pronounce-ments or conscious intentions of individual scholars whose work sometimes may, and sometimes may not, contribute to that movement.

3. As discussed here, neorealism is not just an amalgam of individual scholars' traits or opinions, nor is it the lowest common denominator among them. Rather, my contentions are with respect to neorealism as a collective movement or project emerging in a shared context, having shared principles of practice, and observing certain background understandings and norms that participants mutually accept as unproblematic and that limit and orient the questions raised, the answers warranted, and the conduct of discourse among neorealists—this regardless of the fact that the participants may not be conscious of (may merely take for granted the universal truth of) the norms and understandings integrating them as one movement. In Waltz's now well-known terminology, mine is a systemic, not a reductionist, account of the neorealist system.

4. The term "totalitarian" is, to say the least, provocative. As seen below, my usage is consistent with that of Hans Morgenthau.

5. This is John O'Neill's terminology. The distinction will be elaborated below.

6. Habermas (1976). Of course, the figures cited can hardly be said to occupy one school; in fact, there are very sharp differences among them. Thompson, for instance, would be among the last to align happily with Foucault, "Althusser's former student"; Habermas's rationalism would set him apart from Bourdieu. On the theme of the "economization" of politics, see also Arendt (1958) and Ashley (1983).

7. Karl Popper (1972a,b). As Morgenthau says again and again, the application of every universalizing formulation "must be filtered through the concrete circumstances of time and place" (1948/1978:8).

8. As I shall indicate below, neorealism holds to a very definite, highly restrictive model of social science.

9. A few neorealists are extremely hostile to the use of the *word* anarchy (e.g., as used in Waltz's work), even though they accept the absence of central rule (Waltz's definition of anarchy) as a hard-core assumption. George Modelski takes "world leadership" as his "central concept." Thus, he writes, "we make it clear that we do not regard the modern world as some sort of anarchical society. To the contrary, our analysis clarifies the principles of order and authority that have governed the world for the past half millennium and that, while familiar to historians in each particular instance, have not been previously put together in quite this manner and have generally been unfamiliar to students of international relations. Anarchy could be in the eye of the beholder" (1982:99).

10. Again, neorealists differ, and the words they choose to use is one of the differences. One might speak of order, another of stability, and still another of leadership. The word "hegemony" itself is certainly in some dispute, even though all agree that hegemony (whatever one chooses to call it) follows from power or the distribution of the attributes of power.

11. Popper understands methodological individualism as the principle that "all social phenomena, and especially the functioning of all social institutions, should always be understood as resulting from the decisions, actions, attitudes, etc. of human individuals. . . . we should never be satisfied by an explanation in terms of so-called 'collectives'" (1966:98). Taking states as the living individuals of international life, neorealist statism is understandable on analogous terms.

12. What are we to make of a structuralism, for example, that deploys both

Adam Smith and Emile Durkheim for its authorities without once stopping to consider the contrarieties between the two?

13. Krasner (1982a). In this paper Krasner demonstrates that he is among the most open-minded and criticism-conscious of neorealists. He explores the limits of neorealism; in fact, he goes right to the brink of undermining its statist props altogether. Exploring various relationships between regimes, state interests, political capabilities, and state practices, he comes close to raising the possibility that regimes (principles, norms, and procedures that have some autonomy from the vectoring of state behaviors) might be *constitutive* of states and their interests.

14. I am being careful in my wording here, because neorealists, like most utilitarian thinkers, are slippery about the position they in fact take regarding rational action and the production of order. In a recent review of Mancur Olson's *The Rise and Decline of Nations* (1982), Brian Barry (1983) makes a similar point. He notes that Olson could be offering a "monocausal explanation," a primus inter pares explanation, or an explanation in terms of a factor that is not always the most important but that will always emerge on top when other factors are not too strong (which is not saying much). Barry says that he is "not at all clear what position Mancur Olson himself wants to take." Considering the same three possibilities in neorealist explanations of order, I am not at all sure what positions neorealists mean to take.

15. I hold that *all* social science aspiring to theory has a positivist aspect in the sense given below. This is true of Hegel, Marx, Bourdieu, Foucault, Morgenthau, Alker, and me. Following Bourdieu, even dialectical knowledge contains the objectivistic, the positivistic. As I use the term here, however, a movement is "positivist" if it appears to be a one-dimensional positivism. The issue is not the purging of positivism—the positivist moment is an inescapable moment of all inquiry—but the realization of a more adequate "two-dimensional" or dialectical perspective by bringing the positivist moment into unceasing critical tension with the practical moment such that each side ever problematizes the other. Valuable readings on the subject of positivism and its limits include Radnitzky (1973), Bernstein (1976), Shapiro (1981), Alker (1982), and Adorno et al. (1976).

16. I am not contending that the predisposition toward actor models reflects conscious conformity to a norm; I am saying that social scientists do not conceive of the principle because it is so faithfully observed that, in general, social scientists cannot conceive of thinking about the world in any other ways. The principle at once exhausts and limits the span of active social reasoning. My thinking regarding the irresistible tug of "actor models" is largely sparked by a conversation with Robert North, although I do not know that he would agree with my characterization of this predisposition as methodologically rooted.

17. So dangerous is the term that I must once again hasten to stress that I am addressing the logic of the neorealist movement as expressed in its theoretical discourse and not the consciously held values, intentions, or ideals of individual neorealists. I readily stipulate that Krasner, Gilpin, Keohane, Waltz, and other neorealists are not champions of totalitarianism in their consciously held personal values. I readily stipulate, too, that some neorealists, like Gilpin in his *War and Change,* can moralize at length in their professional writings and do express pluralistic values in their moralizing. The problem is—and this is my charge—that neorealist discourse

grants absolutely no scientific standing to moral norms or practical principles. At best, the moralizing of neorealist scholars is recognized as a proclamation of personal commitments, belief, or faith on the part of individuals, and not as an argument whose truth content is decidable within scientific discourse or groundable within theory. The result is a scientific theory that says no to neorealists' expressed values and yes to totalitarian expectations—hence the aura of quiet despairing (but not theoretically describable irony) surrounding some neorealist arguments. Sadly, many neorealists interpret their own resignation to such a situation as a kind of scientific tough-mindedness, a form of "realism," when in fact their situation is largely attributable to unquestioning acceptance of a moral system: the moral norms of economic reason and positivist science.

18. Some good examples of the agenda-limiting effect of neorealist structuralism are pointed up by Craig Murphy (1983) in his discussion of Stephen Krasner's "Transforming International Regimes: What the Third World Wants and Why" (1981) and Robert W. Tucker's *The Inequality of Nations* (1977).

19. As Wallerstein, Hopkins, and others frequently urge, the modern world system presents itself as only one unit of analysis, an N of 1.

20. A number of tendencies are relevant in this connection. Most can be associated with late capitalist development: "post-industrial" forms of state legitimation according to which the state legitimates itself, not on traditional grounds, but increasingly as an economic dysfunction manager; the fiscal crises of modern states struggling to justify themselves in these terms; the internationalization of capital and the emergence of newly industrialized countries, resulting in a malalignment of world industrial capacity with political-coercive means and traditional symbols of political power; the globalization of the world polity such that hegemonic "responsibility" is ostensibly universal, with no "external areas" remaining for the legitimate externalization of costs; the contradictions exposed through encountering "limits to growth"; the emergence of socialist movements aiming to institutionalize the public political determination of production and exchange but which are also under pressure to rationalize their politics; the Cold War, which institutionalizes the totalization of political competition; and nuclear weapons, which institutionalize the possibility of totalized warfare.

21. As might be inferred from this description, the capitalist power-balancing order addressed in this dialectical competence model is not understood to exhaust the totality of international political reality worthy of theoretical analysis. On the contrary, while it is arguably the dominant mode of order, it is but one point of entry into the theoretical analysis of an international reality that consists of the dialectical interplay and interpenetration of multiple world order.

TEN

The Richness of the Tradition
of Political Realism

ROBERT G. GILPIN

WHAT DO THE FOLLOWING SCHOLARS have in common: Kenneth Waltz, Robert Keohane, Stephen Krasner, Robert W. Tucker, George Modelski, Charles Kindleberger, and the present writer? Very little, you might say, except perhaps that they have all written on international relations from a rather disparate set of professional and political perspectives. How wrong you are, according to Richard Ashley. They are all card-carrying members of an insidious and rather dangerous conspiracy that, like Socrates, is indoctrinating the youth (read graduate students) in false and dangerous ways of thinking. And Ashley, like Karl Popper, E. P. Thompson, and other crusaders against nefarious doctrines before him, seeks to expose their intellectual treachery for the evil that it is.

The heinous and common crime of these perverters of the next generation of graduate students in international relations is "neorealism." This felony may go under other names as well: modern realism, new realism, and structural realism. And, although the purveyors of this false doctrine may clothe themselves in the name and language of the *classical* realism of Hans Morgenthau, Henry Kissinger, and others, they have in fact, according to Ashley, betrayed even the teachings of the venerable realist tradition.

One does not know whether to be bemused or downright scandalized by Ashley's own orrery of confused, misleading, and perplexing propositions. On the one hand, I am flattered to be placed in such distinguished company and to be jointly credited with having had any influence whatsoever on the anarchy of international relations (I mean here the discipline, not the object of study itself). On the other, I feel helpless before my accuser because I am not sure precisely what crime it is that I and my fellow defendants have actually committed. Although Ashley tells us in section 1a that "neorealism . . . is a progressive scientific redemption of classical realist scholarship," he never once informs us of the precise nature of our crime: there is nowhere in the whole indictment a definition of "neorealism." It is, therefore, impossible to know why such a seemingly motley crew as the one he has assembled should be labeled—libeled?— as neorealist. It might have helped if, when describing our alleged lapses from the classical heritage of realism, Ashley had defined realism itself. But although we are all charged with having betrayed the realist heritage, at no time does he tell us what that heritage actually is. As a result, I do not even know why we are all called "realists," much less "neo."

This absence of definition and the density of Ashley's prose present serious problems in coming to terms with his argument. Furthermore, Ashley's method of argumentation makes it exceptionally difficult to respond to his specific points. For example, because we are all alleged to have committed the same crime, quotations from different authors are thrown together to support various specific charges in the overall indictment. Thus, Waltz may be quoted to support one specific charge, Krasner another, and Gilpin yet a third. That Waltz and Krasner should be held accountable for the foibles of Gilpin does not seem to concern the self-appointed Kafkaesque prosecutor. Although I would be the last to deny that schools of thought exist, it is incumbent upon the categorizer and critic to define rather carefully what constitutes the common ground. In the case in point, it is true that the named individuals do hold certain ideas in common, but they also differ importantly on many of the very points Ashley treats. Ashley fails to consider whether the points of agreement or those of disagreement are the more fundamental.

This problem may be illustrated by a brief consideration of Waltz's and my own last books. In his *Theory of International Politics,* Waltz employs a theoretical framework that is, to use Brian Barry's useful formulation, essentially "sociological": Waltz starts with the international system and its structural features in order to explain certain aspects of the behavior of individual states (Waltz 1979). My *War and Change in World Politics* emphasizes the opposite approach, namely, that of economic or rational choice theory: I start with individual state actors and seek to explain the emergence and change of international systems (Gilpin 1981b).

In my judgment, neither approach is intrinsically superior to the other, given our present state of knowledge; the utility of one method or the other depends upon what the scholar is attempting to explain. I find it inexplicable, however, that Ashley argues that these two contrasting methods are both structuralist and somehow identical. But, then, in Ashley's orrery, things are seldom what they seem.

A far more fundamental problem is the basic strategy of Ashley's polemic (the term "polemic" is his, and richly deserved). The strategy works as follows. First, he equates neorealism with a series of particular philosophical positions. Next, he analyzes in turn each position as a surrogate for neorealism. And, finally, employing a ready-made set of standard philosophical criticisms, he dispatches each surrogate and with it its alleged neorealist adherents. Thus, all neorealists are at once structuralists, physicalists, statists, utilitarians, positivists, determinists, and, by virtue of being all these other things, totalitarians and imperialists as well. If Ashley finds a statement by a neorealist that happens not to mesh with one of these philosophical positions, rather than assuming that perhaps the "neorealist" writer does not in fact ascribe to the position in question, Ashley proceeds to accuse the individual of apostasy. One is enmeshed in a Catch-22.

Speaking of philosophy and the clarity that its ancient Greek inventors hoped it would bring to our thinking, what is an accused to make of the following: "For eschatological discourse (evident in phenomenology, ethnomethodology, and some hermeneutical sciences) the objective truth of the discourse lies within and is produced by the discourse itself" (section 2c). Unfortunately, *International Organization* failed to send an English translation with the original text. Therefore, although I am sure that this statement and many like it throughout the article are meaningful to Ashley, I have no idea what it means. It is this needless jargon, this assault on the language, that gives us social scientists a bad name. More seriously, because of the opacity of much of Ashley's prose, I frequently could not follow his argument. (For this reason, if I fail to respond to some of Ashley's more telling points, it is not that I am deliberately avoiding them but rather that I failed to understand them.)

I have been asked to respond to Ashley's criticisms of neorealism because my own name has been attached to his bill of particulars. I do so reluctantly for several reasons. In the first place, I certainly cannot presume to speak for the other defendants. Second, I cannot recall that I have ever described myself as a realist, although I readily admit that I have been profoundly influenced by such realist thinkers as Thucydides, Hans Morgenthau, and E. H. Carr, and have no particular objection to the appellation. But I have also been strongly influenced by Marxist and liberal writers as well. If pressed I would describe myself as a liberal in a realist world and frequently even in a world of Marxist class struggle.

With these caveats in mind I would like to address several issues raised by Ashley's attack. Prior to doing so, however, I shall discuss what I consider to be the essence of realism. Let me state at the outset that, whatever other crimes neorealists may have committed as a group, they have not, as Ashley avers, abandoned the fundamental premises of realist thought.

THE NATURE OF POLITICAL REALISM

I believe that political realism must be seen as a philosophical disposition and set of assumptions about the world rather than as in any strict sense a "scientific" theory. Although a realist perspective may give rise to testable hypotheses and more systematic theories, political realism itself, as Richard Rosecrance once aptly put it, is best viewed as an attitude regarding the human condition. Unlike its polar opposite, idealism, realism is founded on a pessimism regarding moral progress and human possibilities.

From this perspective, all realist writers—neoclassical, structural, or what have you—may be said to share three assumptions regarding political life. The first is the essentially conflictual nature of international affairs. As Thomas Hobbes told his patron, the 2nd Earl of Devonshire, and realist writers have always attempted to tell those who would listen, "it's a jungle out there." Anarchy is the rule; order, justice, and morality are the exceptions. The realist need not believe that one must always forego the pursuit of these higher virtues, but realists do stress that in the world as it is, the final arbiter of things political is power. All moral schemes will come to naught if this basic reality is forgotten.

The second assumption of realism is that the essence of social reality is the group. The building blocks and ultimate units of social and political life are not the individuals of liberal thought nor the classes of Marxism (although in certain circumstances "class" may in fact be the basis of group solidarity). Realism, as I interpret it, holds that the foundation of political life is what Ralf Dahrendorf has called "conflict groups" (Dahrendor 1959). This is another way of saying that in a world of scarce resources and conflict over the distribution of those resources, human beings confront one another ultimately as members of groups, and not as isolated individuals. *Homo sapiens* is a tribal species, and loyalty to the tribe for most of us ranks above all loyalties other than that of the family. In the modern world, we have given the name "nation-state" to these competing tribes and the name "nationalism" to this form of loyalty. True, the name, size, and organization of the competing groups into which our species subdivides itself do alter over time—tribes, city-states, kingdoms, empires, and nation-states—due to economic, demographic, and technological changes. Regrettably, however, the essential nature of intergroup conflict does not.

The third assumption that I believe characterizes realist thinking is the primacy in all political life of power and security in human motivation. As Thucydides put it, men are motivated by honor, greed, and, above all, fear (Thucydides, c. 400 B.C./1951:44). This is not to say that power and security are the sole or even the most important objectives of mankind; as a species we prize beauty, truth, and goodness. Realism does not deny the importance of these other values, although particular realists may. (Nonrealists may as well—realists, after all, do not have a monopoly on vice.) What the realist seeks to stress is that all these more noble goals will be lost unless one makes provision for one's security in the power struggle among social groups.

Given a realism so defined, are the neorealists as ignoble a band of apostates as Ashley would have us believe? In answering this question, I shall discuss only those criticisms that I think lie at the heart of Ashley's case. First, I consider the criticism that the scientific concerns of the neorealists somehow violate the more practical spirit of classical realists. What I propose to show in this connection, and throughout this essay, is that Ashley has a very narrow and constricted comprehension of the variety and richness of realist thought.

THE ISSUE OF METHODOLOGICAL DIFFERENCES

According to Ashley, a major difference between classical and new realists is methodological. The former, we are told, are intuitive in their approach; they remain close to the actual practice of statecraft. In contrast, the neorealists are said to objectify political life and improperly seek to make international relations into a social science. In doing so, however, the new realists, Ashley charges, have abandoned and lost what was most important in the older realism, namely, a respect for diplomatic practice.

Again we run into the critical problem that Ashley does not define his terms, and his argument takes on that closed-loop quality that defies understanding or refutation. If "classical" realists are the members of the realist breed who are intuitive, and "neorealists" are the ones who are scientific, Ashley wins by a tautology. Yet I find realists on *both* sides of this traditionalist/scientific fence, and indeed some versatile ones jump back and forth. In fact, Ashley's quintessence of a classical realist, Hans Morgenthau, can be found at various times on both sides of this methodological issue. The same can be said of most new realists as well. But for the sake of argument, let us consider the several individuals whom Ashley would surely have to call classical realists.

In my judgment, there have been three great realist writers; it is difficult for me to conceive that anyone would deny them inclusion in the tradition. They are Thucydides, Machiavelli, and Carr. (Parenthetically, for such a learned scholar, Ashley holds an amazingly narrow and time-bound conception of the realist tradition.) One finds in each of these writers both intuitive and scientific elements. For example, Thucydides's intuitive insights into state behavior were indeed profound. In Ashley's terms, one could say that he was a classical realist interested in state practice. Yet, as classicists point out, Thucydides was greatly influenced by Greek science and in fact took his method of analysis from it; one should not forget that he is heralded as the first *scientific* historian (and, I would add, the first scientific student of international relations as well). Or take Machiavelli who was, if anything, an observer of state practice but is by most accounts credited as being the first true political *scientist*. As for Carr, the opening chapter of *The Twenty Years' Crisis, 1919–1939*, cries out for a *science* of international relations in order to overcome the problem of war and to institute a mechanism of peaceful change (Carr

1946). If these three writers, spanning the millennia and combining both intuitive and scientific elements in their thinking, are not "classical" realists by anyone's definition, then I do not know who is. And if they are, then Ashley gives too much credit, or discredit, to the new realists as the first realists wanting to put realism on a more scientific footing. In fact, contrary to Ashley, realism in all historical epochs is characterized by its effort to ground the "science" of international relations on the realities of diplomatic "practice."

In this connection, the case of Hans Morgenthau is especially interesting, particularly because he is Ashley's prime example of a classical realist. In his superb *Scientific Man versus Power Politics,* Morgenthau clearly does fit Ashley's very narrow conception of the realist tradition (Morgenthau 1946). The book is brilliant in its exposition of the realist's pessimistic view of the human condition, a judgment that Morgenthau saw confirmed as he observed the failure of the liberal democracies to understand the role of power in the world and to stand together against Hitler before it was too late. But how is one to characterize the Morgenthau who wrote in *Politics Among Nations,* first published two years later in 1948, the following: "Political realism believes that politics, like society in general, is governed by *objective* laws that have their roots in human nature" (Morgenthau 1948/1973:4)? Surely, this Morgenthau would have to be cast into that outer circle of Ashley's *Inferno* reserved for the likes of neorealist objectifiers. (I suspect that the more intuitive Morgenthau was led astray by his Chicago brethren who, beginning with that remarkably creative idealist Quincy Wright and others in the 1920s and 1930s, had been seeking to fashion a science of international relations. Like Ashley, I too prefer the earlier and intuitive Morgenthau.)

It is no doubt true that the new realists are more self-consciously scientific than their classical realist mentors. They do seek to apply social theory to an understanding of international affairs. But, then, so do almost all contemporary schools of international relations. At the same time, however, most, if not all, so-called neorealists also have a healthy respect for practice and intuition. Thus Ashley's notion of a fundamental disjuncture between classical and new realism simply does not hold up under close examination. The realist tradition, for whatever it is worth, is an old one. As distinguished as they are, Morgenthau, Herz, and their contemporaries did not, as Ashley appears to assume, begin it. Within that venerable tradition is far greater room for methodological diversity than is dreamt of in Ashley's philosophy.

THE ROLE OF ECONOMIC FACTORS

I must confess that Ashley's second alleged difference between what he calls classical realism and the new realism astounds me. It is that adherents of the former were uninterested in economic matters whereas the latter are enamored of them. The reason for this contrast, he further argues, is the dual crisis of realism and the world capitalist economy. In my judgment, Ashley's comprehension of these matters is greatly flawed and reveals a superficial understanding of realist thought.

If by "classical" realists one means Morgenthau, John Herz, or Henry Kissinger, then Ashley is most certainly correct. There is an absence of economic concerns in the work of all three scholars. Writing largely during the height of the Cold War, they focused their concerns primarily on national security. The new realists, on the other hand, have been motivated in part by a desire to counter this limitation of postwar realism and to apply the fundamental insights of the realist tradition to the issues that burst on the world scene as the Cold War seemingly abated in the 1970s, and when issues of trade, money, and foreign investment moved to the fore. But Ashley's characterization of this shift in the focus of realism and the reasons for it once again displays his historical myopia.

The new realists may best be seen, I believe, as returning to the roots of the realist tradition. In all historical epochs, realist thinkers have focused on the economic dimensions of statecraft. Thus, Thucydides' *History* can be read as an examination of the impact of a profound commercial revolution on a relatively static international system. The expansion of trade, the monetization of traditional agrarian economies, and the rise of new commercial powers (especially Athens and Corinth), as he tells us, transformed fifth-century Greek international politics and laid the basis for the great war that eviscerated Greek civilization. Everything—well, almost everything—that the new realists find intriguing in the interaction of international economics and politics can be found in the *History of the Peloponnesian War*: an expanding, interdependent "world" economy; the political use of economic leverage, i.e., the Megara Decree;

and even conflict over energy resources, in this case the wheat to fuel men's bodies. These and other economic factors enter into all aspects of Thucydides' analysis of the war and its causes. In spirit and substance he may be said to have been a political economist—perhaps the first— and almost all realists have followed him in this appreciation of the intimate connection between international politics and international economics.

Other examples of the realist concern with economic matters are readily available. Take, for example, the mercantilists of the early modern period. As Jacob Viner tells us, for these realists the pursuit of power and the pursuit of wealth were indistinguishable (Viner 1948). Throughout the seventeenth and eighteenth centuries national interest was identified with and depended upon the achievement of a trade and balance-of-payments surplus. If one wanted to play the game of nations one needed gold and silver to pay for the newly created professional armies of the emergent nation-states and to finance an increasingly expensive foreign policy. Or what about those other realist thinkers, Alexander Hamilton and his disciples in the German Historical School, who identified national power with industrialization and economic self-sufficiency? Perhaps a rather unsavory lot, but realists nonetheless. And then there is my second favorite realist after Thucydides, E. H. Carr, who lays great stress on economic power and economic variables in his classic work in the realist tradition.

To be autobiographical for a moment, this alleged neorealist found in Carr's work one of the greatest inspirations for his own scribblings in the field. He incorporated Carr's analysis of the relationship of international economics and politics into his own work on the subject. In short, contrary to Ashley's allegations, economic aspects of international relations have always been a major concern of realist writers.

From the perspective of this long tradition of realist writings on the intimate connection between international politics and economics, the absence of a similar interest on the part of Ashley's "classical" realists is what is noteworthy and requires explanation. For it was they who abandoned an important component of the mainstream realist tradition. One finds, for example, a scant few pages in Morgenthau on economic imperialism and the economic base of national power. Although he does draw a comparison between realist and economic modes of analysis, as

Ashley points out, this is rather misleading; whereas Morgenthau's realism focuses on the state as actor, economic analysis is based on the individual actor or coalition of actors. (The quotation from Morgenthau is curious in this regard because it is contrary to Ashley's point that classical realists were uninterested in economics.) As for Kissinger, it can truly be said that as scholar and statesman he was almost completely innocent of economic interests or understanding. Indeed, the early postwar generation of American realists, despite their other virtues, had their eyes fixed so firmly on the power struggle between the superpowers that they overlooked the economic relations beneath the flux of political aspirations.

The "rediscovery," if that is the right term, by the new realists of the economic component of international affairs was a response to the surfacing of these economic factors in the 1970s. It was not, as Ashley suggests, due to a crisis in realist thought itself, a crisis somehow intrinsically related to the crisis of world capitalism. On the contrary, realist writers tend to believe that their general perspective on the relationship of economics and politics provides a much better explanation of what has transpired over the past decade or so, and of the reasons for the crisis of the world economy, than do those of their liberal and Marxist ideological rivals.

The essential argument of most realists with respect to the nature and functioning of the international economy, I would venture to say, is that the international political system provides the necessary framework for economic activities. The international economy is not regarded as an autonomous sphere, as liberals argue, nor is it in itself the driving force behind politics, as the Marxists would have us believe. Although economic forces are real and have a profound effect on the distribution of wealth and power in the world, they always work in the context of the political struggle among groups and nations. When the distribution of power and international political relations change, corresponding changes may be expected to take place in global economic relations. Thus, for Carr, the open and expanding world economy of the nineteenth century rested on British power and interest, and when the *pax britannica* was undermined in the latter part of the century by the redistribution of power toward nonliberal states, corresponding economic changes were set in motion that eventually led to the collapse of the liberal world economy.

Ashley's neorealists, including the present writer, have made a similar analysis of the contemporary world economic crisis, in terms of the rise and decline of so-called hegemonic powers. Unfortunately the use of this concept of hegemony and its economic implications have spread as much confusion as light. In particular, the concept has inspired rather oversimplified analyses of the relationship between political hegemony and a liberal international economy. As others have associated me with views to which I do not subscribe, I would like to make clear my own position on this relationship.

As I argue in *War and Change in World Politics,* there is no *necessary* connection between political hegemony and economic liberalism. Historically, in fact, hegemony, or political domination, has been associated with the command economies of empires: why create an imperial system in the first place, if it is not to take control of other economies and exploit them to one's own advantage? The close association between political hegemony and economic liberalism in the modern world began with the political and economic rise of Great Britain. Britain was the most efficient producer of tradeable goods for world markets; its leaders, a liberal, middle class elite, judged the promotion of an open world economy to be in their national interest. It cannot be emphasized too strongly that both political hegemony and economic efficiency are necessary ingredients for a nation to promote a liberal world economy. For the first time in the history of the world these two crucial elements came together in the guise of the *pax britannica* and Britain's global industrial supremacy.

Nor does it follow that the decline of hegemony will lead inevitably to the collapse of a liberal world economy, although the dominant liberal power's decline does, in my judgment, greatly weaken the prospects for the survival of a liberal trading system. This was most certainly the case for the British-centered world economy and may very well be the fate of our own. But what eventually happens depends also, I believe, on factors both economic and political. I shall discuss only the latter, as the more relevant, in the present context. It should be obvious, however, that certain economic aspects of the situation, such as the rate of economic growth or the complementarity of trading interests, are also of great importance in the preservation of economic liberalism.

As I have argued, a liberal international economy rests on three political foundations (Gilpin 1981b, esp. p. 129). The first is a dominant *liberal* hegemonic power or, I would also stress, liberal powers able and willing to manage and enforce the rules of a liberal commercial order. The second is a set of common economic, political, and security interests that help bind liberal states together. And the third is a shared ideological commitment to liberal values. These three elements constitute what I called above the political framework for the economic system. Thus, since the end of the Second World War, American global hegemony, the anti-Soviet alliance, and a Keynesian, welfare-state ideology have cemented together economic relations among the three principal centers of industrial power outside the Soviet bloc—the United States, Japan, and Western Europe.

It was on the basis of this conceptualization of the relationship between international economics and politics that I and a number of other "neo-realists" were highly skeptical of the argument of the more extreme exponents of interdependence theory. Their projections into the indefinite future of an increasingly interdependent world, in which nation-states and tribal loyalties (read nationalism) would cease to exist, seemed to us to be a misreading of history and social evolution. Such theorizing assumed the preeminence and autonomy of economic and technological forces over all others in effecting political and social change. Thus, it neglected the political base on which this interdependent world economy rested and, more importantly, the political forces that were eroding these political foundations.

For many realists, therefore, the crisis of the world economy of which Ashley writes was at least in part a consequence of the erosion of these political foundations: the relative decline of American hegemony, the increasing strains within the anti-Soviet alliance, and the waning of the commitment to liberal ideology. Contrary to Ashley's view that the crisis of the world economy somehow represents a challenge to realism, it is precisely the traditional insights of realism that help us to explain the crisis and the ongoing retreat from an interdependent world economy. The political cement of the economic system is dissolving with the eclipse of American hegemony and related political changes. However, and this is a point that I wish to emphasize, whether or not this deterioration of the world economy continues does not depend solely on structural factors. Market forces and skillful diplomacy do matter in the eventual outcome.

Realists have sought to add the missing political dimensions to other analyses of the interdependent world economy.

OTHER CRIMES AND SERIOUS MISDEMEANORS

Scattered throughout Ashley's article are assorted other indictments of the new realists, especially their alleged departures from the views of classical realists. Among these apostasies are those of statism, structural determinism, objectivism, ethical neutrality, reification of the state, and youthful overexuberance. (As one who has entered his second half-century, I especially liked this last charge.) Under Ashley's close scrutiny no one turns out to be what they seem or thought themselves to be— including, I suspect, the classical realists for whom Ashley claims to speak and whose besmirched honor he seeks to uphold. They would no doubt be as perplexed as I am regarding Ashley's characterization of their views (and everyone else's for that matter).

It may very well be that particular new realists, including me, have committed one or more of the stated crimes. I cannot answer for all of us, and I readily confess that over a span of nearly three decades of professional life my own ideas on many subjects have changed. I shall continue to try, however, as best as I can, to deal with Ashley's criticisms of new realists as a collectivity.

According to Ashley, the new realists, in contrast to his classical variety, are "statist." What does this mean? At times he seems to suggest that new realists worship the state and, therefore, are closet totalitarians. At other times he appears to mean that neorealists, unlike classical realists, believe in an unending state-centric world. I shall assume he means the latter, because it is at least a significant intellectual point whereas the former is polemical innuendo designed to scare easily corruptible graduate students away from the likes of such alleged protofascists as Bob Keohane and George Modelski.

As I pointed out above, I believe that realists of all stripes accept the primacy of the group as the basic unit of political life. In international relations the group-organization of political affairs has most frequently taken the form of the state; in the modern world a particular subspecies of state, the nation-state, has predominated in political life. This does not mean, however, as Ashley alleges, that new realists necessarily believe that the state is here forever. Speaking for myself, I have argued that the modern state and the nation-state system arose due to a peculiar set of economic, technological, and other circumstances. I have argued, further, that just as the modern nation-state is a product of particular historical forces, changes in those forces could bring about the demise of the nation-state. In a changed economic and technological environment, groups, and I emphasize the word, *groups,* might cease to believe that the nation-state continues to serve their security and other interests.

The difference between Ashley and me on this issue of the state and its future can best be understood, I believe, by quoting from an earlier article of his, also attacking the new realists. The quotation from Ashley contains two paragraphs from Morgenthau's *Politics Among Nations.*

> For classical realists, by contrast, such a metaphysical commitment to the state and the states system is, to borrow one of Kenneth Waltz's favorite epithets, a mistaken *reification* of a principle. As discussed earlier, classical realists have their own metaphysical commitment: a commitment to a dialectical and generative balance of power scheme. In the classical realist understanding, this scheme finds expression throughout all levels and in all things of the political universe, among them the modern states system. It is constitutive of the system. The system's tensions—the ever present and contrary movement toward unity and fragmentation, for example— are read by classical realists as a particular historical manifestation of the scheme's own antinomies. But the scheme, as classical realists understand, is not to be reduced to any of the relations it generates, the modern states system included.
>
> Indeed, if one truly grasps the scheme, as classical realists do, then one understands that history cannot be expected to come to an end in some state systemic cul-de-sac whose only exit is by the means endorsed by the system itself. If one truly grasps the scheme, then one can understand how Morgenthau can conclude his discussion of his third "principle of political realism" by saying:
>
> "What is true of the general character of international relations is also true of the nation state as the ultimate point of reference of contemporary foreign policy. While the realist indeed believes that interest is the perennial standard by which political action must be judged and directed, *the contemporary connection between interest and the nation state is a product of history, and is therefore bound to disappear in the course of history. Nothing in the realist*

position militates against the assumption that the present division of the world into nation states will be replaced by larger units of a quite different character, more in keeping with the technical potentialities and the moral requirements of the contemporary world.

"The realist parts company with other schools of thought before the all-important question of how the contemporary world is to be transformed. The realist is persuaded that this transformation can be achieved only through the workmanlike manipulation of the perennial forces that have shaped the past and will shape the future. The realist cannot be persuaded that we can bring about the transformation by confronting a political reality that has its own laws with an abstract ideal that refuses to take those laws into account."

Lest the point be missed: If by statism we mean a metaphysical commitment to the state and the states system suspended beyond the critical force of historically grounded scholarship, then *new realism is a form of statism. Classical realism most emphatically is not.* For classical realism, the state and the states system are themselves 'abstract ideals,' and their realization in concrete form is always problematic, always contingent on the poising and counterpoising of opposing 'perennial forces' generated by an underlying balance of power scheme under the concrete circumstances of time and place. States, in other words, are 'unitary actors' only as an ideal that statesmen would strive to realize but at best only approximate when they succeed in solving the problem of balancing contesting forces which can never be assumed to cease. To say otherwise, to treat states as unitary actors pure and simple, is to engage in a *reductio ad absurdum,* a lie that the leader might tell to the people but never, if he is wise, tell to himself. As Morgenthau was fond of pointing out, to forget this is to take the politics out of the state—something that tyrants would want to do but political scientists should not. (Ashley 1982:26–28)

Ashley's interpretation of Morgenthau's interpretation of classical realism on the nature and future of the state seems to me wrong and unnecessarily complex. I read Morgenthau as simply saying the following: if the nation-state is to disappear, as in the case of earlier forms of the state (empires, city-states, and absolute monarchies), it will do so through age-old political processes and not as idealists would wish through a transcendence of politics itself. The key to his position is contained in the statement that "this transformation can only be achieved through the workmanlike manipulation of the *perennial forces* that have shaped the

past and will shape the future. The realist cannot be persuaded that we
can bring about the transformation by confronting a political reality that
has its own *laws* with an abstract ideal that refuses to take those laws
into account." (With respect to Ashley's charge that neorealists "objectify" where classical realists intuit, what could be more objectified than
to talk about politics having its own laws and to allude to perennial
forces?) I doubt that many new realists would use such language except
perhaps in some metaphorical sense; certainly they would not use it in
the highly determinist manner of Morgenthau himself.

What the latter passage from Morgenthau says, at least to me, is that
if the state or the nation-state system is to be replaced by a larger political
unit, it will happen through the same type of political process that has
historically brought about political change. I accept that. In fact, I wrote
a book whose central thesis was that despite contemporary economic
and technological developments, the essential nature of the political process has not changed over the millennia. In this sense, though I do have
some reservations regarding "objective laws and perennial forces," I consider myself a disciple of Hans Morgenthau.

With respect to Ashley's charges that we new realists are state-centric,
deny the existence of politics, and enshrine the contemporary state as
here forever, perhaps three quotations from my own writing will suffice
to show—putting the point in rather blunt terms—that Ashley has not
done his homework and does not really know what he is talking about.

On state-centricism and the state as political actor:

> The argument that the state (as herein conceived) is the principal actor
> in international relations does not deny the existence of other individual
> and collective actors. As Ernst Haas cogently put it, the actors in inter-
> national relations are those entities capable of putting forth demands
> effectively; who or what these entities may be cannot be answered a priori
> (Haas 1964:84). However, the state is the principal actor in that the nature
> of the state and the pattern of relations among states are the most
> important determinants of the character of international relations at any
> given moment. This argument does not presume that states need always
> be the principal actors, nor does it presume that the nature of the state
> need always be the same and that the contemporary nation-state is the
> ultimate form of political organization. Throughout history, in fact, states
> and political organizations have varied greatly: tribes, empires, fiefdoms,

city-states, etc. The nation-state in historical terms is a rather recent arrival; its success has been due to a peculiar set of historical circumstances, and there is no guarantee that these conditions will continue into the future. Yet it would be premature to suggest (much less declare, as many contemporary writers do) that the nation-state is dead or dying. (Gilpin 1981b:18)

On politics and the political determination of state policy:

Strictly speaking states, as such, have no interests, or what economists call "utility functions," nor do bureaucracies, interest groups, or so-called transnational actors, for that matter. Only individuals and individuals joined together into various types of coalitions can be said to have interests. From this perspective the state may be conceived as a coalition of coalitions whose objectives and interests result from the powers and bargaining among the several coalitions composing the large society and political elite. In the language of Brian Barry (1976:159), collective choice and determination of political objectives are coalition processes (Cyert and March 1963:28). (Gilpin 1981b:18–19)

On the future of the nation-state and the possibilities of larger forms of political organization:

It is not clear, however, what the ultimate effect of contemporary military and economic developments will be on the scale of political organization. The scope of nuclear warfare and the immense cost of a retaliatory force would appear to favor an enlargement of political entities. At the same time, however, an attempt to conquer a small state possessing even a very modest nuclear capability may be prohibitively expensive. Increasing economic interdependence certainly has decreased national economic autonomy. However, it has also meant that states can have access to large markets without the necessity of integrating politically and that states have increased their intervention in the economy in order to protect national values against potentially harmful external economic forces. Although the emergence of global ecological and related problems necessitates a comparable organization of human affairs, the hold of the nation-state concept on the minds of men grows ever more tenacious. The ambiguous effects of these contemporary developments may be noted in three seemingly contradictory aspects of present-day international politics: (1) the emergence of the superpower; (2) the movement toward regional integration; (3) the proliferation of new nation-states and secession move-

ments in older nation-states. These contradictory developments suggest
that the sizes and distributions of political entities in our era have yet to
be determined. (Gilpin 1981b:229)

Of course, we "realists" know that the state does not really exist; in
fact, we knew that before Graham Allison told us so. But, then, as I have
written elsewhere, neither do Allison's bureaucracies, interest groups,
nor even transnational actors exist for that matter (Gilpin 1981b:18).
Only individuals really exist, although I understand that certain schools
of psychology challenge even this. Only individuals *act,* even though they
may act on behalf of one of these collective social entities, the most
important one being the group. But Ashley is certainly correct that we
(all of us, including critics of "neorealists") do write as if some particular
social or political entity really does exist and acts. It is a matter of
convenience and economy to do so. Thus, we speak of the *Soviets* doing
such-and-such rather than listing the individual members of the Central
Committee who in reality did the acting. There is certainly the danger
in this practice of coming to think of the state as an actor in its own
right, which has interests separate from those of its constituent members.
If I have committed this fallacy of reification, I shall attempt to be more
careful in the future. By the same token, however, Ashley should be more
circumspect in attributing various beliefs to the very diverse collection
of *individual* scholars he labels "neorealists."

Two other issues where the new realists are said to depart from
classical realism are those of "free will versus determinism" and "objectivism versus subjectivism." Classical realists, according to Ashley, were
committed to the view that statesmen could change the international
environment; the subjective views of statesmen were, therefore, important. New realists, on the other hand, are accused of believing that
objective structures, such as the number and size of states in the international system or the position of a state in the international hierarchy
of states, determine the behavior of statesmen.

This contrast is absurd. No new realist that I have read argues that
political structure determines all behavior. Nor does any classical realist
argue that indeterminism and subjectivism rule the world. Most new
realists, however, do argue, I believe it safe to say, that structure constrains
and in fact powerfully influences behavior—but so do classical realists,

as Ashley himself well illustrates in his long discussion of the role of the "balance of power" in classical realist thought. As the passage quoted above from Morgenthau attests. Ashley's prime model of a classical realist believes that *perennial forces* and the *laws* of political reality always confront the statesman. No new realist has been more objectivist and determinist than this in setting forth the limits on the freedom of the statesman.

In his earlier article cited above, Ashley made his most vehement attack on the new realists in the following words: *"new realists assume the trans-historical truth, objectivity, and value neutrality of technical reason as an action orienting frame"* (Ashley 1982:32, his emphasis). What he appears to be saying is a criticism frequently made about all political realists, old and new, which accounts in large measure for the strong emotional attacks on realists by Ashley and many others. Many, especially among the younger generation of international scholars, abhor realism because it is believed to be an immoral doctrine at best and a license to kill, make war, and commit wanton acts of rapine at worst. Only the existence of such a belief on the part of its most vocal critics can possibly explain why realism has so frequently been subjected to highly emotional and, I personally believe, irresponsible attacks. Although Ashley, I should quickly add, has not himself been guilty of such behavior, his criticisms do give aid and comfort to those who see realists as immoral monsters.

This rap of moral neutrality bordering on immorality is obviously a difficult one to beat. Do we have a morals test for theories of international relations? I hope not. Fortunately, given the Anglo-Saxon legal tradition in which *International Organization* is published, it should not be necessary to prove one's innocence. Still, if a charge is made and one fails to respond to it, others may tend to presume one's guilt. For this reason, a brief defense of realism as a politically moral doctrine seems called for. In fact, I would argue that a moral commitment lies at the heart of realism, at least as I interpret it. This is not to say, however, that particular individual realists have on all occasions behaved in ways that the reader would regard as morally justified.

Since Machiavelli, if not before, two perspectives on international morality have attached themselves to the realist position. Machiavelli himself has variously been interpreted as sharing one perspective or the other. He has been held to be immoral, amoral, and a moralist.

The first moral perspective associated with realism is what Gordon

Craig and Alexander George characterize as *vulgar* realism (Craig and George 1983). It is the amoralism, or if you prefer, the immoralism, of Thucydides' "Melian Dialogue": in order to discourage further rebellions against their empire, the Athenians put the men of Melos to the sword and enslaved the women and children. It was this type of *raison d'état* behavior that the great German historian, Friedrich Meinecke, condemned in his important book, *Machiavellism* (Meinecke 1957). This amoral version of realism, which holds that the state is supreme and unbound by any ethical principles, is not my own view of realism. Nor, I would venture to say, is it a position to which any of the new realists that Ashley so sweepingly condemns would subscribe.

There is, however, another moral position associated with political realism. As Craig and George remind us, in the early modern period realist writers sought to impose some constraints on the excesses of absolute monarchs (Craig and George 1983:5). According to this interpretation of realism, states should pursue their *national interests,* not those of a particular dynasty or political party. Statesmen are admonished to carry out a foreign policy in the interest of the whole nation and not just in the selfish interests of the ruling elite. Further, it was believed that there were certain rules of prudent behavior that enabled a state both to protect its interests and at the same time to minimize international violence. Certainly Morgenthau is situated in this tradition when he concludes *Politics Among Nations* with a set of "do's and don't's" for contemporary statesmen; furthermore, basing his position on these principles, Morgenthau was among the first to condemn the Vietnam War. What Morgenthau and many other realists have in common is a belief that ethical and political behavior will fail unless it takes into account the actual practice of states and the teachings of sound theory. It is this dual commitment, to practice and to theory, that sets realism apart from both idealism and the abstract theorizing that characterizes so much of the contemporary study of international relations.

I like to think, and Ashley has yet to convince me to the contrary, that the new realists, like their classical forebears, study international practice and theorize about it in part to add to the list of "do's and don't's" formulated by Thucydides, Morgenthau, and others. The new realists thus continue a tradition that political theorists call "advice to princes." For example, some have studied and advocated improvements in international regimes. Others have written on the problem of peaceful change. Still others have dealt with the dangers of nuclear war. This advice may not be very useful and, being realists, we know that it is seldom if ever given serious attention. But to say, as Ashley does, that the new realists as a group are guilty of "moral neutrality" is as baseless as it is unfair.

This last point leads me to make a confession. Ashley is correct. I am "a closet liberal." I do believe in the liberal values of individualism, liberty, and human rights, and I do want my country to stand for and to stand up for these things. I do believe, further, that we social scientists should study war, injustice, and, yes, even imperialism, in order to help eliminate these evils. I do have faith that knowledge as a general rule is to be preferred to ignorance. But I most certainly do not believe, as Ashley alleges, in automatic progress. On the contrary, I am not even sure that progress exists in the moral and international spheres. Indeed, there have been transient international orders that have been more benign and humane than others. I count the British and American eras of world dominance among them, despite the Opium and Vietnam wars and other abuses of power. It is, in fact, precisely this issue of automatic and evolutionary progress that divides most realists from most idealists. Whereas the latter tend to believe that technological advance, increasing economic interdependence, and the alleged emergence of a global community are transforming the nature of international relations, I for one lean toward a belief in Morgenthau's *perennial forces* of political struggle and the limits that they place on human perfection. To me at least, this moral skepticism joined to a hope that reason may one day gain greater control over passions constitutes the essence of realism and unites realists of every generation.

ELEVEN

Reflections on *Theory of International Politics*:

A Response to My Critics

KENNETH N. WALTZ

RICHARD ASHLEY says that older realists, despite some limitations, set a high standard of political reasoning from which I and other neorealists have regressed. Robert Keohane says that I merely reformulated realism and made it more systematic without developing "new ways of seeing" international relations (1983:515; reprinted above, p. 175). Ashley and Robert Cox are highly critical of structural approaches. John Ruggie complains that having started down the structural path, I failed to follow the path to its end (1983, part V; reprinted above). Facing a variety of criticisms, perhaps I can best begin by saying what I tried to accomplish in *Theory of International Politics.*[1] My aim was to do the following:

1. Develop a more rigorous theory of international politics than earlier realists had done.
2. Show how one can distinguish unit-level from structural elements and then make connections between them.
3. Demonstrate the inadequacy of the prevalent inside-out pattern of thinking that has dominated the study of international politics.
4. Show how state behavior differs, and how expected outcomes vary, as systems change.
5. Suggest some ways in which the theory can be tested and provide some examples of its practical application, largely to economic and military problems.

STRUCTURES AND UNITS

Anyone who believes that a systemic theory is required for an adequate understanding of international politics has to distinguish between structural and unit levels. In making the distinction, whether certain components belong at one level or the other is not immediately apparent. By my definition, national political structures are spare, and international-political structures even sparer. The second term of the definition— "specification of the functions of formally differentiated units"—appears in domestic but not in international structures as I conceive of them. This leaves only the first and third terms, the ordering principle of the system—anarchy—and the distribution of capabilities across its units— the states. Ruggie argues impressively, but in the end unconvincingly, for restoring the second term. He tries to show that because I omitted it, both a dimension of change and a determinant of change are missing from my model (p. 148). He seeks to capture both the dimension and the determinant by subtly redefining "differentiation."

Ruggie draws a distinction between differentiation meaning "that which denotes *differences* rather than that which denotes *separateness*" (p. 142). The sociologically "proper" definition of differentiation tells us on what basis the segmentation of an anarchic realm is determined. The second component of international-political structure is thus rescued from oblivion. He then argues that "dynamic density," as defined by Durkheim, should have been included in my model as well, since variations in density may be determinants of systemic transformation.

In our discourse, saying who was more faithful to Durkheim is less important than finding the theoretically most tenable and practically most useful definition of structure. Durkheim is nevertheless an able guide to the elusive prey. He distinguishes between societies of mechanical and of organic solidarity, corresponding respectively to the anarchic order of international politics and the hierarchic order of domestic politics. Durkheim describes a mechanical society as "a multitude of little centres, distinctive and alike" (1893:257). They have their own needs and interests, but they do not interact through their special characteristics in such a way as to become entangled in one another's affairs and dependent on one another's efforts. Each unit does for itself roughly what all of the others are doing. Their lives are characterized by a duplication of effort rather than by a division of labor that would produce their integration. Interactions and exchanges among segments are variable and sporadic. Exchange of products, even if more or less regular, gives rise only to "simple relations of *mutualism* having nothing in common with the division of labor" (1893:282).[2] Like units interact only marginally because of their pervasive resemblance. The more nearly units are alike, the less they can gain by cooperating with one another.

The segments of a mechanical society may grow or may shrink. They may range in size from the clans of what anthropologists call segmentary lineage societies, to villages and cities, to such extensive territorial organizations as nations. The distinction between types of society is not one of size. A society may attain great size, but so long as it is composed of similar segments its unity remains mechanical. Because the parts remain little dependent on one another, any of them can be severed from the whole with little effect on the consciousness, happiness, health, and well-being of the remaining parts (1893:148–149, 261).

A mechanical society rests on the similarity of the units that compose it; an organic society is based on their differences. An organic society promotes the sharpening of individual talents and skills. Different parts of the society make their particular contributions to its general welfare. Units become closely linked because they do special jobs and then exchange goods and services in order to meet their common requirements. The division of labor increases efficiency and promotes the general prosperity. More important still, the division of labor makes for social solidarity. As Durkheim says, "when men unite in a contract, it is because, through the division of labor . . . they need each other" (1893:212). The parts of a highly developed society are tightly integrated. Some parts depend on others for services and supplies that they cannot easily, if at all, provide for themselves.[3] Mechanical societies are loosely linked through the resemblance of their members. Organic societies become closely integrated through the differences of their members.

The division of labor renders "societies possible which, without it, would not exist." Social structure is transformed as society progresses from mechanical to organic unity. From differences of structure predictions can be made. Understanding this enabled Durkheim to make one of the most striking predictions to be found in social-science literature. The sexual division of labor, he writes, establishes "a social and moral order *sui generis.*" The division of labor brings unlikes together. Unlike individuals depend on each other precisely because their different activities, the distinct tasks they perform, contribute to their mutual satisfaction and benefit. Unlikes become strongly glued together because they depend on one another's different abilities and skills. It follows that if the division of labor were to lessen, for example if the roles of the sexes became less distinct, marriage would become less stable, and "conjugal society would eventually subsist in sexual relations preeminently ephemeral" (1893:61). The union of likes is brittle because one's own efforts can replace the other's contributions.

The transition from mechanical to organic society proceeds as more and more individuals come "sufficiently in contact to be able to act and react upon one another. If we agree to call this relation and the active [social and economic] commerce resulting from it dynamic or moral density, we can say that the progress of the division of labor is in direct ratio to the moral or dynamic density of society" (1893:257). Durkheim's view seems much in accord with Ruggie's interpretation. Dynamic density acts as a force that may transform mechanical societies or produce a transition from an anarchic to a hierarchic order. In Ruggie's words, "*the principles on the basis of which the constituent units are separated* from one another" have changed (p. 142, his italics). But for Durkheim this is only because the units themselves have become different. They are no longer similar segments weakly united by their resemblance. They have instead become dissimilar parts of a society strongly united by their differences. Durkheim's transformation of society is not rooted in differentiation defined as a principle of separation; it is rooted in the differences of the parts.

How do simple societies become complex ones? Simple and complex societies are organized according to opposite principles. Complex societies grow out of simple societies and must overcome them. In Durkheim's view, the "segmental arrangement is an insurmountable obstacle to the division of labor" (1893:256; *cf.* 182–185). A structural transformation, the replacement of one principle of order by another, is nothing short of a revolution in social life. How might such a revolution be produced and conducted? Revolution breaks out when the "growth and condensation of societies ... *necessitate* a greater division of labor." Population grows; the struggle for existence becomes acute; war breaks out and becomes more violent the harder the population presses on the resources available. The more acute the struggle, the greater the social progress. The stronger segments of the old society forge ahead at the expense of the weaker. The "triumphant segmental organs" take on the vaster tasks of society; the losers are left with the lesser ones (1893:262–272). The division of labor develops in the struggle and flourishes within the newly integrated society. Durkheim faces up to what revolutions ordinarily entail—fierce and bloody struggle with risks high and outcomes always uncertain.

A few points require emphasis. First, the social segments of the old society must begin to break down before the division of labor can appear (1893:256). Because the new social type rests on such different principles, "it can develop only in proportion to the effacement" of the preceding society (1893:182). The transformation of the old structure begins, as Durkheim emphasizes, only when the segments of a mechanical society are thrown upon one another, only when their fates become tightly entangled because of the intense pressures of the struggle for survival (1893:266). Dynamic density consists not only in economic transactions but also in social ones. It is "a function of a number of individuals who are actually having not only commerce but also social relations, i.e., who not only exchange services or compete with one another but also live a common life." The paragraph is worth completing. "For, as purely economic relations leave men estranged from one another, there may be continuous relations of that sort without participation in the same collective existence. Business carried on across the frontiers which separate peoples does not abolish these frontiers" (1895:114). The transformation of social structure is not produced by the mere mutualism of international trade.

Second, the change in property relations that Ruggie identifies with the shift from medieval to modern politics is significant. It is not for Durkheim, nor I should think for most systems theorists, a transformation of structure. The change Ruggie identifies does not move international society from a condition in which like units are weakly held together by their similarities to one in which unlike units are united by their differences. Only a structural transformation can abolish the international imperative—take care of yourself!—and replace it with the domestic one—specialize!

The redefinition of property relations, however important it may be, cannot produce a transformation of the international system. Dynamic density may have reshaped the structure of property rights, but that took place within different societies, as Ruggie himself says (pp. 148–150). The point is important since it is often thought, wrongly, that any change having widespread repercussions must be a structural change or even a systemic transformation. Ruggie says that he would be surprised if the changes he alludes to—demographic trends, resource constraints, and the like—"do not adversely affect the managerial capacity of bipolarity and, thereby, alter systemic outcomes" (p. 151). So would I. I would be surprised if many different sorts of unit-level changes did not alter systemic outcomes. Ruggie says that I omit such forces. Yet I define a system as consisting of a structure and of interacting units. The question is not one of omission but of the level at which one sees such forces operating. Changes in some or in all of the units will make their relations harder, or easier, to manage. I might add to Ruggie's cogent example a still stronger one: the nuclear revolution in military weaponry. In my view, the two biggest changes in international politics since World War II are the structural shift from multi- to bipolarity and the unit-level change in the extent and rapidity with which some states can hurt others. Surely, the second change, like the first one, has system-wide effects. Wars that might bring nuclear weapons into play have become much harder to start. One must be struck by the fact that over the centuries great powers have fought more wars and minor states have fought fewer. The frequency of war has correlated less closely with the attributes of states than with their international standing. Standing, of course, is a structural characteristic. Yet because of a change in military technology, a change at the unit level, waging war has more and more become the privilege of poor and weak states. A unit-level change has much diminished a structural effect.

Ruggie has described some forces that "adversely affect the managerial capacity of bipolarity." Unfortunately, in doing so he mingles structural and unit levels. Greatly reducing the odds that war will occur among the great and the major powers represents a profound change in the quality of international life, such as only a structural transformation would ordinarily bring. Just what is, and what is not, changed by the nuclear revolution in weaponry? What has changed is this: The international system has become more peaceful, at least at the top. Since the nuclear revolution, states relate to one another differently, yet each state still has to take care of itself as best it can. Nuclear states continue to compete militarily. The continuity of the system, lodged in its structure, accounts for the latter. Nuclear weapons in the hands of some of the states help to account for the former. Nuclear states are loathe to use their most powerful weapons except in the service of peace, that is, for the sake of deterrence. The latter part of Ruggie's otherwise penetrating essay mixes unit and structural matters.

Third, Ruggie is right in saying that for me international structure is not fully generative (pp. 135–136; 148–152). A "generative model of structure" should not be expected to generate all that goes on within a system. Ruggie thinks that structure should contain a logic that accounts for its own transformation and believes that Durkheim's dynamic density reflects "structural effects *and* aggregated unit-level processes" (fn. 45). Ruggie compounds unit-level and structural forces, thus illustrating how difficult it is to keep the levels of a system consistently distinct and separate. Careful though Ruggie has been, his attempt to explain more through structure by increasing its content proves to be the first step down the slippery slope toward reduction. I admire Ruggie's fine and rich account of the historical transition from the medieval to the modern state. The account, however, tells us nothing about the structure of international politics. Durkheim did not confound the internal condition of states with their external environment. Durkheim did not think of dynamic density as part of a system's structure. Dynamic density is a unit-level condition that may burst the bonds of the old system and break its structure apart. Far from thinking of unit-level processes as "all product . . . and . . . not at all productive" (p. 151), I, like Durkheim, think of unit-level processes as a source both of changes in systems and of possible changes of systems, hard though it is to imagine the latter. Neither structure nor units determine outcomes. Each affects the other.

In defining structure, what then are the criteria of inclusion and exclusion? Since not much goes into the definition of structure, a negative injunction is appropriate. Asking whether something is important cannot tell us whether it should be included or excluded. If all that is important for a system were in its structure, then we could ignore the units of the system. We would be saying that structures are determinant, even while knowing that politics is a problematic and uncertain arena of action. Ruggie widens the criteria of inclusion by arguing that property relations, because they affect the way states relate to one another, should be included. His reasoning makes the criteria of inclusion infinitely expansible. Nuclear weapons, as I have said, strongly affect how states relate to one another. So do national ideologies. Surely totalitarian and democratic states relate to one another differently than did the old monarchic states. And one could go on and on.

Still, one might ask why the distribution of capabilities across states should be included in the definition of structure and not other characteristics of states that could be cast in distributional terms. The simple answer is that an international-political system is one of self-help. In a self-help system, states are differently placed by their power. States are self-regarding units. State behavior varies more with differences of power than with differences in ideology, in internal structure of property relations, or in governmental form. In self-help systems, the pressures of competition weigh more heavily than ideological preferences or internal political pressures.

In effect, Ruggie is saying that power does not tell us enough about the placement of states in the system. He is right, but he draws the wrong conclusion. Structures never tell us all that we want to know. Instead they tell us a small number of big and important things. They focus our attention on those components and forces that usually continue for long periods. Clean and simple definitions of structure save us from the pernicious practice of summoning new systems into being in response to every salient change within a system. They direct our attention to the units and to unit-level forces when the particularity of outcomes leads us to search for more idiosyncratic causes than are found in structures.

The world of states is older than any state in it. Thinking only of the modern state system, conventionally dated from 1648, today's states are hardly recognizable when compared with their originals even where their names survive from a distant time. Through all of the changes of boundaries, of social, economic, and political form, of economic and military activity, the substance and style of international politics remain strikingly constant. We can look farther afield, for example, to the China of the warring states era or to the India of Kautilya, and see that where political

entities of whatever sort compete freely, substantive and stylistic characteristics are similar. Ruggie would elevate qualities of the units shared
by some or by all of them to the level of structure. When the units of
an anarchic system develop new qualities through changes of "property
rights," of "social formation," and of "state/society relations" (pp. 149–
152), or presumably through changes in the quality of weaponry, or
whatever, he would have us say that the system has been transformed.
Structures would then no longer show us a purely positional picture of
society. Ruggie would lower the level of abstraction by adding to structures more information about the characteristics of units and of unit-
level processes. Structure, properly defined, is transposable (cf. Nadel
1957:104–109). If we follow Ruggie's advice, structure will no longer
apply to different realms, even where the arrangement of their parts is
similar. We shall also lose another advantage of structural approaches.
Elegant definitions of structure enable one to fashion an explanatory
system having only a few variables. If we add more variables, the explanatory system becomes more complicated, as one sees in Ruggie's
essay. Especially in its last part, theoretical acuity gives way to rich and
dense description.

PREDICTION, POWER, AND THE TESTING OF THEORIES

With Robert Keohane I have only a few disagreements, largely on questions of emphasis. Contrary to his statement, I do not differ with him
over rationality, except semantically. I prefer to state the rationality assumption differently. My preference is based partly on fear that "rationality" carries the wrong connotations. Since making foreign policy is
such a complicated business, one cannot expect of political leaders the
nicely calculated decisions that the word "rationality" suggests. More
significantly, my preference is based on the importance I accord, and
Keohane denies, to the process of selection that takes place in competitive
systems. In structural-functional logic, behaviors are selected for their
consequences (Stinchcombe 1968:85). I fail to understand why Keohane
thinks that selection does not work if the death rate of a system's units
is low (p. 173). Selection does take place more swiftly and surely
when death rates are high, as in a sector of the economy populated by

small economic units. In oligopolistic sectors, the survival rate of firms is higher. Their fortunes nevertheless rise and fall. The market shapes behavior by rewarding some firms and penalizing others. Selection lessens the importance of the rationality assumption, but because selection works less well in oligopolistic than in competitive sectors, we need to know more about oligopolistic firms and are able to predict less surely from market theory alone.

In the international-political system, states wax and wane even as their death rates remain low. In the international-political system, great powers come and go, although not with great frequency. We should keep the notion of "selection" in a position of central importance. Even though constrained by a system's structure, a unit of the system can behave as it pleases. It will, however, fare badly if some of the other parties are making reasonably intelligent decisions. That some states imitate the successful practices of others indicates that the international arena is a competitive one in which the less skillful must expect to pay the price of their ineptitude. The situation provides enough incentive to cause most of the actors to behave sensibly. Actors become "sensitive to costs" to use Shai Feldman's apt phrase, which for convenience can be called an assumption of rationality (1982).

Keohane is surely right to emphasize, as I did, that with the aid of a rationality assumption one still cannot, from national interest alone, predict what the policy of a country might be. Any theory of international politics requires also a theory of domestic politics, since states affect the system's structure even as it affects them. This is why Snyder and Diesing in their excellent study explore information processing and decisionmaking (1977). To do so is fully in accord with, rather than a departure from, realist assumptions. Realist theory by itself can handle some, but not all, of the problems that concern us. Just as market theory at times requires a theory of the firm, so international-political theory at times needs a theory of the state. Yet some successful predictions can be made without paying attention to states. We do not always need to hop quickly from structure to states when looking for explanations. For example, contrary to the expectations of such an experienced statesman as President Franklin D. Roosevelt, realist theorists would surely have predicted the collapse of the allied coalition upon the morrow of victory. Whether alliances cohere or collapse depends more on external situations than on internal characteristics of allies, as their contrasting wartime and peace-time behaviors indicate. The prediction follows from balance-of-power theory. The absence of constraints on American policy for three decades following the war, seen in the light of the same theory, was hardly the anomaly that Keohane takes it to be. Overweening power gives a state the opportunity to act beyond its narrowly defined interests *and* provides incentives for others to try to catch up. Predictions can be made when we can answer this question with some confidence: How would we expect any state so placed to act? In 1950, the People's Republic of China intervened in the Korean War, to the surprise of General MacArthur among others. Yet *any* Chinese government seeing the forces of a great power approaching the Yalu border would almost surely have moved militarily if it were able to. Keohane wrongly emphasizes the failure of realist predictions while rightly emphasizing the limitations of the theory when standing alone (pp. 182–183).

Even when we have failed to predict, theory still helps us to understand and explain some things about the behavior of states. States who lost their great-power status in the course of the Second World War no longer behave as they used to. We tend to think of their postwar preoc-cupation with self, of their inclination to take a free or at least a cheap ride by spending disproportionately little on defense, of their pusillani-mous behavior in the oil crisis following the Middle Eastern War of 1973, as deriving from their political attributes. Instead, such behavior follows mainly from the new structure of international politics. Not unexpectedly, the English historian A. J. P. Taylor assigned structural effects to the unit level and saw them as cause. "For years after the second world war," he wrote, "I continued to believe that there would be another German bid for European supremacy and that we must take precautions against it. Events have proved me totally wrong. I tried to learn lessons from history, which is always a mistake. The Germans have changed their national character" (June 4, 1976, p. 742). More perceptively, Roy Macridis saw the importance of changed position. "To speculate about a Franco-Ger-man war in the 1950s or 1960s," he wrote, "is just as boring as it would have been to contemplate a war between Sparta and Athens under the Roman Empire" (1971:143). If their national characters, and ours, have changed since the war, it is largely because their and our international positions have become profoundly different.

Not only have some states sunk in the international rankings while others have risen but also a great power now is one of two instead of five or more, as was true earlier. The United States and the Soviet Union behave differently from such countries as Germany and Japan because the latter are no longer great powers. The behavior of the United States and of the Soviet Union is also different from the behavior of earlier great powers. A great power that is one among many learns how to manipulate allies as well as adversaries. Great powers have to accommodate some of their number in order to gain strength vis-à-vis others. In dealing with near equals, they design their policies to influence the actions of others. In a crowded field, those who play the great-power game well flourish; those who do not risk falling by the wayside. The situation of the United States and of the Soviet Union is markedly different. Their field is not crowded. The most telling illustration of the difference is seen in the mutual dependence of allies before and during World War II and in the relative independence of the two alliance leaders since, along with the dependence of their associates on them.

Keohane raises the question of properly defining power and holds my definition to be insufficient. He is right. To define power in terms of who affects whom more strongly, is, I think, a move in the right direction; but I did not carry the definition very far. Although power is a key concept in realist theory, its proper definition remains a matter of controversy. On the fungibility of power, however, Keohane and I differ. Obviously, power is not as fungible as money. Not much is. But power is much more fungible than Keohane allows. As ever, the distinction between strong and weak states is important. The stronger the state, the greater the variety of its capabilities. Power may be only slightly fungible for weak states, but it is highly so for strong ones. Did, for example, America's failure to respond to economic pressures with economic or military force show that the United States was unable to translate its capabilities into effective power, as some thought during the oil embargo of the early 1970s, or did it indicate that the United States, more nearly self-sufficient than most countries, was not pressed hard enough to make the effort seem worthwhile? Moreover, in many of the examples Keohane adduces as evidence that Canada, a weak state, prevailed over the United States, a strong one, I suspect that American officials hardly cared about the outcomes or even noticed what they might be. The United States has more levers to pull than other states do but need not always pull them.

Keohane rightly criticizes some realists for assuming that states seek to maximize power (pp. 173–174). He wrongly associates me with them because I point out that a balance-of-power system works whether we find states seeking only the minimum of power needed for security or whether some of them strive for domination. Because the belief that states do or should try to maximize power is quite widespread among realists, I emphasized the error in a paragraph containing these sentences: "Only if survival is assured, can states safely seek such other goals as tranquility, profit, and power. Because power is a means and not an end, states prefer to join the weaker of two coalitions. They cannot let power, a possibly useful means, become the end they pursue" (p. 127).

How one should test theories is the only question on which Keohane and I are far apart. In my simple, and perhaps simplistic, recipe for the testing of theories, given in chapter 1 of *Theory of International Politics,* I may have sounded like a "naïve falsificationist." I should like to correct the impression.

In criticizing my comments on testing, Keohane says that I find it difficult to "state precisely the conditions under which coalitions will change" (p. 172). I think it is *impossible* to do that. Because of the impossibility of precise specification, balance-of-power theory, like most theories in the social sciences, is difficult to test. We should therefore apply a variety of tests. Keohane is bothered by my urging that we seek to confirm theories as well as to falsify them. I do indeed depart from Karl Popper, who insists that only efforts to falsify theories count as legitimate tests. That may be a suitable way to go about testing, but it is not the only way. Errol Harris argues that among natural scientists it is a little used method.[4] Attempts to falsify theories are as problematic as attempts to confirm them. Because of the interdependence of theory and fact, we can find no Popperian critical experiment, the negative results of which would send a theory crashing to the ground. The background knowledge against which to test a theory is as problematic as the theory itself. Popper understood the problem but passed over it in various ways. In science there are no ultimate, or certainly true, statements. Therefore, no test is conclusive; in principle we should test theories *ad infinitum.* One way to avoid an infinite regress is to require not tests but testability. Another way is simply to limit tests on the ground that we are not trying to prove a theory true, but only to disprove a hypothesis (cf. Popper 1935:47–50, 105, 278). Popper's famous example of falsification is the one black swan that disproves the thousands of instances seeming to confirm the proposition that all swans are white. But if the positive statement—this is a black swan—is not proved, the hypothesis is not shown conclusively wrong. As Harris puts it: "We already know that there is and can be no external body of fact—external, that is, to all theory" (1970:353). As Popper once said:

> Science does not rest upon solid bedrock. The bold structure of its theories rises, as it were, above a swamp. It is like a building erected on piles. The piles are driven down from above into the swamp, but not down to any natural or "given" base; and if we stop driving the piles deeper, it is not because we have reached firm ground. We simply stop when we are satisfied that the piles are firm enough to carry the structure, at least for the time being (1935:111).

A theory may help us to understand and explain phenomena and events yet not be a useful instrument for prediction. Darwin's theory of evolution predicted nothing. It did help mightily to explain a changing world. That theories are not merely instruments for prediction opens the way for confirming tests. The inconclusive status of falsification invites us to try other means. Keohane chides me for advocating efforts to confirm theories and at the same time admitting that confirming instances can always be found (p. 172). Because they can be, I insisted on the importance of making tests difficult. This strikes me as being wise counsel since the lower the prior probability of a new piece of evidence, the higher the increased confirmation. Moreover, sound testing does not require one to examine "a universe of cases," as Keohane would have it (p. 172). A small number of cases well studied may be worth hundreds cursorily treated. Insofar as the accumulation of a number of cases is "mere repetition . . . it does not serve to enlighten." Each observation, as Harris has written, is valuable only if it "supplies new information, offers a fresh clue to the form of the total structure" (1970:348). One experiment well designed, one demonstration well conducted, one case carefully examined, may add more to one's confidence in a theory than hundreds of instances looked at hastily.

Testing theories is difficult; interpreting the results of tests is a subtle task. Since results are always problematic, some part of the scientific community has to decide whether enough of an empirical warrant exists to give a theory credibility. Theories gain credibility in a variety of ways—by unsuccessfully attempting to falsify, by successfully attempting to verify, by demonstrating that outcomes are produced in the way the theory contemplates, and by the intellectual force of the theory itself.

Keohane laments realism's lack of a theory of peaceful change, and he calls for more emphasis on norms, institutions, and non-state actors. The structure of a self-help system is defined in terms of its principal actors. The definition does not exclude other components, but merely sets the context of their existence. Empirical and theoretical work often proceeds without consideration of how the structure of the system affects institutions and actions within it. Some states sometimes want to work together to secure the benefits of cooperation. Cooperative projects in the present may lead to more cooperation in the future. But self-help systems do make the cooperation of parties difficult. As Gilpin puts it, "the traditional insights of realism . . . helps us to explain . . . the ongoing retreat from an interdependent world" (p. 312). Rules, institutions, and patterns of cooperation, when they develop in self-help systems, are all limited in extent and modified from what they might otherwise be.

Whether Keohane's conclusion, that *Theory of International Politics* offers nothing new, is valid depends on one's view of the old (p. 175). The behavioral mode of thinking is deeply ingrained in students of international politics. Whether by liberals, Marxists, realists, or behavioralists, the attempt has usually been to explain outcomes through the varying attributes of the acting units. System and structure have become fairly common terms in political science discourse. Only in the most general way, however, had systemic approaches been used to show how a structure shapes and shoves the units of a system. The effects on units of changes in structure had not been identified and examined. I developed a way of thinking that had not been widely familiar. Ashley is partly right; in certain important ways I did break with earlier realist thinking. Keohane is partly right; there is more continuity between earlier realists and me than Ashley noticed. Earlier realists thought of international anarchy simply as setting problems for statesmen different from those to be coped with internally and as altering standards of appropriate behavior. While earlier realists talked about the anarchy of international politics as marking their field of inquiry, they continued to explain international political outcomes in terms of the aims and policies, the actions and interactions, of states and of non-state actors. This remained the dominant pattern of explanation even for those political scientists who began to use the terminology of systems theory.

"PROBLEM-SOLVING" THEORY

I find Richard K. Ashley difficult to deal with. Reading his essay is like entering a maze. I never know quite where I am or how to get out. He is sometimes elusive, shifting from one view to another. In one essay, he quotes me as saying that "the behavior of states and statesmen . . . is indeterminate." He then correctly observes "that there is room for practical action: *Practical realism has partial autonomy*" (1981:220, 222). In another essay, neorealists, apparently including me, are said to "grant to the 'international political system absolute predominance over the parts' " (p. 288). In the earlier essay, he lumps Morgenthau and me pretty much together and tars us with the same brush. In the later essay, he finds more virtue in Morgenthau and less in me. Some of Ashley's comments bewilder me. Like John Herz, I often fail to recognize myself in what he writes about me (Herz 1981:237). In preceding pages, I attended to some of Ashley's complaints. Others are covered in Robert Gilpin's spirited response to Ashley's indictment of neorealism. I shall avoid repetition.

In Ashley's alternative model of international politics, the balance-of-power regime "*produces* sovereign states, who as a condition of their sovereignty, embody the regime" (above, p. 294, his italics). What can this mean? It may mean that states as we know them behave in certain ways because self-help systems strongly encourage some modes of behavior and discourage others. States develop along certain lines and acquire certain characteristics in order to survive and flourish in the system. In a different regime states would be different and would behave differently. But that seems unlikely to be his meaning because it would bring Ashley into agreement with me on a fundamental proposition. Yet I can see only one other way to interpret the sentence: namely, that the balance-of-power regime antedates the units that engage in the balancing! I find this baffling, yet it does seem to be his meaning. Thus a major charge he brings against me is that I understand international structure

> not as a deep, internal relation prior to and constitutive of social actors but as an external joining of states-as-actors who have precisely the bound-aries, ends, and self-understandings that theorists accord them on the basis of unexamined common sense. In turn—and here is the coup—Waltz grants the structure a life of its own independent of the parts, the states-as-actors; and he shows in countless ways how this structure limits and disposes action on the part of states such that, on balance, the structure is reproduced and actors are drawn into conformity with its requisites. But how is the independence of the structural whole estab-lished? It is not established independent of the parts taken together, for it is never anything more than the logical consequence of the parts taken together (p. 287).

This is a pretty fair summary, requiring only a few qualifications. The main one is this: The structure is not "independent of the parts, the states as actors," but constantly interacts with them. Neither the structure nor the units determine, as Ashley seemed to realize in 1981 and had forgotten by 1984.

The root of our differences is exposed in Robert Cox's nice distinction between problem-solving theory and critical theory. Critical theory deals with the "continuing process of historical change" (1981:128; reprinted above, p. 209). Both Cox and Ashley seem to think that my big mistake was to concentrate on the first kind of theory instead of on the second. I have no quarrel with Cox's concern with counter and latent structures, with historical inquiry, and with speculation about possible futures. Ashley and Cox would transcend the world as it is; meanwhile we have to live in it. At the end of his essay Cox speculates about emerging world orders. The likelihood of their realization will vary not only with changing production processes and social forces, which he emphasizes, but also with distributions of capability across states, which I emphasize.

Next to my whole enterprise being misconceived, what bothers Cox and Ashley most is my assumption that states are the units of international politics. They see this as enshrining the state, as freezing the system, and as making it static and eternal. Even though I made abundantly clear that I take the state to be a unit by assumption, Ashley says this: "For despite its statism, neorealism can produce no theory of the state capable of satisfying the state-as-actor premises of its political theory" (p. 279). I have not tried, but surely some neorealist is capable of producing a theory of the state. It would reveal, among other things, one that we already know: The state in fact is not a unitary and purposive actor. I assumed it to be such only for the purpose of constructing a theory. In reality, as I put it: "States pursue many goals, which are often vaguely formulated and inconsistent. They fluctuate with the changing currents of domestic politics, are prey to the vagaries of a shifting cast of political leaders, and are influenced by the outcomes of bureaucratic struggles" (p. 118).

Because I concentrated on "problem-solving" theory and left "critical theory" aside, I had to introduce theoretical concepts. Neither Cox nor Ashley likes the assumption that states are the units of the system. Yet if one is to develop a problem-solving theory about anything, assumptions of this sort have to be made. The alternative is simply to eschew such theories altogether. Would we then know more or less about the social and the natural worlds? In developing a structural theory of international politics, I was most influenced by economists and anthropologists; specifically by microeconomic or market theory and by Emile Durkheim. Obviously, economists in assuming that firms act as maximizing units know that firms in fact do not conform closely to the conception. They know further that forms and modes of economic organization change over the years. The distinction between an assumption and a statement striving for descriptive accuracy should be easy to grasp.

Cox's and Ashley's main objection seems to be that I did not write a theory of domestic politics. Ashley notices that I allow for considerable variety among states but complains that the variety is not a concern of my theory (p. 266). That is so, but only because I essayed an international-political theory and not a domestic one. Not everything need go into one book and not everything can go into one theory.[5] Realizing that I did not write a theory of the state, Ashley and Cox cannot from a theoretical assumption rightly infer what notions I might entertain about the historical origins and development of states and about their possible fates. I find it hard to believe that anyone would think that states will remain fixed in their present condition. But Ashley seems to believe that I hold that odd view. He infers what I believe about states from what I did *not* say about them. In the book he criticizes I abstracted "from every attribute of states except their capabilities" (p. 94). The behavior and practice of states and of statesmen are omitted from international-political theory not because of their unimportance but because their exclusion from the system's structure requires a distinct theory dealing with the politics and policies of states. I see something problematic about this only for those who think that domestic and international politics must be combined in one theory. Someone may one day fashion a unified theory of internal and external politics. Critical theory apparently aspires to do so, but I read in Ashley and Cox only what such a theory might do rather than what the theory is. The theoretical separation of domestic and international politics need not bother us unduly. Economists get along quite well with separate theories of markets and firms. Students of international politics will do well to concentrate on separate theories of internal and external politics until someone figures out a way to unite them.

Ashley accuses me of excluding history from the study of international politics and of immunizing a part of my theory from falsifying tests. In his words: "Despite neorealism's much ballyhooed emphasis on the role of hard falsifying tests as the measure of theoretical progress, neorealism immunizes its statist commitments from any form of falsification" (p. 270). To exclude history from a problem-solving theory is hardly to enjoin the historical study of politics. How can one incorporate history into the type of theory I constructed? Neither Ashley nor Cox gives an answer, but again apparently I should simply not have done what I did but something quite different. Nor does a theoretical assumption about states enjoin anyone from studying them empirically or from theorizing about them. Ashley finds in neorealism "*a historicism of stasis. . . .* a historicism that freezes the political institutions of the current world order" (p. 289). How can any theory have these effects? Ashley has a higher regard for the power of theories than I have. A theory applies only so long as the conditions it contemplates endure in their essentials. If the anarchy of international politics were to give way to a world hierarchy, a theory of international politics would become a theory about the past. Ashley thinks I am reluctant to contemplate "a hierarchy centering power within the grasp of a singular hegemon" because such a concentration would overturn the "fundamental organizing principle of international politics" (p. 277). How could he know this was my reason without asking me? It is true that some of Ashley's neorealists like hegemony better than I do, but that simply illustrates Gilpin's statement that we are a mixed bunch. The influence behind my preference is partly Immanuel Kant and partly Reinhold Niebuhr. Kant feared that a world government would stifle liberty, become a terrible despotism, and in the end collapse into chaos. Niebuhr drew the conclusion from his dim view of human nature that domestically and internationally the ends of security and decency are served better by balanced than by concentrated power. I distrust hegemonic power, whoever may wield it, because it is so easily misused.

Ashley offers an alternative to a neorealist model (pp. 294–297). It looks quite a bit like mine, except that it is wrapped in a capitalist blanket. Does he mean to imply that "a balance-of-power regime" would not exist in, say, a world of socialist states? If this is his meaning, I flatly disagree. Or does he mean that "a balance-of-power regime" would exist but with some differences in the attributes and behaviors of states? No doubt there would be some differences, but not ones of much systemic importance. Balance-of-power politics in much the form that we know it has been practiced over the millennia by many different types of political units, from ancient China and India, to the Greek and Italian city states, and unto our own day.

Critical theory seeks to interpret the world historically and philosophically. Problem-solving theory seeks to understand and explain it. Ashley's critical essay reveals to me no clue about how to write an improved theory of the latter sort. I am sorry that it does not.

CONCLUSION

Systems theory is frequently criticized for being static. It is in one sense but not in others. Self-ordered systems, as Michael Polanyi wrote, are subject to dual control, that is, "control in accordance with the laws that apply to its elements in themselves, and . . . control in accordance with the laws of the powers that control the comprehensive entity formed by these elements" (1968:1311). The latter are the constraints of the system, with the organization of the parts affecting the way the parts function. International-political systems exhibit dual control. Behaviors and outcomes change as interactions among a system's units become sparser or denser, as alliances shift, as nations adapt their policies to one another. These are changes within the system, and often systems dynamics are identified with, and limited to, such changes. What really matters, it seems, are changes in the behavior of states and in their alignments. That is the whole of the story only if *dynamic* is defined as energy in motion. This is the dynamic of the units. Another part of the story is revealed if *dynamics* are thought of as in physics—the action of forces on bodies in motion or at rest. These are the dynamics of the system. Structural changes alter a system's dynamics. Systemic effects cannot be reconstructed from the system's interacting parts since the parts behave differently because they are parts of a system. The constraints and incentives of a system, its dynamics, change if its structure changes or is transformed. To explain outcomes, we have to look at a system's dynamics and not just at the characteristics and the strategies of the units.

Self-help systems are transformed if their organizing principle shifts from anarchy to hierarchy. Establishing a world government would do this. Either all states pooling their sovereignty or some states conquering the others would transform the system. Self-help systems change through consequential variation in the distribution of capabilities among their members. States can more readily change their system than transform it. States fighting wars have immediate offensive or defensive aims. If the aim is to reduce the number of great powers significantly through conquest, then from a system's perspective the aim is to change the system. The result may be produced aside from the intentions of states. The victors in World War II thought of themselves as fighting a defensive war. In doing so, they nevertheless fought a war that changed the system from one of multipolarity to one of bipolarity. Shortly after helping to produce that change, the United States began to promote another one by encouraging Western European countries to unite. From the unit's perspective, one easily understands why. A united Western Europe would be a bulwark against the Soviet Union. From a system's perspective, the aim is an odd one. Why should one of two great powers wish to move the system from bipolarity to tripolarity?

By rewarding behavior that conforms with systemic requirements and punishing behavior that does not, a system's structure works against transformation. This is fortunate only if we are content with the system we have or if we are pessimistic about the costs and consequences of transformation. Changes in, and transformation of, systems originate not in the structure of a system but in its parts. Through selection, structures promote the continuity of systems in form; through variation, unit-level forces contain the possibilities of systemic change. The possibilities of rising in the international system, and the costs and benefits of doing so, vary as systems change; but states decide whether making the effort to advance is worthwhile. Japan has the capability of raising herself to great-power rank, but has lacked the inclination to do so. Systems change, or are transformed, depending on the resources and aims of their units and on the fates that befall them.

Structures condition behaviors and outcomes, yet explanations of behaviors and outcomes are indeterminate because both unit-level and structural causes are in play. Systems are stable if they endure for long periods. They are impressively stable if they survive the disruption of large-scale wars. The bipolar world has been both stable and peaceful— if peace is defined as the low incidence of war among great and major powers, that is, among those states most immediately affected by the structure of global politics. The bothersome limitations of systemic explanations arise from the problem of weighing unit-level and structural causes. To what extent is an effect to be ascribed to one level or the other? One may believe, as I do, that both bipolarity and nuclear weapons promote peace. But one cannot say for sure whether the structural or the unit-level cause is the stronger. The difficulty of sorting causes out is a serious, and seemingly inescapable, limitation of systems theories of international politics.

Structures shape and shove. They do not determine behaviors and outcomes, not only because unit-level and structural causes interact, but also because the shaping and shoving of structures may be successfully resisted. We attribute such success to Bismarck when we describe him as a diplomatic virtuoso. The unification of Germany, fashioned in the fighting of three short wars, shifted the balance of power in the center of Europe. Could that be done without igniting a general war? Given the structure of European politics, few would have thought so before the event. Later, in 1879, Bismarck forged a long-term alliance with Austria-Hungary. Given the structure of European politics, one would have predicted that an alliance made by two great powers would cause a counteralliance to form. Indeed, the Franco-Russian Alliance may have become inevitable with Prussia's victory over France in 1871, as Friedrich Engels thought (1890:48–49). The measure of Bismarck's diplomatic virtuosity is that the Alliance was not made until 1894, four years after his political demise. With skill and determination structural constraints can sometimes be countered. Virtuosos transcend the limits of their instruments and break the constraints of systems that bind lesser performers.

Thinking in terms of systems dynamics does not replace unit-level analysis nor end the search for sequences of cause and effect. Thinking in terms of systems dynamics does change the conduct of the search and add a dimension to it. Structural thought conceives of actions simultaneously taking place within a matrix. Change the matrix—the structure of the system—and expected actions and outcomes are altered. The past causes the present, but the causes are mediated by the present system's structure. The examination of structure tells us how a system does what it does. A structure sets the range of expectations. Like any theory, a structural theory leaves some things aside in order to concentrate on others. Like any theory, a structural theory is limited to making predictions and promoting the understanding of events at a level of generality appropriate to the theory. A structural theory of international politics can fix ranges of outcomes and identify general tendencies, which may be persistent and strong ones but will not be reflected in all particular outcomes. We cannot hope to predict specific outcomes, but if our theory is good, we will see the kind of behavior and record the range of outcomes the theory leads us to expect. From the dynamics of the system we can infer general properties of behavior and outcomes within a system and expected changes in those properties as systems change.

NOTES

1. This essay has benefited from critical readings by my wife, from correspondence and conversation over the years with Barry Buzan, Robert Keohane, and Glenn Snyder, and from searching and suggestive comments by Vinod Aggarwal.

2. States gain from trade because of their dissimilarities. Durkheim dwells on the resemblance of the units of a mechanical society. This may be confusing. One needs to remember that like units are not identical. They may differ considerably

in resource endowment and economic development. Functionally, however, they are like units.

3. Cf. Park: "People live together on the whole, not because they are alike but because they are useful to one another" (1952:80). See also March and Simon: "the greater the *specialization by subprograms* (process specialization), the greater the *interdependence among organizational subunits*" (1958:159).

4. Excellent examples of test by confirmation, mainly from Newton, Lavoisier, and Harvey, are found on pp. 161–178 of Harrris (1970).

5. In a book about foreign policy I concerned myself at length with the effects of internal structural differences on the external policies and behavior of the United States and Britain (1967).

Bibliography

Adorno, Theodore W. et al. 1976. *The Positivism Dispute in German Sociology.*
G. Adey and D. Frisby, transl. New York: Harper Torchbooks.

Aggarwal, Vinod K. 1985. *Liberal Protectionism: The International Politics of Organized Textile Trade.* Berkeley: University of California Press.

Akerlof, George A. and Jane Yellen. 1985. Can small deviations from rationality make significant differences in economic equilibria? *American Economic Review* (September) 75(4):708–720.

Alker, Hayward R., Jr. 1981. Dialectical foundations of global disparities. *International Studies Quarterly* (March) 25(1):69–98.

Alker, Hayward R., Jr. 1982. Logic, dialectics, politics: Some recent controversies. In Alker, ed., *Dialectical Logic for the Political Sciences.* Amsterdam: Rodopi.

Alker, Hayward R., Jr. In Progress. Can the end of power politics possibly be part of the concepts with which its story is told? In Alker, "Essential Contradictions, Hidden Unities." In Progress.

Allison, Graham T. 1971. *Essence of Decision.* Boston: Little, Brown.

Allison, Graham T. and Morton Halperin. 1972. Bureaucratic politics: A paradigm and some policy implications. *World Politics* (Spring) vol. 24.

Anderson, Perry. 1974. *Lineages of the Absolutist State.* London: New Left Books.

Anderson, Perry. 1980. *Arguments within English Marxism.* London: New Left Books.

Andrade, E. N. de C. 1957. *An Approach to Modern Physics.* New York: Doubleday.

Arendt, Hannah. 1958. *The Human Condition.* Chicago: University of Chicago Press.

Aron, Raymond. 1967. What is a theory of international relations? *Journal of International Affairs* 21(2):185–206.

Art, Robert J. 1973a. Bureuacratic politics and American foreign policy: A critique. *Policy Sciences* 4:204–236.

Art, Robert J. 1973b. The influence of foreign policy on seapower: New weapons and weltpolitik in Wilhelminian Germany. *Sage Professional Paper in International Studies* vol. 2. Beverly Hills: Sage Publications.

Ashby, W. Ross. 1956/1964. *An Introduction to Cybernetics.* London: Chapman.

Ashley, Richard K. 1980. *The Political Economy of War and Peace: The Sino-Soviet-American Triangle and the Modern Security Problematique.* London: Frances Pinter; New York: Nichols.

Ashley, Richard K. 1981. Political realism and human interests. *International Studies Quarterly* 25:204–236.

Ashley, Richard K. 1982. Realist dialectics: Toward a critical theory of world politics. Paper prepared for the American Political Science Association meeting, Denver, Colorado, September.

Ashley, Richard K., 1983. Three modes of economism. *International Studies Quarterly* (December) 27(4):463–496.

Ashley, Richard K. 1984. The poverty of neorealism. *International Organization* (Spring) 38(2):225–286.

Avery, William P. and David P. Rapkin, eds. 1982. *America in a Changing World Political Economy.* New York: Longman.

Axelrod, Robert, ed. 1976. *The Structure of Decision: The Cognitive Maps of Political Elites.* Princeton: Princeton University Press.

Axelrod, Robert. 1981. The emergence of cooperation among egoists. *American Political Science Review* 25:306–318.

Baldwin, David A. 1979. Power analysis and world politics: New trends versus old tendencies. *World Politics* (January) 31(2):161–194.

Barnard, Chester I. 1948. On planning for world government. In Barnard, *Organization and Management: Selected Papers.*

Barnard, Chester I. 1948b. *Organization and Management: Selected Papers.* Cambridge: Harvard University Press.

Barraclough, Geoffrey. 1968. *An Introduction to Contemporary History.* Harmondsworth, Middlesex: Penguin.

Barry, Brian. 1970. *Sociologists, Economists and Democracy.* Chicago: University of Chicago Press.

Barry, Brian, ed. 1976. *Power and Political Theory—Some European Perspectives.* London: John Wiley.

Barry, Brian. 1983. Some questions about explanation. *International Studies Quarterly* (March) 27(1):17–28.

Beloff, Max. 1961. *New Dimensions in Foreign Policy.* London: Allen and Unwin.

Berki, R. N. 1971. On Marxian thought and the problem of international relations. *World Politics* (October) 24(1):80–105.

Bernstein, Richard. 1976. *The Restructuring of Political and Social Theory.* New York: Harcourt, Brace, Jovanovich.

Blank, Stephen. 1978. Britain: The politics of foreign economic policy, the domestic economy and the problem of pluralistic stagnation. In Katzenstein, ed. *Between Power and Plenty.*

Boltzman, Ludwig. 1905. Theories as representations. Rudolf Weingartner, transl. In Arthur Danto and Sidney Morgenbesser, eds. 1960. *Philosophy of Science.* Cleveland: World, Meridian Books.

Bourdieu, Pierre. 1977. *Outline of a Theory of Practice.* Richard Nice, transl. Cambridge, England: Cambridge University Press.

Boyle, Francis, A. 1980. The irrelevance of international law: The schism between international law and international politics. *California Western International Law Journal,* vol. 10.

Bozeman, Adda B. 1960. *Politics and Culture in International History.* Princeton: Princeton University Press.

Braudel, Fernand. 1958. Histoire et sciences sociales. La longue durée. *Annales E. S. C.* 13(4):725–753. English transl. in Braudel. 1980. *On History.* Sarah Matthews, transl. Chicago: University of Chicago Press, pp. 25–54.

Braudel, Fernand. 1979. *Civilisation matérielle, économie et capitalisme, XVe–XVIIIe siècle.* 3 vols. Paris: Armand Colin.

Braverman, Harry. 1974. *Labor and Monopoly Capital.* New York: Monthly Review.

Brecher, Michael, with Benjamin Geist. 1980. *Decisions in Crisis: Israel 1967–1973.* Berkeley: University of California Press.

Brenner, Robert. 1977. The origins of capitalist development: A critique of neosmithian marxism. *New Left Review* 104:25–92.

Bueno de Mesquita, Bruce. 1981. *The War Trap.* New Haven: Yale University Press.

Bull, Hedley. 1976. Martin Wight and the theory of international relations: The second Martin Wight memorial lecture. *British Journal of International Studies* 2:101–116.

Bull, Hedley. 1977. *The Anarchical Society.* New York: Columbia University Press.

Camic, Charles. 1979. The utilitarians revisited. *American Journal of International Studies* 85(3):516–550.

Carr, E. H. 1945. *Nationalism and After.* London: Macmillan.

Carr, E. H. 1946. *The Twenty Years' Crisis, 1919–1939.* 2d. ed. London: Macmillan. (The first edition was published in London by Macmillan in 1939.)

Chabod, F. 1964. Was there a renaissance state? In H. Lubasz, ed. *The Development of the Modern State.* New York: Macmillan.

Choucri, Nazli and Robert C. North. 1975. *Nations in Conflict: National Growth and International Violence.* San Francisco: W. H. Freeman.

Cipolla, Carlo. 1970. *The Economic Decline of Empiress.* London: Methuen.

Claude, Inis L. 1962. *Power and International Relations.* New York: Random House.

Collingwood, R. G. 1942. *The New Leviathan.* Oxford: University Press.

Conant, James B. 1947. *On Understanding Science.* New Haven: Yale University Press.

Conant, James B. 1952. *Modern Science and Modern Man.* New York: Columbia University Press.

Cooper, Richard N. 1968. *The Economics of Interdependence.* New York: McGraw Hill.

Cox, Robert W. 1977. Pour une étude prospective des relations de production. *Sociologie du travail* 2:113–137.

Cox, Robert W. 1978. Labour and employment in the late twentieth century. In R. St. J. Macdonald et al., eds., *The International Law and Policy of Human Welfare.* The Hague: Sijthoff and Noordhoff.

Cox, Robert W. 1981. Social forces, states, and world orders: Beyond international relations theory. *Millennium: A Journal of International Studies* (Summer) 10(2):126–155.

Cox, Robert W. 1983. Gramsci, hegemony and international relations: An essay in method. *Millennium: A Journal of International Studies* (Summer) 12(2):162–175.

Cox, Robert W. and Harold K. Jacobson et al. 1972. *The Anatomy of Influence: Decision Making in International Organization.* New Haven: Yale University Press.

Cox, Robert W. and Harold K. Jacobson. 1977. Decision making. *International Social Science Journal* 29(1):115–135. Special issue on international organization.

Craig, Gordon A. and Alexander L. George. 1983. *Force and Statecraft: Diplomatic Problems of Our Time.* New York: Oxford University Press.

Crossman, Richard. 1977. *The Diaries of a Cabinet Minister.* Vol. 3: *Secretary of State for Social Services, 1968–70.* London: Hamish Hamilton and Jonathan Cape.

Culler, Jonathan. 1975. *Structuralist Poetics.* London: Routledge and Kegan Paul.

Cyert, Richard and James G. March. 1963. *A Behavioral Theory of the Firm.* Englewood Cliffs, N.J.: Prentice-Hall.

Cyert, Richard M. and Herbert A. Simon. 1983. The behavioral approach: With emphasis on economics. *Behavioral Science* (April) 28(2):95–108.

Dahl, Robert A. 1961. *Who Governs? Democracy and Power in an American City.* New Haven: Yale University Press.

Dahrendorf, Ralf. 1959. *Class and Class Conflict in Industrial Society.* Stanford: Stanford University Press.

Dehio, Ludwig. 1962. *The Precarious Balance.* New York: Random House.

Deutsch, Karl W. 1966. Recent trends in research methods in political science. In James C. Charlesworth, ed. *A Design for Political Science: Scope, Objectives, and Methods.* Philadelphia: American Academy of Political and Social Science.

Diebold, William, Jr. 1980. *Industrial Policy as an International Issue.* New York: McGraw Hill.

Diesing, Paul. 1962. *Reason in Society.* Urbana: University of Illinois Press.

Disraeli, Benjamin. 1880. *Endymion.* London: Longmans, Green.

Downs, Anthony. 1967. *Inside Bureaucracy.* Boston: Little, Brown.

Dowty, Alan, 1969. Conflict in war potential politics: An approach to historical macroanalysis. *Peace Research Society Papers* vol. 13.

Djilas, Milovan. 1962. *Conversations with Stalin.* Michael B. Petrovich, transl. New York: Harcourt, Brace and World.

Durkheim, Emile. 1893/1964. *The Division of Labor in Society.* George Simpson, transl. New York: Free Press.

Durkheim, Emile. 1895/1964. *The Rules of Sociological Method.* George E. G. Catlin, ed. New York: Free Press.

Eckstein, Harry. 1975. Case study and theory in political science. In Fred I. Greenstein and Nelson W. Polsby, eds. *Handbook of Political Science.* vol. 7. *Strategies of Inquiry.* Reading, Mass.: Addison-Wesley.

Elsenhans, Hartmut. n.d. The state class in the third world: For a new conceptualization of periphery modes of production. Unpublished.

Engels, Friedrich. 1890. The foreign policy of Russian Czarism. In Paul W. Blackstock and Bert F. Hoselitz, eds. 1952. *The Russian Menace to Europe.* Glencoe, Ill.: The Free Press.

Feis, Herbert. 1961. *Europe the World's Banker, 1870–1914.* New York: Kelly for the Council on Foreign Relations.

Feldman, Shai. 1982. *Israeli Nuclear Deterrence.* New York: Columbia University Press.

Fellner, William. 1949. *Competition Among the Few.* New York: Alfred A. Knopf.

Follett, Mary Parker. 1941. *Dynamic Administration: The Collected Papers of Mary Parker Follett.* H. C. Metcalf and L. Urwick, eds. Bath, England: Management Publications Trust.

Fortes, Meyer. 1949. Time and social structure: An Ashanti case study. In Fortes, ed. *Social Structure: Studies Presented to A. R. Radcliffe-Brown.* Oxford: Clarendon Press.

Foucault, Michel. 1970. *The Order of Things.* New York: Pantheon.

Foucault, Michel. 1972. *The Archaeology of Knowledge.* New York: Pantheon.

Foucault, Michel. 1977. *Language, Counter-Memory, Practice.* Oxford: Blackwell.

Foucault, Michel. 1980. *Power/Knowledge: Selected Interviews and Other Writings, 1971–1977.* Colin Gordon et al., ed. and transl. New York: Pantheon.

Fox, William T. R. 1959. The uses of international relations theory. In Fox, ed. *Theoretical Aspects of International Relations.* Notre Dame, Ind.: University of Notre Dame Press.

Fox, William T. R. 1980. Review of Waltz, 1979. *American Political Science Review* (June) 7(2):492–93.

Freidberg, Erhard. 1974. L'internationalisation de l'économie et modalités d'intervention de l'état: La politique industrielle. In *Planification et société.* Grenoble: Presses Universitaires de Grenoble.

Friedman, Milton. 1953. The methodology of positive economics. In Friedman, *Essays in Positive Economics.* Chicago: University of Chicago Press.

Furobotn, Eirik G. and Svetozar Pejovich, eds. 1974. *The Economics of Property Rights.* Cambridge, Mass.: Ballinger.

Galbraith, John Kenneth. 1973. *Economics and the Public Purpose.* Boston: Houghton Mifflin.

Gardner, Richard N. 1956. *Sterling-Dollar Diplomacy: Anglo-American Collaboration in the Reconstruction of Multilateral Trade.* Oxford: Clarendon.

Geertz, Clifford. 1973. *The Interpretation of Cultures.* New Basic Books.

George, Alexander L. 1979. Case studies and theory development: The method of structured, focused comparison. In Paul Gordon Lauren, ed. *Diplomacy: New Approaches in History, Theory and Policy.* New York: Free Press.

George, Alexander L. 1980. *Presidential Decisionmaking in Foreign Policy: The Effective Use of Information and Advice.* Boulder: Westview.

George, Alexander L. and Juliette George. 1964. *Woodrow Wilson and Colonel House.* New York: Dover.

George, Alexander L., D. K. Hall and W. E. Simons. 1971. *The Limits of Coercive Diplomacy.* Boston: Little Brown.

George, Alexander L. and Richard Smoke. 1974. *Deterrence in American Foreign Policy.* New York: Columbia University Press.

Gerschenkron, Alexander. 1962. *Economic Backwardness in Historical Perspective.* Cambridge: The Belknap Press of Harvard University Press.

Gerth, H. H. and C. Wright Mills. 1958. *From Max Weber: Essays in Sociology.* New York: Oxford University Press.

Giddens, Anthony. 1972. *Politics and Sociology in the Thought of Max Weber.* London: Macmillan.

Giddens, Anthony, ed. 1974. *Positivism and Sociology.* London: Henemann.

Giddens, Anthony. 1978. *Emile Durkheim.* New York: Penguin Books.

Giddens, Anthony. 1979. *Central Problems in Social Theory.* Berkeley: University of California Press.

Gilpin, Robert. 1975. *U.S. Power and the Multinational Corporation.* New York: Basic Books.

Gilpin, Robert. 1981a. Political change and international theory. Paper presented at the annual meeting of the American Political Science Association, New York, September 3–6.

Gilpin, Robert. 1981b. *War and Change in World Politics.* New York: Cambridge University Press.

Gilpin, Robert. 1984. The richness of the tradition of political realism. *International Organization* (Spring) 38(2):287–304.

Glucksman, Miriam. 1974. *Structuralist Analysis in Contemporary Social Thought.* London: Routledge & Kegan Paul.

Gourevitch, Peter A. .1978. The second image reversed: The international sources of domestic politics. *International Organization* (Autumn) 32(4):881–911.

Gramsci, Antonio. 1971. *Selections from the Prison Notebooks.* Quintin Hoare and Geoffrey N. Smith, eds. and transl. New York: International Publishers.

Gramsci, Antonio. 1975. *Quaderni del Carcere.* Torino: Einaudi editore. The full critical edition.

Gross, L. 1968. The Peace of Westphalia, 1648–1948. In Richard A. Falk and Wolfram H. Hanrieder, eds. *International Law and Organization.* Phildelphia: J. B. Lippincott.

Haas, Ernst B. 1953. The balance of power: Prescription, concept, or propaganda? *World Politics* (July) 5(4):442–477.

Haas, Ernst B. 1964. *Beyond the Nation State.* Stanford: Stanford University Press.

Haas, Ernst B. 1969. Letter to the editor. *Journal of Common Market Studies* (September) 8(1):70.

Haas, Ernst B. 1980. Why collaborate? Issue-linkage and international regimes. *World Politics* (April) 32(3):357–405.

Haas, Ernst B. 1982. Words can hurt you: Or who said what to whom about regimes. *International Organization* (Spring) 36(2):207–244.

Habermas, Jürgen. 1971. *Towards a Rational Society.* Jeremy J. Shapiro, transl. London: Heinemann.

Habermans, Jürgen. 1974. *Theory and Practice.* John Viertel, transl. Boston: Beacon Press.

Habermas, Jürgen. 1976. *Legitimation Crisis.* Thomas McCarthy, transl. London: Heinemann.

Habermas, Jürgen. 1979. *Communication and the Evolution of Society.* Thomas McCarthy, transl. London: Heinemann.

Halle, Louis J. 1955. *Civilization and Foreign Policy.* New York: Harper.

Harris, Errole E. 1970. *Hypothesis and Perception.* London: Allen and Unwin.

Harrod, R. F. 1951. *The Life of John Maynard Keynes.* London: Macmillan.

Harsanyi, John. 1962. Measurement of social power, opportunity costs, and the theory of two-person bargaining games. *Behavioral Sciences* 7(1):67–80.

Hechter, Michael. 1981. Karl Polanyi's social theory: A critique. *Politics and Society* 10(4):399–429.

Heisenberg, Werner. 1971. Physics and beyond. Arnold J. Pomerans, transl. New York: Harper and Row.

Hertz, Heinrich. 1894/1899. *The Principles of Mechanics.* D. E. Jones and J. T. Walley, transl. Introduction reprinted in Arthur Danto and Sidney Morgenbesser, eds. 1970. *Philosophy of Science.* Cleveland: World Meridian Books.

Herz, John. 1951. *Political Realism and Political Idealism.* Chicago: Chicago University Press.

Herz, John. 1981. Political realism revisited (and "response" in a colloquium). *International Studies Quarterly* (June) 25(2):182–197; 201–203.

Hinsley, F. H. 1963. *Power and the Pursuit of Peace.* Cambridge: Cambridge University Press.

Hinsley, F. H. 1967. The concept of sovereignty and the relations between states. *Journal of International Affairs* 21(2):242–252.

Hobbes, Thomas. 1651/1962. *Leviathan.* M. Oakeshott, ed. New York: Collier.

Hobsbawm, Eric. 1977. *The Age of Capital, 1843–1875.* London: Sphere.

Hobson, J. A. 1902/1938. *Imperialism: A Study.* London: Allen & Unwin.

Hoffmann, Stanley. 1959. International relations: The long road to theory. *World Politics* (April) 11(3):346–377.

Hoffmann, Stanley. 1960. *Contemporary Theory in International Relations*. Englewood Cliffs, N.J.: Prentice-Hall.

Hoffmann, Stanley. 1965. *The State of War*. New York: Praeger.

Hoffmann, Stanley. 1977. An American social science: international relations. *Daedalus* (Summer) 106(3):41–60.

Hoffmann, Stanley. 1978. *Primacy or World Order*. New York: McGraw Hill.

Holsti, Ole. 1976. Foreign policy viewed cognitively. In Robert Axelrod, ed. *The Structure of Decision: The Cognitive Maps of Political Elites*. Princeton: Princeton University Press.

Hosoya, Chihiro. 1974. Characteristics of the foreign policy decision-making system in Japan. *World Politics* (April) 26(3):353–369.

Hume, David. 1742. Of the balance of power. In Charles W. Hendel, ed. 1953. *David Hume's Political Essays*. Indianapolis: Bobbs-Merrill.

Huxley, Aldous. 1952. *Brave New World*. London: Vanguard.

International Organization. 1982. (Spring) 36(2). Special issue on international regimes. Stephen D. Krasner, ed. (This issue was subsequently published with the addition of one article as: Stephen D. Krasner, ed. 1983. *International Regimes*. Ithaca: Cornell University Press.)

Isaak, Alan C. 1969. *Scope and Methods of Political Science*. Homewood, Ill.: Dorsey.

Jaeger, Werner. 1939. *Paideia: The Ideals of Greek Culture*. Vol. 1. Transl. from the 2d German edition by Gilbert Highet. New York: Oxford University Press.

Jervis, Robert. 1976. *Perception and Misperception in International Politics*. Princeton: Princeton University Press.

Jervis, Robert. 1978. Cooperation under the security dilemma. *World Politics* (January) 30(2):167–214.

Johnson, Chalmers A. 1966. *Revolutionary Change*. Boston: Little Brown.

Kahn, Alfred E. 1966. The tyranny of small decisions: market failures, imperfections, and the limits of econometrics. In Bruce M. Russett, ed. 1968. *Economic Theories of International Relations*. Chicago: Markham.

Kant, Immanuel. 1795. *Perpetual Peace*. An edited version appears in C. J. Friedrich, ed. 1949. *The Philosophy of Kant*. New York: Modern Library, pp. 430–476.

Kahnemann, Daniel and Amos Tversky. 1984. Choices, values, and frames. *American Psychologist* (April) 39(4):341–350.

Kaplan, Morton A. 1957. *System and Process in International Politics*. New York: Wiley.

Kaplan, Morton A. 1979. The genteel art of criticism, or how to boggle minds and confooz a discipline. In Kaplan, *Towards Professionalism in International Theory.* New York: Free Press.

Katona, George. 1953. Rational behavior and economic behavior. *Psychological Review* (September) 60:307–318.

Katzenstein, Peter J., ed. 1978. *Between Power and Plenty: Foreign Economic Policies of Advanced Industrial States.* Madison: University of Wisconsin Press.

Kennan, George F. 1951. *American Diplomacy, 1900–1950.* Chicago: University of Chicago Press.

Keohane, Robert O. 1980. The theory of hegemonic stability and changes in international economic regimes, 1967–1977. In Ole Holsti, Randolph Siverson and Alexander L. George, eds. *Change in the International System.* Boulder, Colorado: Westview Press.

Keohane, Robert O. 1982a. Hegemonic leadership and U.S. foreign economic policy in the 'long decade' of the 1950s. In Avery and Rapkin, eds. *America in a Changing World Political Economy.*

Keohane, Robert O. 1982b. The demand for international regimes. *International Organization* (Spring) 36(2):325–356.

Keohane, Robert O. 1983. Theory of world politics: Structural realism and beyond. In Ada Finifter, ed. *Political Science: The State of the Discipline.* Washington: American Political Science Association.

Keohane, Robert O. 1984. *After Hegemony: Cooperation and Discord in the World Political Economy.* Princeton: Princeton University Press.

Keohane, Robert O. and Joseph Nye, eds. 1972. *Transnational Relations and World Politics.* Cambridge: Harvard University Press.

Keohane, Robert O. and Joseph Nye. 1974. Transgovernmental relations and international organizations. *World Politics* (October) 27(1):39–62.

Keohane, Robert O. and Joseph Nye. 1977. *Power and Interdependence: World Politics in Transition.* Boston: Little, Brown.

Kindermann, Gottfried-Karl. 1985. The Munich school of neorealism in international politics. Munich: University of Munich, mimeo.

Kindleberger, Charles P. 1969. *American Business Abroad.* New Haven: Yale University Press.

Kissinger, Henry A. 1957. *Nuclear Weapons and Foreign Policy.* New York: Harper.

Kissinger, Henry A. 1964. *A World Restored.* New York: Grosset and Dunlap.

Kissinger, Henry A. 1968. The white revolutionary: reflections on Bismarck. *Daedalus* (Summer) 97(3):888–924.

Kissinger, Henry A. 1975. Secretary Henry A. Kissinger, interviewed by William F. Buckley, Jr. *The Secretary of State.* Bureau of Public Affairs: Department of State, September 13.

Krasner, Stephen D. 1976. State power and the structure of international trade. *World Politics* (April) 28(3):317–343.

Krasner, Stephen D. 1978a. *Defending the National Interest: Raw Materials Investment and U.S. Foreign Policy.* Princeton: Princeton University Press.

Krasner, Stephen D. 1978b. United States commercial and monetary policy: Unravelling the paradox of external stength and internal weakness. In Katzenstein, ed., *Between Power and Plenty,* pp. 51–88.

Krasner, Stephen D. 1981. Transforming international regimes: What the third world wants and why. *International Studies Quarterly* (March) 25(1):119–148.

Krasner, Stephen D. 1982a. Regimes and the limits of realism: Regimes as autonomous variables. *International Organization* (Spring) 36(2):497–510.

Krasner, Stephen D. 1982b. Structural causes and regime consequences: Regimes as intervening variables. *International Organization* (Spring) 36(2):185–206.

Kuhn, Thomas. 1962. *The Structure of Scientific Revolutions.* Chicago: University of Chicago Press.

Kuhn, Thomas S. 1970. Reflections on my critics. In Imre Lakatos and Alan Musgrave, eds. *Criticism and the Growth of Knowledge.* Cambridge: Cambridge University Press.

Kurth, James R. 1979. The political consequences of the product cycle: Industrial history and political outcomes. *International Organization* (Winter) 33(1):1–34.

Kurzweil, Edith. 1980. *The Age of Structuralism.* New York: Columbia University Press.

Lakatos, Imre. 1970. Falsification and the methodology of scientific research progammes. In Imre Lakatos and Alan Musgrave, eds., *Criticism and the Growth of Knowledge.* Cambridge: Cambridge University Press.

Landau, Martin. 1972. *Political Theory and Political Science.* New York: Macmillan.

Latsis, Spiro J. 1976. A Research programme in economics. In Latsis, ed. *Method and Appraisal in Economics.* Cambridge: Cambridge University Press.

Le Bon, Gustave. 1896. *The Crowd.* Translator unnamed. London: Unwin.

Leach, Edmund. 1961. *Rethinking Anthropology.* London: Athlone Press.

Lebow, Richard Ned. 1981. *Between Peace and War: The Nature of International Crisis.* Baltimore: Johns Hopkins University Press.

Lenin, V. I. 1916/39. *Imperialism: The Highest Stage of Capitalism.* New York: International Publishers.

Lévi-Strauss, Claude. 1946. French sociology. In Wilbert Moore and Georges Gurvitch, eds. *Twentieth Century Sociology.* New York: Philosophical Library.

Lévi-Strauss, Claude. 1967. *Structural Anthropology.* New York: Doubleday.

Levy, Marion J. 1966. *Modernization and the Structure of Societies.* Vol. 2. Princeton: Princeton University Press.

Lichtheim, George. 1971. *Imperialism.* New York: Praeger.

Lippman, Walter. 1943. *U.S. Foreign Policy: Shield of the Republic.* Boston: Little Brown.

Livernash, E. R. 1963. The relation of power to the structure and process of collective bargaining. In Bruce M. Russett, ed. 1968. *Economic Theories of International Politics.* Chicago: Markham.

Luttwak, Edward. 1976. *The Grand Strategy of the Roman Empire—From the First Century A.D. to the Third.* Baltimore: Johns Hopkins University Press.

Lyons, Gene M. 1982. Expanding the study of international relations: The French connection. *World Politics* (October) 35(1):135–149.

Machiavelli, Niccolò. 1531/1970. *The Discourses.* Bernard Crick, ed. Harmondsworth, Middlesex: Penguin.

Machiavelli, Niccolò. 1513/1977. *The Prince.* New York: Norton.

Macpherson, C. B. 1962. *The Political Theory of Possessive Individualism.* New York: Oxford University Press.

Macridis, Roy C. 1971. France and Germany. In Steven L. Spiegel and Kenneth N. Waltz, eds. *Conflict in World Politics.* Cambridge, Mass.: Winthrop.

Mallet, Serge. 1963. *La nouvelle classe ouvrière.* Paris: Seuil.

Mansbach, Richard, Y. H. Ferguson and D. E. Lampert. 1976. *The Web of World Politics.* Englewood Cliffs, N.J.: Prentice-Hall.

Mansbach, Richard and John A. Vasquez. 1981. *In Search of Theory: A New Paradigm for Global Politics.* New York: Columbia University Press.

March, James G. 1966. The power of power. In David Easton, ed. *Varieties of Political Theory.* New York: Prentice-Hall.

March, James G. and Herbert A. Simon. 1958. *Organizations.* New York: Wiley.

Marcuse, Herbert. 1968. Industrialization and capitalism in the work of Max Weber. In *Negations: Essays in Critical Theory.* Boston: Beacon Press.

Martineau, Harriet. 1853/1893. *The Positive Philosophy of Auguste Comte: Freely*

Translated and Condensed. 3d. ed. vol. 2. London: Kegan Paul, Trench, Trubner.

Masterman, Margaret. 1970. The nature of a paradigm. In Lakatos and Musgrave, eds. *Criticism and the Growth of Knowledge.* Cambridge: Cambridge University Press.

Mattingly, Garrett. 1955/1964. *Renaissance Diplomacy.* Baltimore: Penguin Books.

McKeown, Timothy J. 1986. The limitations of "structural" theories of commercial policy. *International Organization,* forthcoming, vol. 40.

Maier, Charles. 1978. The politics of productivity: Foundations of American international economic policy after World War II. In Katzenstein, ed. *Between Power and Plenty.*

Meinecke, Friedrich. 1957. *Machiavellism.* Douglas Scott, transl. New Haven: Yale University Press.

Michalak, Stanley J., Jr. 1979. Theoretical perspectives for understanding international interdependence. *World Politics* (October) 32(1):136–150.

Modelski, George. 1978. The long-cycle of global politics and the nation-state. *Comparative Studies in Society and History* (April) 20:214–35.

Modelski, George. 1982. Long cycles and the strategy of U.S. international economic policy. In Avery and Rapkin, eds., *America in a Changing World Political Economy.*

Moon, Donald J. 1975. The logic of political inquiry: A synthesis of opposed perspectives. In Fred I. Greenstein and Nelson W. Polsby, eds. *Political Science: Scope and Theory.* vol. 1 of Greenstein and Polsby, eds. *Handbook of Political Science.* Reading, Mass.: Addison-Wesley, pp. 131–228.

Moore, Barrington, Jr. 1950. *Soviet Politics: The Dilemma of Power.* Cambridge: Harvard University Press.

Moore, Barrington, Jr. 1966. *Social Origins of Dictatorship and Democracy: Lord and Peasant in the Making of the Modern World.* Boston: Beacon Press.

Morazé, Charles. 1957. *Les Bourgeois Conquérants.* Paris: Colin.

Morgenthau, Hans J. 1946. *Scientific Man Versus Power Politics.* Chicago: University of Chicago Press.

Morgenthau, Hans J. 1948. *Politics Among Nations.* New York: Knopf. (Individual authors have cited the year of the edition that they have used.)

Morgenthau, Hans J. 1958. The escape from power. In *Dilemmas of Politics.* Chicago: University of Chicago Press.

Morgenthau, Hans J. 1970. *Truth and Power.* New York: Praeger.

Morgenthau, Hans J. 1974. Détente: the balance sheet. New York Times, March 28.

Mundell, Robert A. and Alexander K. Swoboda. 1969. Monetary Problems in the International Economy. Chicago: University of Chicago Press.

Murphy, Craig. 1983. What the third world wants: An interpretation of the development and meaning of the new international economic order ideology. International Studies Quarterly (March) 27(1):55–76.

Myrdal, Gunnar. 1960. Beyond the Welfare State. New Haven: Yale University Press.

Nadel, S. F. 1957. The Theory of Social Structure. Glencoe, Ill.: Free Press.

Nagel, Ernest. 1956. Logic Without Metaphysics. Glencoe, Ill.: Free Press.

Nagel, Ernest. 1961. The Structure of Science. New York: Harcourt, Brace and World.

Nelson, Richard R. and Sydney G. Winter. 1982. An Evolutionary Theory of Economic Change. Cambridge: Harvard University Press.

North, Douglass C. 1981. Structure and Change in Economic History. New York: W. W. Norton.

North, Douglass C. and R. P. Thomas. 1973. The Rise of the Western World: A New Economic History. New York: Cambridge University Press.

North, Robert C. 1976. The World That Could Be. The Portable Stanford: Stanford Alumni Association. Palo Alto: Stanford University Press.

O'Connor, James. 1973. The Fiscal Crisis of the State. New York: St. Martin's Press.

Ollman, Bertell. 1976. Alienation: Marx's Conception of Man in Capitalist Society. 2d ed. Cambridge, England: Cambridge University Press.

Olson, Mancur. 1965. The Logic of Collective Action. Cambridge, Mass.: Harvard University Press.

Olson, Mancur. 1982. The Rise and Decline of Nations. New Haven: Yale University Press.

O'Neill, John. 1972. The Hobbesian problem in Marx and Parsons. In O'Neill, Sociology as a Skin Trade. New York: Harper & Row.

Organski, A. F. K. 1968. World Politics. 2d. ed. New York: Knopf.

Organski, A. F. K. and Jacek Kugler. 1980. The War Ledger. Chicago: University of Chicago Press.

Oye, Kenneth A. 1979. The domain of choice. In Kenneth A. Oye, Donald Rothchild and Robert J. Lieber, eds. Eagle Entangled: U.S. Foreign Policy in a Complex World. New York: Longman, pp. 3–33.

Oye, Kenneth A. 1983. Belief Systems, Bargaining and Breakdown: International Political

Economy, 1929–1934. Unpublished doctoral dissertation, Harvard University.

Palloix, Christian. 1975. *L'internationalisation du capital.* Paris: Maspero.

Pantin, C. F. A. 1968. *The Relations between the Sciences.* Cambridge: Cambridge University Press.

Park, Robert E. 1941. The social function of war. In Leon Bramson and George W. Goethals, eds. *War.* New York: Basic Books.

Parsons, Talcott. 1937. *The Structure of Social Action.* New York: McGraw-Hill.

Pepper, Stephen C. 1942. *World Hypotheses.* Berkeley: University of California Press.

Petras, James. 1980. The imperial state system. Paper presented to the American Political Science Association, Washington, D.C., August.

Pinder, John, Takashi Hosomi and William Diebold. 1979. *Industrial Policy and the International Economy.* New York: Trilateral Commission.

Platt, John Rader. 1956. Style in science. *Harper's Magazine* 213(1277):69–75.

Poggi, Gianfranco. 1978. *The Development of the Modern State.* Stanford: Stanford University Press.

Polanyi, Karl. 1957a. Aristotle discovers the economy. In Polanyi et al. *Trade and Markets in the Early Empires.* Glencoe, Ill.: Free Press.

Polanyi, Karl. 1957b. *The Great Transformation.* Boston: Little Brown.

Polanyi, Karl. 1977. *The Livelihood of Man.* New York: Academic Press.

Polanyi, Michael. 1941. The growth of thought in society. *Economica* (November) 8(32):428–456.

Polanyi, Michael. 1968. Life's irreducible structure. *Science* vol. 160.

Popper, Karl. 1934/1959. *The Logic of Discovery.* New York: Basic Books.

Popper, Karl. 1961. *The Poverty of Historicism.* New York: Harper & Row.

Popper, Karl. 1966. *The Open Society and Its Enemies.* London: Routledge, vol. 2.

Popper, Karl. 1972a. Epistemology without a knowing subject. In *Objective Knowledge.* London: Oxford University Press.

Popper, Karl. 1972b. On the theory of the objective mind. In *Objective Knowledge.* London: Oxford University Press.

Rabinow, Paul and William M. Sullivan, eds. 1979. *Interpretive Social Science: A Reader.* Berkeley: University of California Press.

Radnitzky, Gerard. 1973. *Contemporary Schools of Metascience.* 3d. enlarged ed. Chicago: Regnery.

Rapoport, Anatol. 1968. Foreword. In Walter Buckley, ed. *Modern Systems Research for the Behavioral Scientist, A Sourcebook.* Chicago: Aldine.

Ricoeur, Paul. 1974. *Conflict of Interpretations: Essays in Hermeneutics.* Evanston, Ill.: Northwestern University Press.

Rosecrance, Richard N. 1963. *Action and Reaction in World Politics: International Systems in Perspective.* Boston: Little, Brown.

Rosecrance, Richard N. 1981. International theory revisited. *International Organization* (Autumn) 35(4):691–713.

Rosenau, James N. 1966. Pre-Theories and theories of foreign policy. In R. Barry Farrell, ed. *Approaches to Comparative and International Politics.* Evanston: Northwestern University Press.

Rosenau, James N. 1968. National interest. *International Encyclopedia of the Social Sciences.* vol. 11.

Ruggie, John G. 1980. On the problem of the 'global problematique.' *Alternatives* (January) 5:517–550.

Ruggie, John G. 1982. International regimes, transactions and change: Embedded liberalism in the post-war economic order. *International Organization* (Spring) 36(2):379–415.

Ruggie, John G. 1983. Continuity and transformation in the world polity: Toward a neorealist synthesis. *World Politics* (January) 35(2):261–285.

Russett, Bruce M. 1963. The calculus of deterrence. *Journal of Conflict Resolution* (June) 7(2):97–109.

Russett, Bruce M. 1983. International interactions and processes: the internal versus external debate revisited. In Ada Finifter, ed. *Political Science: The State of the Discipline.* Washington: American Political Science Association.

Scheffler, Israel. 1967. *Science and Subjectivity.* Indianapolis: Bobbs-Merrill.

Schell, Jonathan. 1982. *The Fate of the Earth.* New York: Knopf.

Schelling, Thomas. 1960. *The Strategy of Conflict.* New York: Oxford University Press.

Schlesinger, Arthur, Jr. 1960. *The Age of Roosevelt.* vol. 2. *The Coming of the New Deal.* London: Heinemann.

Schumpeter, Joseph A. 1919. The sociology of imperialism. In Schumpeter. 1955. *Imperialism and Social Classes.* Heinz Norde, transl. New York: Meridian Books.

Shapiro, Michael J. 1981. *Language and Political Understanding.* New Haven: Yale University Press.

Shonfield, Andrew. 1965. *Modern Capitalism.* London: Oxford University Press.

Shubik, Martin. 1959. *Strategy and Market Structure.* New York: Wiley.

Simon, Herbert A. 1957. *Models of Man.* New York: Wiley.

Simon, Herbert A. 1969. The Architecture of complexity. In Simon, *The Sciences of the Artificial.* Cambridge: MIT Press.

Simon, Herbert A. 1979. *Models of Thought.* New Haven: Yale University Press.

Simon, Herbert A. 1982. *Models of Bounded Rationality.* Cambridge: MIT Press.

Singer, J. David. 1961. The level of analysis problem. *World Politics* (October) 14(1):77–92.

Singer, J. David. 1969. The global system and its subsystems: A developmental view. In James N. Rosenau, ed. *Linkage Politics: Essays on the Convergence of National and International Systems.* New York: Free Press.

Singer, J. David, Stuart Bremer, and John Stuckey. 1972. Capability distribution, uncertainty, and major power war, 1820–1965. In Bruce M. Russett, ed. *Peace, War, and Numbers.* Beverly Hills: Sage Publications.

Skocpol, Theda. 1977. Wallerstein's world capitalist system: A theoretical and historical critique. *American Journal of Sociology* 82(5):1975–90.

Skocpol, Theda. 1979. *States and Social Revolutions.* Cambridge: Cambridge University Press.

Smith, Adam. 1776/1976. *The Wealth of Nations.* Chicago: University of Chicago Press.

Smith, M. G. 1956. On segmentary lineage systems. *Journal of the Royal Anthropological Institute of Great Britain and Ireland* vol. 86 (July–December).

Smith, M. G. 1966. A structural approach to comparative politics. In David Easton, ed. *Varieties of Political Theories.* Englewood Cliffs, N.J.: Prentice-Hall.

Snidal, Duncan. 1981. *Interdependence, Regimes, and International Cooperation.* Unpublished manuscript, University of Chicago.

Snyder, Glenn H. and Paul Diesing. 1977. *Conflict Among Nations: Bargaining, Decision Making and System Structure in International Crises.* Princeton: Princeton University Press.

Sprout, Harold and Margaret Sprout. 1971. *Toward a Politics of the Planet Earth.* New York: Van Nostrand Reinhold.

Stein, Arthur. 1982. Coordination and collaboration: Regimes in an anarchic world. *International Organization* (Spring) 36(2):299–324.

Sterling, Richard W. 1974. *Macropolitics: International Relations in a Global Society.* New York: Knopf.

Stinchcombe, Arthur. 1968. *Constructing Social Theories*. New York: Harcourt, Brace and World.

Strayer, J. R. 1970. *On the Medieval Origins of the Modern State*. Princeton: Princeton University Press.

Strayer, J. R. and D. C. Munro. 1959. *The Middle Ages*. 4th. ed. New York: Appleton-Century-Crofts.

Taylor, A. J. P. 1976. London diary. *New Statesman* (June 4), vol. 91.

Taylor, Charles. 1965. Hermeneutics and politics. In Paul Connerton, ed. *Critical Sociology*. Harmondsworth, Middlesex: Penguin.

Thompson, E. P. 1978. *The Poverty of Theory and Other Essays*. New York: Monthly Review Press.

Thucydides. c. 400 B.C./1951. *History of the Peloponnesian War*. John H. Finley, Jr., transl. New York: Modern Library.

Tollison, Robert D. and Thomas D. Willett. 1979. An economic theory of mutually advantageous issue linkage in international negotiations. *International Organization* (Autumn) 33(4):425–450.

Toulmin, Stephen. 1961. *Foresight and Understanding*. New York: Harper and Row. (Paperback edition, 1963.)

Trollope, Anthony. 1880/1892. *The Duke's Children*. 3 vols. Philadelphia: Geddie.

Tucker, Robert W. 1977. *The Inequality of Nations*. New York: Basic Books.

Tully, James. 1980. *A Discourse on Property: John Locke and His Adversaries*. New York: Cambridge University Press.

Vattel, Emeric. 1916. *The Law of Nations*. Charles G. Fenwick, transl. In James Brown Scott, ed. *The Classics of International Law*. vol. 4. Oxford: Clarendon Press.

Veblen, Thorstein. 1915. The opportunity of Japan. In Leon Ardzrooni, ed., 1954. *Essays in Our Changing Order*. New York: Viking.

Vico, Giambattista. 1774/1970. *The New Science of Giambattista Vico*. Transl. from the 3d. ed. by Thomas Goddard Bergin and Max Harold Fisch. Ithaca and London: Cornell University Press.

Viner, Jacob. 1948. Power versus Plenty as objectives of foreign policy in the seventeenth and eighteenth centuries. *World Politics* (October) 1(1):1–29.

Von Laue, Theodore H. 1963. Soviet diplomacy: G. V. Chicherin, People's Commissar for foreign affairs, 1918–1930. In Gordon A. Craig and Felix Gilbert, eds. *The Diplomats, 1919–1939*. Vol. 1. New York: Atheneum.

Wallerstein, Immanuel. 1974. *The Modern World System I: Capitalist Agriculture and the Origins of the European World-Economy in the Sixteenth Century. New York: Academic Press.

Wallerstein, Immanuel. 1979. The rise and future demise of the world capitalist system: Concepts for comparative analysis. In Wallerstein, *The Capitalist World Economy*. New York: Cambridge University Press. Originally published in *Comparative Studies in Society and History* (September 1974) 16(4):387–415.

Wallerstein, Immanuel. 1980. *The Modern World System II: Mercantilism and the Consolidation of the European World-Economy, 1600–1750*. New York: Academic Press.

Waltz, Kenneth N. 1959. *Man, the State and War*. New York: Columbia University Press.

Waltz, Kenneth N. 1964. The stability of a bipolar world. *Daedalus* (Summer) 93(3):881–909.

Waltz, Kenneth N. 1967. *Foreign Policy and Democratic Politics: The American and British Experience*. Boston: Little, Brown.

Waltz, Kenneth N. 1970. The myth of national interdependence. In Charles P. Kindleberger, ed. *The International Corporation*. Cambridge: MIT Press.

Waltz, Kenneth N. 1979. *Theory of International Politics*. Reading, Mass.: Addison-Wesley.

Waltz, Kenneth N. 1980. Will the future be like the past? Paper presented to the American Political Science Association, Washington, D.C.

Waltz, Kenneth N. 1982a. Exchange with Richard Rosecrance. *International Organization* (Summer) 36(3):679–681.

Waltz, Kenneth N. 1982b. What causes what? Systemic and unit-level explanations of change. Institute of International Studies, University of California, Berkeley, draft (January).

Watzlawick, Paul, Janet Helmick Beavin, and Don D. Jackson. 1967. *Pragmatics of Human Communication*. New York: Norton.

Weaver, Warren. 1947. Science and complexity. In Weaver, ed. *The Scientists Speak*. New York: Boni and Gaer.

Weber, Max. 1972. *From Max Weber: Essays in Sociology*. H. Gerth and C. Wright Mills, transl. and eds. New York: Oxford University Press.

Weber, Max. 1974. Subjectivism and determinism. A translation of Weber, Roscher und Knies und das irrationalitätsproblem. In Giddens, ed. 1974. *Positivism and Sociology*.

Wight, Martin. 1966. The balance of power. In H. Butterfield and Martin Wight, eds. *Diplomatic Investigations: Essays in the Theory of International Politics*. London: Allen and Unwin.

Wight, Martin. 1973. The balance of power and international order. In Alan James, eds. *The Bases of International Order*. London: Oxford University Press.

Wolfers, Arnold. 1962. *Discord and Collaboration: Essays on International Politics*. Baltimore: Johns Hopkins University Press.

Wolfers, Arnold and Laurence Martin. 1956. *The Anglo-American Tradition in Foreign Affairs*. New Haven: Yale University Press.

Zolberg, Aristide R. 1981. Origins of the modern world system: A missing link. *World Politics* (January) 33(2):253–281.

Index